Historic House Museums in the United States and the United Kingdom

Historic House Museums in the United States and the United Kingdom

A History

Linda Young

ROWMAN & LITTLEFIELD
Lanham • Boulder • New York • London

Published by Rowman & Littlefield
A wholly owned subsidary of The Rowman & Littlefield Publishing Group, Inc.
4501 Forbes Boulevard, Suite 200, Lanham, Maryland 20706
www.rowman.com

Unit A, Whitacre Mews, 26-34 Stannary Street, London SE11 4AB

British Library Cataloguing in Publication Information Available

Library of Congress Cataloging-in-Publication Data

Names: Young, Linda, 1953 June 16 author.
Title: Historic house museums in the United States and the United Kingdom : a
  history / Linda Young.
Description: Lanham, MD : Rowman & Littlefield, [2017] | Includes
  bibliographical references and index.
Identifiers: LCCN 2016036311 (print) | LCCN 2016036647 (ebook) | ISBN
  9781442239760 (cloth : alk. paper) | ISBN 9781442239777 (electronic)
Subjects: LCSH: Historic house museums—United States—History. | Historic
  house museums—United States—Management. | Dwellings—Conservation and
  restoration—United States—History. | Historic house museums—Great
  Britain—History. | Historic house museums—Great Britain—Management. |
  Dwellings—Conservation and restoration—Great Britain—History.
Classification: LCC E159 .Y685 2017 (print) | LCC E159 (ebook) | DDC
  363.6/90973—dc23
LC record available at https://lccn.loc.gov/2016036311

Printed in the United States of America

~

Contents

~

Preface

What Is It About House Museums?

This book is a history of the museumization of historic houses, about the creation and development of a genre of museum, akin to art museums, national museums, natural history museums, and so on. The latter are similar institutions focusing on different bodies of knowledge, presented via distinctive epistemologies. House museums are the same, yet different. The difference springs from the defining and framing role of the house as not only a museumized object (with all its contents and sometimes its setting) but also a "home," an idea loaded with personal, social, and cultural meanings. Connecting this idea to the context and process of the museumization of many, many houses builds up a field of evidence, inviting interpretation as a remarkably persistent nationalist project.

The museumization of houses is a business that has enchanted and employed me for a great part of my professional life as a curator, teacher, and researcher, lurking in the crossover of the disciplines of history, art history, historical archaeology, museum studies, and cultural heritage management. I lucked into museum work in the early 1980s, first in Sydney, then later in Perth. At the Western Australian Museum I encountered my first house job, the museumization of the Samson House, recently bequeathed to the museum. The work I did in and on the house included cataloging, with colleagues, the house's vast indigenous collection and brought it under managed control, but it left open a question: What does all this stuff mean?

In subsequent years I cataloged two houses in South Australia: Martindale Hall in Mintaro and Collingrove in Angaston. The three assemblages led me to further house museum research that explored various explanatory theories and methods. The experience also fed into my PhD, a sociological history of middle-class culture interpreted through the consumption of domestic furnishings and other performative dynamics. Some years later, teaching at the University of Canberra, I began an approach toward the house museum as an institution, producing a survey of Australian house museums. This attracted a PhD student, Charlotte Smith, with whom I began to focus on distinguishing subsets in the class of house museums; she wrote a thesis on what we then called "Great Man house museums" (Smith 2002). As Dr. Smith, she moved back to more general curatorial work, and I picked up the broad topic of house museums again. The book of my PhD (about middle-class construction via cultural capital; Young 2003) had taken the initial thesis argument into transnational comparisons between Australia, the United Kingdom, and the United States; I rashly decided to do the same with house museums. (If I were to start again, I wouldn't do this; the topic is too big to do it justice.)

The present book began with that inchoate question: What is it about house museums? (refined to: Why museumize houses?). Put more hypothetically, what are the foundational motives of house museums? How do such motives distinguish houses from other museums, and each other? Historicizing the genre of house museums was surprisingly untrodden country. House museums have generated a big and beautiful literature of souvenir and coffee table books, often focusing on a single house, sometimes addressing a number of similar or nearby houses. Their texts are variably useful to the cultural historian. The most practical resource was the numerous guides or listings of museums in specific cities, states, counties, regions, and nations—some published in hard copy, others available online. I had established a huge hard-copy file of Australian house museum source material in the 1990s; mercifully, in the 2000s, the Internet enabled international access and electronic file storage. A number of research assistants commenced gathering data, following guidebooks and online lists of house museums in the United States and the United Kingdom, and interpretive models began to suggest themselves.

There were many discussions with Charlotte, then seemingly the only other person in the universe with a broad interest in and knowledge of house museums; we chewed over the organizing concept of the motivations of the founders of house museums and the contexts in which they operated. I tested the themes that came forth on house museums in three national "middling" regions: forty in Victoria, fifty-eight in Wisconsin, and thirty-one in the East Midlands (Young 2007). The exercise clarified the characteristics that suggested meaningful directions of understanding; for instance, it was not worth recording data leading to the observation that large, high-style houses predominate everywhere. One category was abolished, one was added, and several changed names. The method of persistent hoeing and raking of the data, turning over and enlarging the lists, adding historical detail and the evidence of contemporary inquiries, was long and slow but rich.

The database continued to expand. The sources were enhanced by cross-checking house and other websites; invaluable Wikipedia entries, articles, and books; and emails and Skype conversations with curators. I squeezed house museums into the topics of museum and heritage conference papers, where friendly listeners suggested further sites. The ICOM Committee for Historic House Museums, DEMHIST (Demeures Historiques), was especially supportive; its prior project on classifying house museums changed direction partly through my input. The Attingham Summer School on Country House Studies (2007 session) filled in a crucial gap in my knowledge and opened up a tremendous source of advisors and contacts. Thanks to travel for conferences and holidays, I visited house museums in the United Kingdom and the United States, though far from all the sites I've written about. This is disturbing because real-time visiting always made a difference to my understanding; I remain excruciatingly aware that my sources have their limits. I encountered Anne Trubek, another lister and analyst of house museums, who was writing A Skeptic's Guide to Writers' Houses (2011); we exchanged lists, and I acknowledged to myself at last that I would never have a total score of house museums but that perhaps, at about five hundred, I had enough. That was a relief.

The interpretive typology that structures this book took shape, and I began writing chapter after chapter, now based in Melbourne at Deakin University. Five species of house museum had taken shape, based on the motivations of their founders. They proved remarkably persistent through time. The types brought with them characteristic disciplinary and professional frameworks, with the consequence that the continuity of the final book might seem jagged. As a museologist and cultural historian of the nineteenth-century British world, I knew a little about much of the spectrum and relished the further research into English and American literature, elite and vernacular cultural registers, the history of great collectors, and the prehistory of social history. I found it very difficult to get journal articles accepted for publication during the long writing period. Referee reports often objected that the topic was far too big, even when I thought the pieces addressed one aspect, of one species, in one nation. In a time when the taste is for microhistories, I'm out of step. I hope the concept of this book is more convincing than the would-be articles; maybe now I can frame articles in relation to a big picture that exists in the public sphere.

The major contribution of this book is to complicate the topic of house museums within the body of museum studies. "The museum" is a generic abstraction in too many studies, especially by nonpractitioners. Frequently they mean art museums, with little understanding of the historical and practical idiosyncrasies of the museumization of artworks or of the differences between art museums and other genres. Thanks to colonialist archaeology, ancient objects destined for metropolitan museums tended to be the biggest and best trophies rather than the fragments that characterize excavation in practice; hence archaeological relics in museums are frequently written about as art. In other contexts, commentators mean ethnographic museums, or collections based on the kind of imperialist collecting that shaped the meaning of anthropology. Writing about natural history and science museums explicates the clearest identity in contrast to museums focusing on the arts. But between arts and social sciences, the acknowledgment of profound difference has been woefully absent in the surge of attention paid to museums as cultural vectors since the 1990s. Of course, there are common characteristics in the theory and management of museums in general, but the analytical disciplines applied to different bodies of collections demand specialized consideration.

House museums exhibit the same range of disciplinary variety. As a rule, it's simply overlooked, and the habit of writing about "the house museum" takes its cue from the character of the case in question. One exception stands out: writers' house museums. An International Committee on Literary Museums was established by ICOM a few years before the International Committee on Historic House House Museums—a testament to the vast spread and strong identity of writers' house museums. (The ICLM welcomed the subset of composers' houses into its fold in 2014.) Here is one subspecies of house museum that self-identifies as particular; the specialist theme of literary houses has also been taken up as a theme of tourism. Will the invention of the typological vocabulary identified in this book make any difference to how house museum people understand their particular sites? It ought to, in the interest of institutional self-knowledge and recognition of commitments in common with other house museums, and because awareness of varieties implies distinctive museological practice (Young 2012). The motivation that inspired the foundation of a house museum need not determine its future for ever after, but it is likely to have shaped the conditions in which the house developed. That's worth knowing.

~

Acknowledgments

My heartfelt thanks to so many people, and especially:

In the United Kingdom:
Janet Allan; John Barnes; John Beckett; Adam Busiakewicz; Gillian Crawley; Susan Dalloe; Helen Dorey; Anna Forrest; John Goldsmith; Carolyn Hammond; Rosalinda Hardiman; Natalie Hill; Carmen Holdsworth-Delgado; Mary Hollern; David Hopes; Howard Hull; Rachel Hunt; Eleanor John; John Lewis; Hilary Lowe; Denise Maior-Barron; Denise Melhuish; Nick Molyneux; Louisa Moore; Gerallt Nash; John Powell; Malcolm Smith; Sarah Staniforth; Craig Statham; Rob Wake; Duncan Walker; Dan Watson; Annabel Westman; Audrey Winkler; Matthew Withey; Jacquie Wright.

In the United States:
Irene Axelrod; Sid Berger; Seth Bruggeman; Heather Clewell; Elinor Curtin Cameron; Karen Daly; Jennie Deer; Kathy Dickson; Kendra Dillard; Tammy Duchesne; Kristie Erickson; Juliette Fritsch; Ami Ghazala; Peter Gittleman; Brooke Guthrie; Donna Ann Harris; Wendy Hubbard; Kim Ivey; Mark Johnson; Tom Johnson; Laura Keim; Charles G. Kellogg; Sarah Kennel; Mary Knapp; Dean Lahikainen; Anne Lane; Debbie Lawton; Teri Mandic; Shana McKenna; Carl Nold; Linda J. Park; Dennis Pogue; Jennifer Pustz; Laurel Racine; Shax Riegler; Jennifer Robles; Kevin Rose; Stephen Seals; Patrick Stenshorn; Robert Sutton; Susana Tejada; Anne Trubeck; Eva Ulz; Cary Weisner; Patricia West McKay; Sally Zimmerman.

In Australia:

Martin Green; Louis le Vaillant; Clive Lucas; Charlotte Smith; Laurajane Smith; Peter Watts; Andrea Witcomb; David Young.

~

CHAPTER ONE

Is There a Museum in the House?

House and *museum* may seem, at first, to be opposite ideas. Yet pairing them contains a counterfactual expression of the separation between the private and the public, the particular and the universal, the mundane and the exceptional. Connecting *house* and *museum* requires either domesticating the institution or institutionalizing the home. In practice, both effects are present, constructing uncanny parameters for the house museum. Precisely because the house normally shapes home life, the house museum offers a personal take on the theme of the museum, whether its topic is the lives of individuals, the forms or designs within which domestic lives are lived, or the crossover of collecting from institution to home. At the same time, the aura of the museum suffuses the house museum with institutional authority, validating the domestic story as something of significance in the public interest. The counterpoint of these two themes and their ramifications permeates the study of house museums.

This book shows how museum presentation of homes embodies an agenda of exemplary politics relative to the national sphere. It argues that the act of transforming a house into a museum—museumization in shorthand—introduces the distinctive "museum way of seeing": the objectification of the house and all it contains and refers to, relative to the visitor (Alpers 1991). Thus the house museum projects a purposeful story into the public sphere, usually in a national frame of reference, or sometimes in the microcosm of the local. The conventional domestic scope of the house emerges as the vehicle of larger narratives about the character of the nation or the locality.

Following a Gramscian view of cultural manifestations that generate consensus among the public, house museums are shown as devices that promote a civic sense of identity (Hoare & Smith 1971, 323–24). In practice, a visit to a house museum produces knowledge grounded in the common experience of *home*, which contributes to collective identity and affirms national or local characteristics. Thus house museums make the abstractions of nation personal, material, visible, and visitable in the familiar form of home. Visitors actively choose (or might decline) to identify with the presentation, and to acknowledge (or not) a shared heritage. This agenda, I argue, is the major frame of house museums in the transnational Anglo tradition.

This framing works because home, manifested in the house, contains the individual, idiosyncratic, interior signs of national identity, thus enabling house museums to represent a spectrum of personal contexts of nation. This is possible because the domestic sphere is where everyday life occurs for most people; it is vastly, unspeakably familiar. And yet the habits of home life are not merely domestic. They are crucial elements of habitus, the set of psychic, cultural, and material conditions that inexplicitly but absolutely structure the practice of everyday life (Bourdieu 1977, 78–80). Habitus, or lifestyle, is not exclusively based in homes, but homes are crucial fields of habitus. This book suggests that habitus informs the agency by which the museumized house can evoke a powerful range of meanings among the visiting public. The house museum invokes home to tap into the diverse domestic experiences and emotions of segments of the population by enabling negotiations about social identities.

How is a house translated into a museum? House museums can be envisaged as a genre in the taxonomy of museums, a type equivalent to art museums or zoos. They are a small proportion of the total, maybe 10–15 percent of all museums, but the genre is very diverse. Having reviewed many hundreds of house museums in the United Kingdom, the United States, and Australia, I distinguish five "species" on the basis of the motivations inspiring their foundation. The categories are not incontestable and more than occasionally cross over into each other. Nonetheless, they provide a fruitful system with which to analyze and understand the spectrum of house museums. I suggest that house museums are established to recognize the heroic character of an inhabitant, to conserve the aesthetic quality of the building itself, to enable the universalizing gesture of particular collections displayed in the house; to interpret the significance of social history in the domestic sphere, and to manage the aristocratic English country house, an almost redundant form that nevertheless wields much influence on other house museums.

In the process of translation, house museumization generates the peculiar consequences of exhibiting *home*, thus provoking the suite of oppositions cited above. The act of exposing the house as a museum, "for looking at," sets up a double perspective for visitors: they observe simultaneously a specimen and a construct, a "natural" artifact and a curated exhibition. The crossovers in perception induced by this form of total-environment exhibition conduce to the ritual aspects of house museum visiting. The formal procedures of admission and controls on access within predispose visitors to collude with the ideological frame of the presentation. Visitors suspend doubts or disbelief for the duration of their visit, in ways that are not required of a visit to a general museum. This ritualized experience engages the special capacity of the house museum for representing collective identities.

The differences between the genre of house museums and other museum types are not greater than the similarities. However, they inflect characteristic modes of operation on house museums that can be described as distinc-

Anne, Neeha, and Linda contemplate dinner at Como House, Melbourne, 2015. A velvet rope separating visitors from displays is the emblem of the polite house museum—it says, "Here, but no farther; look, but don't touch." The polite visitor acknowledges its implication that what is on the other side is for contemplation of the admirable past.
Photo courtesy of David Young.

tive house museologies. Houses smaller than palaces are not easy to open to the public *en masse*, usually having been designed for use by a family group. Where historic furnishings and fittings survive, their significance makes them particularly valuable and hence at risk from exposure to modern tourism. The demands of site security and visitor safety impose further constraints in many houses. Historic buildings are inevitably expensive to maintain at the high standard expected by custodians and visitors, as are the grounds around them. Managing these conditions in the public interest often diverts curatorial attention from the ideological implications of museumized houses. Hence this book asserts the conviction that there is more to house museums than the perception of gracious antiquity or the restoration of former glory.

To set the scene for this argument, I explore the dual structures of the house as home and as museum, and the agency of both home and museum as shapers of national identities. Having demonstrated how identity construction operates in both circumstances, I introduce the significant characters of museumized houses as species of the type. The material reality of houses translated into museums demands acknowledgment in order to contextualize a discussion of the implications of displaying a house. The exhibited house launches frank exposure as well as intimate experience, realized via different technologies of display to those employed in the general museum exhibition. Out of these differences emerge the specialized perspectives and skills of house museologies.

House, Home, and Identity

"Be it ever so humble, there's no place like home," tinkles the song that expresses one of the warmest ideas of comfort and happiness that humans know. A home is not necessarily a house, and a house is not necessarily a home, not all the time, or to all its inhabitants (Blunt & Dowling 2006). But the material expression of a dwelling and the imaginary of home are so closely intertwined that they are often elided in a multitude of contexts. The idea of "home" infuses many applications: the geographical place we inhabit, on small and large scales; the physical house, or abode (to acknowledge non-house forms of dwelling); the performance of life therein; the construction of self-identity, and by extension, social identities. To begin with, home is the place where we live, inside the familiar four walls, but home also extends outward: to the hometown, the homeland, and even planet Earth as our home in space. "Our house is our corner of the world," writes Gaston Bachelard, arguing that home is a state of mind that creates intimate space in the universe, anchoring humans literally and figuratively (Bachelard 1994, 3–4).

The idea of home as one's primal place in the world gives it a role in the construction of identity as an individual and a social being. Here it is necessary to distinguish *house* and *home* in order to unravel the complexity of the dual idea. A *house* is a structure made or modified to give shelter to humans—a space, in a place; whereas a *home* is an emotional affect—"my" place in space. The interplay between people and their natural, built, and social surroundings is the subject of environmental psychology, which shows how ideas, values, feelings, and memories of places produce a distinctive aspect of self-identity. Place identity describes the individual's incorporation of place into the larger concept of self. This is an insight that is more intuitive than articulate. In fact, it is a condition that Harold Proshansky, one of the founders of environmental psychology, acknowledged might be better understood by artists than behavioral scientists (Proshansky, Ittelson, & Rivlin 1976, 493–94). Yet the intuition that place has important effects on self and others explains why it is meaningful for people to visit the locations where admired people lived or important aesthetics are enacted, as pilgrims, students, or tourists. The same significance inspired the nineteenth-century category of "homes and haunts" literature, which enabled armchair travelers to experience the geographies and landscapes traversed by national heroes and believe thus they see deeper into heroes' souls.

If cognitions about the physical world frame everyone's daily experience, then the dwelling is certainly a major element of life. Predating the development of environmental psychology, Martin Heidegger posited in a 1954 essay, "Building, Dwelling, Thinking," that dwelling is the fundamental character of human existence in the world, and that humans dwell by building (Heidegger 1993, 347). The idea of building a house as the holistic frame of existence is attractive, though it characteristically ignores women, implicating them as either the inspiration or the biological urge of housing the (male) self. Iris Young therefore proposes the extended act of inhabiting the dwelling and enacting the routines that shape daily life as a more inclusive way to understand human ontology. She names it home making, and argues that it is informed by normative values of shelter, nurture, growth, and privacy, which support personal and collective identity formation (Young 1997, 161–64). By these means, home becomes the performative and experiential dimension of dwelling, quickening the house with human consciousness.

Other people, too, have roles in establishing the idea of home. The interplay of relationships within the house sets up variables that differentiate the lived experience of home conventionally framed by family. Before the twentieth century, *family* could refer to all the inhabitants of a house, a meaning now reduced to the nuclear unit of immediate relations. But even today, a household may consist of head, partner, dependent or adult child, sibling, elderly relative, visiting friend, servant, or tenant—and each one's experience of the same home is likely to be different. The basis of difference is relative power in the social dynamic of the household, substantiating the individual's sense of belonging (or alienation). Being acknowledged as part of an intimate social group is a key to human selfhood, and home is its most basic site. So profound is the identity of self in the supportive group that the concept of home can exist wherever there are vital others: one can be at home at work, on the road, on holiday. At the same time, the intrinsic spatial dimension of home can also be experienced alone as a comforting presence on the strength of its associations—or, in a dysfunctional home, the opposite. Humans make home, home makes humans.

The house that is the shell of home can be used both materially and rhetorically as a symbol of identity. Where the individual has a measure of power in the household, the design, decoration, or management of the house expresses and represents the self: call it taste or character. By contrast, the absence of personal control in institutional living denies individual identity—which may be the institution's purpose. Deliberate unhomeliness is employed as punishment in the jail, mortification in the hermitage, remolding of personality in the army barracks. Even very unpromising spaces can be transformed into home by the power to introduce touches of self into one's house or room, and to close the door to control access. With this agency, the individual can express a sense of identity that is contingently attached to the notion of home (Mallet 2004, 82–83). This is usually the sense that curators hope to present by preserving or re-creating the historic home environment, and that visitors expect to encounter when visiting.

The physical form of the house or abode may be easier for subsequent generations to recognize and understand than the material impression made by its inhabitants. A house is the product of demographic variables and cultural norms: wealth, class, and ethnicity may determine its location, size, material, design. In the light of these effects, the dwelling can be called a personality-forming environment, by being large or small, on the right or wrong side of the tracks, well maintained and therefore secure or dilapidated and unsafe, and so forth. The details of these conditions need to be made explicit to visitors because they change through time and vary according to culture. But the implications of domestic life in wealth or poverty, in or out of the social mainstream, and with differing traditions of culture, are also sufficiently familiar to people today to appreciate them as sources for the sense of identity.

House, Museum, National Identity

Museums in all their forms have proven to be influential media among the cultural apparatus that generate communal meanings, social narratives, and collective public identities. Carol Duncan and Alan Wallach argue that the great national "universal survey" museums presented the riches and curiosities of foreign lands in order to instill a sense of mastery by nationals over the culture of primitives (Duncan & Wallach 1980). Public art museums, proposes Duncan, enabled the people to savor cultural privileges that were once the exclusive domain of kings, and thus to assert themselves as citizens of the democratic state (Duncan 1995). Tony Bennett shows how museums mobilize references to selected events from the ancient and recent past to create national stories to which moderns can relate (Bennett 1995; Bennett 2004). Each type of museum—art, ethnology, natural history—invites visitors to presentations in which abstract values are contextualized in narratives, backed up with evidence drawn from experts, and demonstrated with authentic objects. The stories thus presented often take on mythic characteristics as the foundational explanations of the national "us," and the objects displayed adopt the status of relics—sacred demonstrations of the myth. Insofar as visitors concur with the representation, they unite in a common understanding and a collective identity.

The house museum is a museum type that peculiarly demonstrates and promotes national identity or its small-scale parallel, local identity. As the homes they once were, house museums symbolize individuals and families, as the homeland symbolizes the nation. As museums, they provide a visible and visitable form to a domestic vision of the nation ideal (Geisler 2005, xiv–xv). However homely the welcome, the visit to a house museum is more highly controlled and ritualized than to other museums. Museum visiting has often been likened to a pilgrimage: at the end, visitors feel a sense of achievement or fulfillment, having made a journey to commune with a significant idea embodied therein (Horne 1984). In these ways visitors experience the house as a special, even sacred, place. The religious overtones are not incidental.

The eighteenth-century Enlightenment initiated the transfer of religious forms into secular practice. Rousseau coined the term *civil religion* in 1762 to describe a means of unifying the citizens who acquiesce in the social contract by endowing the state with sacred authority that provides a religious dimension to national life· The idea furnished the French Revolution with symbolic goddesses and real-life heroes, to be served with ceremonies and temples in neoclassical styles. A century and a half later, Robert Bellah analyzed the forms of patriotism in the United States as the same transference

The Codman House, Lincoln, Massachusetts. The land now known as the Codman Estate was purchased in 1708 and remained in the extended family (with a
generation's gap) until 1969. The present house enlarged and remodeled an older
one in 1790, as the country and summer house of the first of five generations of
Boston Brahmin Codmans. Furniture and decorative schemes of every era survive
in the house.
Photo by David Bohl, courtesy of Historic New England.

of religious ideas and practices to the service of the secular republic, noting
that these had been practiced with energy since the American Revolution
(Bellah 1967). American patriotic civil religion now contains a repertoire of
prophets, martyrs, sacred events and places, rituals and symbols, incorporating biblical archetypes of the chosen people, the Promised Land, and, via the
trauma of the Civil War, sacrificial death and redemption. A large fraction of
these patriotic forms are expressed and celebrated in museums and heritage
sites. In Britain, the formats of civil religion are also comprehensive, invoking the state religion and the monarchy to provide rituals for popular myths
of the national imaginary, based on a relationship of many centuries' standing. In particular, the ceremonial surrounding members of the royal family
provides daily events through which the people come in contact with British
majesty, in person, on television, and in magazine photo spreads. The myths

of national character they embody—once attached to the Empire, and still powerful in cultural fields—are also expressed in museums.

Nationalism and patriotism can be defined separately for rhetorical purposes, but as devotion to the nation, they mean the same thing. The highly focused topics of house museums are particularly eloquent in representing the nation, conveying patriotic meanings via a repertoire of techniques to engender high feeling. Magico-religious sentiment is one. Contrary to the expectations of pioneering sociologists, secular principles have not yet displaced the popular taste for faith and magic, and it is not hard to find magico-religious structures and practices in nationalist environments, including house museums (Young 2012).

Another mode of adding sentiment to nationalism is the aestheticization of humble or utilitarian forms, such as vernacular housing. This process discovers previously unrecognized beauty in local artifacts and asserts it to represent national distinctiveness. The Scandinavian development of folk museum parks encapsulates this strand of nationalist values as found in houses. Yet another mode is the contemporary appraisal of house designs by notable architects, interior designers, and their less defined predecessors as artworks in themselves. In the art history tradition of identifying national schools of art, even internationalist modernism in design is museumized as artwork statements of "British" or "American" character. In another vein, munificent gifts of art or property to the state, made by individuals for the improvement and enjoyment of fellow citizens, as well as for continuing glory of the individual, constitute a group of houses that are museums in themselves due to the donor's rich collecting. Sometimes named *ego-seums*, the extravagance of the gift celebrates not only the noblesse of the donor but also the wealth of the state that can enable individuals to achieve such heights of philanthropy.

Two more techniques of bringing patriotic effect into the domain of house museums can be seen as opposite sides of a coin. The opening up of stately homes appears to indicate a democratizing of aristocratic culture by giving access to all; by contrast, the celebration of ordinary people's lives in houses interpreted for social history significance elevates the anonymous characters of history into the pantheon of the nation. What had once been the patrimony of a great family headed by one individual per generation was unexpectedly transmuted in the 1960s into the national heritage of England, and promoted as a special contribution of English culture to world culture. At the same time, the social history turn elevated the historical significance of the poor, the marginal, and the excluded from conventional history, calling forth the sympathies of a new generation of social justice advocates. The demand for equal representation in the state cultural apparatus seemed

difficult to achieve, owing to the poor and ephemeral nature of their possessions, but generated a new art of re-creation based on documentary and pictorial records. Tenement houses, industrial barracks, and workers' cottages
have joined the corpus of older styles of house museums to enlarge the span
of national identities depicted via houses.

Species of House Museum

In the light of the foregoing discussion of the implication of home in the
construction of individual identity, and of museums in the construction of
national identities, the house museum is revealed as a particularly charged
form. While they share a common relationship to aspects of national identity, it is useful to subdivide the species of house museums by the motivation
of their foundation.

Hero Houses
These are houses of great men (and sometimes women) whose achievements
are acknowledged as forming, improving, and even redeeming national existence and character. A hero doesn't need to have inhabited a house for very
long to leave an aura of greatness; occasionally, the hero may have merely
visited the house commemorated for his or her presence, as in the "Queen
Elizabeth/George Washington slept here" phenomenon. The heroes whose
houses are museumized are invariably figures of national or local fame.

Artwork Houses
Artwork houses are preserved and museumized for the sake of their design,
which may be high style or vernacular, ancient or modern, famed for the
interior and/or exterior quality. Artwork houses display certain formal characteristics claimed as particularly expressive of national or local character,
and hence are important for distinguishing national identity. Technological
innovation, ingenuity, skill, and workmanship may also have a part in defining what makes a place worth museumizing for design qualities, though, in
practice, high style is the overwhelming characteristic.

Collectors' Houses
These are houses in which a collection, usually of antiquities or art, is developed with such a connection to its house-vessel that its integrity requires
the shell as well as the contents. The result is a self-contained essence of
museum-in-a-house, referring particularly to the individual collector and
casting her or him as a figure especially important for national insight, taste,

or character. In this species, many collectors explicitly donate the house and collection to the state, or it is offered by heirs, thus stressing the personal gesture to the state.

Social History Houses

The modern expression of social history is realized in houses deliberately selected to represent more humble strata of society than those representing the previous species of house museums. The restorative justice element of social history house museums focuses on both anonymous and known individuals, and it veers between a heroization of Everyman/woman and a personal story in which the big history may be lost in the welter of the particular. The species of social history houses addresses demotic aspects of national identity.

Country Houses

Country houses are aristocratic houses of Great Britain, products of a multigenerational development of house, furnishings, collections, and gardens. Country houses (more realistically considered palaces on once-feudal estates) are (in the English-speaking world) a phenomenon particular to the United Kingdom, but they have had enormous influence on the international idea of what a house museum is or should be. The significance of country houses as national icons might now lie less in their own history than in their widespread museumization after World War II and their acclamation as peak artifacts of national culture.

Not-Very-Important Houses

There remains a large rump composed of pale imitations of the others. On examination, they are often found to be houses that became available and were seized by enthusiastic advocates without much heed to justifiable significance. Ancestor veneration often drives such house museums, sometimes endowing them with positive spiritual or communal feeling, focused on nonspecific antiquity (contrasted to consciously constructed history). There is a vast number of not-very-important house museums.

The term *house museum* is in common use in the United States and Australia, but less in the United Kingdom. The idea as it is understood in the New World is clouded in Britain by the overwhelming image of the country house. Hailed in a 1820s poem as "the stately homes of England," the phrase was colored in a parody by Noel Coward, and drifted into the language of mass-marketing culture; *stately home* is used by the cognoscenti with a slightly mocking inflection (Hemans 1827).[1] It is matched by a certain prejudice hovering over the notion that a country house might be a museum—the specter of the dead, dusty repository of museum stereotype militates against perceiving historic houses as museums in the professional sense. Not all country houses *are* museums; some owners can afford to keep them as private residences, and others prefer to pay for the huge costs of maintenance by marketing their houses as venues for commercial events and hospitality. But to the non-British mind, there is no question that the National Trust's and other agencies' country houses are house museums, as are the private houses that open with professionally curated presentations.

That said, the meanings contained in the country house ideal have had a tsunami effect on house museums in the rest of the world, despite removal from their United Kingdom context and filtering by colonial and postcolonial circumstances. The long, particular conditions of aristocratic property display expressed in the castles, palaces, and country houses of Britain encapsulate a lifestyle that still enchants modern people's dreams. It came into mass consciousness when country houses opened as tourism destinations after World War II, and it flourishes in film and television, fantasy as well as reality. Country house style came to seem the very model of what is valuable enough to be conserved, a self-fulfilling definition of what *should* be conserved. Thus in Britain the ideal of elegant housing with ancient lineage shaped both fashion and heritage practice (Cornforth 1988, 12–19). And regardless of the specificity of Britain's country houses to Britain's history, Britain's ex-colonies sought to mold their own monuments along the lines of the best of British. This was assisted by continuing adherence among the New World ruling class to the decorative style of antique furniture and rich textiles on English/European lines. The country house ideal filtered the vision of both decorators and preservationists across oceans.

Luckily for the national cultures of the United States and Australia, the social history movement that stormed professional museums in the 1980s inverted the focus of heritage significance. It by no means wiped out or replaced the country house ideal, but it ushered in a new phase of exhibiting nonaristocratic inhabitants and museumizing humble houses. Antiquity or primal standing is an influential value in Western culture, but in the ex-colonies the ancient tended not to be very glamorous. Social history bolstered New World antiquity, explained the absence of aristocratic people and culture, and enabled the glorification of such unlikely heroes as Puritans and convicts. Humble buildings and material culture have the disadvantage of being flimsy and ephemeral, so dedicated museumization of their history was often shaped by archaeology and reproduction, exemplified by Plimoth Plantation in Massachusetts. At the same time, the colonies created wealth for some, and their (relatively) fine houses were among the first to be identified by communities and heritage agencies for museumization.

The habit of museumizing the relatively grand produced a situation in which any available house with some pretension to style and a collection of antique furniture seemed capable of plausible museumhood, on the grounds that it was, relatively speaking, a country house or stately home. Since such houses belonged to the rich, who tended to have the influence and power that led to fame, they also represented the most respectable vestiges of local or national history. Continuous family occupation of the same house was less common in the socially mobile New World than in the Old, so fine old houses often demonstrated a history of use by several families. Where democratic values existed alongside a taste for ancestral grandeur, this made museumization apparently more representative by including more characters

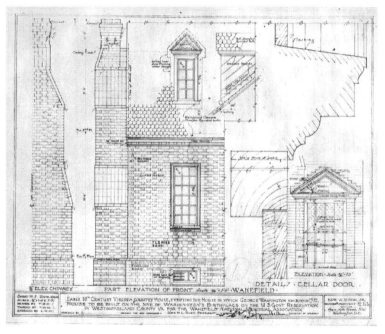

Sheet 7 of plans for a speculative reconstruction of George Washington's birthplace home, Northern Neck, Virginia, 1928, by Edward Donn. The large brick house built to these plans in 1931 was largely based on nearby Gunston Hall. Wakefield, the house in which George Washington was born in 1732, burned down in 1779. The project to construct a "replica" indicates the strong desire for a nativity story for the first president of the United States.
Photo courtesy of the Library of Congress, Prints & Photographs Division, HABS, VA, 97-____, 3–4.

who fulfilled the national mythology of immigrants making good. But the language of house museum interpretation has always tended to aggrandize achievement in terms of the richness of furniture rather than contextualizing it within the story of immigration. Grand-ish houses have thus acquired grand-ish histories to validate their existence as house museums, where little grandeur was ever evident in reality.

To museum professionals, this appears to be the revenge of the country house on New World imitations. Yet such a judgment fails to explain the continuing affection that some communities, or segments of communities, hold for their not-very-important house museums. Unfortunately, even more communities are finding that the not-very-important house museum in their neighborhood is *not* of much significance to them, and plenty are floundering (Harris 2007, 3–19). Energetic staff determined to make them locally relevant can rescue some, but many deserve museum euthanasia.

The Morphology of House Museums

A basic definition of a house museum is to say it is a dwelling, museumized and largely presented in its domestic function. This opens up the range from a hut to a palace, and could include institutional dwellings such as convents and jails (though to reduce the scope slightly, they are not discussed in this book). Several further characteristics of the museumized form of a house need consideration. Must a house museum be furnished, or can an empty house make a meaningful museum? Are original furnishings necessary, or can a re-created assemblage fulfill legitimate functions? Does a reproduction house count as a house museum? How much restoration makes a reproduction? What about ruins? The answers depend on circumstances, but houses demonstrating all these conditions appear in this book. A house museum may be presented in as-found condition, stabilized as-found, restored to a known condition, or re-created to a provisional condition; empty, furnished, or part furnished; fitted with original furnishings (as found or rearranged), or re-created with appropriate period material, or with reproductions; or wholly or partially furnished to different historic periods. If the significance of the site is constituted by its domestic purpose, the interpretive aim is to express some aspect of domestic culture, and the management regime complies or aims to comply with professional standards, then a house can be called a house museum.

Houses are intricate artifacts, comprising real estate, built fabric, arranged or decorated settings, items of furnishing, household equipment, and fittings. They contain the intangibles of human associations past and present. Sometimes a house museum continues to be inhabited, or partially inhabited, by residents, who might be caretakers or previous owners with lifetime occupancy or other residential agreements. Houses that come to museumization with a full or large quantity of furnishings and fittings require intensive management to determine the extent and condition of the collection, and then to assess how it can be securely exhibited for public access. Houses that come as a shell, even a ruin, may need the attention of architects and conservators to restore significant form (if, *pace* Ruskin, this is possible) before the long process of gathering appropriate furnishings or exhibits commences. Framing the house itself, most houses occupy a curtilage larger than the immediate footprint of the building, frequently with integral gardens, outbuildings, and estates. Managing the house museum therefore includes property and environmental management of the entire site. These are the range of conditions that make it appropriate to talk of specialist house museologies as the scope of conserving, researching, interpreting, and exhibiting a house museum for the purpose of study, education, and enjoyment, in the words of the ICOM definition of a museum.

As a result of all the foregoing conditions, houses are costly to conserve, demanding to maintain, and frequently difficult to open to large-scale visiting. In conservation treatment terms, it is unwise to separate the structure and the contents, though this can be difficult to prioritize. The problems of, say, hanging conserved pictures on damp walls, or continuing to expose old textiles to even occasional sunlight, can only be resolved by decision following an analysis of risk. It often results in limited display options unless or until expensive conservation standards, or the use of reproductions, can be introduced. The house structure and outbuildings require constant maintenance, necessary repairs, and improvements as specified in the overall management plan. Gardens need specialist horticulturists and regular gardeners to develop and maintain them to a level that meets the significance and interpretive goals of the place. Larger estates of farm, wood, or bushland bring tasks that demand experienced property management personnel. This range and mix of knowledge necessary to operate a house museum indicates one aspect of how agencies such as the National Trust in Britain and Historic New England in the United States have grown: having developed specialist infrastructure to manage complex sites, they can (to some extent) service sites using economies of scale. The absence of such resources indicates why amateur and underfunded sites cannot achieve the standards that are both necessary and expected in house museums.

Enabling visitors to access the house is a primary purpose of house museums: a place that is too small, too precious, or too fragile to allow access can be a specimen but not a museum. The compromise between access, preserva-tion, and safety is the central dilemma of opening a house to visitors. The challenge is to introduce many people into spaces generally designed for a small number. Most dwellings are built for family-scale use, and even a big extended family house tends to have more, rather than bigger, spaces. Even a palace, though it may have galleries capable of taking large numbers of visitors in historical times and now, has private apartments and servant quar-ters on a smaller scale. Hence the techniques of mass people management are often necessary in popular house museums: prescribed one-way routes; a number of thematic routes to spread the load; timed admission based on maximum carrying capacity; admission only to spaces big enough to take the numbers; and booked tours to satisfy specialist interests in less accessible parts.

House museums face the awkward fact that they come "as is"—a fully formed product, almost never developed in response to customer needs or de-sires. It is a major challenge of institutional survival for many house museums to entice sufficient paying visitors to maintain their operations. Some close; some revert to private ownership with occasional open days; many struggle to find sponsorship deals and grant funding; perhaps the majority get by on less than enough. The marketing perspective urges house museum managers to develop aspects of the heritage resource in directions that accord with what the public wants to see and do when it decides to visit the homes of the past. On a different plane from the abstractions of nationalist meaning, market research shows that visitors want a pleasant excursion with family or friends, and that the intellectual content of the visit is only one of several condi-tions that contribute to a satisfying visit. The others have much to do with the social and physical contexts of visiting. Provision of access and activities suitable for sociable looking and interaction includes seating, personable guides, cafés, and clean toilets. Orientation areas and visitor centers have proved themselves in achieving goals in visitor education, physical comfort, and transitional modification of behavior, helping to put both visitors and managers at ease. Visitors who are comfortable, aware of what they are about to see, and reminded that their next step is into a special environment are safer and more aware and more receptive, proving that the customer focus is good practice in all dimensions of house museum management.

The curatorial presentation and interpretation of a house museum is gen-erally intended to be subtle and unobtrusive. The presuppositions and limits of such a goal were thoroughly disrupted by the critique of the new museol-ogy, pointing out that the inexplicit values of dominant ideologies underlie the museum as a representational medium (Vergo 1989; Smith 2006). This reality is evident in lapses in the technical aspects of presenting a house, quite as much as in the content. The intact house is almost invariably presented without comment beyond noting that it is rare, allowing the implication that what the visitor sees was always there. The "editorial" housekeeping of collection registration, conservation, and security is rarely made visible in the public sphere. Almost without comment, the re-created house museum presents as if it were original, and thanks to the highly specialized knowledge required to assess the authenticity of furnishing schemes, few visitors notice, unless egregious anomalies infiltrate the *mise-en-scène*. At the same time, the magico-religious atmosphere of many house museums conduces to the wishfulness of some visitors to believe they are indeed in the literal presence of the past. Credulity or complicity? This question introduces an investigation of the twin acts of exhibiting and looking in house museums.

The Exhibited House

"A house is a machine for living in," wrote Le Corbusier in 1923 (Le Corbusier 2007, 151). This book is a study of houses that have shifted from their usual purpose of accommodating the lives of their inhabitants to being displayed for public inspiration, edification, and pleasure. To paraphrase Corbu, a house museum is a machine for looking (at). In this, the displayed house constitutes a social relationship between exhibitors and viewers, mediated by artifacts. The act of looking in the house museum is conditioned by two particularities of the house as such: it is (usually) located in situ, and it possesses the integrity of a whole (except when it doesn't, as considered below). Knowledge formed in this environment is a product of the resource itself, the narrative frame constructed by institutions and their curatorial agents, the technologies of collection and display, and the agendas of visitors. Whether venerably patinated or shiny-bright restored, the exhibited house demands close analysis to recognize the effects of these mechanisms. Its raw materials and parameters are the authenticity of the house and the integrity of the contents; its levers are the naturalization of what is exhibited and the suppression of time. The following discussion explores these four elements and their permutations.

The claim to authenticity on the basis of in-situ location is grounded in the conventional expectation that a house is permanently sited in space until it is demolished. The claim is undermined in many circumstances; yet it miraculously retains credibility with managers and visitors. In the most extreme case, even when the house is gone, its site may continue to carry associations recognized in, for instance, a plaque that grants honor to the location. In practice, almost any house is portable, depending on the budget available to move it, and a surprising number of historic houses are relocated in the course of museumization. The potential to move a house is often what "saves" it for museumization: the commercial value of its site can justify the costs of removal, especially if the move satisfies regulations or public interest demanding preservation. In other scenarios, an abandoned house might collapse forever if not "rescued" for museumization. Through all such transformations, observed practice shows that relocated houses can assert the same degree of museum authority as the house in situ. Even more surprisingly, so can a brand-new replica. How is it possible to subvert the place or even the fabric of a house and yet sustain its truth-claim to authenticity? The metaphysics of this question are interrogated in chapter 7, but it seems that the professional norms of museology and the expectations of visitors can be satis-

Steve ponders Wordsworth at home in Dove Cottage, Grasmere, Cumbria, 2009. Everyone who visits Dove Cottage knows a line or ten of Wordsworth. This is where the poet wrote, "I wandered, lonely as a cloud," to introduce his joy at coming across "a crowd, a host, of golden daffodils." You know: "And then my heart with pleasure fills, and dances with the daffodils." From 1804 to today . . .
Photo courtesy of Stephen Liddle.

fied with certain compromises in the practice of conserving history for the perceived public good. The exhibited house is not just a social interaction but also a relationship of complicity.

Similar license applies to the credibility of the contents of house museums. Even when houses contain collections that are substantially intact, it is very common to re-create room settings. In many houses, the collection is largely or entirely introduced to represent what could have been there. A few provenanced objects may have made their way back to the house after museumization, the kind of small objects that survive as souvenirs and keepsakes—spectacles, jewelry, family Bibles, inkwells. They come to serve as touchstones that validate the rest of the re-created ensemble. These examples demonstrate how, in the eyes of managers and consumers, the mantle of museum-authorized meaning is endowed with the power to legitimate re-created furnishings. Furthermore, the totality and unity of the house display make it seem particularly real and appropriate for this end. The risk of old museum-style taxonomic displays being perceived as "dead" plagues the house museum, and both curatorial hand and visitor eye strive to overcome static display. The former inserts costumed interpreters, fresh flowers, and casual disorder to indicate an on-going human presence. Visitor books show that visitors are highly inclined to adopt the view that the scene is "as if the inhabitants had stepped out for a moment." This charming delusion is a testament to the power of things over people, a condition exercised to its capacity in the intact or mimetic environment of the house museum.

Curators are willing to reconstruct what is lacking in order to produce a coherent scenario, in the way that art restorers reproduce the missing pieces in a broken object to make it intelligible. Both acknowledge, with philosophical justifications and practical conventions, the artifice required to achieve a more ideal representation; however, practices such as *tratteggio* to indicate conjectural infill are more standard procedure in art conservation than in constructing social history displays. The careful methods of furnishing plans based on meticulous research are indicators of the good faith of house curators, but unknown and unavailable objects in the setting are almost never publicly acknowledged. It doesn't seem to matter. For their part, visitors are surprisingly willing to suspend disbelief and to be delighted by the constructed product. Despite the rhetoric of the apparent "real thing," house museums, even if substantially a re-creation, require and receive complicity between the museum and the public.

Framed by this unspoken bargain, the material culture of the house can truly be called, in the phrase of Alfred Gell, a technology of enchantment (Gell 1992). Gell referred to the dazzling effect of overwhelming complexity, beauty, and riches produced in order to engulf beholders and sway them to the exhibitor's purpose. Sharon Macdonald describes this power in museumized sites as "enchanted looking" and proposes that the process of mystification that produces it needs to be addressed with an eye to the political agency of institutions (Macdonald 2005, 224). Certainly, the history of museumization demonstrates a predilection to find significance in the houses of the dominant culture, evident in the overwhelming proportion of large size and high-style houses among the sum of house museums (Young 2007, 65–69). But even among small and vernacular houses, as already suggested, the domestication of national themes in order to encourage the viewer to identify with nationalist consensus constitutes the foremost agenda.

Like any museum specimen, the exhibited house is selected out of the stock of its kind, for a reason that usually refers to just one moment or aspect of its history. The power to select and interpret is the crucial exercise of institutional museum authority, locating or reiterating the house theme within the national narrative. Although only the tiniest proportion of houses is ever excised from use to become museum-style specimens, the consequences of selection and museumization are many. The rationale for museumization often mandates that the house is restored to a certain period of its career, a process that may obliterate prior and subsequent uses, the better to frame the exhibition within. A period restoration may also isolate the museumized house from others among which it stands, which bear the signs of modern use. Equally challenging, surroundings may have altered, as when suburbs swallow a once-rural cottage or a one-time estate shrinks to the gardens around the house, or less. All these cases chart transformations that aim to suppress ongoing time by eradicating the adaptations that time brings to any structure that survives. For the act of shaping the physical house to display a certain moment, year, or period inevitably requires erasing subsequent changes, and often demands active reconstruction to achieve the known or putative form of the chosen era.

Here begins the dilemma of restoring the past in order to display it. Evidence may be available, but there is never enough. For each step that comes closer to historical reality, a gap remains between it and the unknown, pointing to the essential impossibility of reestablishing past time. That museums continue to try to display the past speaks to the conviction that it is worthwhile in order to visit history in situ. In fact, this claim is often the theme of house museum advertising: having extracted the house from its conventional purpose and the present time, the crucial moment of transformation into a historic site is the public invitation to come and look. Both inside and out, the metaphor of frozen time is often applied to historic houses. Sometimes it carries a sense of wonder; at other times, it is an accusation of cold irrelevance. I suggest that it is more appropriate to think of time pruned to a single bud, containing the promise of a future that the visitor already knows. Does it matter? The argument against interventionist restoration is that of ethical archaeology: exposure of one era destroys all others and closes off subsequent investigation of anything else. For this reason, reversibility is a key tenet of contemporary conservation philosophy, though pragmatic conservators admit that it is more honored in the breach than the observance. Meanwhile, the philosophical historian observes that each generation makes use of the resources of the past in ways that are relevant to its present, and time moves on, leaving a palimpsest.

Having negotiated time and space, the house museum presents a unique duality, a plural basis of display: it is a house *as* display and a house *for* display. From the outside, the house is on display; yet, on the inside, it is so normal and complete that it does not seem to be on display. Of course, it is, and far from untouched. Viewing the house from outside or walking around it, looking at its features, illustrates how a house can be perceived as a specimen, an artifact, an object. The curious experience of the house museum is that the specimen transforms into a museum—not just the abstract shell of a museum but the shell of the house's essential purpose as a home. In other words, the house constitutes the intelligible context of its exhibition. Technically speaking, the contents of the house are specimens on show; yet the constellation of the whole appears to possess such coherent totality that it is hard not to see it as a "natural" formation, an artifact in itself. The house provides an authentic context for displaying its contents: the kitchen is full of cooking utensils, the dining room displays how the inhabitants consumed their food, the bedrooms are furnished for sleeping—more or less as modern people understand these acts of daily life. Visitors know that no food is prepared or eaten here and no one sleeps in the beds, but they suspend disbelief in order to participate in the experience. They use the double lens of the house museum to look at the house *as* and *for* display.

The consequences highlight the difference between the house museum and the conventional museum. The general museum focus on the display of labeled specimens seems so self-evident that it can obscure the values implicit in its institutional ethos, a prime field of critique. By contrast, the house museum offers maximal context, sheer display in situ, signaling full and frank exposition of household values. Thanks to the visible habitus, the whole ensemble itself communicates meaning to the visitor in a different way to individually labeled items of furnishing. Looking at the interior, the implications of fashionable or out-of-date arrangement, messy or tidy presentation, poor or affluent setting, point to insights into the character and experience of the household that inhabited it. To comprehend such conditions implicit in domestic arrangements may require historical knowledge many visitors don't possess, calling for interpretation under the museum aegis of education. Nonetheless, the ongoing familiarities of domestic living enable a level of confidence in understanding the exhibited house, unequalled in any other kind of museum. Even the difference between objects, styles, and arrangements then and now can promote the state of mindfulness that predisposes people to be aware of and responsive to information and interpretation. Perception of the house interior thus involves interplay between looking in the mode of the museum and apprehending in the mode of the house or home.

Some risks follow from this conflation of ways of seeing. First is the cognitive dissonance of looking at domestic goods that are so familiar to the viewer ("Grandma had one of those") that they challenge the museum effect. How can something so ordinary be important? This question proves the strength of the effect in provoking the response. It can be explained in terms of the traditions that color the popular concept of a museum, in particular the character of the museum as treasure house. If the museum is defined by material of "museum quality," its contents must be rare and precious and worth lots of money, which is irresistibly attractive to contemplate. Grandma's iron is discordant in this sense, though her antique chair might fulfill the fantasy. Nonetheless, all but the most dismissive visitors can usually make the transition from an object's value in money to its significance in history, and in doing so they achieve one of the museum's educational purposes.

Second is the overwhelming totality of the contextual exhibition, so convincing that it seems natural and uncrafted—not an exhibition at all. The integrity of excellent room re-creations tests this problem with the question: What is authentic? Even in houses with a high degree of intact contents, a conservator or curator will have "edited" the place for structural stability, public access, and (almost certainly) a vision of coherence. Practical requirements such as safe floorboards, flow paths through rooms, and security for fragile artifacts determine some replacements or changes in location of original material. Small acts to rationalize or improve strange or clumsy arrangements are almost impossible to resist, even though they disturb the integrity of the archival fond of an intact collection. Such changes are small and may be necessary, and they are rarely explicit to the viewer. In re-created house museums, the apparent perfection of the total environment is frequently more than convincing to visitors, who assume they are seeing "the real thing." After all, the museum is the guarantor of authenticity, isn't it?

House Museum Visitors and Their Visits

Visitors are not unaware of the constructed nature of the house museum display. They choose to make the visit, pay for the ticket, leave bags at the door, and perhaps put on booties to protect the carpet from visitors like themselves. Yet they are likely to suppress their awareness of artifice to some degree, feeling a mixture of privilege, pleasure, or solemnity, as they step into the imaginative role of inhabitants or friends of the household (Smith 2009, 41). This state of willing disbelief or imaginative hedonism is not total; visitors can swing between the spectator personality and the imaginary self *because* the house is on display. The experience is different from visiting a friend's house or going home after work because one has relationships to tend and tasks to do in those houses, which usually take priority over admiring the decor. But it is very similar to visiting a house for sale, where potential buyers are invited to imagine themselves living here while they simultaneously consider the logistics of whether this house actually suits their needs. The visitor doesn't have to *like* the taste displayed, just as in the house museum. In fact, criticizing the taste on display may be part of the onlooker's persona, and one of the most satisfying elements of the visit.

"The old house movement appeals to the public more widely than any other branch of museum work," wrote the director of the American Association of Museums in 1939 (Coleman 1939, 74). Despite fears of a surfeit of heritage these days, his opinion is still valid, as house museums remain icons of local identity, popular destinations, and cynosures of history and taste, regardless of whether these attributions are deserved. Unfortunately, such truths apply most to the passing trade, for (though gardens and grounds are well-used) familiarity can breed oblivion among many house museum neighbors and locals. At the same time, the majority of house museums would not open at all without the vast commitment of local volunteers to guiding, housekeeping, gardening, shop-keeping, and serving the tea and scones in the café. Still, for the uncommitted, it requires vigorous programs of events, exhibitions, activities, festivals, fairs, and reenactments to lure locals into regular engagement with their house museums. In marketing terms, the question arises: "Who wants house museums?"

In the era of museum sensitivity to social inclusiveness and cultural diversity, much angst has resulted from the truth that house museums appeal most to an apparently exclusive, older, female, and middle-class audience. In practice, this demographic looms large in all museum audiences, with the exception of motor museums. Without diminishing the responsibility of museums to make themselves accessible to the widest possible social spectrum, it should be noted that school students and sociable groups of adults are also large components of the average house museum audience. Many an adult visitor to a house museum makes and enjoys personal connections that might be called nostalgia or reminiscence, that enable the satisfaction of reflecting on one's own life in relation to officially preserved history. Even in grand houses, visitors who judge how much they like or dislike the color of the sofa upholstery in relation to their own living rooms cast themselves as equal agents in the history of taste.

There are many answers to the question, "What motivates house museum visitors?" Writing of country houses, Adrian Tinniswood suggests that, to the regret of specialists and connoisseurs, most visitors come not to appreciate the finer details of Tudor paneling and Georgian portraits but to engage in creative fantasy (Tinniswood 1989, 191–93). This view follows the trend toward seeing museum visitors as active creators of their own experiences, informed by personal history and agendas. It leads to a very attractive conclusion: that visitors come to mine the house for the raw materials of imaginative bricolage and to share the experience with their family and friends. Laurajane Smith interprets the findings of her interviews with country house visitors to show that they visit in the persona of their family culture and thus find reassurance in affiliation with or deference to the original aristocratic inhabitants (Smith 2006, 138–41). I understand this as a peculiarly British condition; I doubt that it applies in the New World. There is little other analysis of visitors specifically to house museums, and it is likely that the data on museum visiting in general applies to the house species as well (Merriman 1991, 42–56). But in the chapters that follow I explore evidence for visitation connected to the particular purposes of the different species of house museums discussed in each chapter. These include the memorial visit to the house of a hero, where sentiment and knowledge combine in reverence or, where there is insufficient personal connection, a simulacrum of reverence. The effects of the postmodern taste for celebrity hints at the possibility that the fake intimacy contemporary people can enjoy with celebrities may now color visits to heroes' houses with another kind of imagined relationship.

The Rest of the Book

The argument that national identity frames and shapes the genre of house museums in a number of idiosyncratic expressions constitutes the rest of the book that follows. Threads of the ideas reviewed in this chapter bob in and out, not all with conclusive findings. The first chapter comprises studies of the five genres: heroes' houses, artwork houses, collectors' houses, social history houses, and country houses. I confess I largely sidestep the ungainly segment of house museums I have described as insignificant. (Their problems are management challenges, not to be much assisted by analysis of typologies.)

The second and third chapters survey the primal house museum species, the dwellings of heroes. The pilgrimage tradition and its mores is a central theme, developing in the conditions of nineteenth- and twentieth-century economy and culture. The rising forces of mass, democratic, secular society in the different but kindred environments of the Old World and the New gave to the pilgrimage model new focuses and mediums. The nature of the heroes commemorated in their houses demonstrates the shift from a feudal world to one where political states overhauled local identities. The national project engulfed previous religious and monarchical loyalties, and house museums were in the vanguard of its public presentation by showcasing the heroes of the state. The aura of national leadership was easy to find in heroes' houses, and the ambit of leadership increasingly encompassed cultural as well as political manifestations. The growth of mass literacy provided an eager citizenry of readers, which was transnational from the early nineteenth century. As colonial and former-colonial writers began to address local conditions, they established the scene for academic standard-setters at the turn of the twentieth century to proclaim them as the voices of distinctively national literatures. Celebrating the nation's writers generated the biggest class of hero house museums to this day—and they are still being created. Other nationally famous creative personalities are museumized in their houses too—artists, musicians, inventors, scientists—but in nothing like the quantity of writers. A parallel sphere of heroes' house museums opened up in the later twentieth century to acknowledge the heroes of previously marginalized social sectors such as people of color and women, and cultural manifestations such as popular music and film. It is hard to know whether this development demonstrates that house museums occupy a strong, vital position in public culture or if it represents a catch-up appropriation of a share of the markers of power. I suspect the latter. There remains much to investigate in the field of heroes' houses.

The fourth chapter introduces the category of artwork houses and the question of national aesthetics. The idea of national style or styles was held dear in various times and places, but its imprecision and wishfulness usually undermined its chances of having a wider effect. Nonetheless, many an institution tried to define, express, and promulgate the values of national style. The vernacular and the elite were both found to be suited to the role. Houses turned out to be useful vehicles for this agenda, as buildings big enough to fulfill the monumental role but small enough to be extracted from utilitarian purposes for display. In recent years, the concept of design has taken on more specialized meanings and acquired a broader public interest. Its connections with art, insofar as they are different things, suggest that design too can be harnessed to the national project by retrospective selection and display. Just as paintings were regrouped in national schools when palaces laden with artworks were turned into museums, so certain houses of virtuoso or representative design have been retro-attributed with national character. This is part of the transformation of the category of British country houses from conspicuous consumption as evidence of owners' wealth and power to representing an alleged characteristically English aesthetic. Scholarly connoisseurs invested this translation with revisionist authority; it has been mightily successful. Reattribution is a fertile source of new perspectives, and I employ it myself by nominating various country house museums into the class of artwork house museums. I do not deny that this is an instrumentalist intervention in order to make my case, and acknowledge that the examples used can be employed in other categories as well.

Chapter 5 visits the most direct conjunction of house and museum, collectors' houses. It is right to consider them as a category of house museum rather than generic museum because they commenced their existence as dwellings and usually frame their distinctiveness by reference to domestic origins, even if they take on the title *museum* or *collection*, as at Sir John Soane's Museum and the Frick Collection. The works were acquired and placed in the house, but not (usually) exhibited to the public until after the death of their collectors or their heirs. Collectors' house museums constitute the smallest species of house museum for not many collections survive their collectors, and even fewer remain in situ. The ones that do are overwhelmingly collections of art and antiquities, the kind of material whose quality and monetary value is high enough to justify keeping a house out of domestic use in order to display it in permanent museum mode. Natural history or artifact collections are much harder to justify for such permanent display in situ, and generally survive by unusual chance rather than design. The national frame of a collector's house museum is a little attenuated. In claiming the mantle of a great museum (for collectors' house museums comprise the very finest quality material), they gesture to their models-cum-comparators, the great museums of the state. By placing her or his collection in the public sphere after a lifetime of private pleasure, the collector becomes a benefactor, not just contributing individual works to established museums but contributing on the level of the entire museum. The consequent philanthropic reputation polishes the memory of the collector, who lives on in public esteem. A collector's house museum is the ultimate in grand national gestures.

In chapter 6, this story tracks and reaches the social history revolution of the mid- to late twentieth century, the chief mode of modern museum history, with particular applications to representing the material domestic world. Social history's startling arrival on the scene of museum interpretation belies several strong older modes of collecting and exhibiting domestic life, first via folklore and next via industrial archaeology. In the United States, the phenomenon of women's lineage societies, whose contribution to patriotic culture inserted the uncelebrated women of history into the national story, had adopted house museums as their special project. The maternalist democracy of depicting ordinary women contains all the contradictions of conservative feminism, and the movement's political influence waned before social history overtook its remaining house museums. In such ways the impact of social history on house museums was less about hardware than about introducing critical politics to explain the lives of women and other power-less social groups. The politics shifted toward cultural identities by the turn of the twenty-first century, emerging with a restitutional agenda to locate and present suppressed histories in historic sites, especially houses. A commitment to social justice accompanied the search for new classes of people's homes to museumize. Recognizing the history of slavery in house museums remains the most obdurate theme.

Chapter 7 springs from the challenge to present social history in house museums where little material evidence survives, generating the solution of interpretation. Heritage interpretation is delivered in a myriad of media, but whatever the medium, the limited presence of original fabric problema-tizes museum credibility, which almost always relies on exhibiting "the real thing." That problem is authenticity. For all that the idea of authenticity is acknowledged as slippery, it contains such intuitive truth that it's very hard to avoid. The spectrum of foundational motives that activates house museums, plus their doubled orientation to site *and* collection, present an exceptional field in which to examine the paradoxes of authenticity. This field contains the narratives that house museum managements select for the public, and the techniques that carry the narratives, both of them constitut-ing interpretation. The field also contains the processes of managing house museum fabric, which almost always involve interpretive decisions about restoration and reconstruction, outside and in. The whole apparatus chal-lenges the assumed singular truth of "authenticity," especially at the far ends of living history, experimental archaeology, and museum theater. Hence I come to the view that the authenticity of house museums is a construct, highly negotiated among the experts who museumize them, with the aim of presenting visitors with a credible insight into history and heritage. In the end, credibility lives or dies in the minds of the visiting public. Hence we can regard authenticity as a judgment co-created between professionals and visitors. Its focus shifts in different types of house museum, the ideal challenged by so many variables that only the innocent can hold on. The rest of us must grapple with the limits of history in space and time and acknowledge them frankly to visitors—who, it turns out, are very capable of recognizing reality, suspending and reinstating disbelief, joking with the mismatches, and drawing conclusions from the experience.

Chapter 8 reviews the museumizing history of British country houses. Country houses have been well analyzed in architectural, cultural, and social history, but some points remain to be made about the country house as a museum. The first is that country houses that are open to the public on a regular and reasonably substantial timetable (more than occasional weekends), and present interpretive services about the cultural value of the place and its contents to visitors, are museums. Whether they are inhabited is irrelevant to museum status, for many resident caretakers, maintenance staff, or tenants occupy house museums. This needs to be said, on account of the old and persistent prejudice against calling country houses *museums*, dating from the earliest years of the National Trust's Country Houses Scheme in the late 1930s. It is based on mystification of the house due to the magic endowed by the presence of aristocratic owners. This is snobbery based on the hollow privilege of ancestry. Not all country house museums resist or resent the title, but the antimuseum attitude is past its time. More important is the impact of country houses on the genus of house museums in the popular imagination in the Old World and the New. The image of the stately home is widely perceived as summing up the essence of what a house museum could and should be, regardless of historic contexts. The country house ideal has become a straitjacket on other house museums.

The last chapter embarks on a difficult category: insignificant house museums, a painful topic. In the United States, it is recognized in the question, "Are there too many house museums?" The question emerged as a public topic in 1996 and received much well-informed consideration, leading to several strategic directions for sustainability. But the global financial crisis in 2008–2009 undermined the whole field of problematic museums, and the situation has not completely settled since then. In the United Kingdom, there are relatively few house museums other than country houses, a problem mainly perceived as market saturation and, occasionally, as a tax dodge. In both nations, the cruelest fate afflicts not the poorest-resourced, volunteer-led house museums, which are effectively outside the commercial economy, but the houses owned and managed by local government authorities. Consequently, in the United Kingdom, state ownership is transmuting to charitable agency status. In the long term, this may push some English house museums into the wasteland of unsustainability, as in the United States. The free-enterprising United States might or might not prove more resilient. My approach to the sad problems is recourse to professional assessment of heritage significance, a long-term judgment that can see endangered places fall off the twig if decay goes too far for too long. However, I know it is easier to prescribe closure than to enact it. I rather suspect that more house museums will survive, if in emaciated condition, than will disappear. On a theoretical level, the crisis pushed along a trend in the British world to develop public policy cases for the value of museums. The "too many house museums" discussion in the United States rehearsed traditional civic virtue arguments, culminating in calls for local relevance. By contrast, the British search pursued first the economic case for the strengths of the creative economy and, more recently, the public value of culture and especially museums in the cause of social integration. Both are big stretches for house museums as a species. But their core business of representing the past in the present is, on the basis of the revitalization around the turn of the twenty-first century of numerous older house museums, as flexible as the idea of authenticity. I think there is hope for house museums.

Notes

1. Felicia Hemans: "The stately homes of England,/How beautiful they stand,/Amidst their tall ancestral trees,/O'er all the pleasant land!"
   Noel Coward: "The stately homes of England,/How beautiful they stand,/To prove the upper classes/Have still the upper hand."

CHAPTER TWO

~

Heroes' Houses

The Home of the Nation Personified

Heroes are the secular gods or saints of the nation or of its civic subsets: provinces, regions, towns. The transformation of their houses into museums celebrates the collective identity and cultural community of the nation through the ritual of visiting. In this way, the visitor discovers or acknowledges the hero's achievements and understands them as qualities, events, or products that express a dimension of national character. The history of heroes' house museums is a history of national dreams, myths, and ideologies. This and the next chapter investigate the nature and history of commemorating and celebrating the great by preserving their houses. It is a phenomenon that constructs purposeful narratives of greatness in the context of domestic circumstances, despite many shortfalls, errors of fact and interpretation, repetition and elision. The house—almost any house, however long or briefly it was inhabited—serves as a means for the public to approach and commune with a Great Person or hero.

The idea that the home environment shapes an individual resident's development is common sense to some degree, though its limits are often stretched by a desire to explain outstanding characteristics. Equally common is the desire to find the mystical imprint of a hero's occupation of a house, expressed by a regular trope of the genre, as in this example relating to the homes of composers: "The masters lived in houses that still resonate those mute and mysterious harmonies, the famous silence which, after the last chord has been sounded, remains that of a long-departed genius" (Gefen 1998, 7). In the imagination of the visitor, it might be possible to see prefigurations or psychic remnants or to ascribe environmental causes to the hero's life and works that are derived from exposure to particular furnishings, rooms, structures, gardens, streets, towns, and more. Yet looking for the logical end of this list demonstrates the problem: Where do you draw the line in searching for the causal effects of home environment? Lives are at least as much shaped by family dynamics, economic standing, social constraints, ethical values, and the love and happiness present (or not) in the household. Other than economics, which determines the standard of living, these qualities are not readily intelligible in building or furnishing fabric.

That said, it is often only the material remains of the house that can be museumized to celebrate a hero. To this end, it is not accidental that the apparatus of religion has been adapted to the cause. In effect, the way in which the civil public responds to heroes' houses is not only kindred to the pilgrimage of the faithful to saints' shrines but also a direct continuation with that tradition. Indeed, it may connect to a deep structure of the human psyche that relies on magical thinking to provide comfort and confidence in negotiating the world. Despite the disenchantment asserted by modernity over older mentalities, the habit of magical thinking has many survivals in the modern world, underlying creations of postmodernity such as celebrity.

The appropriation by house museums of the psychology of veneration and the continuing power of magic gives them special strength as agents of a nationalist agenda. It is no surprise that the Great Men and occasional Great Women recognized by posterity in their dwellings today constitute a sizeable segment of the repertoire of heritage, and new Great Persons and their houses are steadily added to the stock. The fact that the public still seeks and apparently enjoys evidence of the greatness of heroes in their museumized houses indicates a complex blend of belief and wishfulness at work in the modern world. The taste for inspecting the domestic conditions in which admirable people lived is more than common sense, for its logic as presented by house curators and interpreters is essentially grounded in the practice of communing with relics. The key concept in this kind of reliquary thinking is authenticity—an idea with deep but flexible meanings in the practice of cultural heritage management (further taken up in chapter 7).

Dilemmas flow from the assumption that authentic connection has a particular role in validating, understanding, and maintaining the hero's house. The apparatus of managing the genuine suggests how the houses of heroes come to be thought of as shrines, and thence how they stray into the frame of magic, perhaps equally the intention of founders and guardians as well as in the public mind. A thread of ego runs throughout: heroes are, by definition, driven personalities. The domestic function of the house opens up a sense of intimately privileged connection between visitor and hero. Indeed, visitors are often motivated by some urge of personal identification with the hero, and in the aura of heroic numen, perfectly rational moderns can find themselves beset by deep emotion. Yes, I acknowledge that I, too, have quivered in Jane Austen's bedroom and Handel's rehearsal room.

What Is a Hero, and Why Do Nations Want Them?

Litterateurs and philosophers have addressed this question almost simultaneously with the foundation of heroes' house museums, and not by coincidence. The ur-theorist of Great Men, historian Thomas Carlyle, defined the characteristics of heroes through his commentaries on a set of lives in order to demonstrate his conviction that both history and humanity need transcendent leadership (Carlyle 1841). Some of his specimens seemed distinctly peculiar to his audience in 1841: Odin, Mohammed, Cromwell, and Napoleon showed that Carlyle populated his argument with myths, pagans, and national enemies as well as more conventional examples of the great and good. He concluded that heroes are men who advance their communities at vital moments in history, thanks to leadership that is visionary, resolute, and spiritually informed, despite inevitable human flaws. The splendid characters of this ilk not only merited hero veneration on their own account or for the histories they shaped, he argued, but also satisfied a deep longing for inspiration in the hearts of ordinary folk. His view was mystical and patriarchal: "We all of us reverence and must reverence Great Men, the one fixed point in . . . history, otherwise . . . bottomless and shoreless" (Carlyle 1841, 21).

Thus Carlyle articulated the rationale underpinning the idea that a visit to a hero's house attaches the visitor to a heroic historical narrative, joining the present to the glorious past. And while Carlyle never envisaged this outcome, of his ten exemplary Great Men, all but the prophet Mohammed are today commemorated in house museums (and often other museums as well), in which the national dimension of their achievements is the major frame of presentation.[1] Commentators steadily modified Carlyle's analysis of the hero throughout the nineteenth and twentieth centuries, producing new takes on the spectrum of house museums. The importance of cultural leadership was introduced in the 1880s: "Rembrandt must teach us to enjoy the struggle of light with darkness," wrote philosopher-psychologist William James. "Wagner teaches us to enjoy peculiar musical effects; Dickens gives a twist to our sentimentality, Artemus Ward to our humor; Emerson kindles a new moral light within us" (James 1917, 176). As another roll call of heroic figures by which to gauge the house museum standard, all these men but the comic wit, Artemus Ward, have houses preserved in their honor today.

In another attempt to explain the human drive to revere heroes, Edward B. Tylor, first professor of anthropology at Oxford, observed that hero myths are universal among the elements of primitive religion. He argued that they remain visible in religion, serving a social need for role models of transcendent capacity, even (or especially) if touched by imperfection and tragedy (Tylor 1958). Tylor's case studies displayed enough common elements to describe a "hero pattern" across cultures, an idea refocused by Joseph Campbell's project on mythic archetypes in *The Hero with a Thousand Faces* (1949). In the post–World War II world, the scope of studies of mind became infused with Freudian approaches to the unconscious, shifting the motivation of hero cults from heartening the soul to individual ego-satisfaction via projection and identification, evoking connection to the inner self and easing its integration in society. Campbell's analysis proved influential, especially for confirming the potential of the common man to achieve hero status, already enabled by new democratizing standards of society.

The lure of revisionist categorizing of heroes persisted. In 1957, literary critic Northrop Frye contrasted powerful heroes with further classes of distinctly fallible heroes (Frye 1957). These small or inglorious heroes came to historiographic attention via the new social history of the 1960s–1970s and were slowly translated into house museums celebrating Everyman heroes of the everyday. With the range of heroes now enlarged and the filter of psychology universally applied, the contemporary critic Bruce Meyer interprets the hero in literary history as a state of being, a projection of potential, a manifestation of desires—even as ourselves (Meyer 2007, 27–41).

The possibility that the reader—or visitor—recognizes flecks of self as having heroic quality indicates a very different approach to the concept of heroic inspiration than Carlyle had in mind. Yet a direct intellectual line can be traced to Ralph Waldo Emerson, who met and admired Carlyle in the 1830s when *On Heroes* was developed in lecture form, and himself wrote "Heroism" in 1841. It was the seventh of Emerson's subsequently gathered *Essays*, outlining the principles of Transcendentalism, and in it he reviewed the heroes of ancient Greece and Rome, proposing, "All [their] great and transcendent properties are ours . . . we [Americans] are already domesticating the same sentiments" (Emerson 1907, 145). If the contemporary individual contains the capacity to recognize herself or himself in the persona of the Great, it is an effect of mid-nineteenth-century New England mysticism, as well as early twentieth-century psychology and the identity politics of the

1960s–1970s. The sum of these insights provides a fertile environment for the continuing growth of hero house museums.

Heroes, Authenticity, and Magic

Many and long-held religious traditions of sacralizing the houses and smaller relics of heroes feed into the modern practice of house museums. The perspective that rationalizes Christian veneration of its heroes, or saints, is twofold: saints inspire faith on the basis of their tribulations and steadfastness, and they have the power to intercede with the godhead on behalf of other mortals. Though divine intercession is not available via secular heroes, it is a small step to conflate the defining characters of religious saints and their earthly counterparts as sources of inspiration. The houses of saints and heroes can be described validly as shrines, presenting the legend, site, and relics of the subject in directly parallel formats. The manners of the church similarly frame the ways that visitors respond to hero houses: solemn, impelled by (possibly attenuated) faith, fascinated by material proof, and moved by the numinous aura of the erstwhile inhabitant.

The authenticity of the shrine and its contents guarantees this encounter. Yet can the truth be known for certain? This troublesome question plagues the power of relics, epitomizing the challenges to knowing authenticity. In the end, truth depends on proof by miraculous intervention, acquiescence to authoritative word, or unquestioning blind faith. Except for the first proof, the same conditions obtain among civil relics. Outside these inconclusive parameters, the arguments against authenticity as an absolute are blunt. Logic asserts that if something exists in certain conditions, it is authentic within those conditions. A range of possible authenticities demonstrates that unless limits are specified (contingently admitting the existence of other limits), a judgment of authenticity is an argument of conviction. In other words, recognizing authenticity is a choice, a belief, an act of faith.

Faith is the essential dynamic of authenticity (further discussed in chapter 7). There is no rational means of guaranteeing the authenticity of relics and sacred sites, but there is plenty of evidence that demonstrable inauthenticity has little impact on the experience of a visitor who possesses faith, or merely has a positive anticipation (Phillips 1997, 165–70; Lowenthal 2008). Reams have been written on the notion of authenticity from the secular point of view of understanding and managing heritage objects and places as relics; despite all this, as Peter Howard concludes in a textbook discussion, "Authenticity is a slippery topic" (Howard 2003, 61, 227). I believe it is now more useful to focus on the faith that creates the perception of authenticity rather than a myriad of tests and standards that can never be proven. The point is not to condone or condemn faith, but to recognize its power among museum and heritage visitors who come with reverent expectations.

At root, faith is underwritten by magical thinking. Among the fundamental strands of magic is the principle of sympathetic magic, named in 1890 by James Frazer in terms still recognized today. He identified two laws of magical effect, achieved by similarity and contagion. The magic of similarity enables effects to be worked on distant people or objects by conducting rituals on a simulacrum, like punishing a voodoo doll to cause harm to a real person. The magic of contagion enables transmission of the magical essence inherent in certain items and places through contact, as with touching a saint's bone and feeling empowered by it (Frazer 1890). Faith in contagious magic is perhaps more present in contemporary popular culture than in similar magic, but there can be little doubt that magical thinking is as familiar in the modern West as it ever was or is in ancient and other cultures.

The concept of magical contagion underlies not only the cults of relics and pilgrimage in the Christian Church and the museum/heritage agency apparatus that manages civil relics and historic sites but also the taste for collecting relics of modern heroes and visiting the scenes of their fame. Such faith does not need to be total and explicit, thanks to the human capacity to hold contradictory beliefs. And as the proliferation of museums and heritage places shows, official state and cultural agencies are ready and eager to endorse the value of encounters between people and the contagious good of relic objects and places. Today, in the secular environment, the virtue of the encounter is couched in terms of inspiration or education rather than in the language of religion.

Magic being what it is, an effective visit to a hero's house needs to be fuelled with the faith to perceive its meaning and authenticity. The skeptic finds it easy to be unimpressed by the insignificance of much that is presented as reliquary. At the very least, a positive expectation is necessary to be touched by the aura of the hero through contact with his or her walls, spaces, furnishings, and possessions. Framed by this expectation, the material culture of the house does indeed function as a technology of enchantment (Gell 1992). This describes the effect on the visitor of encountering the totality and depth of the hero's house, and experiencing a disarming sense of wonder and communion. The concept is eloquent in connecting magical power to a carefully contrived physical structure. The belief that the hero walked through this very door, sat at this very desk, slept in the very bed, and left his veritable dentures on the bedside table can envelop the visitor's consciousness with awe and pleasure. Is it authentic? Is it contagious magic? Is it a set decked with antique furnishings and operated by elaborate back-stage controls? Who can be sure?

Museumizing Heroes' Houses

The secular history of museumizing the houses, furnishings, and personal materials of heroes is an early to late nineteenth-century phenomenon in both Britain and the United States. There was some knowledge among Americans of early efforts in the United Kingdom, especially of Shakespeare's birthplace (Hodgdon 1998, 196–97), but no direct contacts among house museumizers are known; the circumstances of the first American house museumizations of George Washington sites were entirely local. Nonetheless, the cultural dynamic that informed developments on both sides of the Atlantic reflected the same urge to strengthen the national identity through exposure to the relics of national heroes. At the same time, the taste for seeking or acknowledging the greatness of heroes had been presaged by the pilgrimage tradition of visiting the burial sites and tomb monuments of admired persons, a practice that expanded in the new sphere of public culture in eighteenth-century London (Watson 2006). Insofar as tourism was available to the leisured in the first half of the nineteenth century, it included literary sites as well as grand scenery and great country houses (Sears 1989, 62–63; Tinniswood 1989). The latter required genteel standing and a tip to the housekeeper, but the owners of common houses with poet- or author-hero associations could make a sideline or even a considerable income from tourists by allowing access and selling souvenirs. The following case studies survey how the first generation of heroes' houses became museumized, with some comparisons and variations.

Sir Walter Scott's Abbotsford
The construction in the 1810s–1820s of a Gothic Scottish baronial mansion on the site of a country cottage eventually bankrupted the great novelist, Sir Walter Scott; luckily, the house remained in the family thanks to the legal stratagem of settling it on his son. The house was open to respectable visitors during the author's hospitable lifetime, though even he was often irritated by the tourist hordes, as described by a guest in 1825: "The house used to be literally stormed; no less than *sixteen* parties, all uninvited, came in one day ... The tourists roved about the house" (Wainwright 1989, 150). The library, where Scott wrote *Waverley*, *Rob Roy*, and *Ivanhoe*, was formally opened by his family to the public in 1833, just five months after his death, gradually

followed by the opening of other rooms. To some degree, this addressed necessity, for Abbotsford remained a family residence as well as a popular shrine. It is not clear when an admission charge was instituted (shifting from a tip to the servant who opened the door), but the fee redefined the visit as a public commodity rather than a graceful favor; it is one index of calling Abbotsford a museum. At last, in the early 1850s, the family built an adjacent house for themselves and opened the entrance hall, study, Chinese drawing room, armory, dining room, and gardens. As a result of these developments, the Gothic fantasies of Abbotsford can be said to be the first fully public hero's house museum in Britain.

Abbotsford was particularly suited for museumization thanks to Scott's taste for collecting ancient and exotic heraldry, armor, and weaponry. Much of this material came from the 1819 sale of William Bullock's "Egyptian Hall" museum in London, acquired for Scott by Daniel Terry, the actor-agent who had adapted the early Waverley novels for the stage. Bullock was the brother of George Bullock, cabinet maker and furnisher of Abbotsford,

Abbotsford House, near Melrose in the Scottish Borders, by Thomas Shepherd, 1829. The battlemented profile of Abbotsford expressed Sir Walter Scott's vision of wild, heroic, medieval Scotland in 1820s masonry. The walls are set with fragments of ancient sculpture and architecture, in the spirit of the collections indoors. Scott's fans loved the house as much as his literary output.
Engraving (Corson 1590), courtesy of Edinburgh University Library.

and himself a dealer in antiquities (Altick 1978, 241–42; Norman 1962, 525). Further material came from the souvenir market of returned East India Company veterans; some items had a modern Waterloo provenance; a gun, sword, and dirk were reputed to have belonged to the folk hero Rob Roy. The collection was (and is) presented as a medieval armory, with pieces arranged as trophies to conjure the booty of old battles. With overtones both gory and chivalrous, chiming with the spirit of his romantic but highly moral tales, Scott created at Abbotsford an early expression of medieval fantasy, mixing taxonomic display with decorative effects (as did Sir John Soane with his collection of architectural fragments displayed in his house in London). In fact, the Abbotsford collections and their integration into the decoration of the house made it one of the great romantic interiors of Britain, and an exemplar of invented antiquity (Wainwright 1989).

Abbotsford long remained a private house museum, though its history in this mode illustrates the difficulty of heritage as a sustainable income source. The last resident family member died in 2004, at which point no one in the extended family wanted to take over the management of the house and museum. Thus the site and most of its collections were transformed into the Abbotsford Trust in 2007. Professional planning and Heritage Lottery funding have now secured its future as a museum (English 2005).

Scott was a towering figure as a poet and novelist in the early nineteenth century, a powerful cultural and intellectual force. As a modern commentator observed, "To have been alive and literate in the nineteenth century was to have been affected in some way by the Waverley novels" (Raleigh 1963, 10). But at a time when literary admiration of Sir Walter Scott has declined, it is easy to imagine that a visit to Abbotsford in the twenty-first century is less likely to be the vehicle of heroic enchantment and more a sight constructed purely by the tourist gaze. To the naive, Abbotsford can seem to be a medieval reverie; for the connoisseur, it is a magnificent Victorian pastiche. Only the reader of nineteenth-century romantic literature recognizes in it the shades of Scottish glory that moved Scott and his readers. Contemplating Scott fifty years after his death, Leslie Stephen asked, "Will our posterity understand . . . why he was once a luminary of the first magnitude, or wonder at their ancestors' hallucination about a mere will-o'-the-wisp?" (Stephen 1892, 138). More than a hundred years since Stephen asked that question, Scott, the inspirational hero-poet, has dwindled into an item of English literary history, English language ascendancy, and English hegemony in Scotland. But as a star in the constellation of English literature, Scott's hero status is indubitable.

Shakespeare's Birthplace

Shakespeare has been the star of English poetry and drama since his death in 1616, so he was well set for heroization via a house. His legendary birthplace in Stratford-upon-Avon had been celebrated ever since the actor David Garrick initiated festivities in 1769 to mark (slightly belatedly) the two hundredth anniversary of the Bard's birth. A cottage industry catering to pilgrims was well established by the late eighteenth century (Watson 2006, 56–63). Carlyle articulated the Victorian vision:

> We can fancy him as radiant aloft over all nations of Englishmen, a thousand years hence. From Parramatta, from New York wheresoever . . . English men and women are, they will say to each other, "we produced him, we speak and think by him; we are of one blood and kind by him." (Carlyle 1841, 132–33)

This is the real stuff of hero worship, and to facilitate the opportunity for all and forever, a campaign by a committee of local and London worthies organized to purchase the house of Shakespeare's birth in 1847. They had been optimistic that the government would adopt the house as a national memorial, but the British state never did; after the rapture of winning at auction, it took the committee nearly thirty years to pay off the bank loan. Indeed, the house languished until two benefactors emerged with sufficient funds for restoration. It opened as a museum in 1864, the year of Shakespeare's tercentenary (Fox 1997; Thomas 2012).

The committee's approach indicates a shift in expectations as to how visitors should perceive the national poet; indeed, that the experience should be more constructed than left open to individual modes of reverence. The house was remodeled in the 1850s, with the removal of partial brick cladding and reconstruction of the gables shown in a drawing of 1769, though haphazard funding made it an anxious process. The interiors received attention in 1862, with the creation of a library and museum on the ground floor, and the whole ensemble opened in 1864. The experience of visiting Shakespeare's birthplace was now set in a Tudor burgher's residence, introduced by historic books, pictures, and relics, which visitors passed through to the sacred focus of the house, the birth room. This shrine was empty for many years, making the scratched window graffiti left by earlier visitors an attraction in its own right; subsequent visitors joined the ritual by adding their own signature graffiti to the walls. Meanwhile, the committee established the structure that framed governance of the birthplace until the mid-twentieth century. The property was conveyed to the Stratford Corporation to be managed by a Trust of ex-officio representatives including the mayor, the lord lieutenant,

Shakespeare's birthplace, Stratford-upon-Avon, c. 1850, Shakespeare's father's house (where it is presumed the poet was born), after acquisition but before restoration and the removal of houses on either side. The lady ticket-seller and guide is just visible at the counter.
Photo courtesy of the Folger Shakespeare Library, New York.

the vicar, and the Stratford Grammar School headmaster, plus several life trustees from the previous committee. The first ticket assistant was appointed in 1871, and shortly afterward, the first librarian. Receipts finally began to exceed expenses in 1879.

At the same time, there was a ready eye to further property with Shakespeare associations in Stratford and its environs—a proclivity that came to shape the Trust's vision and Stratford's real estate. The first addition was the land where New Place (Shakespeare's last home, where he died) had stood; the adjoining Nash's house, occupied by his granddaughter Elizabeth Nash and her first husband; and a nineteenth-century theater built nearby, which was demolished to expose the entire New Place site, then excavated in the early 1870s. Nash's house was re-created as a jettied Tudor town house in 1912; it has had a mixed career involving sundry displays and domestic settings. The farmhouse belonging to the yeoman Hathaways, the family of Shakespeare's wife, Ann, had been on the tourist circuit since the 1840s and was purchased in 1892, complete with a significant collection of Elizabethan furnishings. However, the terms included life tenancies that meant the entire house was not fully opened to the public until 1926. What was thought to be Shakespeare's mother's family farmhouse entered the galaxy of shrines in 1930; with its barn, outbuildings, and the adjoining Glebe Farm, which turned out to be the real Mary Arden's house, it has become the Shakespeare Countryside Museum. The "only remaining property with Shakespeare associations which was not in the possession of the Birthplace Trust" was acquired in 1949: Hall's Croft, the home of Shakespeare's daughter Susannah and her husband, Dr. John Hall, which became an educational and social center for Shakespeare events (Fox 1997, 109).

The Trust also acquired small houses in Stratford and larger houses and their estates bordering the outlying properties to preserve urban scale and rural ambience. They housed Trust offices, staff apartments, and other tenants, and drove what has become the large maintenance arm of the organization. The physical growth and diversification of the Trust was accompanied in the post–World War II era by a surge in educational and scholarly programs, backed up by an increasingly important library. This range of modern functions impelled the establishment of the first Shakespeare Centre, opened in 1961 and extended in 1981. By the mid-twentieth century the Shakespeare birthplace Trust had become a major player in Stratford town planning, managing the impact of tourists with toilet blocks and big new car parks; the route of freeways was diverted to avoid impinging on historic ambience, and in 1988 the birthplace precinct was pedestrianized.

No British hero's shrine compares to the complex in Stratford-upon-Avon. The rare survival of ancient buildings with reliable (if extended) connections to a great hero inspired and enabled a voluntary organization to make the most of the popular taste for civil shrines. Consequently, Shakespeare's birth room has been revised and re-presented many times in the 150-year history of the organization. It began empty; two Elizabethan coffers and a bust were inserted in 1899; the first re-created furnishing scheme was introduced in 1950; and Tudor colors and textiles were added in 2000. The steady progress from minimal intrusion into sacred space toward more and more explicit representations of the poet's life follows modern museological trends in interpretation, and describes a model that many smaller hero house museums would emulate if they could.

Thanks to the Trust, Shakespeare tourism drives the local economy, with ever-increasing opportunities for other businesses to profit by the Bard, such as the "Shakespearience" multimedia show, the Othello café, the Food of Love patisserie, and more (not to mention the Royal Shakespeare Theatre, founded in 1879). Yet Stratford's house museums are still central to the experience: Shakespeare is not only a *bona fide* hero of English literature but also a transnational hero of the English language, appreciated through relics, re-creations, and reverence.

George Washington's Houses

George Washington is the most house-museumized leader in the Western world, and in this he leads a battalion of subsequent US presidents. (He is exceeded only by Mao Zedong.) Washington's charisma inspired the first two historic house museums established in the United States, among the earliest in the world, and still has the potential to inspire more—as at the boyhood home site, Ferry Farm, Virginia, where archaeology identified the foundations of the original house in 2008, immediately inciting schemes to reconstruct it. Washington has been called the clan totem and tribal leader of the United States, but it is his reputation as the Father of the Nation that endows him with the familial and domestic contexts that suit representation via house museum in especially apt ways (Schwartz 1987, 4–9; Marling 1987).

Washington's plantation house at Mount Vernon, near Washington, DC, on the Potomac River, became the object of hero-memorialization in the 1850s. It had been the focus of small-scale patriotic tourism ever since his retirement from the presidency in 1797; Washington, and later his widow, Martha, often treated even unknown visitors to tea (Burns 2007, 182–83). Washington relations inherited Mount Vernon, in whose ownership it declined as a farm and residence, stirring occasional public calls that the government should acquire it as a memorial. Great-nephew John Washington offered it to the federal and Virginia governments three times between 1846 and 1853, but his price was consistently rebuffed (West 1999, 6). The house was already acknowledged in these ways as a sacred site of American republicanism, when the cause of its preservation was taken up in 1854 by Ann Pamela Cunningham, a gentlewoman of South Carolina; she established the Mount Vernon Ladies' Association (MVLA) of the Union to raise funds to buy and open the house. The history of the MVLA's campaign has been told from numerous perspectives, so it is recounted here only in summary as an introduction to the breadth of Washington-based house museums, and as an introduction to the tradition of museumizing houses associated with subsequent presidents (e.g., Lossing 1870; Page 1910; Rogers 1928; Thane 1967; West 1999; McLeod 2010).

The concatenation of political and cultural circumstances shaping the MVLA project in the United States in the 1850s has no parallel in house

Mount Vernon, near Alexandria, Virginia, by Currier & Ives, c. 1859. Mount Vernon had been a Washington family property for two generations before George Washington came to live there, soon after acquiring full ownership; he rebuilt the plantation house to its current form in the 1770s.
Lithograph courtesy of the Mount Vernon Ladies Association.

museum history. In the anxious decade of constitutional struggle over slavery that preceded the Civil War, Cunningham envisaged that Mount Vernon could be presented as a national symbol of unity between North and South. More than that, she saw it as a resolution that could be provided uniquely by women in their role as agents of domestic morality and peace. Money was raised via the female economy of bazaars, balls, and theatricals, and contributions came from individuals, schools, businesses, and state legislatures. John Washington was at length persuaded to accept the MVLA as purchaser of Mount Vernon, and the sale was finally achieved in 1860.

It was too late for the house to become a unifying national symbol. The Civil War erupted in 1861, and Mount Vernon stood in its path. A (Southern) farm manager and a (Northern) lady resident (with chaperone) were installed to maintain the crumbling fabric and open the house as a museum when possible, assisted by several of the plantation slaves who had been freed by George Washington's will and now worked as free labor (Casper 2008). Mount Vernon survived the Civil War unscathed, though ever more dilapidated, and Ann Cunningham returned to nurture it as a shrine. When she retired in 1874, she exhorted her comrades to maintain the sacred place by resisting "the vandal fingers" of progress in order to preserve the essence of the Father forever (Marling 1987, 83).

Mount Vernon is often called the United States' first house museum, but, in fact, the magic of Washington's association had already justified the state's acquisition of Hasbrouck House, Newburgh, New York, in 1850 (West 1999, 4). It led the way in a subclass of shrines: Washington's headquarters. The Revolutionary War took the general and the Continental Army from Massachusetts to New York, New Jersey, and Pennsylvania, and with each move, Washington commandeered a suitable large local house from which to manage the campaign. The war moved on, but as soon as Washington left such a house, no matter how short his stay, nothing was ever the same again. Frequently the structure became known simply as "Washington's Headquarters" (regardless of how many others may have been within twenty miles), and the owners often preserved the furniture and fittings that Washington had used (Hosmer 1965, 78).

One was the Ford Mansion, Morristown, New Jersey, headquarters for six months during the "Hard Winter" of 1779–1780. When it came up for sale in 1873, the house was acquired by the Washington Association of New Jersey and gradually furnished with Washingtoniana and other material thought to be correct. Since 1933 the Ford Mansion has been part of the Morristown National Historical Park, focusing its interpretation on the long rigors of the War of Independence. It was refurnished according to plan in 1974, a scheme criticized in 2003 for suggesting occupation by a nuclear family of four rather than the thirty-odd who squeezed in with Washington, Mrs. Washington, his staff and servants, and the Ford family (Marling 1987, 73–74; *Morristown National Historical Park* 2007, 16–17, 26, 40). The shift from a focus on relics touched by the hero to relics in a historical context became more explicit over the years, characteristic of modern attempts to constrain magical attraction to historical narrative. Meanwhile, six more houses vaunt Washington Headquarters status in their stories of heroic museumization: the Vassall-Craigie-Longfellow House, Cambridge, Massachusetts (HQ: 1775–1776; later inhabited by H. W. Longfellow and museumized mainly in his honor, 1913); the Morris-Jumel House, New York, New York (HQ: 1776; later HQ of the enemy Royal Army; museumized 1903); the Jacob Purdy House, White Plains, New Jersey (HQ: 1776, 1778; museumized 1963); the Moland House, Hartsville, Pennsylvania (HQ: 1777; museumized 1980s); the Isaac

Potts House, Valley Forge, Pennsylvania (HQ: 1777–1778; museumized 1976); the Dey Mansion, Wayne, New Jersey (HQ: 1780; museumized 1930); and the Hasbrouck House, Newburgh, New York (HQ: 1782–1783; museumized in 1850).

And that's not all. The desire to understand and connect with the great man led to investigations and museumizations of the houses that had shaped his very genealogy. The Washington family plantation on Pope's Creek (later named, and now known as, Wakefield), Westmoreland County, Virginia, had been inhabited by three generations when the future president was born in 1732. Though George Washington lived there until the age of just three, and the house burned down nearly fifty years later, a descendant, Josephine Wheelwright Rust, founded the Wakefield National Memorial Association in 1923 to build what she asserted would be a replica of the house on the site (Bruggeman 2009). It was presented to the US government in 1932 for the bicentenary of Washington's birth, and assigned to National Park Service management. For the next twenty years, NPS archaeologists and managers disputed the authenticity of the so-called Memorial House with the descendent organization, expressing the contest, ferocious on both sides, between celebratory and professional history. A much-praised program in the 1960s–1980s of costumed, living history on the theme of colonial rural lifestyle, including occasional references to slavery on the plantation, did not diminish the overwhelming effect of the Memorial House on visitors as the apparently real—or at least faithful replica—house (see illustration on page 13). This continues to be the case, leading to a new interpretive theme, once again focused on appreciation of the original hero: "George Washington was the transcendent leader of the American Revolutionary era whose actions were crucial to the establishment of the United States as an independent nation founded on principles of universal liberty" (*George Washington Birthplace National Monument* 1999, 7). Aside from the racial omission inherent in this goal, it is hard to see how it can divert the Memorial House from anything other than interpreting Washington's ongoing reputation as the beatified parent of his country.

In the grand project to grasp the spirit of George Washington, two houses have been museumized in England, as homes of the hero's ancestors. Over generations of turmoil in people's lives and in buildings' careers, the associations of these houses in relation to the great man are, to say the least, slender. But there is magic in the history of the family name. It is derived from the Anglo-Saxon village of Wæssaingatūn, adopted in Middle English form by William de Wessyngton, whose descendants made the village and themselves into Washingtons. They inhabited a manor from the twelfth century to 1613, but what is now called Washington Old Hall, near Durham, post-dates the presidential ancestors. Nonetheless, it was acquired in a derelict state by a Preservation Committee in 1936 and restored with American aid until being passed to the National Trust in 1957 (Fedden & Joekes 1984, 238–40).

Always of minor gentry status, the Washington family grew prosperous and spread widely in northeast England. A Lawrence Washington built Sulgrave Manor in Northampton on property acquired after the dissolution of the monasteries in the 1530s. But the fourth-generation Lawrence died in poverty, having been condemned as a Royalist in the years of the Commonwealth, when Sulgrave changed hands. His son, John Washington, sailed for Virginia in 1656, where he married Anne Pope; they became the great grandparents of George (Smith 1933; Otte 2011). Meanwhile, Sulgrave declined into a ruinous farmhouse throughout the nineteenth century until 1914, when it was purchased by the British Peace Centenary Committee to mark the centenary of the Treaty of Ghent that ended the War of 1812 between the British Empire and the United States, acknowledging the national independence of the United States. With British and American funds, and an endowment raised by the Colonial Dames of America, it was officially opened in 1921. Over the next decade, the missing half of the Tudor house was reinstated and interiors refurbished and furnished. New visitor facilities and garden design were undertaken in 1999, described variously as "money spent with panache" and "a George Washington theme park," but, either way, it testifies to the conviction that the Washington magic endures (Jenkins 2003, 552). George Washington's only trip outside the continental United States took him to stay in Barbados for two months in 1751; Bush Hill House in Bridgetown was identified in 1977 and acquired by the Barbados National Trust, which restored and opened it to the public in 2007.

Log Cabins and Abraham Lincoln

The national mythology of the United States is represented foremost by its presidents, whose houses have been comprehensively museumized. The First Citizen of the nation embodies the symbolism of democracy, and its myths have both shaped and been shaped by dwellings inhabited by presidents, exemplified by America's primal story of the rise from log cabin to White House. The log cabin trope acquired political clout in the 1839–1840 presidential campaign between Martin van Buren and William Henry Harrison. When the latter appropriated a newspaper columnist's dismissive description of him as enjoying a barrel of hard cider in his log cabin in Ohio, the humble house was seized upon as the epitome of the virtuous, self-sufficient pioneer spirit. Harrison—by birth a scion of the Virginia planter aristocracy—died in Washington after barely a month in office; his log cabin—which by the time he became president was a much-enlarged genteel clapboard mansion—does not survive. Though cynically created, the symbolic log cabin rapidly achieved a central place in American democratic mythology as the mark of a man of the people; its magic has been conjured up in electoral politics ever since.

The log cabin symbolized the American dream that any boy could aspire to become president, though historical evaluation of the social origins of those who made it to the White House suggests that less than 10 percent could claim log cabin or equivalent social origins (Pessen 1984, 68). Not many huts survive, of course; log cabins and other forms of modest cottage tend to be impermanent buildings. And the careers of the handful of poorer men who achieved political success enabled all of them to acquire the much more substantial houses that have become National Historic Sites, managed by the National Park Service. But the imagery of humble origins has had enduring political appeal.

The most famous log cabin in the United States is, or represents, the birthplace of Abraham Lincoln on the site of Sinking Spring Farm, near Hodgenville, Kentucky. The single-room, notched-log cabin is so precious that it is museumized not as a house but as a sacred relic, and enclosed in a neoclassical temple. Lincoln was born there in 1809; his family moved on when he was two years old. The cabin logs were said to have been reused on an adjacent farm. An entrepreneur purchased them and the Lincoln site in 1894, and reerected the cabin on site in 1895. Thereafter the logs were demounted, reconstructed, and exhibited around the country for some years. The site was sold in 1905, and the logs also passed on in ownership. In 1906, a benefactor acquired the property, established the Lincoln Farm Association, and the cabin logs returned in triumph. The Association commissioned the temple to house the yet-again-reconstructed cabin, and when it opened in 1911, transferred the site to the state. It shifted to US federal government ownership in 1916, and it has been managed by the National Park Service (NPS) since 1933 (Peterson 1968).

The authenticity of Lincoln's birthplace was initially founded on the affidavits of old-timers; dissenters were not asked to testify. All doubt was sidelined at the time when the Lincoln Farm Association began its commemorative project, and again when the National Park Service took control. In 1948, an amateur historian published a critical analysis of the presentation, arguing that the cabin was a hoax. The Park Service responded with its own research, which supported the critique, though not the implication

Abraham Lincoln "symbolic birth cabin" at Sinking Spring, Hodgenville, Kentucky. Logs held to be those that constituted the birthplace and first home of Abraham Lincoln (from 1809–1811) were reconstructed around 1910. The resultant cabin was enclosed in a memorial temple structure, inaugurated in 1911.
Photo courtesy of the National Park Service.

of intent to deceive. But recognizing that the cabin had metastasized into a key element of the legend of the martyred president, which could not simply be abolished, staff introduced a descriptive qualification, calling it the "traditional" birthplace of Lincoln—making a distinction with *authentic* that probably escaped most visitors. Presentation of the cabin within the temple is today more forthright: it is referred to as a "symbolic" birthplace and paired with a second cabin, ten miles away at Knob Creek, where Lincoln lived between the ages of two and seven. The Knob Creek cabin is frankly a replica, fully furnished, as is a third Lincoln childhood cabin near Lincoln City, Indiana.

Lincoln's adult family house in Springfield, Illinois; Ford's Theatre in Washington, DC, where he was assassinated; and the Peterson House opposite, where he died, are also NPS sites. The village of New Salem, Indiana, where he lived as a young single adult but never owned a house, has a historic park of relocated cabins, known as Lincoln's New Salem (discussed in chapter 7). Rounding out the ancestral dimension of the family, the Lincoln Log Cabin State Historic Site near Charleston, Illinois, is a replica of the house inhabited by Lincoln's father and stepmother long after he had left home. Knob Hill, New Salem, and Charleston were all constructed by the Civilian Conservation Corps as Depression-era relief programs in the 1930s. The abundance of houses associated with Lincoln points most obviously to the sacral character of the hero's touch and the faith it evokes; yet all contain an element of the real history of the man, a "factual" basis of belief. As Dwight Pitcaithley, former chief historian of the National Park Service, reflected on the mediating role of the authorizing agency, "The public's perception of the Lincoln cabin is important to the nation's image and an indispensable part of the nation's ritualistic public tribute to its own humble origins" (Pitcaithley 2001, 252).

Herbert Hoover's Houses

The dyad of Washington as father and Lincoln as martyr of the nation set a high bar for the heroization of other presidents. The case of Herbert Hoover, thirty-first president (1929–1933), is outlined here to examine a less significant incumbent's house museumization. It demonstrates the mix of local boosterism, electoral propaganda, sincere admiration, and civil religion that propelled the museumization of many other presidential dwellings. Hoover became president with a reputation for progressivism and efficiency, grounded in his professional background as an engineer, and followed by public service as Secretary of Commerce and "Under-Secretary of Everything Else." At the same time, he managed humanitarian crises effectively and was hailed as a civilian hero personifying modern American values. With a dual reputation as the "Great Engineer" and the "Great Humanitarian," he led the Republicans to presidential victory in 1928, only to encounter the Wall Street crash a few months after his inauguration. His anti-intervention strategies failed to resolve the economic and social problems created by the Great Depression, and Hoover lost the 1932 election to Franklin Roosevelt. Hoover is generally ranked in the lower echelons of presidential league tables; nonetheless, he wore the mantle of First Citizen and thus takes a place in the American patriotic spectrum (Leuchtenburg 2009).

But Herbert Hoover and his wife, Lou Henry Hoover, had been assiduous in constructing that place even before he was elected president (Bearss 1971). He was born in 1874 in West Branch, Iowa, the son of a Quaker blacksmith and merchant. The family moved into the house in 1879, shortly before his father died, and after his mother's death four years later the three children were spread among relatives; Herbert grew up in Oregon with an uncle and aunt. (The Hoover-Minthorn House in Newburg, Oregon, opened as a museum in 1955, managed by the Colonial Dames of America; it displays the furnished bedroom of the future president.) Stanford University and marriage made him a Californian, and he lived in Palo Alto after a career in mining in Australia and China. (The Palo Alto house, designed by Lou Henry Hoover, is now the official residence of the president of Stanford University. The mine manager's house at Gwalia, Western Australia, was built for Hoover in 1898; it is open as a museum and bed-and-breakfast.) By the early 1920s, Hoover, as secretary of commerce, was the most famous son of West Branch. Though the cottage in which he had lived to the age of four had been moved and incorporated into a larger structure in front, its current owner was well aware of her house as the birthplace of the great man and welcomed public interest. Mrs. Hoover visited the site in 1921; Hoover himself visited in 1923 and toured old haunts, strategically accompanied by photographers. He made a grand homecoming after accepting the Republican nomination in 1928, artfully asserting his heritage of humble origins in the Midwest. In that year, some seventeen thousand people paid ten cents each to be shown through the cottage. A cascade of civic rituals acknowledged the house as a shrine: the local chapter of the Daughters of the American Revolution planted a memorial stone in front; a number of artists visited to paint it. (The most famous was by Grant Wood—*The Birthplace of Herbert Hoover*, 1931, Minneapolis Institute of the Arts. Hoover disliked the picture.) A replica of the house based on measured drawings was shown at the Iowa State Fair.

Mrs. Hoover was now intent on constructing a domestic legend for the president. The Hoover family quietly tried to buy the house from 1930 onward, succeeding in 1935, and the cottage was made public in 1939. It was relocated to its original site, minus the 1890s two-story house in front; unclad to reveal the board and batten construction under the modern weatherboards; and guarded by a caretaker residence at a discreet distance. A massive bronze statue of veiled Isis, which had been presented by the grateful Belgian nation to celebrate Hoover's first famous humanitarian project of food aid in 1914, was moved from Stanford University to the cottage site. Ownership of the whole complex was now transferred to the Herbert Hoover Birthplace Society, later Foundation, established by Mrs. Hoover. Aided by Iowa state funding, the site expanded: Jesse Hoover's blacksmith business was reconstructed to contextualize the family income; the old Friends Meeting House and, later, the West Branch schoolhouse were relocated to the site, both appropriately furnished to add the dimensions of religion and learning to the Hoover legend; trees were planted and picnic tables installed; a stone gateway introduced a new, winding approach; and gravesites were planned for both Hoovers. The Herbert Hoover Presidential Library opened in 1962, operated by the federal General Services Administration, which soon acquired ownership of the whole site from the Foundation; in 1971 the National Park Service took control. The rationale for preserving the house and other buildings today is summarized in the statement of significance: "Herbert Hoover's experiences and associations with his family and the community of West Branch influenced his personality, work ethic, spiritual and moral character, and ambition" (*Herbert Hoover National Historic Site* 2004, 6). Undeclared, and hardly to be expected in a modern professional management plan, is the leap of faith that empowers the house with the magical essence of America.

Captain Cook's Cottage

The gaps between the material presence of an old house, its connection to and influence on its inhabitants, its perception as a memorial by a willing public, and the standards of modern house museum management suggest how insecure is the practice of history and how strong are the habits of magical thinking in relation to heroes' houses. The case of the house of the father of Captain James Cook, Royal Navy explorer and acclaimed British "discoverer" of Australia, is almost comical in the elisions, stretches, and denials of evidence that fail to undermine its continuing popularity. In this, not–Captain Cook's Cottage constitutes determined evidence of the national project and the civic desire for heroes. Most remarkably, the cottage is located in Melbourne, having been translated from Yorkshire in 1933, and is thus the oldest house in Australia, predating white settlement by nearly fifty years. It can now be said confidently that the cottage was never inhabited by James Cook (it was built after he left home, but it is possible that he visited his parents there), that only half the house as it was built was relocated, that the structural accommodations to this severing render it almost unrecognizable, and that the 1930s rearrangement of the interior thoroughly gentrifies the social origins of the national foundation hero (Young 2008).

Cook spent part of his youth in the village of Great Ayton, though not in this cottage; his birthplace in nearby Marton claims him equally, and it has a dedicated Captain Cook Birthplace Museum. The cottage in Great Ayton, and the ruins of his birthplace in Marton, became famous in a small way for their associations with the Cook family, especially after he died in 1778 at the hands of Hawaiian warriors. But his fame merged into the generic Valhalla of British imperial heroes until it was resuscitated in New South Wales in 1870, the centenary of his "discovery" and claiming of Australia for King George III. In fact, Cook had landed only briefly on Australian shores and left no marks other than those on maps and the recommendation that Botany Bay would be a fine place for a colony. On this advice, a First

Fleet of convicts and Royal Marines established the settlement of Sydney in 1788. The British colony survived and gradually expanded, until gold discoveries spelled the end of convictism, the introduction of constitutional self-government, and the growth of immigration, urbanization, and prosperity. The colonists began to contemplate their potential identity as a nation, unfortunately one tainted by its convict genealogy; they needed a respectable history and found it in Captain Cook. From the 1860s he took his place in statues, imagery, place names, and the public imagination, joining peculiar marsupials and upside-down seasons as emblems of the British antipodes.

In 1933 an event occurred that brought Captain Cook into high focus again: his father's house in Great Ayton had been partially demolished for road widening and its owners were selling off the remaining portion. A Melbourne magnate and philanthropist heard of the sale and determined that the cottage should be acquired for his state of Victoria (the Australian colonies having federated in 1901). A rationale for its acquisition was constructed on the argument that the first segment of the Australian coastline observed by Cook's 1770 expedition was what had later become the state of Victoria. Since Victoria's capital, Melbourne, was about to mark a hundred years of settlement, he offered the funds to enable Melbourne to become "the proud guardian of the one-time home of the man who had made that

Captain Cook's father's cottage, Melbourne, Victoria, c. 1934. The central portion of this 1756 structure is the relic of a double-cell house with a through-passage, the remains of which are enclosed as an awkward lean-to corridor on the outside. But Captain Cook might have crossed its threshold when visiting his old parents—and that made it sacred to Australians.
Photo courtesy of the State Library of Victoria.

Centenary possible—Captain James Cook" (Gill 1957, 8–12). For more than twice the price offered locally, the cottage was sold, disassembled, packed up, and shipped to Australia.

What arrived was half of a two-part house accessed by a shared through-passage, which was preserved as a lean-to corridor to provide a front door. Other changes were the addition of a byre for animals at the other end, improving the downstairs fireplace recess into an inglenook, and constructing two tiny partitioned areas as separate bedrooms: one up, one down. Appropriate antique oak furniture was purchased in York, and a colonial revival aesthetic of homespun curtains and whitewashed walls completed the representation of a house suitable for a yeoman farmer and his wife, with anachronistic separate bedrooms for their daughters and seafaring son. Under the proud name of Captain Cook's Cottage, it opened in 1934 to civic rapture, but after a hectic year of attention, the cottage subsided from a spectacle to a curiosity. There followed years of near abandonment, vandalism, rescue, and restoration in time for the 1970 Cook bicentenary. It was the beginning of professional heritage management in Australia. Since the cottage's historical claims to James Cook were acknowledged as thin, the focus of interpretation shifted to the scientific conservation of the built fabric and an imaginative garden setting. When a new management plan was developed in 1993, purist understanding went so far as to eliminate from its assessed significance any reference to James Cook, seeing the place instead as a metaphor for white settlement, Indigenous dispossession, and 1930s imperial loyalism. Guides responded that the inchoate social memory of Cook as the source of a collective national past persisted among visitors, and interpretation drifted back to the familiar myth. The fact is, the cottage is meaningless without Captain Cook, and he can be incorporated easily in an act of faith—visitors believe in Captain Cook because they want to. This is a reality that historic house museum management must engage with, everywhere.

The Houses of Thomas and Jane Carlyle

The stories of enshrining heroes turn again to historian Thomas Carlyle. With unexpected poetic justice, the third hero's house museumized in Britain was his birthplace, a house in Ecclefechan, in southern Scotland, opened to the public in 1881. The house he shared with his wife, Jane, in Cheyne Row, Chelsea, for thirty-eight years inspired an unusual campaign to bring it into public ownership, brought to fruition in 1895. A hundred years later, Jane Welsh Carlyle's birthplace in Haddington, East Lothian, was museumized in 1984. More recently, the house in which they spent their first married years, Craigenputtock, was optimistically promoted for World Heritage listing on the grounds of the Carlylean presence and the inspiration of the wild, lonely landscape he enjoyed (and she endured) there.

It is a considerable legacy of house museum fame for a pair of anachronistic heroes. Thomas and Jane Carlyle are known today largely by academic historians and litterateurs of the Victorian age, but they were key personalities in intellectual England and Scotland in the mid-nineteenth century: Thomas, the magnificent historian of revolution, empires, and heroes; Jane, the witty and practical housekeeper, hostess, and letter-writer. Thomas's politics now seem romantic, racist, and antidemocratic, and memoirs and extant letters show that he treated Jane badly. Jane gave herself the task of nurturing ungrateful genius, paying a price in repression, depression, and illness, but conducted an alternative life in conversation and correspondence.

Exploration of the circumstances of these museumizations reveals insights into the general phenomenon of heroes' houses. Three factors stand out: family advocacy and activism to preserve the house; the anguish of raising money to secure the house in public ownership; and the inertia of celebrity in modern tourism. Sir Walter Scott's family is an example of the first; Shakespeare's birthplace an example of the second; the survival of near-forgotten writers' house museums points to the third. In the Carlyle case, Mary Aitken Carlyle, wife of Thomas's nephew, was the first agent of house immortalization. She was his housekeeper and amanuensis after Jane died and inherited most of the furniture when Thomas died. It was she who managed the translation of Carlyle's birthplace in Ecclefechan into a memorial museum, in 1881, the year of his death.

Carlyle's literary and personal reputation had already sunk in his later years and suffered a bruising battle of postmortem biographical accounts, but Mary Aitken Carlyle was not alone in tending the flame of his greatness. A Carlyle Society had already been established in London (it still exists, now based in Edinburgh), but when an otherwise unknown Manchester merchant began a campaign to rescue the Chelsea house its members resisted the call, apparently out of snobbery. At least, this was the impression of the man himself, George Lumsden, whose frank account of his efforts appears in the *Illustrated Memorial Volume of the Carlyle's House Purchase Fund Committee,* published in 1896, soon after the house opened. As a contemporary account of the travails endured by would-be pilgrims to secure their shrine, the

Memorial Volume is rare. Lumsden recounts how he went looking for Carlyle's house on a visit to London in 1894:

> My wish to see the House . . . will be easily understood by most of those who are likely to read this narrative . . . I wished to see Carlyle's House because one of England's greatest men had lived and worked in it, the man whose influence upon my own life had been . . . determinative . . . All was dingy and dirty . . . [but] to me whatever its state or circumstances, it was holy ground. (Anon. 1995, 1–2)

Lumsden discovered that the house was to be sold in a few months' time, and resolved with a friend that it should be acquired and preserved. Their first efforts to reach influential gentlemen and the elite press were in vain, but after they sent letters to 450 provincial papers, the campaign was noticed by *The Times*. The younger Mrs. Carlyle contacted Lumsden; one member of the Carlyle Society responded; the emperor of Germany promised £100 (in acknowledgment of Carlyle's German histories); and a committee of the great and the good was established at last. Over five months of "begging and preying," as the treasurer described it, enough was raised to buy, repair, and open the house.

The *Memorial Volume* contains a commentary on the layout of the rooms and the furniture, as well as a catalog list of each item: in this dedicated focus can be seen the essentially fetishistic quality of heroes' house museums. The attention paid to "the chairs they sat on and the cups they drank from, their umbrellas and their chests of drawers" moved Virginia Woolf, who acknowledged Carlyle's narrative greatness but ached for the wasted talents of Jane Carlyle (Woolf 1975). Nonetheless, she contributed an annual subscription to the Memorial Trust (Laniel 2008, 124).

Carlyle's House on Cheyne Row demonstrates the difficulty that private trusts encounter in trying to sustain their objects—it's a struggle today and it always has been. In 1936 the Memorial Trust transferred ownership and operation of the House to the National Trust, whose managerial expertise and economies of scale keep it going today. But this lesson did not discourage the gesture of the late Duchess of Hamilton and the Scottish Tourist Board in organizing the opening of the house in which Jane Welsh Carlyle was born, in the town of Haddington, and presenting several rooms as a memorial to her in 1984 (Anon. 1984). It was an act of restorative justice that acknowledged the woman who maintained the great Thomas Carlyle, and whose correspondence is still being published. Further, at least by implication, the house as a monument to Jane criticized "the horrible domestic tradition which made it seemly for a woman of genius to spend her time chasing beetles, scouring saucepans instead of writing books," as Woolf wrote in 1923 (Woolf 1966, 320–21). However, Jane's house has not survived as a museum, having closed in 2004. Its short life shows that the making and sustaining of heroes is not guaranteed by house museumization.

Note

1. References to Mohammed's house in Mecca can be found occasionally on the Internet. In 2005 it was said to have been demolished for new construction, but evidently leaving a low-walled, ruined site.

CHAPTER THREE

~

Heroes' Houses

Literary and Other Identities

As typified by the Carlyles, the largest proportion of hero house museums is dedicated to writers. It is hard to be definitive about this figure, but at least twice as many writers are celebrated in their houses as are the heroes of other arts, science, or achievement, in both the United Kingdom and the United States. What is the special significance ascribed to the dwellings of writers?

Writers as Heroes

The answers to this question have more to do with the nineteenth-century construction of English literature as a body of evidence of national achievement and identity than with individual authors. The post-Renaissance English tradition of poets and dramatists—of whom Shakespeare was doyen—spoke in their time to the literate and the urban, while the Greek and Latin classics dominated formal learning. Both streams of knowledge were largely confined to men. The development of the novel from the mid-eighteenth century, though decried by the learned, introduced a new species of more-or-less sanctioned fiction, which generated a new and growing community of readers. The emotional role of fictional narratives coincided with the aesthetics of early nineteenth-century Romanticism, the cult of feeling that enabled "the capacity to gain pleasure from self-constructed, imaginative experience" (Campbell 1987, 85). Within this mindset, the notion emerged that literature need not be confined to noble, religious, or civic causes but could explore the personal and the everyday to find meaning, truth, and even sublimity.

The political applications of such an influential medium became evident in the maturity of Victorian novels that engaged in critique of the modern world or its recent past through humor and realism, as in the works of Charles Dickens, Elizabeth Gaskell, and George Eliot. Novelists and poets may rarely have envisaged themselves as popular leaders, but in articulating and characterizing ideas that resonated with growing segments of the public, their books—and hence their names and pseudonyms—became the vehicles of national and indeed transnational conversations among readers. In appealing to the nonlearned as well as the educated, reading novels enabled vastly more people than ever before, women as well as men, and especially members of the expanding middle class, to participate in the public culture of ideas. In this way, a familiar body of literature came to frame a consciousness of the modern world. Furthermore, the idiosyncratic pleasures of books as personal companions fed the popular love of literature that became a mark of humane British culture (Doyle 1989, 8–10).

The ideal of an educated, literature-loving society was in reality confined to a class—the middle class—that was increasingly mobilized throughout the nineteenth century as its members engaged in intellectual and managerial labor in the industrial market economy and the concomitant empire. Their world required an education in English comprehension and fluency rather than in Latin grammar. Hence it was in the halls of the Scottish universities that the concept of a nonclassical literature was first taught in the later eighteenth century, under the name of rhetoric and belles lettres, to give metropolitan polish to Scots students (Crawford 2000, 1–8). In England, what is today known as English, then still under the rubric of "rhetoric," was taught at London University (the secular alternative to Oxbridge) from its foundation in 1826. (The energy and popularity of English literature were ignored by the two ancient universities until 1904 and 1919.) One of the first expressions of public educational reform, the study of English letters in London, was a means of spreading high literacy and respect for written culture among the youth of the middling sort, civilizing them for public life. Thus evolved the bourgeois myth of the polite, educated nation, speaking a standardized form of English and recognizing a canon of culture with deep national roots and an imperial mission (Doyle 1989, 10; Court 1992, 14). The Ruskinian conflation of beauty with truth imbued Victorian literature with a moral compass, by which its readers could be confirmed in their task to live, model, and transmit British values throughout the world. This imperial perspective motivated an inexplicit agenda to perceive English literature as the expression of British civilization itself. Colonial Britons thus recognized their direct kinship with the motherland, and the colonized learned the virtues of their occupier by comparison with the benighted condition of native cultures.

Not until the end of the nineteenth century did academic standards of comparison and evaluation begin to be applied to English literature. A shift from rhetoric to criticism enabled the institutionalization of difference between high and popular culture, validating the former as the sphere of the universities. Here, the giants of the eighteenth century, such as Joseph Addison and Samuel Johnson, who had themselves established the canon of William Shakespeare, John Milton, and Edmund Spenser, joined the literary curriculum. Their cohort of writers in new media—the critics, journalists, and novelists who initiated the bourgeois public culture that challenged the tradition of aristocratic cultural leadership—gradually followed (Kramnick 1998). But though the formation of the English literary canon was most actively tended in academe, other spheres also shaped it, especially writers and readers. Their opinions were backed by real market power, but the ideological hold of the gatekeepers of high culture in the universities was more enduring, even in the early twentieth-century period when vernacular literature still seemed déclassé.

British Writers' Houses

Literature as the privileged bearer of British national identity was well established in the public sphere by the middle of the nineteenth century (Young 2015). The private trust acquisition of Shakespeare's birthplace demonstrates the material application of this claim. But the even earlier public opening of Sir Walter Scott's house demonstrates a parallel representation asserted by *readers* about the nature of Englishness—for despite the Scottish setting of the Waverley novels, their central story was the lost cause of the romantic Scots nation, which ever gave way to the noble justice of the English crown. In such ways, the rise of the author as the hero of literary history indicates not only aesthetic acknowledgement but also national consciousness. Writers' houses were endowed by museumization with the further status of literature's nationalist capacity. That power was witnessed by the acquisition of two more Shakespeare sites, book-ending the public opening of houses inhabited by John Milton in 1887 and William Wordsworth in 1890. The first half of the twentieth century saw more than twenty writers' houses opened to the public as museums: dwellings inhabited by William Cowper, Dr. Johnson, Dickens, and Samuel Taylor Coleridge were museumized in the first decade; by John Keats, Dickens again, Izaak Walton, and the Brontë sisters,

Charlotte, Emily, and Anne, in the 1920s; by Lord Byron, John Ruskin, T. E. Lawrence, J. M. Barrie, a fourth Shakespeare site, Wordsworth again, and Rudyard Kipling in the 1930s; by Jane Austen, Thomas Hardy, Beatrix Potter, Vita Sackville-West, and the fifth Shakespeare house in the hard years of the 1940s.

There were at least thirty writers' house museums in the British public domain before World War II. Their variety along the spectrum of the seventeenth- and eighteenth-century literary canon, nineteenth-century novelists, and twentieth-century moderns demonstrates the importance of availability and advocacy as the drivers of house enshrinement, rather than any consistent program of national recognition. By comparison, the *Blue Guide to Literary Britain and Ireland*, which identifies both real-life and fictional places, discussed an acknowledged selection of 185 "writers of imaginative literature," of whom just 45 had been memorialized in their houses when the guide was published in 1985. Author Ian Ousby often notes the destruction of significant houses in the Great Fire of London in 1666, the Blitz in 1940–1941, and the bulldozer shovel of urban development. He occasionally mourns more recent losses, as for the previously mentioned museum-less George Eliot: "It is unfortunate that so few of the houses she lived in survive; the loss of The Priory near Regent's Canal, where she presided over afternoon teas for famous and aspiring writers, leaves a specially important gap" (Ousby 1985, 236). Ousby and his readers had come to expect that great writers would—even should—be commemorated in houses.

They could bask in this expectation thanks to a triad of mechanisms for managing the extraction of houses from everyday living stock and translating them into museums. A few made their way into the bosom of the National Trust, which addresses the challenge of keeping up historic house museums on a large scale that offers some economies and strengths. Slightly more migrated into ownership by local authorities, with mixed fortunes; culture and heritage do not always fare well among the traditional local government priorities of roads, rates, and rubbish. Private trusts are still the most frequent legal means of constituting house museums in the United Kingdom, and even the most successful exist on a treadmill of fund-raising.

Small trusts established in the early to mid-twentieth century have done the hard yards to get and keep their houses going. There is no consistent exemplar of a house museum trust, but the history of Brantwood, the Cumbria home of John Ruskin, involves elements that are both common and unique. Like so many houses, it owes its museum career to one passionate soul. Ruskin had lived in Brantwood with his niece Joan Agnew and her husband, artist Arthur Severn, and their family; he left the house to Joan when he died in 1900. After her death in 1924, Arthur began to sell the contents, and John Whitehouse bought them. Whitehouse had come under Ruskin's spell as a young man; he had a short career as a Liberal MP, and in 1919 he established Bembridge School on Ruskinian principles. The School Trust funded Whitehouse's Ruskin collection, including more of Brantwood's contents and, after Severn's death in 1931, the house itself. Some rooms were opened in museum form, while Bembridge used Brantwood for summer field schools and spent the World War II years nearby. After the war, Whitehouse was in his seventies and anxious to secure the Ruskin legacy. He passed Brantwood to Oxford University, but after a short period of benign neglect, he reclaimed it and in 1951 established the Brantwood Trust. He died in 1954, and for the next twenty years the house consolidated its purpose as an educational resource for a number of schools while maintaining the exhibits in the front rooms. The revival of scholarly interest in Ruskin, a new caretaker couple, and a new chair of the Brantwood Trust pushed the house toward a more public focus on its Ruskin heritage in the 1980s. Bembridge School closed in 1996, and the Ruskin collections formed by Whitehouse were transferred to a new Ruskin Foundation. The archive went to Lancaster University, where a dedicated library to house it opened in 1997. Artifacts, furniture, and memorabilia returned to Brantwood, where a museum director was employed for the first time, and the house worked through the steps of formal museum accreditation, improving conditions such that J. M. W. Turner watercolors on loan from other collections once more hang on Ruskin's walls. The house now commemorates the great man's myriad interests, with re-created rooms and public programs in art, writing, gardening, and nature (Hull 2010).

The museum career of Newstead Abbey near Nottingham, ancestral home of Lord Byron, demonstrates some characteristics of the segment of houses that came into public ownership via local government. The poet Byron inherited Newstead unexpectedly at the age of ten; after his coming of age, he lived there on and off from 1808 to 1814, steadily spending the estate's income to the extent that selling it became his financial salvation. A very rich friend, Thomas Wildman, bought it in 1817; he spent a huge amount on the ruined abbey and an early Victorian Gothic house beside it, designed by John Shaw. The Wildmans saved both Byron and the house, and they sustained the Byron myth after the poet's death in 1824, building up a large collection of memorabilia to add to the original furniture (Wildman 1857; Beckett 2002, 283–99). When Wildman died in 1859, Newstead was sold to another wealthy man, William Webb, who continued to maintain the heroic legacy of Byron and of his own friend, the Scottish explorer of Africa, Dr. David Livingstone. The house passed to Webb's children and eventually a

grandson, who, after World War I, sold off much of the estate for development and subdivided the house into apartments. The abbey ruins, the Great
Hall, and the Byron rooms were sold to Sir Julien Cahn, Nottingham businessman and philanthropist, to present to the Nottingham Corporation in
1931. The Corporation had acquired Wollaton Hall, an important Elizabethan mansion, in 1925 for conversion into a natural history museum and was
evidently committed to developing cultural services for the people of Nottingham. However, at Newstead it was found that local council-style utilitarian maintenance could not keep the estate in the condition it merited. On
advice from the National Trust, the Corporation commenced a long-term
program to buy back the subdivided house and, where possible, the old estate
to rebuild a critical mass of character and curtilage. The management regime
shifted from librarians and council gardeners to curators and estate managers
in the 1970s–1980s, so it was well placed to benefit from devolved government funding programs in the early 2000s. This was fortunate, for Newstead
has never been within the urban boundary of Nottingham, and the civic authority had long harbored ambivalent feelings about it, as is common among
agencies where houses are noncore business.

Meanwhile, in Scotland: Robbie Burns

In Scotland, the nationalist politics of language had generated a body of
museumizations nearly as old as, but counter to, the teaching of English in
the Scottish universities. Robert Burns, the Ploughman Bard of Ayr, wrote
proto-Romantic verse in Lallands (Lowlands Scots), Scottish English, and
standard English in the late eighteenth century. He was not the first such
poet, but he achieved vast fame in Scotland, England, and, thanks to the
Scottish diaspora, the world for expressing the autonomy of the Scottish
voice within the United Kingdom (Andrews 2004). Burns's picturesque rise
from agricultural laborer to acclaimed poet was accompanied by a difficult
career as a failing farmer. He was eventually rescued by a government clerk-
ship, but also by a calling to Masonic solidarity and good-time drinking, none
of which damaged his reputation as the voice of native Scottish culture.
The traditions of Burns Suppers and his Hogmanay songs are buttressed by
countless Burns monuments around the world and, in Scotland itself, by
three house museums. His birthplace cottage at Alloway speedily became a
hallowed place after his death in 1796. A sign marking the event had been
installed by 1805, and the closet bed in which the poet was born was shown
when the cottage was reincarnated as a pub, introducing a commoditization
of the hero that flourishes to this day (Watson 2006, 68–69). Keats visited
in 1818 and was enchanted by the humble cottage but appalled by its use;

Burns Cottage, Alloway, Ayrshire, c. 1910. Poet Robbie Burns (1759–1796) was born in this humble cottage. He passed his life in Lowland Scotland, moving so frequently that the area is now speckled with Burns house museums, including Tarbolton Bachelors' Club, Ellisland Farm, and the house in Dumfries where he lived for the last five years of his life.
Postcard, private collection.

he called it "a flummery of a birthplace!" (Wilson-Costa 2009, 47). Other visitors were more ready to be moved:

> And I have stood beside the pile,
> His monument—that tells to Heaven,
> The homage of earth's proudest isle
> To that Bard-peasant given! (Halleck in Bates 1882, 249–51)

A formal Trust assumed management of the site in 1881, making Alloway coeval with Carlyle's birthplace as Britain's third-oldest hero house museums. Now managed by the National Trust for Scotland, the birthplace cottage recently had dioramas removed in favor of spare symbolism, quotes painted on the walls, and clever multimedia installations, bolstered by a new museum off site. Further memorializing Burns, the house where he died in Dumfries was museumized by the Town Council in 1903, under the care of a Burns great-granddaughter; it had a rocky career as a museum but has been regularly open since 1944. Ellisland Farm was an unsuccessful agricultural venture for Burns and his young family between 1788 and 1791; it was acquired by a philanthropist and gifted to the nation in 1921. Interpretation at all three sites focuses on the songs and poems composed there, always stressing the Scottish character of Burns's language. Burns and his poetry stand for Scotland to this day.

Writers, Fame, and House Museums

British writers' houses museumized in the first decades of the twenty-first century show no signs of challenging the inexplicit tradition of the national virtue of English literature. Rather, the imprimatur of a house museum seems to have been drawn into asserting the significance of lesser-known figures. A prime example is Clare Cottage, home of John Clare, the Northamptonshire "peasant poet" reevaluated in the later twentieth century as equally important as Keats and Wordsworth; his house was opened in 2005. The beguiling, whitewashed, thatched house was formerly divided into tenements, in one of which Clare was born in 1793 and later lived with his wife and six children; the last thirty years of his tortured life were spent in a madhouse. The garden and countryside about the house are now presented as resources for understanding Clare's poetry, which was once called "rural" and is today framed as "environmentally sensitive." Clare's manic depression and the spare introversion of his later prose and poetry appeal to the psychological awareness of modern people, as well as representing the pain and reality of then-untreatable mental illness. Formally unlettered, rural, laboring, and ultimately mad, Clare personifies many aspects of physical and psychological powerlessness that make him a restorative emblem of the inclusive cultural politics of today.

Another specimen of revisionism is Elizabeth Gaskell, who was once regarded as a second-order novelist among the Victorian pantheon. Her house in the suburbs of Greater Manchester underwent a long restoration to open in 2014, and it exemplifies the contemporary forms of writer's house memorialization. The house had come to the attention of heritage agencies as an important, because largely intact, specimen of 1830s Italianate villa design; it had fallen into disuse, and its literary associations were drawn into a rationale for preservation. It was the author's home from 1850 to her death in 1865, the place where she wrote most of her major works, and was visited by other eminent writers. Gaskell's fame rocketed in the 2000s thanks to "the *Cranford* effect," set off by BBC television adaptations of *Cranford*, *Wives and Daughters*, and other novels—another example of an ever more influential phenomenon in the modern consumption of Victorian fiction. Having introduced a vast new dimension to literary tourism, films have generated a plethora of sites with the potential to connect readers/viewers/

visitors to the author and story. (Filmmaking is also now valuable business for heritage houses and sites.) Film tourism could seem inauthentic in displacing the grounded historical connections of authors to sites, but in a triumph of popular culture transformation, it may instead constitute a vehicle of neocollective memories (Pucci & Thompson 2003, 9–10). Gaskell herself was the subject of similar memory seeking by her nineteenth-century readers, who sought Cranford in Knutsford, her childhood home and burial place, and in biographies such as Mrs. Ellis Chadwick's *Mrs. Gaskell: Haunts, Homes, and Stories* (1910). The modern revival of Gaskell's Manchester house is a project of an offshoot of the Gaskell Society, populated by readers with sentimental as well as scholarly attraction to the author. In them, the shrine aspect of the house motivates a good part of the task of raising the funds for the costly apparatus of a modern house museum: room re-creations, offices, a study center, café, and all the services necessary to make them work. The pleasures of imagining tea with Mrs. Gaskell in the room where she wrote sustain the responsibility.

Yet at the same time, the houses of some museumized authors have declined in attractiveness. A case in point is Shaw's Corner, the Hertfordshire retreat of George Bernard Shaw, complete with his "writing hut" in the garden. He used it as a weekender from 1906 to his death in 1950. Shaw himself offered the house to the National Trust, with additional memorabilia from his London house but without an endowment; hence he authorized the sale of any parts of the collection necessary for fund-raising. After a big opening year in 1951, visitation fell and the silver was sold in 1952, followed by photographic equipment and furniture. The house has remained open, but the challenges are many, and not just economic. Shaw's commentary and dramatic works are subjects of specialist interest today; he is no longer taught in schools, and other than *Pygmalion*, his plays are rarely performed, though the site organizes summer outdoor productions. By the metrics of popularity and rational calculation, it is difficult to justify the continuing costs of keeping Shaw's Corner open. But here the onus of curatorial management of the past for the future comes into play. It is the sacred role of a trust to carry on through shifts in fashion: Shaw's cultural hero status might be passé today, but he was a highly influential thinker in his time and no one can tell if or when his star will rise again. It is the museum's role to wait out history.

American Writers' Houses

Americans sought to develop a distinctive literature in a process similar to that of the Scots (Crawford 2000). Colonial literature had been essentially rhetorical, with religious or political agendas, but from the late eighteenth century onward a handful of writers, responding to new literary forms in England, set their poems and stories in American contexts. Calls for a distinctive American literature followed the great events of the Revolution and the War of 1812, in which the polity began to share the kind of sentiments and experiences that evolved into a national identity. In this spirit, the *Analectic Magazine* and the *North American Review*, the first native literary journals, commenced in the 1810s, edited by emerging writers such as Washington Irving and William Cullen Bryant and publishing their own and others' poetry, fiction, and essays. Irving and James Fenimore Cooper, commonly agreed to be the first American novelists, gained fame with youthful works in America. They subsequently traveled to Britain and Europe, where their new works, including novels set in the United States, were well received; returning home, both enjoyed enormous national popularity. The tide of consciously American writing now surged through the nineteenth century: the New England poets, the Transcendentalists, the Dark Romantics, vernacular humorists, elite realists, and rare spirits like Emily Dickinson. New literary journals, especially the *Atlantic Monthly*, carried their work, employed writers as editorial staff, and engaged in the great campaign of the antebellum period, abolition. Both American literature and its nation were effectively of the North. The character of the South, shaped by the plantation economy and slavery, was conservative, and many Southerners with literary ambitions moved north. Slavery, the defining lens of Southern society, generated a small apologetic fiction published locally, and the resistance genres of slave narratives and fiction, written of necessity in the North or in England.

Writing in America, then, was a dynamic project in the nineteenth century. Commentators called for a national literature, yet disagreed about whether American writing could be true "literature" or distinctively American, or both (Hutner 1999, 1–4). If it was a problem, authors and readers soared above it as ready producers and consumers, and the argument eventually came to rest in academe. As in Britain, writing in the contemporary vernacular was not embraced in the old colonial colleges until the early twentieth century, other than in the genres of rhetoric and belles lettres, and even then American books were admitted with some reluctance. The *Cambridge History of American Literature* began at Columbia University and took shape as four volumes between 1917 and 1921 (it directly followed the publication of the *Cambridge History of English Literature* in seventeen volumes from 1907 to 1917), proving that a creative, rather than merely civic, literature existed. But American literary specialists did not assert the academic respectability of the study of American writers until the 1920s (Shumway 1994, 148–50; Vanderbilt 1986).

The anguish provoked by this topic in universities mattered little among the public culture of readers, who knew what they liked. They liked the New England poets. They admired the learned voices—Henry Wadsworth Longfellow, James Russell Lowell, Oliver Wendell Holmes—and they loved the homely Quaker poet, John Greenleaf Whittier. Unlike the others, Whittier was relatively unschooled and never traveled abroad, but alongside his poetry, he made a career as a journalist, which took him into Massachusetts state politics where principle made him a militant abolitionist from the 1830s. Whittier's natural metier was rural, but he gladly put his pen to the cause and churned out poems in the voice of enslaved misery; he was also a forthright activist in the cause. For thirty years, Whittier's poetry stirred the pages of the abolitionist press; yet simultaneously he wrote bucolic New England lyrics and personal reflections, culminating in the heartfelt reminiscence of "Snow-Bound: A Winter Idyl." The poet became a New England institution, celebrated in several Whittier Clubs: his seventy-fifth and eightieth birthdays inspired festivals of public tribute. He died in 1892,

Haverhill, Mass. Poet Whittier's Birthplace, "Snowbound".

The Whittier family homestead in Haverhill, Massachusetts, c. 1900. Poet and abolitionist John Greenleaf Whittier (1807–1892) was born in this house, the site he recalled in his poem "Snow-Bound" (1866), an elegy to rural life. He moved to Amesbury, Massachusetts, around 1845, and that house was also museumized soon after his death. Postcard, private collection.

and his birthplace, the family farm of five generations (which had been sold when his father died), was purchased and presented to the Haverhill Whittier Club in 1893. This constitutes it as the first writer's house museum in the United States. Five years later, a group of women established the Whittier Home Association to open his Amesbury town house, the second American writer's house museum. Both houses still contain family furnishings: the original material of the Amesbury house remains in situ, and other material has been repatriated to the homestead.

Starting in 1886 as a private association of the most respectable citizens in Haverhill, the Whittier Club survives today, with an open membership, dedicated to maintaining the homestead as a New England farm to celebrate the poet's pastoral sentiments and values. It holds two annual meetings: in summer, members eat strawberries and ice cream in the garden, and in winter, they recite "Snow-Bound" by the very fireplace conjured in the poem.

The Whittier Home Association, guardian of the Amesbury house, was founded by one wing of the preexisting Elizabeth H. Whittier Club, a women's club named in honor of the poet's sister, friend, and housekeeper; when the house became available, the Home Association established a separate existence. Whittier left the house to his niece; she didn't live there and readily agreed that the Home Association should lease and open it, for the poet's goods and furnishings remained inside. She left the house to her son, who in 1904 added a modern house behind the old structure, leaving the front rooms to be managed by the Association to celebrate the memory of Whittier. When this occupant died in 1917, his heir sold the entire house to the Association. The Association is still an active guardian, with a mission "to engage diverse audiences in the life-story of Whittier in his roles as a Quaker, a Writer and an Abolitionist" by way of managing the house collection of artifacts and archives and conducting programs of lectures, music, and poetry.

Both Whittier organizations represent the American Victorian movement of middle-class and female cultural activism. Though unspoken, their dedication to the good old ways of New England suggests the widespread anxiety of the late nineteenth/early twentieth century period that American values were under threat from the avalanche of immigrants then sweeping in from eastern Europe. Rightly proud and proudly patriotic, they upheld the virtues of the Puritan founders and Revolutionary stalwarts of the nation; this generation had been ennobled in their own time by achieving the abolition of slavery, even at the cost of Civil War and its aftermath. Such consciousness made the simple pleasures of countryside New England even sweeter, and Whittier's poetry even more poignant. The rustic aesthetic burnished the immigrant education goals that were especially dear to the women's clubs of the era. To this end, the conservation of model homes such as those that had molded John Greenleaf Whittier were regarded as an appropriate, even natural, civic task for genteel women. Whittier's personal life was actually introverted, childless, and radical, as much as it was upstanding and some-times lyrical, but he also had deep rural roots that could be exemplified in his family's farmhouse and his own modest weatherboard house. It made the houses sound candidates for the project commended by the General Federa-tion of Women's Clubs to its members, to preserve "all that is good in the civilization of the past" (Wood 1912, 312).

Patricia West traced a similar history of female club agency in the pres-ervation of Louisa May Alcott's family home, Orchard House in Concord (West 1999, 55–68). Orchard House could have been the third writer's house museum in the United States but that it took ten years to raise enough money to buy and restore the house where *Little Women* was written. Visitors have blissfully ignored the abyss of discrepancies between the real Alcott and the fictional March families since 1912, proving yet again that the appetite for warm fiction easily overrides the cold facts of history.

Instead, the third writer's house to be museumized was the poet Henry Wadsworth Longfellow's childhood home in Portland, Maine. It was bequeathed to the Maine Historical Society in 1901 on the death of its owner, his younger sister. Like Whittier's Amesbury house, the direct family connection endowed the house with family furniture of a four-generation provenance, though Longfellow himself left the place at age fourteen to at-tend college. He traveled, taught languages at Harvard, and wrote poems so popular they soon enabled him to live on his author's earnings, in Craigie House, Cambridge, which was museumized by his family in 1913. Historical epics such as "The Song of Hiawatha" and "Evangeline" made Longfellow the most popular poet of nineteenth-century America; admirers mobbed his house during his life and after his death. His children resolved to preserve the house and its furnishings via a trust, commemorating not only Longfel-low but also George Washington, who had occupied the house as his head-quarters during the Siege of Boston in 1775–1776. A Longfellow grandson dedicated thirty years as curator, gathering family archives that made the house a research destination for scholars as well as a site of popular acclaim. It was donated to the National Park Service in 1972.

Sectional Literary Houses

The power of preserving a house to mark and celebrate the literary identi-ties adopted by a nation is evident in the first Southern literary museumiza-tion, in 1913: the Atlanta, Georgia, house of Joel Chandler Harris, the white author of the Uncle Remus tales of slave folklore. In the voice of the "venerable old darkey," Harris brought rural black dialect to national and international awareness in his stories of animal tricksters. The genius of the Uncle Remus corpus lies in using the dialect of the enslaved to define and proclaim the difference of the South: Harris invoked the language of the oppressed as a characteristic that naturalized oppression. For such reasons, he was condemned in the later twentieth century as a cultural thief, though also occasionally hailed as a subversive who acknowledged black resistance in his tales of the successes of Br'er Rabbit over his enemies. The subversive animals themselves introduced a new trope to European literature, providing a model for subsequent authors' animal characters, such as Jemima Puddle-Duck and Peter Rabbit (Southern expressions adopted by their English creator, Beatrix Potter). The museumization of Harris's house, named the Wren's Nest, vividly represented one pole of "the counter-narrative of the Old South," softening slave tradition into quaint tales that were acceptable throughout the country (Geisler 2005, 5). Remolded for a new century, the Wren's Nest now conceives its mission as maintaining the legacy of Harris and the heritage of African American folklore, appropriately realized through storytelling programs.

The other pole of the Old South is embodied in the Margaret Mitchell House and Museum, representing the loss of the dream of gracious white plantation culture. Mitchell wrote most of *Gone with the Wind* in apartment no. 1 of a subdivided Atlanta house, where she lived from 1925 to 1932, several years before the manuscript was published. The building itself was already run down when Mitchell lived there (she called it "The Dump") and had been abandoned, burned out, and slated for demolition when a local activist gathered support to preserve it in 1994. Burned and rebuilt yet again, the site of Mitchell's apartment is said to be intact, and since 1997 it has been re-created to show her typewriter at the ready in the front room. The rest of the house is occupied by exhibitions and a busy Center for Southern Literature, offering creative writing workshops, book clubs, author lectures, and youth writing programs. (Further *Gone with the Wind* fantasy and memorabilia occupy private museums and Tara lookalikes elsewhere in Atlanta and nearby.) In 2004, the Margaret Mitchell House merged with the Atlanta History Center (formerly Historical Society), giving it a strong collegial base for a confident future (Harris 2007, 129–34).

The regional identity of the South, as expressed in the concept of southern literature and represented by writers' house museums, is sustained by some ten establishments (two for Flannery O'Connor), mainly founded since the 1980s. In New England there are about twenty (two for Robert Frost).

Br'er Rabbit gestures to "The Wren's Nest" of Joel Chandler Harris, in Atlanta, c. 1910. Harris (1845–1908) was a journalist in Georgia for almost all of his life. In the 1880s he began to publish African American folktales in the Deep South Gullah voice of "Uncle Remus." The stories were largely written in this house in Atlanta, museumized in 1913. Postcard, private collection.

Both South and North nurture Mark Twain houses (his boyhood home in Missouri and an adult house in Connecticut); they exemplify the political significance of domicile as a cultural identification, for the individual as well as the state. Continuing acts of shrine creation via literary houses constitute vivid evidence of sectional identity: Emily Dickinson in 2003; Flannery O'Connor (number 2) in 2004; Eudora Welty in 2006; and Henry Thoreau in 2010.

By contrast, the tale of westward expansion recounted in Laura Ingalls Wilder's *Little House* books is normatively American. No less than eight house museums represent the stories, bringing together topics that speak to the complex nature of the museumization of writers' houses. It is no cliché to call Wilder a much-loved author, adored by children, especially girls, since her first book was published in 1932, and cherished by adults (grown-up girls). Her semi-autobiographical series of eight books (plus four published posthumously) follows the Ingalls family's homestead quest from Wisconsin to South Dakota in the 1870s–1880s. The houses they inhabited were mainly impermanent vernacular structures, only one of which remained in situ until the home of her adult life, Rocky Ridge Farm in the Ozarks. The fictional aspects of Wilder's childhood in the books (and nine television seasons) match the conflation of life and artifice in the replication of her homes long gone, presenting readers/visitors with deadpan "realities" that cannot sustain close analysis. Yet metaphysics matter little in the face of continuing delight in the books and enthusiastic visitation to the sites, witnessed by many blogs.

Wilder was guided by her journalist daughter Rose Wilder Lane to produce best-selling stories of pioneer determination in the face of hard fortune: Pa Ingalls could always take out his fiddle to resolve chapters of pain and trauma, and the family moved on. The movement was literal, and there are replica dwellings where Laura was born in Pepin, Wisconsin (the Little House in the Big Woods, built 1974); Independence, Kansas (the Little House on the Prairie, built 1977); and Walnut Grove, Minnesota (the dugout on the Banks of Plum Creek). Original houses occupied by the family can be visited in Burr Creek, Iowa (by the Shores of Silver Lake), and De Smet, South Dakota (the Little Town on the Prairie, and the site of the Long Winter, where the Laura Ingalls Wilder Memorial Society is based). In Mansfield, Missouri, is the house that Laura and Almanzo Wilder built after ten married years marred by infant death, illness, drought, fire, and slump; gradually their Rocky Ridge Farm grew from a cabin to a spacious farmhouse. Their daughter Rose aimed to ease the Wilders' hard life in 1928 with the profits of her own successful writing career when she had a new house built on the farm to Sears Roebuck kit plans, in smart Old English style. Here Rose encouraged her mother to begin writing—or possibly ghosted—the books that became the *Little House* series. But after eight years in the bright new house, the Wilders chose to return to their old farmhouse, where Almanzo died in 1949 and Laura in 1957.

The Wilder Home Association was founded almost immediately to acquire the farmhouse, with Rose's help. A museum was built on the site in the 1970s, and in 1994 Rock House was also purchased. The site of the Plum Creek dugout house was identified in 1947 by artist Garth Williams, whose renderings of Laura's life still appear in most editions; the property owners have since preserved the depression in the ground, and a reproduction dugout features as a nearby tourist attraction. The De Smet houses were acquired in 1968 and 1973; the replica houses all date from the 1970s. No other American writer is as thoroughly museumized as Laura Ingalls Wilder. Her stories are comfortably plain and reliably moral; she concluded a standard fan letter in the 1950s, "Every American has always been free to pursue his happiness, and so long as Americans are free they will continue to make our country even more wonderful" (http://www.laurasprairiehouse. com/research/lettertofans.html). This message remains popular today, buttressed by wagon rides and Laura look-alike competitions. Little houses can carry big stories.

Local Heroes

House museums prove to be fertile material for celebrating identity at the local level. The threshold of hero status is a frankly relative concept, and so is the border between national and local fame. Nonetheless, there seems little risk in suggesting that (almost random examples such as) Charles La Trobe, first governor of the colony of Victoria, Australia, or Jonathan Bailey, founder of the town of Whittier, California, are *local* heroes, of limited significance outside their regional spheres. The meanings of "local hero" become clear when tracing the history of how each came to be commemorated in a house museum.

Charles La Trobe was a scientifically minded gentleman, posted in 1839 by the Colonial Office as superintendent and later governor of the district in southeast Australia that in 1851 became the colony of Victoria. He brought a prefabricated wooden cottage with him and lived in it with his family until they left the colony in 1854. The house barely survived the travails of time, but a wall and the colonial-built additions were relocated and rebuilt in 1963 and again in 1998. Now managed by the National Trust, it contains original furniture and other material. La Trobe returned to England but remains important in the history of Melbourne as the first personification of organized British power, and in that sense, represents the origin of the modern state. Jonathan Bailey was an Ohio Quaker farmer and church leader, elected head of the company formed in 1887 to establish a California Quaker community, named Whittier after the poet. The company purchased a ranch with a cottage built there after the Mexican-American War, now known as the Jonathan Bailey House. The settlement flourished, exporting "Quaker" brand fruit all over the United States and pioneering the Californian walnut industry. The house was transferred to the City of Whittier in 1975 and is managed as a branch of the Whittier Historical Society; it contains several Bailey family items of furniture. "This small, dignified home furnished much of Whittier's early history and is a symbol of our heritage," concluded the Society website (since disappeared), expressing a now well-formed local identity.

Both buildings housed founding figures, the first of a state in Australia, the second of a city that is now part of Greater Los Angeles. La Trobe's Cottage housed governmental power in a tiny colony that grew in his term from three thousand souls to seventy-six thousand. Bailey's house hosted the first services

Birthplace of Maria Mitchell in Nantucket, Massachusetts, preserved by the Maria Mitchell Association, established in 1902, c. 1910. Mitchell (1819–1889) achieved fame by discovering a telescopic comet (not visible to the naked eye) in 1847. The family home was museumized by the Maria Mitchell Association in 1903 and has grown into a science education complex with two observatories, a natural history museum, and an aquarium, as well as the house.
Postcard, private collection.

held by the Friends in their new community, and sustained its social life in the first decade. Such functions enabled and encouraged the new towns to develop, and museumizing each house about a hundred years later constitutes a communal claim to historic identity—a microcosm of the foundation of the nation. Can this statement of a primal house museum in local identity be extended into the historic identities of other communities of interest?

Part of the motivation to commemorate heroes in their houses is the luster that reflects on the community when a local son or daughter makes good, but an important further constituency of interest in museumization is the hero's professional, intellectual, or spiritual community, which draws social identity from celebrating its foundational heroes. A pair of astronomers' houses offers food for thought on the social nature of "local heroes." The Nantucket, Massachusetts, birthplace of Maria Mitchell, first professor of astronomy at Vassar College, was museumized in 1903. Mitchell was a self-taught astronomer who discovered a comet in 1847; it brought her international fame and (as a woman) ground-breaking membership of scientific learned academies. Family, friends, and Vassar alumnae formed the Maria Mitchell Association to "preserve the legacy of a Nantucket native" via community education programs in astronomy and natural history, and the preservation of her birth-place; both association and house continue to this day. On the other side of the Atlantic, the foundation of the Herschel Astronomy Museum in Bath commemorates siblings William and Caroline Herschel, who came to Britain from Hanover as musicians but whose amateur astronomy brought more fame to both. William discovered the planet Uranus in 1781 with a telescope of his own design, from the garden of the small Georgian house that is now the museum. Here, too, Caroline conducted observations that resulted in the discovery of eight comets and other astronomical bodies; she also revised and corrected the first star catalog in the early eighteenth century, publishing the new edition in 1798. William became astronomer to the king, and George III also paid Caroline £50 p.a. for her work as William's assistant. In 1828 she received the Gold Medal of the Royal Astronomical Society. A group of enthusiasts formed the Herschel Society in 1977 with the aim of acquiring and opening the Herschels' house, achieved in 1981. The Society remains a trustee of the museum, its board thickly populated by Fellows of the Royal Astronomical Society, evidence of the foundational hero status of the Her-schels. (Maria Mitchell met William Herschel's astronomer son John on her first trip to Europe; he gave her a page from Caroline's notebook, still among Maria's papers.)

Another house-museumized hero-in-his-vocation is John Muir, the con-servationist who lobbied for the protection of Yosemite, cofounded the Si-erra Club in 1892, and is often called "the father of national parks"—a sacred figure to a community of American wilderness lovers and environmental activists. Even they might be surprised to know that two houses have been museumized to celebrate Muir and bestow honor on their locations: his birth-place in Dunbar, Scotland, from which he departed for America as a child in 1849, and the house of his later life in Martinez, California. The latter, once the citrus ranch of his wife's family, had become dilapidated and was threat-ened by suburban development in the 1950s. Two activists bought the prop-erty, created the John Muir Memorial Association, and succeeded in 1964 in having the site adopted into the National Park Service as a monument to Muir and his ideals. The preservation of the Scottish birthplace house was a partnership between a trust (which had been holding wild lands in the Scottish highlands and islands since 1983), a local association (dedicated to upholding Muir's vision since 1994), and local government. The house opened in 1981 and was redeveloped to include an interpretive center with historical, art, and children's programs in 2003. Acknowledging the localized contingency of fame, Dunbar's John Muir Association wrote some years ago on its website, "For many millions of Californians, John Muir is as famous as Alexander Graham Bell or Andrew Carnegie, two other Scottish emigrants, and his writings are as celebrated as those of Robert Burns or Robert Louis Stevenson. Yet in Britain he is largely unknown, and even in the land of his birth few Scots have heard of him." The construction of a transnational hero through the museumization of his houses is clearly underway here.

The cases of John Muir, Maria Mitchell, and William and Caroline Herschel demonstrate the power of social identification that is generated by a shared hero, functioning as a symbol of an interest group and a focus for publicity and education. Perhaps few in the imagined communities of national park lovers, Vassar graduates, and astronomers have any idea that these "heroes" of their fields are commemorated in house museums. But if and when they become aware, they are likely to feel a twinge of recognition that brings a sense of community identity.

The Heroes of Suppressed Cultures

The public assertion of heroic quality implied by the foundation of a house museum has a considerable history in political advocacy. The birthplaces and residences of outstanding representatives of long-suppressed segments of society, notably women and people of color, is not a recent phenomenon. Starting with the preservation of Cedar Hill, home of black abolitionist Frederick Douglass, in 1903, the house museum has been adopted to mark the achievement of the erstwhile and otherwise excluded. With this motivation, it is clear that a purpose of house museumization is less the systematic restitution of the dispossessed to the public sphere as much as a claim for recognition of the great individual. (This topic emerges again in chapter 6.)

As was often the pattern among early-twentieth-century hero house museumizations, family led the way in preserving Frederick Douglass's house. Douglass, who was born into slavery in 1818 and escaped from bondage in 1838, made his mark as an eloquent abolitionist in New York, traveling the country and the world. His stark autobiographical account of the treatment of America's enslaved people was published in 1845 and became an international best seller. He was a (not uncritical) adviser to Abraham Lincoln, and after the Civil War he occupied several political appointments. Douglass moved to Washington, DC, in 1877 after his house in New York was attacked, and he purchased the house he named Cedar Hill, where he died in 1895. After his death, his second wife bought the house from his children: "The house is to be kept just as it is for a 'memorial hall' of the earliest efforts in the cause of human freedom," she told a journalist in 1897 (Hinds

1968, 22). To achieve this, she established the Frederick Douglass Memorial and Historical Association, which opened the house to the public in 1903. The mortgage was eventually paid by the National Association of Colored Women, and in 1962, the National Park Service assumed management of the property. The house has had several restorations over the years, and still contains a high proportion of Douglass's furnishings. The museumization was a significant tribute to an African American man whose narrative of personal witness gave tremendous weight to the abolition movement, backed by his biting oratory and commentary. His house was funded by his speaking income and depicts the satisfactions of having built his own achievement in the interests of the oppressed, for which he is still celebrated today.

Subsequent house monuments to black heroes were the product of more complex negotiations, challenges, and compromises, bearing on decisions about the character of a "hero" and the availability of a suitable house. The history of the memorialization of Booker T. Washington demonstrates this dilemma. Washington, born in 1856, clawed his way from childhood enslavement to being principal of the Tuskegee Institute in Alabama, the first higher education school for blacks and staffed by blacks. In this role, Washington practiced his conviction that education was the most important route to black equality, and he was a mighty speaker in the cause, criss-crossing America on fund-raising tours. By the time he died in 1915, Tuskegee was a thriving institution, and he had been the preeminent African American spokesman of the previous twenty years, with support among the southern black community and powerful white sponsors. Yet his "racial diplomacy" was born of compromise and collaboration, which opened him to criticism by advocates of a more vigorous campaign for civil rights. Washington's grave at Tuskegee and a monumental statue titled *Lifting the Veil* (of ignorance) commemorated him in the environs of his most important achievement, but it was 1940 before his memory received wider public recognition when he became the first African American to be depicted on a postage stamp.

In 1945 the Burroughs Plantation near Roanoke, Virginia, where Washington had been born, came up for sale (Mackintosh 1969). Tuskegee indicated it could not afford to buy, and family friend and former Tuskegee professor Sidney J. Phillips purchased the property and established the Booker T. Washington Birthplace Memorial the next year. Phillips sold the property to the trust for a dollar, and a replica slave cabin was created on the site with funds from the state of Virginia, opening in 1949. A demonstration farm and memorial trade school were established nearby, bringing in income by means of a mop factory, chosen as a symbol of Washington's ideals of cleanliness and labor. In 1953 the National Park Service was requested to take over management of the site but declined on the ground that no object or building still existed there relating to Washington's residence, and that "the birth site is not as equally impressive as the man" (Mackintosh 1969). The Birthplace Memorial went bankrupt in 1955. Sidney J. Phillips purchased the site yet again and chartered the Booker T. Washington National Monument Foundation, promoting it with a letter-writing campaign to Congress. Within a year a House of Representatives committee criticized the Park Service and recommended that the Foundation should be supported: both houses passed the measure, and President Eisenhower signed the bill to authorize the Booker T. Washington National Monument. Since 1957 the site has been re-created as a middle-class tobacco farm, representing the great man's enslaved childhood via replica cabins, farm buildings, farm animals, and a kitchen garden. A visitor center goes some way to satisfying the professional aims of the Park Service as a heritage interpretation organization, the front-line agent of memorialization. Contemporary interpretation via costumed actors now frames a participatory theatrical presentation that is more sympathetic to the reality that the site is a set as much as it is sacred ground.

Professional standards had determined the NPS reluctance to operate the site, though staff acknowledged the reality that the life of the enslaved left few remains, and that the absence of structures could tell as much history as it suppressed. At the same time, the popular taste for material reality had already been asserted on the site when the Birthplace Memorial built a replica kitchen cabin, shaping subsequent presentation. Some tropes of heritage can prove irresistible, especially when they engage audiences effectively. This is a besetting challenge of museumizing birthplaces of the enslaved. It has generated further sites where re-creations and other devices are developed to interpret lives, such as the George Washington Carver National Monument in Diamond, Missouri, opened in 1943. Slowly, slowly, the national narrative of African American emancipation and achievement has now effected several generations of house commemoration. The earliest subjects were the abolitionist heroes who were born enslaved, such as Harriet Tubman's Brick House, associated with her Home for Aged and Indigent Colored People, in Auburn, New York, preserved and opened in 1953. Fifty years later, the site was transferred to NPS control as a National Historical Park in 2016.

Since the later twentieth century, houses associated with black achievers in government, business, and the arts, and the heroes of the civil rights struggle, were translated into house museumhood. The process was strengthened from the 1980s by the impact of social history perspectives on museum and site presentations, traced in chapter 6. The account here indicates how the tradition of heroic signification by enshrinement was deployed by the marginalized, first as an element of doing honor within their own community, and second, as an assertion of communal dignity in the dominant society.

The museumization of houses associated with women's rights heroes followed the same track. Thus the house of Susan B. Anthony, in Rochester, New York, sold after she and the sister with whom she lived had both died, was purchased by the Rochester Federation of Women's Clubs in 1945. They opened a small museum, more recognized by historic markers than visitors. The house organization gradually professionalized throughout the 1980s and 1990s and began to receive federal grant funds in 2000; the site now comprises four houses on Madison Street, Rochester, enabling the contemporary requirements for a visitor center, teaching and event spaces, and office accommodation. Number 17 was Anthony's home during the most politically active period of her life, and, reflecting the resource constraints of a single woman in the nineteenth century, it was her base of operations for suffrage campaigns across the United States. Hence it was the scene of dramatic events such as her arrest for voting in 1872. As she was not pursued for refusing to pay the $100 fine, she was unable to argue in a higher court that women had the legal right to vote under the provisions of the recently passed Fourteenth and Fifteenth amendments to the Constitution. Anthony did not live to see women's vote achieved, but the current Susan B. Anthony House mission statement aims to keep her vision alive.

Anthony's house museumization sprang from the reformist tradition of women's clubs; the 1970s second wave of radical feminism, riding the tide of the success of the civil rights movement in the United States, stimulated unprecedented formal responses by state apparatus. The National Park Service identified Seneca Falls, New York, location of the 1848 Convention that produced the Declaration of [Women's] Rights and Sentiments, based on the Declaration of Independence, as a potential new historic park in 1978 (Wellman 2003). It noted that local people had recently formed the Elizabeth Cady Stanton Foundation to rescue the house of one of the Convention's foremothers. Also identified in Seneca Falls were the remains of the Wesleyan Chapel, where the Convention was held, and the M'Clintock and Hunt houses, homes of other women connected with the event. Several anxious incidents intervened between the formal recommendation of the park and its opening in 1982, including fear that the new Reagan administration would freeze all action, but the Park Service proceeded and the site has gone from strength to strength. Judith Wellman, historian with the newly constituted Women's Rights National Historical Park at its opening, wrote twenty years later, "Historic preservation reflects contemporary values, and the new emphasis on sites related to women's rights reflected a profound change in

American life, towards a renewed awareness of the importance of women, past and present" (Wellman 2003, 247). It may be added that the ways in which the present makes use of the past itself constitutes an interpretive act. The preservation of the park inevitably staked the claim of the Seneca Falls Convention as the primal moment in the women's rights struggle in the United States, though events in other places, both before and after, could make equally plausible claims. The house museums of the individuals concerned, thanks to their long occupation, can tell the broader story.

House museum commemorations of suppressed cultures and their political activism are notably more scarce in the United Kingdom than in the United States. Slavery, mainly a matter of offshore trade, introduced a small black presence in Britain, acknowledged in museum exhibitions rather than in historic houses. The suffrage struggle is celebrated in institutional establishments, including funding schemes, rather than in dedicated museums. (A statue of Emmeline Pankhurst was raised in 1930 in London.) And just one postcolonial immigrant has so far bequeathed a house to the public domain. Khadambi Asalache, Kenyan poet, novelist, artist, and civil servant, bought a small, run-down terrace house in South London in 1981 and proceeded to adorn the interior with fretwork inspired by African, Islamic, and British design in a cosmopolitan fusion of cultures. Assessed as an embodiment of the social, political, and artistic history of the British colonial experience in the twentieth century, the National Trust began to open this fragile house in 2013.

The issue of representing the subversive sexuality of certain heroes demonstrates the current state of the impact of identity politics in house museums. Queer sexuality is considered by some to be an aspect of private life irrelevant to an individual's public acclaim and by others to be centrally important in understanding the individual's character and achievements (see chapter 6). Either way, conventional prejudice has long prohibited references to known or inferable gay sexuality in heroes' houses—though it is taken up in popular media. James Loewen, gadfly sociologist of American historical misrepresentation, makes an unprovable but highly suggestive case that President James Buchanan was gay, and he notes that the topic is utterly suppressed in tours of his house, Wheatlands, in Lancaster, Pennsylvania. Loewen's expeditions through historic sites asking awkward questions enable him to document similar stonewalling at Willa Cather's childhood home in Red Cloud, Nebraska. He observes that even hidden homosexuality influenced the sensibility, values, and careers of any number of notable Americans (Loewen 1999, 341–45, 113–16).

In the semisecret way of historic gay culture, a house museum in Wales was, in its time, and is now in its museum incarnation, perceived by some as a lesbian monument. Plas Newydd was the home of the "Ladies of Llangollen." The Ladies were Anglo-Irish gentlewomen, Lady Eleanor Butler and Miss Sarah Ponsonby, who eloped to avoid conventional marriages and set up home together in Wales in 1780 and lived there for nearly fifty years. Their frank romantic friendship was a phenomenon of voyeuristic interest to many literati of their own time, who visited to take tea, and to historians of sexuality ever since (Meem 2000, 334–36). Butler and Ponsonby decorated their six-room house inside and out with antique carved oak panels retrieved from house and church fittings and furnishings, creating an imaginative Tudoresque pastiche. (A subsequent owner further enriched the antiquarian decor.) Plas Newydd is now owned and opened as a house museum by the Denbighshire County Council, having been acquired for its antiquarian significance in 1932.

In Staten Island, New York, the picturesque but decaying family home of photographer Alice Austen, at the entrance to New York harbor, was saved from demolition and acquired by the New York City Department of Parks and

Plas Newydd, home of the Ladies of Llangollen, c. 1910. The Ladies, here depicted in riding habits, adorned their cottage with carved oak collected from houses, furniture, and ornaments. The postcard shows the form in which the house was museumized in 1933, having been much enlarged and further decorated by successors. The Ladies' original cottage comprised the western third of the present house; none of their furniture remains.
Postcard, private collection.

Recreation in 1975; it has been operated by the Friends of Alice Austen since 1985. Austen was a life-long amateur photographer of New York City, though she never sold her work, being genteelly well off. She lived in the house from 1866 to 1945, when financial disaster sent her briefly to a paupers' home. Photos rescued by the local historical society from her household sale and put on exhibition were recognized as the work of a major documentary artist, raising enough money for small comforts in her last years. Austen was outed in a gay anniversary exhibition at the New York Public Library in 1994. The house museum "was thrown into a cultural war. One side urged that the museum should become a center for lesbian and feminist studies and the other argued that Austen's personal life was personal" (Rutberg 2010, 6). She had lived with Gertrude Tate since 1917, and some of her photos depict the couple and their friends in cross dress. Insofar as heroes are figures identified by others who create community and identity out of their shared admiration, the Ladies of Llangollen and Austen and Tate might be called heroines of sexual politics. The couples' relationships are now acknowledged in interpretation in both houses, but the significance of their sexuality is as much in the eye of the beholder as in the management of their houses. So who makes a hero?

Popular Culture Heroes

The rate of house museumizations that continues every year demonstrates how convincing is the urge to memorialize the great in the sphere of home, and it is not confined to the great of history. Certain heroes of twentieth-century popular culture are celebrated in house museums, some even before death, the usual trigger for memorialization. Paul McCartney represents this category. He is flanked by John Lennon and preceded by Elvis Presley, the key figure in this story.

Graceland, in Memphis, Tennessee, is the Abbotsford of the twentieth century. Like Sir Walter Scott's mansion, Graceland was opened by Presley's family some years after he died in 1977. Unlike Abbotsford, visitors had never been permitted in before, and the opening was scripted to make money for the ailing estate. From 1982 onward it did just that, and it has since become the keystone of a massive themed development. By some definitions, the profit-making motive excludes Graceland from good standing as a museum. But for the purposes of this study, it would be willfully blind to ignore it: *The Elvis Encyclopedia* claims Graceland is the most visited house in the United States, after the White House (Victor 2008, 208).

Visiting Graceland is driven by Elvis's unparalleled status as a hero of popular culture, a poor boy killed by success who became the object of multitudinous projections of desire. His early music expressed the essence of American mid-twentieth-century music, hybridizing black rhythm and blues and southern country music into rock'n'roll: there is little argument that Elvis Presley personifies American rock'n'roll. The globalizing technologies of the recording industry, radio, television, and film thrust him into international stardom, whence he also became emblematic of the United States as a superpower after World War II. In the 1950s and 1960s, Elvis represented America to poor whites, the new class of teenagers, and their imitators around the world. Beyond music, a cult of fandom acclaimed him during his life and after, and fans are fervent about him to this day. Not only Graceland but also Presley's birthplace in Tupelo, Mississippi, and the Memphis social housing apartment in which he lived as a teenager have been preserved and opened as historic houses.

Graceland secures the myth of Elvis. Aged twenty-two, he acquired the house in 1957. "Graceland was big, showy, see-it-from-the-road, old-lace-and-honeysuckle, pseudo-plantation South—a thoroughly modern house, in other words," writes Karal Ann Marling (1996, 145). She argues that its "rock'n'roll heaven aesthetic" nonetheless constitutes an assertion of good ol' southern home values that anchored a self-creation from white trash poverty to *Gone with the Wind* grandeur (Marling 1993). Parts of the house were redecorated after Presley's death by his ex-wife, though other parts retain the inhabitant's own taste, such as the "jungle room" styled in "Polynesian Primitive" with green shag carpet and an indoor waterfall. Graceland is also where Elvis died and is buried with his parents and grandmother. The house thus possesses the ultimate ingredients of a shrine, and some of it is too sacred for public exposure. The bedroom floor is closed to visitors, thus maintaining a secret that keeps the fans breathless while avoiding the potential for on-site hysteria. Emotional homage is managed more practically at the grave, set in a "Garden of Meditation" with pool and columned arcade and plenty of space for floral tributes. High feeling is further dissipated by the route of more and more exhibits—gold records, stage costumes, cars—behind the mansion.

Aside from tightly controlled marketing strategies, the representational edifice of Graceland is, to a unique degree, a creation of fandom. Presley's power in this sphere relies on the versatility of his memory: rockabilly rebel, all-American boy, B-movie idol, patriotic GI, Las Vegas superstar, or, by another set of observers, white trash, an ugly Other. While legions of fans visit Graceland to commune and celebrate, there is also a stream of ironic spectators, whose taste echoes the largely disdainful academic literature on the Elvis phenomenon. Either way, what happens at Graceland is of major significance in contemporary culture because, as one commentator writes,

"Debates and conflicts over who Elvis is and what he means are comparable to the debates over what America is and what America means" (Doss 1999, 259). The truth of this claim was already acknowledged by the listing of Graceland on the National Register of Historic Places in 1991.

A similar imprimatur elevated 20 Forthlin Road, Allerton, Liverpool, from fan fame to transnational shrine when the National Trust purchased Paul McCartney's boyhood-and-teenage home in 1995. A modest row house on a Council estate, part of the rebuilding of war-devastated Liverpool, it was the site of the first song-writing efforts by McCartney and John Lennon. By 1963, the year the Beatles hurtled into superstar status, crowds on the suburban footpath day after day had made life difficult in Forthlin Road; Paul moved on and the family moved out. Thirty years later the house came up for sale. Urged by public interest and an acknowledgment that "pop music is now almost half a century old and has helped to transform British popular culture," the house represents a living hero as well as a genre of housing that has not otherwise been preserved (Garnett 1998, 16). The house in which John Lennon spent much of his youth came onto the market a few years later, but the Trust declined to buy it on the grounds that no important music was composed there. Thereupon Lennon's widow, Yoko Ono, bought and re-created it to 1950s form and gave it to the Trust in 2002. The Lennon house is more posh than the McCartney house, and it is equally a specimen type that is not otherwise preserved: a 1930s suburban semidetached house (Garnett 2003, 5). This is, of course, incidental to the fervor of fans who visit for a sense of communion with their heroes, sometimes at a highly emotional pitch.

Many heroes of another age are known only vaguely, if solemnly, by today's audiences. The kind of ardent communion observed in the houses of contemporary popular heroes seems to be fed by the discourse of celebrity in the form of a curated vision of the private life of someone "well known for being well known." The highly personalized presentation of the hero's domestic circumstances corresponds with the populist style of personal revelation that encourages onlookers to consider themselves intimate participants in another person's life. Theorists of celebrity concur that the interaction generated between celebrity and beholder is a site of elaboration of cultural identity that contributes to the integration and normalizing of identity construction (Turner 2006, 23–26). To explain this observation, a way forward is suggested by the parallels of religion and celebrity culture, both of which are draped in the tradition of magical thinking. The mode of honoring the spectrum of saint-to-hero-to-celebrity demonstrates a shift from revered distance to (pseudo-)up-close vantage to a hero in the house museum. Whether this can persist through time remains to be seen. Its power in the present proves the enduring attraction of the hero house museum.

CHAPTER FOUR

Artwork Houses
and National Aesthetics

The idea that national style can be expressed in the design arts has accompanied the nationalist project for almost as long as the consciousness of nationalism itself. However, the phrase *national style* is easier to cite than to define. As is typical of many aspects of nationalist identification, anything deeper than cursory attention discloses that a "national" style is one of many that could have been selected for the role. Furthermore, the circumstances of one style's identification by *cognoscenti* have more to do with inventiveness than discovery, as shown in the history of ascribing tartan cloth to Scots tradition (Trevor-Roper 1983). Nonetheless, the idea of national style has a record of enthusiastic adoption in circumstances in which a distinctive nationality is found to be desirable or necessary. The case of the promotion of the rustic housing of the Zakopane region of Poland in the late nineteenth century as the inspiration for a proudly *Polish* style shows the lure of the indigenous in asserting the spirit of the nation (Crowley 2001). This spirit inspired the turn-of-the-twentieth-century museumization of houses for the sake of their vernacular architectural character, understood to be not just local but also national, in both the United Kingdom and the United States. Tony Bennett argues that the museum role of "nationing" by historicizing territory and territorializing history is among the institution's most persuasive achievements (Bennett 1995, 141). The claim to national style represented by domestic architecture shows that the house museum can be another powerful vehicle of the nationalist capacity of museums.

At the other end of the spectrum of style, houses designed by the most creative minds of their ages often came to be assessed in the early twentieth century as expressing the spirit of the nation. Vernacular works tend to be connected closely to the tradition of place, whereas the fine or academic arts flourish in the hothouse of the cosmopolitan fashion cycle. Nonetheless, by defining these works as British or American or Polish, high-style products can be attached to the idea of nation to bring the luster of elite creativity to national identity. The intellectual structuring of artworks is the business of the discipline of art history, and like many branches of the humanities, art history often finds itself bolstering the claims of nations with cultural bulwarks. Art and architectural historians and connoisseurs who advocated the museumization of fine houses often cited them as the "best of English style" or "characteristically American" design to fix their significance in the scale of the nation. This claim works because the ability of nominated houses to take on iconic stature as benchmarks of architectural design is guaranteed by the principles of creativity and authenticity that underpin the art museum's authority and can be transferred by its authority (Phillips 1997, 92–93, 207).

Thus high-style and vernacular houses came to be museumized largely in order to express national character and identity. Aesthetics was rarely the *only* reason the visibility of these houses was revived, but design as demonstration of national identity was expressly the discourse employed to explain why they were so worthy. Especially in the field of high style, the genre of artwork house museums can be subdivided by a variety of inflections on the concept of design. A few house museums are the self-designed houses of designers, such as Lord Burlington's 1726 Chiswick House in outer London and Walter Gropius's 1938 house in Lincoln, Massachusetts. Then there are specimens commissioned by individuals from great modern architects, including the Farnsworth house in Illinois by Mies van der Rohe and some twenty-five houses by Frank Lloyd Wright. Further houses are preserved for their significant internal decoration and/or fine original furnishings, such as the Victorian Italianate Victoria Mansion in Portland, Maine, and the Arts and Crafts Standen in West Sussex.

Adding an incidental element to the genre of artwork house museums, many a British country house can be held up as a textbook specimen of built style and virtuoso interior design: Kedleston Hall, Derbyshire, for example, is a superlative specimen with its grand Palladian north front and Adam south front and interiors. Superb design was a key element in fulfilling owners' requirements for taste and magnificence, but the aura of aristocracy and large landholding inhering in such houses also connects them to the political and economic history of England as reasons for making them into museums.

Thus Kedleston is also significant as the ancestral home of the Curzon family and site of the Indian collections of Lord Curzon, viceroy of India from 1899 to 1905. The formal splendor afforded by wealth and power is similarly displayed in the mansion "cottages" of Newport, Rhode Island, where barons of the Gilded Age summered in extravagant high style.

The disciplines of art/architectural history define two more categories under which certain aspects of historic houses have come to be museumized: interior design and middling-class taste. Interior design is to Architecture what the decorative arts are to Art: less prestigious and female-associated expressions of the same field of practice. High-style interior design tends to be classified primarily by artist, artisan, workshop, or merchant, as an Adam scheme, *boiseries* by Grinling Gibbons, a Morris interior, a Herter Brothers fit-out. Nonetheless, the larger scope of the overall site tends to be inexplicitly or secondarily understood by specialists as a national manifestation of taste.

There is practically no classification system for contemplating the evidence of popular taste in interior decoration because it falls only fractionally within the bailiwick of the most edgy investigations of aesthetics. The study of less-than-high style strays into the ground of the history and sociology of popular culture. Thus the social sciences pay more attention than do the arts to the small but significant fraction of middling-class house interiors preserved for the sake of their furnishing or decorative intactness: interiors that are not rich and stylish enough to be considered Art, yet very clearly show evidence of human creative artifice. This kind of style without a capital S is difficult to define, but it can be seen in examples such as Miss Toward's Glasgow tenement house and Mr. Straw's house in Worksop, which can be considered in the frames of class, consumerism, taste, and popular culture. But I propose that these interiors merit inclusion in this chapter because, as manifested in house museums, they are analogous to the rationale for the preservation of high-style interiors: they provide evidence of the spectrum of aesthetic consciousness in the home.

This rainbow of specimens also shows how easy it is to conceive of the practice of preserving houses for the essence of their design as a manifestation of the scopic enterprise of collecting, making literal the claim to "curatorial management of the built environment," to cite James Marston Fitch's definition of historic preservation (Fitch 1982). The conviction that houses should be collected and displayed for their representative design qualities indicates how intensely they can be perceived as artworks. That is to say, even the modest decoration of houses can be presented in the vocabulary of art history as style exemplars of time, place, technique, and ineffable inspiration, as evidence of individuals' domestic creativity. In the microcontext of the period room, Trevor Keeble points to the same museumizing impulse, dictated by the creed of art history, that the high-style products of esteemed creators are ipso facto worthy of representation and display in a museum (Keeble 2006, 3). This insight can be extended to the products of popular creativity. In similar vein, the social-distinction-creating role of artworks guaranteed as authentic, thoroughly unpacked by David Phillips (1997), is clearly the inspiration of a segment of visitors to artwork house museums. Whether this perception can be likened to the interest of visitors to public inspections of houses-for-sale—stickybeak curiosity about other peoples' lives and tastes—is worthy of future investigation.

Whether it is high style or middling taste, visitors require three-dimensional experience to apprehend the artwork house, provoking the characteristic house museological challenge of enabling both access and preservation. How to facilitate engagement yet protect fabric drives the argument between conservation and restoration. It can be sidestepped to some degree in the context of the "social life of things," whereby houses can be seen to pass through a trajectory of newness and fitness, enlargement or reconstruction, decline and dilapidation, and destruction or resurrection as heritage or museums (Appadurai 1986, 13). But it is a challenge of management to make this happen. The activities of the architects and curators who conduct the museum transformation reveal the field of heritage and museums as a hive of contemporary cultural production, nurturing the public canon of great and representative architectural objects made public and exhibitionary.

Vernacular-Style House Museums

In traditional cultures, distinctions in dress, building detail, and other forms with the capacity to carry semiotic markers served social functions in small, conservative communities over long periods of time. Identifying one such tradition to represent national unity was an entirely political strategy, and was usually the work of urban elites. Proposing a certain style of bonnet or carved bargeboard or painted cupboard as especially characteristic is as much a unifying myth as the adoption of a particular hero as founding father of the nation. The unity of sharing is an "imagined" bond, in Benedict Anderson's famous phrase; such symbols are "invented traditions," in Hobsbawm's and Ranger's telling. They are as crucial in defining nations as the historic territory, common economy, and legal rights and responsibilities that form the dictionary definitions of "nation." The mundane dimensions of clothing, buildings, and furnishings give concrete applications to the abstractions of nationalism.

Folk dress, housing, and domestic decoration were seized upon by nineteenth-century scholars, artists, and politicians in northern and central Europe as evidence of inherent national character (Vale 2008; Taylor 2004, 200–201; Gerle 1993). Experts asserted that a common aesthetic proved the existence of cultural unity, which in turn justified the establishment of a national state over specific geographic regions. The history of Skansen, the great open-air folk museum of Sweden, demonstrates the power of gathering and displaying folk culture in establishing ethno-nationalist consciousness (Rentzhog 2007, 18–19). Sweden had little need of popular nationalism, having been a successful imperialist state for hundreds of years. But the impact of Artur Hazelius's collecting and display at international exhibitions, the Nordiska Museet, and Skansen, impelled similar collecting in Norway, which had sought independence from Sweden since 1814. The Norsk Folkemuseet of relocated traditional houses commenced in 1894 with a strongly nationalist agenda, asserting that the vernacular culture of the coastal strip of Scandinavia represented a distinctive Norwegian people (Rentzhog 2007, 52–58). Similar schemes followed in post–World War I Hungary, Poland, Czechoslovakia, Estonia, and Latvia, aiming to establish national identities in the wake of the collapse of the Austro-Hungarian Empire and the revolution in Russia (Rentzhog 2007, 38–40).

No such nation-building movement was at work in England at the same time, but the romantic tinge of Nordic cultural revivalism still touched the British Isles. The focus on design as an inspiration to create house museums began with the National Trust in the 1890s, whose founders favored the later medieval vernacular as the premier form of national expression. It was welcomed as representing the essence of "Old England," with its implied critique of the modern age. The case was different from both Norway and Britain in the United States, where, around the turn of the twentieth century, the tired, poor, huddled masses of eastern and southern Europe were enacting the world's greatest-ever voluntary migration. In the United States, design-motivated house museums focused on the very late medieval vernacular, which had been translated to the first colonies in America. "What could be more American than architecture inspired by indigenous buildings of the seventeenth and eighteenth century?" as Wendy Kaplan puts the question with some irony (Kaplan 1993, 55). The answer is clearest when understood to mean "anything Anglo," in contradistinction to that of other "races" then claiming US citizenship.

In imperial Britain there was little need to define national identity via traditional artifacts in Skansen-style museums in the nineteenth century—though it is no coincidence that the first folk museums were eventually

Alfriston Clergy House, East Sussex, 1894. A National Trust committee inspects the first "indigenous" English structure acquired by the organization in 1896. It looks much tamer today.
Photo courtesy of National Trust Images.

established in the Isle of Man in 1938 and Wales in 1946. However, the romance of traditional cultures in general, and old English links to Norse culture in particular, imbued the Arts and Crafts movement with a new vision of the beauty of local vernacular buildings. In the 1840s, romantics considered a cottage more beautiful if it had Gothic detailing, but by the time William Morris acquired Kelmscott Manor in 1871, a broader sense of simple Old Englishness had begun to infuse the aesthetics of advanced taste.

The earliest house museum conserved for the sake of its form is the National Trust's first building acquisition, the fourteenth-century Clergy House at Alfriston, East Sussex. Reporting on its purchase for £10 in 1896, Trust founder Octavia Hill described it as "tiny but beautiful." A commentator, looking back on the first fifty years of Trust acquisitions, offered the house and a cohort of additional vernacular cottages as visible proof of Englishness manifested in architecture: "They look, and are, indigenous" (Oliver 1945, 78). The Arts and Crafts movement attributed its dearest values to medieval vernacular buildings: unpretentious design and honest craftsmanship in a snug domestic sphere. It was a vision whose appeal was at its peak in the

1890s and early 1900s. The museumization of such houses confirms Peter Mandler's schema of elite tastes in English historic building conservation in the late nineteenth century: neither "Olden Time" Gothic/Elizabethan nor cold, proud Georgian, but cozy, informal vernacular on a domestic scale—a homely vision of British character (Mandler 1997, 135).

Until 1935, the National Trust's building acquisitions were almost entirely medieval or Tudor; they were (on the whole) small, and most were not only unfurnished but also uninhabitable. The Trust's initial motivation had been to hold places of historic interest or natural beauty in the public interest, safe from privatization or development "for the everlasting delight of thousands of the people of these islands" (Waterson 1994, 37). Gardens and grounds were open to the public as a setting for looking at the buildings, which were let to tenants, thus meeting the Trust's objective of securing their future. Sites such as the Priest's House, Muchelney, Somerset, purchased in 1911, remain tenanted to this day and are open for just a few days per week over summer.

The story of the first large house the Trust acquired—Barrington Court, Somerset—demonstrates the challenges of managing its property portfolio before the development of strong policies. A plain and ruinous mid-sixteenth-century manor house, its cause was advocated by another of the Trust's founders, Hardwick Rawnsley, in essentially national-romantic terms. Purchase and initial repairs in 1907 cost £11,500, but it was still neither publicly accessible nor habitable. Thus, the house waited until 1920 for, as Simon Jenkins writes, a sugar daddy. Sugar magnate Colonel Arthur Lyle leased the house for ninety-nine years and funded a major restoration, including paneling it with his own collection of historic woodwork. The third generation of Lyles let it to an antiques dealer as an atmospheric showroom from 1986 to 2008. The house then returned to the National Trust fold for open display. For many decades, Barrington Court was thought to be an early sixteenth-century house, and in 1945 James Lees-Milne called it "one of the earliest instances of 'architecture,' for it shows symmetry and style" (Lees-Milne 1945, 63). Subsequent reattribution to fifty years later makes this claim less important. Historic photos of the place suggest that its pretty skyline of chimneys and finials and pleasant texture of Hamstone masonry, perhaps coupled with its sorry state, cast Barrington Court as a piece of Old England in need of saving, with the National Trust riding to the rescue. The costs and problems it caused haunted subsequent Trust acquisitions of large houses for many years.

The National Trust acquired several icons of essentially vernacular style in the interwar period (though they were outnumbered by acquisitions of the houses of heroes, always a more popular type of historic house museum). Montacute House in Somerset was the first: a late Elizabethan pile, abandoned to be sold for scrap even though it had been lavishly restored by a tenant, it was saved by the Society for the Protection of Ancient Buildings and accepted by the Trust in 1931. Another was Little Moreton Hall in Cheshire, transferred in 1938. One of Britain's finest timber-framed Tudor manor houses, it is still presented almost unfurnished to highlight the craftsmanship of its framing and paneling. Such acquisitions entered easily into the discourse of picturesque Englishness, though at the same time they were collected and displayed as specimens of architectural excellence.

A parallel vision of the power of the style of buildings to express the spirit of nation developed among some antiquaries of New England. George Dow, secretary of the Essex Institute of Salem, Massachusetts, since 1900, introduced local architectural fragments and period rooms into the Institute's exhibition galleries from 1907. He soon moved on to bigger schemes, and in 1910 he engineered the removal to the Institute's site of the John Ward House—America's first Skansen-style house relocation. The house was built in 1684, enlarged about 1730, and had been rebuilt inside and out, requiring major works to re-create it to a suitably ancient form. It was furnished to the 1700s period with antiques and reproductions, and a lady custodian dressed in a homespun costume led guided tours. Pioneering a different track toward the preservation of American house forms and values, the Society for the Preservation of New England Antiquities (SPNEA, since 2004 Historic New England) was established in 1910. By 1915 it had acquired four properties, all remaining in situ but conserved and secured. The early portfolio is exemplified by the third acquisition, the Boardman House in Saugus, Massachusetts. Built about 1687 by a not-very-important local carpenter, and a place in which nothing of great import ever happened, the Boardman House was described as "a magnificent specimen of our early architecture which has come down to us practically unchanged" (Appleton in Hosmer 1965, 244). Like the Ward House, it owes nothing to high style, but its construction reveals the building systems of the Old World coming into contact with New World materials and techniques.

An architectural essence of Englishness, translated to New England with timber cladding, justified collecting and preserving such houses for posterity. In this way, the Society always maintained a more consciously historicist perspective on the houses it campaigned to preserve than did the National Trust in Britain. The SPNEA's presiding genius, William Sumner Appleton, saw pre-Revolutionary houses in terms of type and rarity, but he was also moved by historical associations and the potential to read buildings as

John Ward House in situ, Prison Lane, Salem, Massachusetts, c. 1900, and as relocated and restored at the Essex Institute, c. 1912. Timber-framed houses are technically straightforward to dismantle and reconstruct, thanks to the system of joints that shapes the structure. Here the two large front gables were reinstated in 1912 to illustrate the late medieval aesthetic for which the house was valued.

Photo (a) courtesy of David M. Rubenstein Rare Book & Manuscript Library (Frank Cousins Photographs), Duke University, Durham, North Carolina; photo (b) courtesy of the Phillips Library (Salem Streets, folder 58), Peabody Essex Museum, Salem.

historic documents (Holleran 2001, 227–28). With this mindset, the system-atic museumization of American vernacular buildings took off from a more advanced point than the 1840s picturesque interest in colonial-era buildings that had inspired a poet to praise a crumbling Virginia church: "Remnant of Olden days, best, lowliest style!" (Maynard 2000, 339–40). For the SPNEA, the preservation of style was primarily a scientific, rather than an emotional, commitment.

Conservation, as practiced by both the National Trust and the SPNEA, observed the standards of minimal intervention advocated by the Society for the Protection of Ancient Buildings (SPAB), expressed in its Manifesto of 1877:

> To put Protection in the place of Restoration, to stave off decay by daily care, to prop a perilous wall or mend a leaky roof by such means as are obviously meant for support or covering, and show no pretense of other art, and other-wise to resist all tampering with either the fabric or ornament of the building as it stands. (SPAB 1877)

This is a purist and materialist agenda, an approach that reinforces the pre-cious character of original fabric above all other values in a historic building, paying homage to its status as a sacred relic or a rare artwork. In the glow of such aura, meanings are often overwhelmed by sheer visible presence.

But in the early twentieth century, seeing vernacular houses as authentic indigenous-hence-national architecture rather than junk, relics, or history introduced a new perspective for displaying the "legacy" of the past.

High-Style House Museums

Nonetheless, the history of museumizing historic houses for the sake of design swung quickly toward high style after its early engagement with the vernacular. In Britain the story is complicated by the tribulations of the great country houses, whose upkeep became unsustainable for many owners after World War I (this story is taken up in chapter 8). Suffice it to say that style was just one among a complex of attributes by which the country house rescue movement was justified. More important for the history of exhibiting architectural style is the series of shifts in educated British taste that rehabilitated interest in neoclassicism following the peak of the Arts and Crafts movement, itself a reaction to eclectic Victorian taste. English esteem for Georgian, baroque, and mannerist architecture was resuscitated very slowly, as can be seen in the date limits of the Historic Monuments Commission, founded in 1908 to record historic buildings up to 1700, creeping forward to 1714 (the accession of George I) in 1921, acquiring discretion to consider buildings up to 1850 in 1946, and not losing the date barrier entirely until 1963. These shifts in appreciation of style represented the advanced taste of a new, professional eye, distinguished from popular taste, and thus defining a new take on class as a function of the possession of cultural rather than financial capital. Its demarcating ramifications can be followed in the fashions of period preservation for the rest of the century.

The National Trust's acquisition of country houses expanded hugely following the National Trust Act of 1937, which enabled the organization to hold tax-free endowments for great houses transferred to it while allowing owners to continue to live on site as tenants. Some of this 1940s–1950s torrent were houses whose design significance added important substance to the public knowledge of English architecture, such as Knole, Kent (acquired by the Trust in 1946); Attingham, Shropshire (acquired in 1947); and Osterley Park, Middlesex, from the 1760s to the 1780s (acquired 1949). Why these and not others? James Lees-Milne explains that one of the first tasks of the National Trust's Country Houses Committee in 1936 was to respond to a government request for a list of houses considered of "undoubted merit" to gauge the dimensions of the proposed tax-exemption scheme. The Committee came up with a list of 230 houses, which inevitably took on a canonical air, though Lees-Milne later acknowledged it was hastily compiled by a small group of cognoscenti at a time when there was little comparative knowledge of country houses (Lees-Milne 1992, 7). They were informed by the discourses of connoisseurship and architectural history, and steeped in a reverent nostalgia for the historical role of the aristocracy in English life.

It was a different story in the United States. High-style houses of the colonial and early republican eras were entering the collections of the Essex Institute, the SPNEA, and other organizations with a preservation mission, such as the Daughters of the American Revolution, from the late 1910s. High style is, of course, a relative judgment in comparison with the scale of architecturally significant British houses. But in the context of the fine house stock of the United States, the growth of fashion-informed and wealth-enabled architectural design in the eighteenth century produced what came to be perceived in the late nineteenth century as a distinctive American aesthetic, expressed in domestic as well as public buildings. Perceptions of Colonial Georgian and later neoclassical architectural idioms were transformed from merely olden days forms, variously considered crude or charming, to become the inspiration for the Colonial Revival aesthetic. They were endowed with the virtue of American history to inform models of modern beauty.

House museums were among the touchstones of the Colonial Revival. Art museums such as the Metropolitan in New York began seriously building Americana collections, including architectural woodwork, from the 1910s (Hosmer 1965, 226–28). In the same period the SPNEA and the Essex Institute acquired whole houses. The SPNEA's first high-style house was its fourth acquisition: the first Harrison Gray Otis house in Boston, designed by Charles Bulfinch, whose later work on the Capitol in Washington, DC, confirmed his preeminence as an architect. The Otis house was purchased in 1916, though restoration took several years and then the house had to be rolled backward thirteen meters to accommodate road widening. By 1925 it housed the SPNEA headquarters as well as museum rooms. Surveying the scene in 1919, Appleton outlined the range of houses he'd like to preserve, starting with "houses of superlative architectural interest of the type of the Pierce-Nicholls house in Salem MA, or the Moffatt-Ladd house in Portsmouth NH" (Hosmer 1965, 262–63).

As it happens, the Colonial Dames of America had already acquired the latter in 1911 (its illustrious occupants included a signatory to the Declaration of Independence). The former, under threat of demolition, had been installed at the Essex Institute in 1917. Appleton probably appreciated their aesthetic significance most, while the houses were valued by their new institutional owners mostly for their historical associations. But that changed as the first American architectural historians began to publish in the 1920s. Sidney Fiske Kimball discovered the architectural originality of Samuel McIntire, who called himself a housewright and wood carver when he built the Pierce-Nicholls house in 1782 and 1801. Kimball called its style "postcolonial," acknowledging the stylistic impression of the politics of the Revolution; the term *Federal* style seems to have appeared in the 1970s (Kimball 1922, 145). McIntire's Gardner-Pingree house of 1805 joined the Essex Institute collection in 1933; McIntire design is now celebrated as the cynosure of Old Salem. The Moffatt-Ladd house is acclaimed on its website as "one of America's finest Georgian mansions." The consciousness of *American* high style was securely established.

"Only a handful of [American] houses had been saved by 1926 as architectural monuments," wrote Charles Hosmer (1965, 269). The preservation of houses in the United States in the interwar/ World War II period was overshadowed by the great historic village projects sponsored by collector-philanthropists: Williamsburg, Greenfield (since 2003, The Henry Ford), Cooperstown, Sturbridge, and Deerfield (Hosmer 1981, 74–132). Colonial Williamsburg especially became the nursery of both scholarship and practice of historic buildings preservation, training historians, architects, and archaeologists. The major perspective for preservation in these contexts was history rather than style. But American history was as importantly formed in the nineteenth century as in the eighteenth, and the middle three of the aforementioned villages came to focus on the Federal and Victorian periods. Such focus pushed American preservationists to acknowledge the integrity of Victorian design well before their English counterparts, with important consequences for house museums.

The Recognition of Victorian Style

Even preservationists were less than enthusiastic about initiating the museumization of Victorian houses: to make it happen, the taxonomic logic of preservation for the sake of coherent style had to override taste. The earliest examples were the results of efforts of individuals, often family members, recognizing that the houses left behind by reclusive old relatives constituted important evidence of Victorian taste and merited preservation for their unusual integrity. The Merchant's House in New York City (belonging to the Tredwell family) was built in 1832; it was occupied by the generation of builders, and then by their youngest child, who died there in 1933. Architecturally, it is a conventional specimen of an affluent city row house, with Greek Revival detail in the public rooms; further significance lies in the degree of intactness in the furnishings, fittings, decoration, and personal material still in situ. The whole was purchased by a member of the extended family and opened as a museum in 1936, as memorial to "the old merchants" of late eighteenth and early nineteenth-century New York (Knapp 2016). It appears to be the earliest museumization of Victorian form for its own sake in the Anglo world.

Two conditions explain the museumization of Victorian mansions in America well before it happened in Britain. First, the relative antiquity of houses induced greater preservation interest in museumizing Victorian houses in the United States than in the United Kingdom, where Elizabethan country houses defined the conventional idea of a historic house. Second, the English habit of the new rich moving up in the world by buying an old country house contrasted with the preference of each new generation of American millionaire to build his own mansion. Yet families do not always thrive forever: whereas some English family lines died out, leaving their houses available for new buyers, a significant proportion of the splendid American houses that have been museumized occurred, as in the case of the Merchant's House, after the death of only the second generation. It is not an uncommon pattern among house museums to find that, after the parents who built it, an unmarried child or children lived in the new house until their death, when, without direct heirs, the house was acquired by a preservation group. This was also the case at, for instance, the 1851 Campbell house, St. Louis, Missouri (museumized in 1943); the 1864 Lockwood-Mathews House, Norwalk, Connecticut (1966); and the 1852/1870s Chateau sur Mer, Newport, Rhode Island (1969).

The value of Victorian design revived in professional awareness in the later twentieth century, but it was a painful process. In England, it endured first the anti-Victorian movement of the 1930s, which facilitated a reaction in favor of Georgian taste, previously condemned as un-English and exclusive and now rehabilitated as elegant and civil (Mandler 1997, 265). The importance of Georgian style was asserted with the formation of the Georgian Group in 1937 to identify and protect buildings that had been popularly condemned as soulless. It was quite the opposite in the United States, where Georgian style expressed the elite taste of colonial North America and continued to be valued in all its manifestations. But even the Georgians drew the line at 1837, the year of the coronation of Queen Victoria. Not until 1958 was the Victorian Society founded in London, in which time and place it was a somewhat subversive taste.

The Victorian Society's inspiration lives on in the Linley Sambourne House in Chelsea, London, an 1870s terrace house decorated in high Victorian Aesthetic style, which survived largely intact through three generations.

Like the Merchant's House, the Sambourne House was inhabited by a first and second generation; it passed then to the status of a *pied á terre*, occupied occasionally. Here, at a party in 1957, the incumbent grandniece proposed that Victorian taste merited profile raising by an advocacy group, from which the Victorian Society emerged (Filmer-Sankey 1998). (The Victorian Society in America followed in 1966, in outraged response to the destruction of Penn Station, New York City.) The Sambourne House was later sold to local government and opened as a museum in 1980 (Robbins, Suleman, & Hunter 2003, 44–46).

The 1970s became the decade of popular rapprochement with Victorian and Edwardian design, in both Britain and the United States. The SPNEA had been offered an odd 1854 circular house with neoclassical details in 1921, of which it was said, "The present is probably fifty years too early for anything of [this] kind, since to most people that period represents the very quintessence of the ugly" (Appleton in Lindgren 1995, 158). This was an acute observation on prevailing fashions in taste. It could barely have been foreseen how, fifty years later, urban development threats to historic buildings of all periods would transform the field of architectural preservation from arcane interest societies into the popular heritage movement. The late twentieth-century heritage push definitively revalued Victorian design. It changed the face of historic preservation from an emphasis on sheer antiquity to the aestheticized standard of design integrity. At the same time, architectural history was influenced by the new "grassroots" style of social history that advocated personal and contextual approaches; it opened up new interest in Victorian gardens, interiors, and furnishings as well as buildings.

In this environment old houses acquired new value, leading to the gentrification of inner city, largely Victorian, suburbs on both sides of the Atlantic. Appreciation of Victorian style benefited from the popular interest in building conservation, enabled by the abundance of Victorian houses and informed by a new literature on nineteenth-century built forms and decorative techniques and how to reproduce them. Thanks to knowledge developed in the field of conservation architecture, and sensitized by media attention to preservation projects, countless city dwellers well off enough to buy houses set out to restore them. And so did heritage and museum agencies and community groups. The museumization of houses on the grounds of design took off.

The National Achievement in Art: Great Designer Houses
The buildings of great designers have always been admired by those in the know, but until the twentieth century the glory of great design accrued to

the owner rather than the designer. Le Corbusier was the first artist-hero to achieve museumization with the Villa Savoye (built in 1928, near Paris) in 1959, deploying the preservation of modernist architecture in the service of French cultural prestige (Murphy 2002, 68–80). The esteem of professional architects drove the preservation of further houses via museumization, exemplified by the saving of the Glessner house in Chicago designed by Henry Hobson Richardson in 1887. Resisting its threatened demolition in 1966, the purpose-formed Chicago School of Architecture Foundation purchased the house and began to make it suitable for visitors. The endorsement of national and city landmark status came in the 1970s, and the house museum was incorporated as an independent agency in 1994. Another pivotal Chicago house, the Charnley house by Louis Sullivan, 1891, was acquired in 1988 by the architectural firm Skidmore, Owings and Merrill, and, in the spirit of tribute, converted for limited office use by SKM. The house shifted into semimuseum public accessibility when presented as its headquarters to the Society of Architectural Historians by a philanthropist in whose honor it is now known as the Charnley-Persky House. The Charnley house was partly

Glessner House, Chicago, c. 1887. The Glessner house, a muscular Romanesque Revival design by Henry Hobson Richardson, 1885–1887, was admired from the first, as shown by the presence of this image in the Architecture Department of Cornell University.
Courtesy of the A. D. White Architectural Photographs, Acc. No. 15/5/3090.00155, Cornell University Library.

drafted by the young Frank Lloyd Wright, then working in Sullivan's office; the extent of his impact on the design continues to be argued.

But Wright's fame is more than comprehensively addressed by the museumization of at least twenty-five of his houses (from a total output of about 430, of which some 260 survive) (Weintraub & Hess 2005, 13). Of the museum houses, more than half have become so since the 1990s—a telling comment on the public demand for architectural culture. Their designs span his career, from 1889 to 1958, covering Shingle, Chicago, Prairie, Western concrete block, California, and Usonian styles. The oldest house is Wright's first home and studio in Oak Park, Illinois; his later homes, the two Taliesins in Wisconsin and Arizona, took on museum functions after his death, as well as housing his architectural fellowship. Among the other Wright-designed museum houses are peak works such as the Martin house (1903) in Buffalo, New York; the Robie house (1908) in Chicago; and Fallingwater, in Bear Run, Pennsylvania (1937). Fallingwater was the first Wright house to be museumized, in 1963; Edgar Kaufmann Jr., son of the designer's original clients, presented its contents and grounds to the Western Pennsylvania Conservancy. The Martin and Robie houses, quintessential large Prairie houses, suffered from institutional adaptation and deterioration; foundations rescued them in 1992 and 1997, respectively.

It is said of Wright houses, "Few houses of equal fame have embodied more conspicuous faults. Many of Wright's plans defy reasonable furniture arrangements, many frustrate even the storage of reasonable and treasured possessions. In many cases severe problems afflict the architectural fabric: leaking roofs, unserviceable detailing, even structural inadequacies" (Hildebrand 1991, 15). Anecdote suggests that many of the Wright houses came to be regarded by their owners as so unlivable that museumization was their only means of preservation. This may contain some truth, but the idea that twenty-five of them merit eternal life as house museums speaks to a larger myth of Frank Lloyd Wright as the transcendent creative spirit of America (McCarter 2006, 8). Undergirding his mythic grandeur is the Frank Lloyd Wright-Prairie School of Architecture Historic District, Chicago, which attracts large visitation. The district was listed on the National Register of Historic Places in 1973 with a claim as the largest concentration of early modern architecture to be found anywhere in the world. It asserts a definitive counterclaim to the primacy of the Old World in cultural status.

Only one other designer glows with such a popular aura in the English-speaking world: Charles Rennie Mackintosh, hero of Scottish design. Mackintosh's professional career was short, effectively from 1895 to about 1915; following scholarly reappraisals in the 1950s, his apotheosis occurred in 1973 with the foundation of the Charles Rennie Mackintosh Society (Howarth 1952; Pevsner 1968). Four critical houses by Mackintosh have been museumized, and they introduced two unique museological realizations.

The first is the interior design and some furniture of Mackintosh's own Glasgow house, designed with his wife, Margaret Macdonald, in 1900–1906. The house was demolished in the 1960s, but two floors of its layout and interior were re-created in the Hunterian Art Gallery of the University of Glasgow in 1981. The second is the Mackintosh-Macdonald competition design, "House for an Art Lover" of 1901, a creative exercise for a German art magazine that had a profound influence on the Vienna Secession and Werkstätte. Ninety years later, the house was constructed in a Glasgow park from the presentation drawings, requiring inventive reverse engineering to establish many structural details (Cosgrove 2004). The new house museum contains interior decoration, fittings, textiles, and furniture as shown in the competition portfolio. The project was a labor of love by a dedicated admirer, supported by local artists and architects; besides its public rooms, it houses a branch of the Glasgow School of Art. The third, more conventional house museum is Hill House, outside Glasgow, one of Mackintosh's few major commissions, built in 1902–1903 and still complete with its Mackintosh-Macdonald designed furnishings; it was bequeathed to the National Trust of Scotland in 1982. The fourth house is the 1916 renovation of a small terrace house in Northampton, number 78 Derngate; it was rescued and restored in 1996. Mackintosh, Macdonald, and their fellows now have a gallery in Glasgow's Kelvingrove Museum, and a dedicated bus enables tourists to make a comprehensive pilgrimage to Mackintosh sites in the city. Mackintosh style is assuredly part of the modern national identity of Scotland.

Conserving Architectural History

The museumization of houses is generally a reactive rather than proactive business: a house becomes available, an individual or interest group conceives that it merits extracting from daily use as a style specimen, and (if the planets line up) it may happen. Occasionally, museums attempt to construct rational schemes of art history typology in appropriate historic houses, but the record shows this is a difficult program to sustain. Sidney Fiske Kimball used his position as director of the Philadelphia Museum of Art (PMA) to incorporate whole houses as well as period rooms into the PMA's coverage of American art. And the Victoria and Albert Museum (V&A) made a brave sally into this area in the second half of the twentieth century.

Kimball, one of the first generation of architectural historians of America, became director of the newly organized Philadelphia Museum of Art in 1925. He introduced a chronological arrangement into the grand new building, enabling the "pageant of art," as he called it, to be traversed via galleries of artworks and period rooms. He also noted that the dozen-odd historic houses in Fairmount Park nearby could be deployed to illustrate the evolution of American art from the seventeenth to the nineteenth century. The park had been created in 1812 to protect the Schuylkill River waterworks from industrial pollution; it grew to a huge size over the years. Thus the city of Philadelphia acquired ownership of more than twenty fine old houses, which were used in the nineteenth century as residences for park staff and as picnic resources for city folk. The historic and artistic significance of many of them was well known. The Park Commissioners began restoring Mount Pleasant in 1923, and Kimball himself was assigned one, Lemon Hill, to live in and restore as a perk of his new job. Noting that several of the houses were of the highest quality, Kimball envisaged "a chain of fine old houses, appropriately furnished from every period of the colonies and the Republic" to enhance the Museum's collections (Kimball 1926a, 155; Roberts & Roberts 1959, 70–72).

The PMA became responsible for just two houses, Mount Pleasant and Cedar Grove, but, in association with the Fairmount Park Commissioners, the museum also advised volunteer groups on the restoration and furnishing of the others and lent appropriate furnishings. Mount Pleasant was furnished with Philadelphia furniture, ceramics, silver, and historic textiles from the PMA collections and private loans, as a branch museum of "American art on the eve of the Revolution," opening in 1926 (Kimball 1926b, 197–216). Cedar Grove was relocated to Fairmount Park in 1927, furnished with its Morris family collection of baroque, rococo, and Federal-style Philadelphia-made furniture; it opened as a branch museum of colonial art and architecture (Anon. 1928, 4–14). From at least 1960 onward PMA trained and managed guides conducted tours of nine houses, as described each year in the annual report. Kimball's successors maintain the relationship with the Fairmount Park houses to this day, a rare long-term connection between a major museum with expertise in interior design and historic architecture on the ground.

Among the country houses accepted by the UK government in place of family death duties in the immediate post–World War II period, and transferred to the National Trust, were Osterley Park and Ham House, both near London and both with very significant furnishings. The V&A purchased the collections, and the museum took on the curatorial management of the houses. First Ham, and then Osterley, came to the attention of Peter

Thornton, keeper of the Department of Furniture and Woodwork (and, de facto, historic houses), and his cohorts. From the 1970s to the 1990s, they conducted innovative campaigns of archival research into understanding each house in its most stylistically significant period: Ham House, with its major ensemble of seventeenth-century furniture, paintings, and ornaments, and Osterley Park as the product of its redecoration by Robert Adam at the end of the eighteenth century. Inventories of the times were used to reinstate furniture and pictures from the V&A collections, set within wall coverings and paint colors described in contemporary accounts. These pioneering exercises in "authentic decor" (as Thornton's 1984 book was titled) shocked some and startled more. A "battle of colours" ensued over the Adam schemes at Osterley, where strong pastels disturbed the prevailing assumption that neoclassical stucco must be white. A further campaign at Ham House in the 1990s reinstated unfamiliar bright tones and (to some modern eyes) garish graining and gilding, which challenged visitor expectations of great historic houses. The vivid re-creations asserted interpretive decisions to depict

North drawing room at Ham House, West London, 2014. Ham House was rebuilt and opulently decorated in the 1670s; it survived to a rare degree and passed to the National Trust in 1948. The house's decorative schemes became an object of the V&A-inspired "authentic decor" movement of the 1980s–1990s.
Photo by, and courtesy of, Leigh Kemp.

important moments of style rather than generations of taste. Thornton's forceful curatorial choices represent the tension between radical and conservative approaches to the presentation of historic style. They introduced a rage for "authentic" colors and finishes that swept the world of architectural heritage in the later twentieth century (Thornton 2007; Jervis 2013, 383–96).

The success of re-presenting Carolean Ham House and neoclassical Osterley Park suggested a vision to complete the V&A collection of specimen galleries *and* houses with a nineteenth-century exemplar. Mentmore Towers seemed the obvious candidate when it was offered to the government in lieu of inheritance taxes in 1974. A neo-Jacobean mansion built in Buckinghamshire in 1852 for Baron Mayer de Rothschild, Mentmore was furnished with Rothschild family treasures and a further collection of outstanding European fine arts. But the government declined to accept the house, and frantic attempts to save it came to naught. Sotheby's auctioned Mentmore and its collection in a famous sale in 1977, for millions of pounds. "If only the government had purchased Mentmore for £2 million when it was offered two years ago!" wrote V&A director Roy Strong (1997, 187–89). The drawn-out struggle over Mentmore exemplified the continuing fragility of Britain's great houses, topic of the V&A exhibition "The Destruction of the Country House" in 1974, which shaped the later twentieth-century rebirth of country houses as national heritage (see chapter 8). Meanwhile, the costs of operating Ham and Osterley as branch museums led in 1976 to government instructions to return full management of the houses to the National Trust (Strong 1997, 161, 319). The collections, officially vested in the V&A, were transferred to the Trust in 2002. The story illustrates a general truth that large museums are such complex organisms that additional responsibility for smaller museums is often more than can be managed well. However, the vision and expertise that the PMA still brings, and the V&A brought, to their house museums initiated long-lasting advances in the presentation of historic design.

The intellectual critical mass of large museums such as the PMA and networks of houses like the National Trust certainly facilitated bold steps in design-focused heritage. The SPNEA welcomed the offer of the Gropius house in Lincoln, Massachusetts, by Walter Gropius's widow, Ise, in 1974, subject to her life tenancy. Designed by the expatriate in 1937–1938 in pure Bauhaus style, it had been an object of study and admiration in the United States from the first, and became acknowledged as a key source of American modernism. The house finally opened to the public, fully furnished with original items, in

1985. Today it is the most visited Historic New England property, reaching design and fashion buffs as well as the historic house visitor constituency. A similar place in the history of architectural design in Australia inspired the museumization of the Rose Seidler house in Sydney in 1988. Harry Seidler transported Bauhaus modernism from Harvard to Australia, and he demonstrated it in a 1947 house for his mother, provoking joy among progressives and alarm among traditional builders. Mrs. Seidler was induced to abandon her fine Viennese furniture to live more starkly in tune with her son's taste; many furnishings still survive in the house. Another Bauhaus refugee, Mies van der Rohe, built the house that is, arguably, the pinnacle of domestic modernism in America: the Farnsworth house in Plano, Illinois, designed in 1947, built in 1951, and museumized in 2003. Long hailed as the uttermost refinement of Mies's vision, its status as an artwork and style exemplar ahead of a dwelling (livability within its sheer glass walls was always problematic) justified the transformation.

It was much more problematic to initiate the preservation of modernist design in the United Kingdom. There, the public response to the conservation of modernist buildings long contained a strong current of hostility, underlain by the trauma of post–World War II austerity, urban clearance, and planning visions (Kindred 2007, 1–2). There was bemusement and even bitterness among many members when the National Trust acquired 2 Willow Road, Hampstead, in 1994, complete with furnishings and artworks. One of three houses in a terrace, the whole was designed in 1938 by German émigré architect Erno Goldfinger in an uncompromising modernist style. This had fallen so far out of British public favor by 1991, when his heirs offered the house to the Trust, that only intellectual determination to preserve "an aspect of the cultural life of Britain between the Wars" carried the day for preservation (Waterson 1994, 246). But interest turned in the 2000s. The Trust acquired the high-style modernist Homewood (also designed in 1938) in affluent London exurbia in 2003; it opened in 2008. "Visitors have responded extremely positively to Willow Road—'More modern houses, please' is often the request in the visitors' book," wrote the curator in 2004 (McKay 2004; McKay 2006, 154).

The effects of taxonomic architectural history are predictably strong on the museumization of houses for the sake of aesthetics. By contrast, houses preserved as museums to represent popular or broadly fashionable tastes are exceedingly rare. One specimen of the latter is the 1929 Adamson House in Malibu, California, a Spanish Colonial Revival house sumptuously decorated with tiles made by the owner's business, Malibu Potteries (Dowey 1995). Another is the 1925 Casa del Herrero in Montecito, California, described in the first paragraph of its website as "one of the finest examples of Spanish Colonial Revival architecture in America" (http://www.casadelherrero.com). The quintessential California style, Spanish Colonial flourishes introduced a touch of Hollywood glamour into suburban houses of the interwar years around the world—though little in the spheres of design history or house museums. Even the breathtaking Hearst Castle, the complex designed for William Randolph Hearst in San Simeon, California, by Julia Morgan between 1919 and 1947, is acknowledged more for the collections it houses than its design (and is discussed in chapter 5). However, interest in the Spanish Colonial Revival could yet arise as time makes good examples scarce, and thus could follow in the footsteps of the revaluing of Victorian styles.

Aesthetic Peaks: Designers' Own Houses

Designers' own houses constitute a small subset of house museums, as the purest expression of the aesthetic dimension of the genre, presenting architectural artworks of the highest order and authenticity. Chiswick House, London, is the oldest specimen that can be so called: designed in 1726–1729 by Lord Burlington, "the architect Earl," as his *casina*, a house for elegant recreation rather than daily living. It declined in institutional ownership from 1892 until taken over by the Ministry of Works in 1948; since then, English Heritage has restored it. Designers have rarely been so affluent that their own houses were on the Chiswick scale, nor, until the later twentieth century, were they or their skill so valued that their houses were preserved as museums.

This summit of fame and chance has been achieved largely through the affection of subsequent owners. The Craftsman Farms site—the house, workshop, and self-sufficient farm founded by Arts and Crafts designer Gustav Stickley in Parsippany, New Jersey, in 1908—was sold in 1915 when Stickley became bankrupt, to a family that cherished the Craftsman ideals for seventy years. Threatened by suburban development, the site was acquired by local government and incorporated as a foundation in 1989 to preserve and interpret Stickley's vision of the American Arts and Crafts movement. A similar survival story describes the Red House in Kent, home of William Morris from 1860 to 1865. The house was recognized as a lodestar of the Arts and Crafts movement from very early days but required significant restoration after official wartime (ab)use. It was then acquired by an architectural family who loved it for fifty years, until the National Trust purchased it in 2003.

By this time, professional consciousness of great designers' products had already been at work in the United States for thirty years. Frank Lloyd

Wright's house and studio in Oak Park (1889) entered a long period of research and restoration after its acquisition in 1974 by the National Trust for Historic Preservation (NTHP) and the foundation that became the Frank Lloyd Wright Preservation Trust. It was neither the first nor the last Wright house to become a museum, but it illustrates both the sentimental and the seminal nature of designers' own houses as preserved icons. The 1925 house of Eliel and Loja Saarinen at Cranbrook Academy of Art, Bloomfield Hills, Michigan, is another example. Demobilized in 1977 as the school president's residence, it constitutes a fusion of Arts and Crafts, art deco, and modernist sources, expressing overlooked hybridizing trends in twentieth-century design history.

The first twenty-first-century artwork house museumization is Philip Johnson's Glass House in New Canaan, Connecticut, designed in 1949. Given to the NTHP in 1986 with a life interest, Johnson lived there until his death in 2006; it opened to the public the next year. Aiming for a purpose beyond sheer house exhibition, the organization (philipjohnsonglasshouse. org) proclaims its mission as "a catalyst for the preservation of modern architecture, landscape, and art." This vision hearkens to the nineteenth-century aspiration of art museums to inspire the public via provision of visitable artworks (and to distinguish the sheep from the goats by their capacity to appreciate the art). In comparison, artists' museumized houses comprise a small subset of the larger category of the museumized houses of heroes, but they tend to be normal houses made into public shrines as opposed to possessing the special character of designers' own houses, where the house is both the constitutive artwork and the functional shell of the museum.

Authentic Style: Houses with Intact Decorative and Furnishing Schemes
The cycle of new generations and fashions usually sees houses with old decorative schemes replaced by new ones, though the grand schemes of wealthy houses have always had more chance of surviving thanks to their quality and prestige. Occasionally these mainly nineteenth-century interiors survive (the survival of older decorative schemes on anything less than a palatial scale is very rare) and are recognized for their integrity, even when they are glaringly out of fashion. As design ensembles, such houses have grown in scholarly and professional esteem. They are increasingly acknowledged as authentic records of historic taste. Intact (or largely intact) specimens are especially valuable for the documentary context they offer to the art historically defined masterpieces. While some intact houses *are* masterpieces, such as the Gamble House in Pasadena, California, others might be called merely fashionable: stylish and expensive, but mainstream.

The house known as the Victoria Mansion in Portland, Maine, demonstrates this condition. An Italianate villa built as a summer house, it was
decorated and furnished by the New York design firm Herter Brothers in
1860, with furniture, wall paintings, artworks, carpets, gas lighting fixtures,
stained glass, china, silver, and glassware, of which more than 90 percent is
still intact—taste in a time capsule. The house was inhabited by three generations but faced demolition before a passionate individual who recognized
its importance and used his own funds to save it for posterity rescued it in
1940. Having opened it as a museum, William Holmes transferred it to a trust
in 1943; both interior and exterior were heavily restored in the early 2000s.
Herter Brothers furniture exists in many houses and museums, but none as

**Turkish smoking room, Victoria Mansion, Portland, Maine, in 1935 and
2010. Twin photos, seventy-five years apart, depict the survival of a
spectacular 1860 interior. The painted walls were cleaned and details
regilded in 2007, the curtain fabrics reproduced in 2008, and the passe-
menterie re-created in 2009. This Turkish nook appears to be the first,
and perhaps the oldest, of its kind in an American building.**
Photo (a), on the left, courtesy of the Library of Congress, Prints & Photographs Division, HABS ME, 3-PORT, 15–13; photo (b), on the right, by J. David Bohl, courtesy
of Victoria Mansion.

complete as at Victoria Mansion: it would have been a cover feature in the *Architectural Digest* magazine of its time.

The evolution of the museum-informed management of intact interiors is evidenced at Brodsworth Hall in Yorkshire, another 1860s Italianate mansion inhabited by three generations. Described by Mark Girouard as "the most complete surviving example of a Victorian country house," it is decorated with rich finishes, silk-paneled walls, lush furniture, horse paintings, twenty-four marble sculptures acquired at the 1865 Dublin Exhibition, and an exceptional range of decorative and domestic textiles, as well as household equipment (Allfrey 1999, 116). English Heritage acquired the house as a last resort in 1990, for without an endowment the National Trust could not afford to take it on. Brodsworth confirmed a new standard of veneration for authentic style in the professional rhetoric of historic preservation when the decision was made to stabilize rather than restore the interiors. The aesthetic of the pleasure of ruins, or at least the appreciation of patina, currently represents the summit of educated heritage architecture taste. It constitutes the opposite pole to the naïve astonishment of visitors who expect restoration to a house's "former glory": a taste distinction that often puts professional practice at odds with public expectations. Nonetheless, twenty years on, some of the most fragile materials at Brodsworth are reaching the end of their lives, testing the limits of the sustainability of the preserve "as is" ethic (Allfrey & Xavier-Rowe, 2012).

The challenge of affording the preservation of significant intact interiors persists also on a smaller scale. 7 Hammersmith Terrace, London W6, is an Arts and Crafts interior in a humble Georgian row house; it was the home of typographer and printer Emery Walker, member of the Art Workers' Guild, the SPAB, and the Arts and Crafts Exhibition Society. His daughter, and then her companion, maintained the collection of furniture, ornaments, textiles, and memorabilia of William Morris, Philip Webb, and others, until the 1990s. The small house is unconserved by comparison with the great Morris monuments such as Standen and Wightwick. Had timing been more fortuitous, it is said that the National Trust would have chosen to put its resources into the Emery Walker House rather than the Red House on the grounds of intactness. This is typical of the dilemmas of chance that haunt preservation agencies. Now owned by an independent charitable trust, the house has been open to booked visitors since 2005, and its future is gradually becoming more certain.

The chances that govern the survival of intact decorative schemes and stylish houses also frame the history of the museumization of the Gamble House in Pasadena, California. One of the icons of the American Arts and

Crafts Shingle style, it was designed in 1907–1909 by Greene and Greene. Docents recount that it was saved for preservation when the second-generation inhabitants contemplated selling in 1966 but overheard potential buyers discussing painting the exquisite Japanesque interiors white. Mercifully, the house was taken off the market and donated to the City of Pasadena to be managed by the University of Southern California. Since then, its burnished interiors of teak and mahogany, jewel-like leaded art-glass windows, and exquisite details of craftsmanship have brought countless visitors to a transcendent experience of wonder and delight (Bosley 2002). It is a beautiful house, and it is poignant to contemplate the fragility of such beauty in the voracious maw of the real estate market. How many excellent interior designs have been lost to demolition and insensitive renovation?

Thanks to less exposure to the risks of time, twentieth-century houses and interiors ought be more prevalent among the body of intact houses conserved for the sake of design, but they are still relatively few. To some degree this is a matter of how a historic house is viewed at the moment of its museumization. Calthorpes' House in Canberra is largely presented in the social history trope of domestic life in the then newly established capital of Australia. But because it was furnished essentially in one shopping trip to a big store in Sydney in 1927 and maintained by a dedicated housewife for fifty-two years, it remained a consistent ensemble of popular interwar "Jacobethan" interior decoration. Family members recognized its integrity, and the house was acquired by a local government heritage agency and opened in 1985. It is often met with surprise by visitors whose expectation of a historic house is high-style antiquity, but interpretation focuses their attention on the significance of modern consumerism by a middle-class household. The interpretation could easily have an aesthetic dimension that reviews popular fashions and tastes—but that is a scarce perspective in design history as presented in house museums, anywhere.

Postscript: Dennis Severs's House
Dennis Severs's House is an artwork in itself rather than a house museum, but it is worth discussing here because it plays on the concept of museumizing a house and, in blurring some perceptions, clarifies others. Severs himself lived in and created the house from 1979 to 1999, and bequeathed it to a local trust. Situated in a small Georgian terrace in Spitalfields, London, the house presents as a museum, with rooms dressed in eighteenth- and nineteenth-century styles. Several generations of a fictional family inhabit the house, initially presented as affluent Huguenot silk weavers; their fortunes decline as the visitor climbs the stairs to the garret, where Dickensian rags and boards draped in cobwebs indicate dire poverty. Severs invited

friends and visitors to experience his creation with him in noisy parties, or in contemplative silence, which is the mode enjoined on visitors today. Entry numbers are controlled, and hip young guardians in each room try to keep out of the way of visitors, who are unconstrained by barriers. The rooms are painted in rich, dark colors, densely furnished, and lit by candles and oil lamps. Ephemeral elements such as fresh fruit, artfully half peeled or bitten into, lie amid the objects, and items of period clothing are strewn here and there. Smells of food, spice, and tobacco infuse some spaces, and the sounds of footsteps, laughter, or a cat occasionally ripple by. The thick arrangements of objects invite peering, which reveals little typed notes to the visitor, chiding one for looking more than imagining. The whole appears to be a conventional, albeit extravagantly furnished, house museum with unusually free access.

Most visitors love Dennis Severs's House, and many a tourism article extols its magical character in counterpoint to dead, frozen house museums. Some curmudgeons loathe it. Severs's own premise was "As an artist, my canvas is your imagination," and "You either see it or you don't." Explaining the house, Peter Ackroyd writes in the introduction to Severs's house-cum-personal autobiography, "The house in Folgate street is not a museum piece but a living thing"; "It is a revenant, a retrieval, with its own laws of growth and change" (Ackroyd 2002, ix). The words of both artist and commentator are suggestive but opaque. While the house is ultra-materialist in its massing of objects, the artist's intent is noisily ethereal, and the visitor is teased and taunted with this opposition. Whether it delights or frustrates is in the mind of the beholder. One sees the quirky, the charming, the weird, the unexpected. There are jokes for those who recognize them, such as the Grinling Gibbons–style swags hung in the salon, which are actually composed of walnut shells, star anise seed pods, tiny pine cones, and such. There are literary references such as Tiny Tim's pathetic crutch in the garret. There are clever gestures to artworks, as in the dregs-laden table reproduced from the Hogarth picture above the mantelpiece in a sitting room. Foolish or fascinating?

Furniture historians and house curators often feel uneasy about Dennis Severs's House for its boisterous misrepresentation of historic lifestyle. However, online tourist reviews and blog comments indicate that visitors see the house as an artwork rather than as a credible museum. Indeed, it is true pastiche, a riff on the period room. A comparison with Handel's House in central London demonstrates the very opposite interpretive style: here imagination is required to fill the correctly spare spaces with knowledge based on an introductory video and personal knowledge. Is understanding better served by one or the other?

CHAPTER FIVE

~

Collectors' Houses

Egos and Afterlives

The segment of house museums preserved for the sake of the collections they house is small relative to other types, and disproportionately celebrated. There is a charismatic allure in the personalities of collectors who resolved to bequeath their collections to the public, located in situ in the homes they had inhabited, sometimes with the injunction that content and/or arrangement should not change. Such a prescriptive vision for the future of the alter ego that inhabits most collections belies the more muddled reality that obtains in the long term, as this chapter shows in several variations on the theme. The dynamic of the transformation of private collections into the public sphere is a central factor in the particular character of collectors' house museums. In transferring their houseloads of art to the public, collectors created a genre of "national collection house," blending refined taste with energy and wealth, made democratically available to all. An analogy is evident with the interpretation of the nationalization of royal palaces as symbolic gestures of public ownership of and citizen attachment to the most elevated resources of the land (Duncan 1995, 22–26). Collectors' house museums in the United Kingdom and the United States demonstrate certain continuities but also differences and disparate feedback relationships. Understanding begins by surveying how collecting and the resultant collections were incorporated into the domestic lives of collectors, a living and therefore mutable process. The political implications of collections and their domestic settings suffuse the study of collectors' house museums and the questions that emerge from them. The question of the motivation to collect inevitably arises first.

A multitude of motivations have been proposed to explain the urge of individuals to collect, from psychopathology to play (Pearce 1992, 48–53; Muensterberger 1994, 3–13). But at the root of all, most authorities observe a singular, visionary agency in the collector's self, generating an alter ego composed of desirable objects, intrinsically satisfying to the collector and unified in his or her mind. Considered thus, the act of making a collection serves as a means of self-definition via material culture deployed as a public or semipublic statement. This is an aspect of the agency of the material in human life, examined profoundly by Susan Pearce; she concludes that "bewitchment" may be the most apt description of the relationship between collector and collection (1995, 170–73), describing as it does both an unworldly state and a mysterious motivation. The history of collections made and maintained in the collector's own house, and subsequently transformed into an ongoing house museum, exposes a spectrum of domestically framed collecting and collections, and exposes the characteristics of their occasional survival. It addresses the multigenerational dynamic of British aristocratic collecting, which established the paradigm for a genre of similar collecting by the new rich in the mid- and late nineteenth century. It identifies the colossal influence of the Wallace Collection, peculiarly formed at a nexus of aristocratic tradition, escapist irregularity in France, and reintegration into English culture. This model of collecting by the super rich was taken up in the new home of capital, the United States, from the early twentieth century, establishing a fabulous roll of collectors' houses bequeathed as public museums (Cannadine 2014). The practice continues to this day, its products wittily named "ego-seums" (Alberge 2010). In addition, certain maverick and primeval histories of other house collections cast oblique lights on the mainstream and give definition to the overall narrative of house collections in situ.

As a rule, the "extended self" of a collection dies with the collector. Collections are commonly redistributed to heirs as discrete objects or realized as cash; thus the works themselves return to the market, while specific items might be bequeathed to individuals or institutions. As noted in earlier chapters, the absence of direct heirs is a major factor in the museumization of house collections. It is the primary reason why collectors' house museums are overwhelmingly the legacy of the childless. That said, a few collectors have bequeathed their collections, but not their houses, to form a new museum, usually named for themselves—for example, the Bowes Museum near Durham and the Getty Center and Getty Villa (officially the J. Paul Getty Museum) in Los Angeles, built for eponymous collectors. Few collectors can afford to endow their collections as entities that persist into the future, and even with plenty of money, the transition to public museum is rarely easy. A huge endowment is generally vital, but where the collection is agreed to be outstandingly significant, public resources are surprisingly often drawn into maintaining the whole. Consequently, the kinds of collection that are sustained in situ as a collection tend to be composed of the most valuable kinds of objects in the relevant milieu: usually elite artworks and antiquities. In this light, it is evident that copious wealth underlies the phenomenon of collectors' house museums. Several are derived from fortunes that were the richest in their times, enabling the most conspicuous forms of consumption via grand houses and superb furnishings. Depending on the social dimension of wealth, versions of these peaks of possession and display could be realized at many price points. The Rothschild Waddesdon Manor in Buckingham-shire was formed on a different financial order from the Russell-Cotes Art Gallery in Bournemouth, though the spirit is the same (as is the comparison of the Frick Collection in New York City to the Charles Allis Art Museum in Milwaukee).

The disposition to collect usually manifests first in the collector's home, where it may be justified as decoration or show. The former opens up a clear subset of collectors' house museum, where the collector's devoted taste informs the acquisition of particular objects to contribute to a creative ensemble. The house may become a total artwork in itself, a *Gesamtkunst-werk*—the dream of totalizing architects such as Frank Lloyd Wright, and of certain gifted collectors such as Charles Paget Wade of Snowshill Manor, Gloucestershire. The chance of such arrangements surviving their creators' deaths requires that subsequent owners recognize the collection's expressive quality as worthy of preservation, and/or can afford to suppress (or satisfy) their own characters in the owner-artist-decorator's creation, as at Beauport, in Gloucester, Massachusetts. Where art collecting begins as the vehicle of presenting a magnificent front to the world via superlative pictures in the home, the collector's own agency may be much or little. But even if the lat-ter, there is plenty of evidence that the bewitching nature of collecting can come to work its charms on mercenary moguls. Educated by dealers and their peers, some unlikely characters have found themselves enchanted by the great art that came their way and in some cases, overtook their lives.

The binary of the private and the public is a pivotal frame of all house museums. To museumize a house is to put private life on exhibition—though admittedly, there is a spectrum of private-to-public spaces within all houses. One ingredient of the modern attraction of house museums is visitors' relish in gaining otherwise exclusive access, with the opportunity to look at what is customarily concealed from public gaze. Even to access the more public rooms of a private house offers the scopic pleasure of comparing one's own tastes and standards with those of (usually much richer) others. In practice, there is a complex range of conventional thresholds within the private house. Domestic public rooms are spaces dedicated to presenting the inhabitants in "at-home" condition, implying the absence of worldly artificiality, and as such have a long history of carefully composed show. To this day, "best" furniture and decorations are mobilized in the most public rooms to prove the style and taste of the occupants. Where display is a large consideration, prestigious material en masse, in the form of collections, introduces the purest form of conspicuous consumption.

As mentioned, among the species of house museums, collectors' house museums are the smallest category (Higonnet 2009). They tend to come to museumhood through a conjunction of chances, and those conditions introduce a particular lens to the phenomenon of collecting. The fundamental connection of collecting and collections to museums makes the confluence worth evaluating in the context of museology. Hence the following account traces a history of collectors' house museums that employs the psychology of collecting, the sociology of individual collector-residents, and the context of each house's transformation into a museum.

A Historic Spectrum of House-Based Collecting

The concept of collecting exists across a range of "gathering" behaviors: hoarding, parsimony, plunder, attachment, play, classification, exhibition, artistry. The latter three describe the motives of practically all collectors' house museums, with the bewildering exception of Calke Abbey, in Derbyshire, and, to put it in perspective, the besetting collections of Arlington Court in Devon. At Calke, several conventional collections are nested within a multigenerational habit of introverted hoarding. Here the unusual context of a great house with a hereditary order of succession and associated income enabled four of the last six generations of owners to simply close the door on the preceding occupants' acquisitions and take up life in another part of the house. Such an accumulation is a rare survival, more confounding than enlightening. What Calke shows in its sheer mass of stuff is a range of collecting in registers from the conventional to the manic, and the ways collections could be incorporated into everyday life by, literally, compartmentalizing.

Previously notable only for their wealth, a strain of "congenital unsociability" emerged in the Harpur (later Harpur-Crewe) family in the seventh baronet, Henry, who inherited as a young man in 1789 (Garnett 2000, 37).

He gave himself to natural history, in the form of specimens; by 1800 the house contained some two hundred vitrines of birds, fish, shells, fossils, and minerals. His son George succeeded him, and recalled "under God's blessing, after 19 years labours . . . I have at last cleansed the Augean Stables of Calke" (Garnett 2000, 39). He made improvements to the house and collected orthodox paintings of landscapes, horses, and family portraits, but also added to the taxidermy collection; by his death in 1844, the number of display cases had doubled (Garnett 2000, 42). The ninth baronet, John, displayed much of his grandfather's personality and tastes, giving his life to stock breeding and ornithology, both celebrated in taxidermy. His successor, Vauncey, reverted to the extreme form of introverted eccentricity, such that at his death in 1924 mounted specimens in glass cases totaled several thousand. Taxidermy now inhabited every floor of the house. The house then passed to his daughter Hilda, who, to pay inheritance taxes, sold a quantity of specimens and some of the valuable books that accompanied her forefathers' collecting; she herself seems to have avoided the collecting obsession. Her nephew Charles succeeded her, displaying the family isolate character but not the acquisitive one. After he died, childless, in 1981, his brother, Henry, also childless, initiated a long process by which the house and estate came into the ownership of the National Trust in 1985.

Calke survives because the last Henry Harpur-Crewe made the call to try to preserve it rather than conduct another Herculean clean up. His judgment was backed by the decision of the Trust and other agencies that the assemblage was of sufficient cultural significance to merit the time, money, and energy required to stabilize it for public access. In essence, the Calke collections are typical of the kinds found in many a great house of the eighteenth- and nineteenth-century period and strange only in their excess. If the Calke collections of Sir Vauncey suggest insatiability or obsession, it is germane to compare them with those of Rosalie Chichester and her father, Sir Bruce, a family of similar baronet status and wealth, seated at Arlington Court in Devon. The house is fitted with elements of several generations' worth of furnishings and decorative schemes, including treasured eighteenth-century tapestries that predate the current building. Parts of the 1820s building were grandly Victorianized inside in the 1860s, and decorated with yachting pictures, models, and souvenirs celebrating the family's trips to the Mediterranean in a luxury schooner. In adulthood, ships, boats, and traveling to exotic parts became Rosalie Chichester's life, along with her care of the Arlington estate, which she embraced with a sense of duty and noblesse oblige (Anon. 1996, 29–31). But she also developed "a mania for collecting," comprising at her death: two hundred model ships; about four hundred pieces of pewter;

seventy-five cabinets of shells and shellwork; fifty punch ladles; thirty tea caddies; hundreds of genteel knickknacks (snuffboxes, paperweights, and the like); close to a hundred animal sculptures in decorative and semiprecious materials; and much more, including souvenir spoons (Marsh 2004). She bequeathed everything to the National Trust in 1949. Like the collections at Calke Abbey, the substance of the Arlington Court objects is mainstream, this time in the context of decorative arts and antiquarian crafts. It comprises types of material culture associated with elite, moneyed taste, though applied without much discrimination. In terms of content, the Harpur-Crewes and the Chichesters were part of the continuum of aristocratic collecting, discussed below. To modern minds, such collecting may suggest the impaired self-control of addiction, linked with the personality disorders that underlie obsession.

A similar suspicion could apply to two more house collections, gathered by men of a different order of wealth and class. Sir John Soane and Sir Walter Scott were self-made men, middle-class professionals who were knighted toward the ends of their lives. Their houses and collections became public, and in that sense museumized, in the 1830s—chronologically, they are the first two house museums in the United Kingdom. Their status introduces the social group that thereafter became the fountainhead of collectors' house museums: the new rich.

It is easy to perceive the generator of the extended self in both Soane's and Scott's purposely designed houses, and in the substance of their collections. Soane collected to construct himself (the son of a building tradesman) as a gentleman, an heir to the classical tradition of architecture, a learned designer and teacher. He was a golden youth at the Royal Academy, which launched his career with a Grand Tour studentship. He was gifted and lucky, especially to marry the heiress of a property portfolio built by the City of London's Surveyor of Paving (Palmer 2002). As a rentier, Soane had no need to earn his income and accepted only prestigious jobs and appointments. His collecting was prodigious: as an antiquarian, he focused on Egyptian and classical antiquities, bolstered by plaster casts, displayed in decorative compositions on the walls, together with a sideline in the medieval; as an architect, he acquired a massive archive of his own and others' designs and models; as an academician, he collected contemporary English paintings, sculpture, and drawings. A few items were extremely rare and valuable; some were job lots purchased for effect: effect he certainly envisioned, notably via a three-night open house in 1825, lit by hundreds of hired lamps. This theatrical gesture points up the degree to which Soane perceived the collection-adorned house as the stage for his own performance as the great man of British architecture.

Classical antiquity had useful multiple meanings for Soane and his audience: it represented the refined and educated taste of eighteenth-century elite culture, it was the aesthetic frame of modern nineteenth-century design, and it spoke to a vision of past and present that was thoroughly romantic. Soane permitted his friend Mrs. Barbara Hofland to add flourishes of sensibility to the second edition of his own dry catalog, retitled *Popular Description of Sir John Soane's House, Museum and Library*. She articulated a cultivated emotional response to the collection. Thus, to introduce the solemn, affective tone of a visit, "It is evident that the hand, or rather the mind, which has arranged the beautiful fragments, massive pillars, ancient sculptures and various decorations around us intended that sentiment to pervade our bosoms, proper to the visitants of the dead" (Hofland 1919, 26–27). For all its antiquarian scholarship, Sir John Soane's Museum was a deeply romantic statement of the relationship between antiquity and modern England.

Walter Scott (the son of a solicitor) collected to materialize his poetry and novels, which is to say his fame, with relics and props of the Scottish antiquity that he created, celebrated, and reveled in. His house, Abbotsford, has been called "the *Waverley* novels in stone," referring to its pugnacious but ultraromantic turrets and battlements (Brown 2003, 5). The same vision shaped the collection with which he furnished it (judiciously interspersed with modern conveniences): a fantasy of a lordly castle decked with arms,

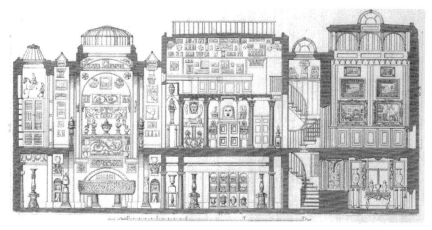

Section through Sir John Soane's Museum, 1827. This section shows the layout of major pieces in Soane's collection but glosses the dense reality, where corners, reveals, returns, vaults, and interstices are loaded with smaller pieces.
Plate VIII in John Britton, *The Union of Architecture, Sculpture and Painting: Exemplified by a Series of Illustrations, with Descriptive Accounts of the House and Galleries of John Soane* (London, 1827); courtesy of the Trustees of Sir John Soane's Museum.

armor, and relics of ancient Scots buildings, events, and people, joined in a pastiche of oak-grained, plaster-molded hall and armory. His primary collecting focus on relics of the sorties and battles of mythicized Scottish history was embellished by the contexts of international and modern weaponry. Indian and Asian blades came to his collection via veterans of the British wars in India (his soldier son died on a return trip from India), and he toured the site of the Battle of Waterloo to acquire helmets and other relics. All were arranged in heraldic style evoking the trophies of victory. Scott's other collecting was rich in objects made sacred by association with Scottish figures and other heroes, especially Napoleon and Shakespeare. This spirit crossed over with his own reputation as a literary lion in mutual heroic gifts between himself and Byron: a gold-mounted dagger from Scott and a silver urn containing "dead men's bones from certain sepulchres within the long walls of Athens" from Byron (Wainwright 1989, 163). In conjuring the bellicose fortitude of Scottish resistance to English domination (which in his novels was always safely put down in the name of the English crown), Scott's house and collection gave form to the romantic spirit to which he gave voice in his poetry and (first of the kind) historical fiction.

The Laird of Abbotsford cherished his identity as such, and in his stage-set house, he played to an audience of tourists, which didn't fade when he died in 1832. The fans' enthusiasm impelled the Scott family to open the hall and study the next year, then the library and armory. In the 1850s, the family moved into a new house immediately adjacent, and transformed old Abbotsford into a pilgrimage-cum-tourism business that remained family operated until 2004. Only then was the whole transferred to an independent trust and set on the track to modern professional management. The museumization of Soane's house and collection was incomparably more calculated. Soane sought and his friends delivered an Act of Parliament in 1833, which vested both house and collection in a trust for the benefit of the nation. The bequest took effect on Soane's death in 1837. By the end of World War II its value had shrunk and costs expanded, to the point that government was convinced to contribute an annual allocation (Stroud 1984, 111). The Act specified that the house should be maintained "as nearly as possible in the state in which Sir John Soane [left] it" to guard the genius of its founder (Summerson 1981, 69). No. 13 was opened to the public, first for two days a week, rising to five days a week in 1947; the self-contained front half of no. 12 was left to the nation to be rented out to make an income for the museum (it was taken back into museum use in 1969); and the self-contained front half of no. 14, let to tenants in Soane's day, was bequeathed to his family (the museum bought it back in 1996). The reclaimed front houses and other spaces in the complex underwent significant reworking in the 2010s to pro-vide contemporary standards of museum access and services and to restore the Soanes' private apartments. The rooms at the rear across all three houses were joined to form two levels of museum and picture rooms. Soane's and Scott's houses are now important specimens of Romantic decor, based on their founders' collecting.

The threads of collector practice at Calke, Arlington, Abbotsford, and Soane's Museum, woven into the history of houses preserved as a genre of museum, introduce and confirm some important themes in grasping the dis-tinction of collectors' houses. The creative possibilities of collections as the media of what might be called a decorated house or an installation artwork are strong. The startling, sometimes disturbing, possibilities of fetishistic accumulation indicate a theme of obsession that hovers at the far edge of ec-centricity. It displays an evident, though not always intelligible, effect, with which the museum visitor might or might not choose to engage sympatheti-cally (a privilege of the onlooker perspective). The number, diversity, and intensity of objects collected in all four cases is surprising even to the modern mind accustomed to abundant material culture. The thought that the collec-tions would not have been preserved had they been composed of acorns or pieces of string clarifies the sense of what is generally considered museumiz-able; yet it also confirms the focus of museum practice on objects rather than visitors. Financial value is one element of this mixture, but it's not impossible to conceive of a contemporary museum collecting a pathological hoarder's house, or maybe one room of it, as a specimen of extreme consumption.

A case that veers toward extreme collecting is the project of Richard H. Jenrette, a retired New York investment banker. In 2006, he began to transfer his forty-year-long hobby of restoring old houses into a collection of historic house museums, the American Classical Homes Preservation Trust. A self-named "house-aholic," Jenrette ascribes his interest to his view that the Federal neoclassical style is the "national style" of the United States; that he grew up in the South, watching *Gone with the Wind*; and that he has been captured by the charms of restoration, including reinstating a remarkable fraction of original furnishings (Jenrette 2005, 11–15). He lives between several of these houses, and all can be booked for group visits; the two already formally transferred to the ACHPT are open at regular hours. Jenrette writes that "the others will be given to the Foundation as my tax and personal circumstances dictate" (American Classical Homes Preservation Trust 2015). His fortune is derived from innovation in financial research, investment strategies, and use of technology in the money market in the 1960s–1990s. Polished by the culture of old New York, he enabled himself to

Richard H. Jenrette in front of Edgewater, Barrytown, New York, 1999. Only a very rich man can afford to collect and furnish historic houses as Jenrette does. Lord Peter Palumbo did it, too, for a while (Le Corbusier, Mies van der Rohe, Frank Lloyd Wright) but sold off most of his acquisitions.
Photo by Douglas Baz, courtesy of the Classical American Homes Preservation Trust.

collect antique houses and furnishings for fun, profit, and public inspiration. Relishing the material beauty of such objects, he notes that he is "a little at variance with current thinking by some of our friends in today's museum world" in subscribing to an ideal of "restoring things to their former glory." In this, Jenrette might be called an artist rather than a curator or collector, suggesting what may be a fuzzy intersection between the three.

The Original Ideal: Collecting for the British Country House
Whether acquired for decoration or show, the dominant concept of a fine collection displayed in the collector's home springs from the prototype of the stately homes of England. More accurately thought of as palaces than mere houses, the lure of the aristocratic model is easy to appreciate: it signals the grandeur that demonstrates wealth, power, ancestry, and legitimacy. The ideal is, inevitably, shaped by the fluctuations of context and history. Critical to the phenomenon in the United Kingdom is the legal device of male primogeniture with entailed property succession, through which the eldest legitimate male heir inherited titles and estates, a kinship structure devised to preserve and consolidate family wealth. Land ownership was the basis of aristocratic wealth, generated by rents, shares in agricultural produce, and profits from resource industries such as coal. Effectively managed, income from these sources (plus intermittent royal favors, court and government posts, and the fruits of strategic marriages) enabled a noble family to live according to its lord's taste, at a standard of appropriate splendor, and to transmit the improvements to future generations. Thus occasional generations among titleholders built or rebuilt family homes and collected splendid contents to adorn them. Relatively few collecting aristocrats were motivated by informed interest and acquired portraits almost exclusively. Many more, often including the king, acquired artworks because it was expected of a great lord that he would possess the finest furnishings and decor. Prestige accordingly joined visible wealth as qualities reflected on the collector by ownership of an accumulation of superb goods. Yet another dimension of house-and-collection significance arises from the intergenerational continuity of valuable items so long associated with family history that they become regarded as heirlooms. The notion of generations past represented in such objects constitutes them as evidence of the ancestral power, boosting the standing of each new head of the family.

The houses and goods gathered by the Cavendish family (earls, then dukes, of Devonshire) offer an exemplary study of aristocratic collecting to adorn the family seats. A notable seven out of twelve generations of dukes since 1694 dedicated considerable amounts of what was frequently among the largest fortunes in England to acquiring treasures for their houses: paintings and drawings, manuscripts and engravings, printed books, splendid furniture, gold and silver plate, oriental ceramics, and other luxury goods. (Almost all the dukes were similarly devoted to racehorses and hunting, further forms of luxury spending.) At the turn of the eighteenth century the first duke had Chatsworth converted from an Elizabethan mansion to a baroque palace. It contained grand rooms, decorated with murals by the favorite house artists of the age, with sculpture, stucco, and carved decoration by the best artisans. The second and third dukes added significant Old Master drawings and antique gems and coins. The third duke oversaw the rebuilding of Devonshire House in London; furnishings and paintings shuttled between the two houses. The next outstanding collector of the line was the fourth duke, whose marriage brought additional vast estates and the valuable art collection of the late Lord Burlington to Chatsworth. The sixth duke acquired a number of important private libraries, and in the 1820s he oversaw the construction of a grand new wing at Chatsworth. Not until the eleventh duke inherited in 1950 did another collector emerge. This one had first to clear massive succession taxes, achieved via transfer of property and artworks in lieu; he restructured Chatsworth as a trust and established a new business for the house as a tourism attraction. It was successful enough to enable him to revive the traditions of aristocratic patronage as a collector of contemporary British art, a practice followed by the current, twelfth duke (Blunt 1979, 17–21; Obee 2008, 60–66).

The example of the Cavendish family's development of Chatsworth demonstrates the complex of money and taste that constitutes a habitus—in this case, a disposition to live like a lord. For anyone who aspires to a similar condition, a great house fitted with furnishings and artworks, magnificent in themselves and reinforced by the authority of ancestral provenance, constitutes an essential base for ambition. Consequently, the new rich of every generation have invested in aristocratic housing, habits, and marriage partners to polish their money with the glamour of the nobility (Wilson & Mackley 2000). In practice, the reality of living like a lord tends to induce an aura of lordliness, acknowledged by many and resisted only by the imitated class and its lackeys. Their defensive response has always been to denigrate the cultural understanding of the aspirant (Davidoff 1973). But by dint of inserting self, and educating children, into the most expensive and exclusive practices, such as etiquette, horse sports, and collecting, truly enormous fortunes have proved an effective way of becoming refined. It appears to be an enduring route: upwardly mobile billionaires follow it to this day.

The New Rich as Collectors

From the late eighteenth century, the industrial economy of Britain, and its associated apparatus of finance, distribution, and transport, generated a dramatic tide of new fortunes. Entrepreneurs expanded their businesses, reinvested the profits, arriving at a point where expenditure on comforts and even luxuries was no longer an extravagance. A few continued to live close to their enterprise, but many had grand houses built in elegant suburbs or the countryside; they, or their children, were on the way to becoming gentlemen (Macleod 1996, 20–30; Crook 1999, 7–31). This new middle class was inspired to create a moral and genteel culture informed by the virtues of honest work, civic responsibility, and private virtue, in distinction to the tastes of an aristocracy sometimes regarded as decadent. Nonetheless, they were ready to adopt aristocratic standards of consumption as the ideal criteria of desirable living. That meant buying property of appropriate grandeur, adding commensurate furnishings, acquiring horses for carriages and for hunting, and funding wives and daughters to advance family honor via elegant self-presentation and entertainments (Young 2003, 88–94). Collecting art was an especially efficient vehicle of converting financial to cultural capital, enhancing the reputation of the individual and his possessions. In the absence of a long line of forebears represented in portraits, the new rich of the industrial north and financial south favored the realist landscape and genre modes of contemporary English artists. Indeed, it seems that early and mid-Victorian industrialists' and financiers' prodigious demand for art that was moral in content and finely worked in style both nurtured and sustained the new English School of Landseer, Mulready, Wilkie, and others soon joined by the Pre-Raphaelites (Macleod 1996, 88–129). The great Victorian art museums of Manchester, Birmingham, Liverpool, and other industrial city art galleries today contain the fruit of their preferences.

Art collecting is among the sophisticated activities that enable the new rich to express not only their wealth but also their taste, thus identifying themselves with the old money elite—if they can do it correctly. The acceptable standard is a variable threshold of cultural knowledge and performance—that is, the cultural capital that is as distinctive as financial capital in structuring the individual in the field of social life (Bourdieu 1986). Building up cultural capital by collecting art entails the essential medium of very expensive goods, specialized knowledge and the experience to use it, and the right environment in which to display the agent's capacity. A fortune and a mansion could be enhanced by self-education via dealers, peers, and wives, though acknowledgment by the elite was far from guaranteed and would-be aspirants could always be resisted with cultural snubs. However, persistent money and the political power it attracts transformed the new rich into the dominant class in the long run. Where collecting is part of the process, it can be naturalized into genuine passion, as art commentator Mrs. Anna Jameson observed of new collectors in the 1840s: "The wish to possess is followed by delight in the possession. What we delight in, we love; and love becomes in time a discriminating and refined appreciation" (Jameson 1844, xxvii).

The new rich businessmen of early to mid-nineteenth-century England who took to collecting art overwhelmingly sprang from petit bourgeois backgrounds. As upright men with a characteristic culture of public responsibility, many eventually bequeathed key works to their cities' art galleries. Two, Robert Vernon and John Sheepshanks, both childless, gave primal collections of contemporary English art to, respectively, the National Gallery (1847) and the Victoria and Albert Museum (1857), the first great donations to then-new institutions. Just one house of this kind of collector has survived as a house museum: George Holt's house, Sudley, in Liverpool. Holt died in 1896, leaving the house and collection to his daughter, Emma Holt, who bequeathed them to the Corporation of Liverpool in 1944. Holt and several brothers had founded shipping lines and became very rich; they were exemplary citizens (magistrates, mayors, civic philanthropists); and they were collectors. George Holt began collecting in middle age. When he died, an obituary described him as "another conspicuous example of the fact that the pursuit of commerce is naturally compatible with the pursuit of refinement and intellectual interests," an assertion that was still contestable in some circles (Macleod 1996, 213). Holt's collecting had begun with English genre paintings. He purchased Sudley in 1883, and hung it with the newly flourishing taste for eighteenth-century English portraits, along with a line of modern academic classicist and Pre-Raphaelite works, landscapes, and the odd French name. Diane Macleod shows how typical was this mixture among the new rich of industrial England: contemporary, realist, improving, godly, loyal, and British (1996, 209–66). Emma Holt's bequest consisted of the house and 148 works, the major part of her father's collection (Bennett 1964, 2–5). Since museumization, the house has served a range of civic functions as well as being the site of the collection. It has been cared for as a municipal asset more than a *Gesamtkunstwerk*, but its original lincrusta wallpapers and dark green tones survive in the reception rooms. This is a sad but not-untypical fate of local government-owned collectors' house museums: the building is perceived as a container, subject to workmanlike renovation every few decades; the artworks are managed separately, almost independently of the ensemble. The loss to the particular history of the house and collector is severe.

Sir Merton Russell-Cotes embodied another variety of the new rich businessman, with another rationale for collecting art. In 1876, he and his cotton-heiress wife, Annie, bought a grand hotel in Bournemouth. Their Royal Bath Hotel became the most fashionable in town, noted for stylish decor and embellished with its owners' collection of art and far-flung travel souvenirs. The leading hotelier of the town, Russell-Cotes was a dedicated civic booster; he advocated development, became mayor in the 1890s, and was knighted in 1897. East Cliff Hall, a fancifully grand residence, was built next to the hotel on the cliff front above the beach. In 1905, a large part of the hotel art collection was sold, but about a third (more than two hundred works) was installed in the new house. Here one admirer described it as "a miniature Wallace Collection, and much more varied in its exhibits" (Waterfield 1999, 864). The Russell-Coteses announced they would bequeath the house and collection to the people of Bournemouth as an art gallery when they died, and had three spacious galleries added to the house for their large history and biblical paintings. In 1922 the benefaction was realized, and the home and its galleries transmuted easily to public use. The luxurious decorative scheme of the house remains reasonably intact, and it is densely furnished with paintings, antiquities, ethnographic curios (especially Japanese), ceramics, furniture, and fittings. The original entrance hall is surmounted by a gallery level, closely hung with paintings and punctuated by white marble sculpture. The contrast of domestic-scale and gallery-scale hang is a striking demonstration of the difference between the private and public presentation of artworks (Bills 2001, 47–50).

The Super Rich as Art Collectors

Three British plutocrats of the late nineteenth century left collections in houses. Sir Richard Wallace, Lord Iveagh, and Baron Ferdinand Rothschild possessed immense wealth, on a scale equivalent to their American contemporaries, the millionaires of the Gilded Age. Two of the latter, Isabella Stewart Gardner and Henry Clay Frick, created and bequeathed their houses as museums, as did several lesser millionaires. The prototype, inspiration, and cynosure of all of them were the Hertford collections—the source of the Wallace Collection.

What became the Wallace Collection could have been a traditional, if spectacular, country house collection but for a triple-generational taste for French style. Its history demonstrates how the museum that came into public ownership in 1897–1900 trod a complicated path through family idiosyncrasy (Lasic 2009). Although it was the product of aristocratic wealth, a mass of social ambiguities shaped the bequest to the nation as a claim to

The Main Hall of East Cliff Hall, c. 1908. This view shows the segment of the hotel collection presented to the city of Bournemouth in that year, hung in a thick display of beauty, taste, morality, and money that redounded to the donors' fame.
Photo courtesy of the Russell-Cotes Gallery and Museum.

respectability via philanthropy. The Wallace Collection is a subset of multigenerational aristocratic collecting by the Marquesses of Hertford. It was defined by the well-funded and dedicated collecting of the fourth marquess, a reclusive expatriate in Paris, and was enlarged through strategic collecting by his illegitimate son and heir to everything except the title, Richard Jackson, who took his mother's name, Wallace (Ingamells 2004; Hughes 1981). Soon after inheriting in 1870 he moved to London, where much of the accumulated collection had been stored in the family townhouse (more remained in his father's chateau and apartment in Paris). After nearly fifty years in France, Wallace transformed himself into an English gentleman, parliamentarian, and philanthropist, and he was created a baronet in his own right. In a gesture perceived as magnificent public largesse, he lent the Hertford collections, rich in Old Master and modern English paintings, miniatures, French ceramics and furniture, and European arms and armor, to the Bethnal Green Museum for several years while the family house in London, renamed Hertford House, was refurbished.

Wallace died in 1890, having planned to present his collection to the nation but shying away from the idea when he heard that the government might decline it on account of the cost of a building and an endowment (Hughes 1981, 49). Hence he left everything to his wife; it was her will that decided the bequest, comprising the fine and decorative arts on the first two floors of Hertford House. "Never yet has a nation come into an artistic heritage so rich, so varied and so comprehensive," wrote a commentator in 1913, an opinion that stands today (Rutter 1913, 13). Lady Wallace required provision of a museum in central London and specified that it should be maintained as a closed collection. The lease of Hertford House, all other property, and the rest of the collection were left to the Wallaces' private secretary, in the event that the gift and its conditions were accepted by the Conservative government. An advisory committee recommended that the Wallace Collection should remain in Hertford House by buying out the lease and the freehold; thus the Collection opened in 1900. The trustees of the Wallace Collection were imperious to a degree unusual even among the boards of Britain's national museums. Largely aristocrats, they resisted professional advice for their own vision of how the collection should be displayed (Lasic 2009, 179–80; Poole 2010, 91–92). This was in the conventional manner of town house galleries, meaning that the bedrooms and service rooms evaporated and artworks were redistributed for display in the customary national categories rather than in Wallace's own hang. Security mandated that the furniture be stripped of most of its lavish load of *objets de virtu*, which reappeared in vitrines. Nonetheless, contemporary commentators proclaimed a conviction that Hertford House remained a domestic space: "The character of the house has been but little interfered with. It retains much of the atmosphere characteristic of the home of a man of taste, and it has taken on less than might have been expected of the museum aspect," insisted a leading art critic (Baldry 1904, 18). This is a wishful claim; in fact, Hertford House has always been treated preeminently as a display space, with rare gestures to its historic form (Gaynor 1984, 74–79).

The Iveagh Bequest and Kenwood House in which it is displayed constitute a different type of house collection. It springs from the enormous wealth of the Guinness family brewing business, as nurtured by the fourth-generation Edward Guinness, who became super rich by taking the company two-thirds public in 1886. He thereupon retired and dedicated himself to philanthropy, the Conservative Party, and advancing in English society. In the four years of 1887–1891, he purchased 212 Old Masters and English eighteenth-century portraits to furnish his Mayfair house (Bryant 2003, 10–12). Guinness was ennobled four times between 1891 and 1919, when he became the Earl of Iveagh. After a lifetime of benefactions in housing and education, he rescued Kenwood House, Hampstead, in 1925, when the house and its parkland fell under threat of development. Iveagh furnished the house with about a quarter of his paintings and bequeathed it to the nation when he died in 1927. Thus Kenwood is less a collector's house than an art collection exhibited in a house. Yet its residential scale enabled the principle articulated by the director of the National Gallery (ex-officio a trustee of Kenwood) in its first catalog: "In a series of living rooms it is possible to group or to isolate, to give prominence to a masterpiece, and relative obscurity to things of less importance. Many of the pictures will gain immensely from not being treated as museums specimens. Hanging in the congenial surroundings of an old country mansion, they will appear in the setting for which they were designed" (Holmes 1928, xvi). Unfortunately, Kenwood's damp walls exposed works to a risk that was monitored nervously for years. It did, however, result in several pictures being restored, including cleaning, which pitted the taste of professionalism against the general trustee taste for old-varnish "brown" paintings, in another contest between experts and public guardians (Bryant 2004, 42–44). After the war, Kenwood's management devolved to the body that became English Heritage. Under this administration, the house received a second art bequest, the Suffolk Collection of Jacobean portraits, and has been semifurnished with material purchased from the house's last family owners, the earls of Mansfield. Thus, as a house museum, it lies at the museum end of the spectrum, even while its house nature is stressed in the presentation of two collections.

The opposite is the case at Waddesdon Manor, Buckinghamshire, an original and intact expression of le goût Rothschild, the opulent, French-inspired decorative aesthetic subsequently adopted by the transatlantic super rich (Hall 2014). Ferdinand Rothschild was a fourth-generation member of the English Rothschild family; he dedicated himself to collecting after his wife died in childbirth. When he came into independent wealth in 1874, he began building his own extravagant neo-Renaissance mansion in the Vale of Aylesbury, where five other Rothschild relatives also established country houses. Ferdinand collected primarily to furnish Waddesdon and his London townhouse, while maintaining a taste for the precious objets his father had collected. He sought the same French furnishings acquired by (not yet Sir) Richard Wallace on behalf of Lord Hertford and pursued the predilection for eighteenth-century English portraits, of the kind later taken up enthusiastically by Lord Iveagh. A Liberal and a democrat, Rothschild approved the private-to-public trajectory of great collections: "Collectors may deplore the fact but it should be a source of gratification to the public that most fine works of art drift slowly but surely into museums and public galleries. In private hands they can afford delight only to a small number of persons" (Rothschild 1897, 68). Yet, when he died in 1898, he left the house to his younger sister Alice, aside from the Waddesdon Bequest to the British Museum, comprising nearly three hundred medieval and renaissance objets de virtu. Alice Rothschild guarded the legacy of the house for twenty-four years. She carefully refurnished the room in which Ferdinand had kept the treasures that became the Bequest and established a housekeeping regime that persists to this day. She selected a great-nephew to inherit, James de Rothschild, in 1922. "Never can any man have had less incentive, or need, than Jimmy to make a personal collection of works of art," wrote his wife (Rothschild 1979, 104). The only significant changes they introduced were some modernization of drains and electricity, and the incorporation in 1936 of a share of the collection of Jimmy's father, Edmond, from Paris. But Waddesdon had never been, and never could be, anything but "a subsidised pleasure palace" (Hall 2002, 300). Jimmy began negotiations for its future with the National Trust after World War II. At this time, the house was both relatively modern and defiantly old-fashioned; nonetheless, the integrity of its collection was admitted, and some authorities recognized its ensemble quality (Hall 2002, 249–51). Jimmy's death in 1957 made the house a bequest rather than a gift, and it opened to the public in 1959. Twenty years later, Mrs. Jimmy (as she was known) wrote a rare account of the intricate business of converting the house to a museum role (Rothschild 1979, 139–48).

The trials of conversion were avoided at Fenway Court, Boston, for the house now called the Isabella Stewart Gardner Museum was designed for the purpose, with small private quarters on the top floor. Gardner was sixty when construction of her house museum began in 1900, immensely rich in her own right as well as having inherited her husband's fortune. She had begun collecting art in the 1870s but shifted to a different register after 1894, when she acquired a Botticelli on the advice of Bernard Berenson, who focused her attention on Italian masterpieces. Gardner also collected in the gamut of Old Masters, sculpture, manuscripts, decorative arts and architectural fragments, as well certain moderns. Gardner's collecting motivation has been subjected to more analysis than any other of her contemporaries (see Matthews 2009),

The Gothic Room, Fenway Court, c. 1926. Fenway Court, Isabella Stewart Gardner's house museum, did not open fully to the public until after her death in 1925. Until then, at her husband's request, Sargent's famous and contentious portrait (1888) was hung in one of the private rooms.
Photo by T. E. Marr & Son, courtesy of the Archives, Isabella Stewart Gardner Museum, Boston.

and while it certainly shared in the prevailing dimension of very expensive prestige, she was so entirely the genius of the total arrangement of the house that it can well be understood as her own artwork, a theme that reemerges below. She was appropriately delighted by a friend's birthday tribute in 1911: "You are, not only the lover of Art, and the Collector, but the Artist, having built the house and having arranged all the objects which it contains in the order and unity of a single idea" (Goldfarb 1995, 20). The museum opened to a very limited extent from 1903, not becoming fully public until Gardner's death in 1924. The caprice of the house was set permanently by her will, generating management dilemmas resolved in 2012 with a subtle new building in the back garden (Pfeiffer 2012, 50–56).

By contrast, the Frick Collection in New York developed as the Wallace Collection of the United States, equivalent in quality, cost, and style. Henry Clay Frick was a ruthless and immensely successful tycoon, an archetype of the "squillionaires," as termed by Bernard Berenson. However, his ambition was decisively different from Wallace's in planning a future public museum with the explicit aim of self-memorialization (Quodbach 2009). This aim took shape with the construction of Frick's new house in 1913–1914. His collecting had begun with conventional contemporary French paintings in the 1880s–1890s but made a dramatic shift in 1899 when he acquired his first (since reattributed) Rembrandt and his first eighteenth-century English portrait. Frick was now in the style league of the British plutocrats, and their taste grew ever more marked in his collection. He was chiefly interested in paintings but acquired the characteristic French furniture, ceramics, and bronzes of the goût Rothschild from the collection of J. P. Morgan, who died as Frick's mansion was rising; the dealer Joseph Duveen supervised the interior decoration. Frick himself died in 1919; the museum opened in 1935, after Mrs. Frick died. His huge endowment had already nearly doubled, enabling construction of two more galleries, plus other spaces, to convert the house to a satisfactory museum; further enlargements took place in 1977, 2011, and 2016. Frick chose not to specify a closed collection, and today, nearly a third of the works on display postdate the collector himself. Not all tastes appreciated the quasi-domestic setting of the Frick Collection. A commentator wrote of the newly opened museum, "The paintings are lost in the background. That may have satisfied the tastes of Renaissance princes, or even of American millionaires during the first part of the present century, but it no longer meets today's standards of presentation" (Ryskamp et al. 1996, 29). The judgment was deliberately provocative in the early years of Modernism, but it proved to be a lonely view, for the Frick ideal inspired generations of American collecting.

A span of degrees was evident as mere millionaires applied the essentially French taste of the great American collectors to their own lavish houses. More than a handful were transformed into house museums throughout the twentieth century. Most owners had absorbed the lessons of the 1898 American interior design text, *The Decoration of Houses*, by Edith Wharton and Ogden Codman Jr. The authors asserted that the ideal model of good living derived from Renaissance Italy (admitting that it was not a viable form for the northern United States), followed by French and English neoclassicisms, claimed to make the beautiful comfortable. Encouraging aspirational standards, they noted optimistically that "the bourgeois of one generation lives more like the aristocrat of a previous generation" (Wharton & Codman 1898, 2–5). One of the most effective means of achieving the lifestyle of a "mellower civilisation," they recommended, was collecting. It communicated to onlookers an ineffable mix of taste and money: "The qualities implied in the ownership of such bibelots are the mark of their unattainableness" (Wharton & Codman 1898, 187). Grand examples of millionaire collecting in this vein came into the public sphere as house museums throughout the twentieth century: Ca' d'Zan, Sarasota, Florida, in 1946; the Charles Allis Art Museum in Milwaukee, Wisconsin, in 1957; the most spectacular of all, Hearst Castle, San Simeon, California, in 1958; and Shangri La, Hawaii, in 2002. (The years cited represent the moment of transition that followed a lifetime of collecting; the house museums actually represent older collecting careers than the dates might suggest.)

Such American collectors' house museums add to the argument of this book that house museums address a national identity agenda. Some authors connect the phenomenon to the triumphant sense of America buying up the best of the old world to demonstrate the equivalent splendor of the new (Higonnet 2009, 81; Holler & Klose-Ullmann 2010, 92). This vein of public giving sometimes exemplifies an archetype of American individualist success, though many more collector house museums arose from second- and third-generation fortunes than the handful of self-made multimillionaires. The latter is a small fraction, represented by Alfred Barnes of the Barnes Foundation, Henry Frick, and John Ringling of Ca' d'Zan. Gift giving may be perceived as philanthropy, but sociologists analyze it more brutally as the motor of a cycle of social obligation (Mauss 1990). In the case of exceptional gifts to the public, the return is in the currency of enduring prestige, which rises above the mundane crudity of making a fortune. Thus Barnes is presented even today as creating a product "to prevent infant blindness" (Barnes Foundation website 2016)—in fact, a gonorrhea treatment; Frick is remembered less as a notorious robber baron, and Ringling as more than a circus impresario. These perspectives were not in the consciousness of the collectors but in being perpetuated by their collections, it is not far fetched to suggest that their individual histories are superseded by their alter ego-collections.

The House Adorned with Collections

The story of the late nineteenth/early twentieth century era of the rich and super rich creating art museum houses to be bequeathed to the public tends to overwhelm the continuity of another strand of collecting practice, in the tradition of Sir Walter Scott's and Sir John Soane's houses. I distinguish them from the trophy-art collectors as individuals whose collecting was driven by more or less idiosyncratic aesthetic tastes, applied to the environment of their houses, in which they constructed a kind of installation artwork: the adorned house. That collecting is integral to the conscious aesthetic of furnishing a house is agreed by the handful of historians of domestic furnishing and decoration, though it's clear that collecting for one's house may rise from diverse inspirations (Praz 1964, 25–26; Rice 2007, 277–82). The meanings of their collections to the collector-inhabitants tend to connect to aestheticism, historicism, nationalist sensibility, and, of course, the ego. It also needs to be stressed that collecting for an adorned house that survives into museumhood is inevitably a function of wealth, though not necessarily in the league of Iveagh and Frick.

Antiquarian tastes inspired most of the house adorners. In the United Kingdom, in 1897, Frank Green, a third-generation scion of an industrial fortune, acquired the house long known as the Treasurer's House, located in the cathedral close of York Minister. Green was thirty-six and unmarried, and for the next thirty years he worked on the structure and its furnishing, presenting it on his retirement to the National Trust. He lived in the house (with a ghostly visitation of Roman legionaries in the basement) and held grand entertainments there; it was a vehicle of social prestige, as well as his passionate hobby (Hilyard 2000, 30). Green "improved" the house's accretion of architectural styles from medieval to early eighteenth century by demolishing nineteenth-century additions and developing a then-novel scheme of period rooms: the Queen Anne Drawing Room, the Tudor Dressing Room, and so forth, plus a central great hall, which he felt certain had been there. The vision required structural remodeling throughout his occupation of the house. His furnishing schemes were the product of continuous buying and selling of antiques and revising wall finishes and textiles, improving and finessing period character. In this, Green was at the forefront of the taste for Old England, bolstered by new expertise in the history of English furniture and decoration. The Treasurer's House was much admired: visited by the Prince of Wales in 1900 and written up in *Country Life* in 1906 and 1922.

Collecting historic furniture in a systematic way to furnish period room settings, as Frank Green did, marks a commitment that would be unfeasible for most householders. The bulk of furniture hinders the possibility of placing more than the number of items one actually needs in the rooms one has available. For where paintings are relatively convenient forms to collect and display, a sequence of chairs, let alone tables or beds, would be impossibly obtrusive in most settings. Even Sir Walter Scott and Sir John Soane, who shaped their houses in antique styles and collected antique objects, bought modern furniture for comfort and convenience in their drawing and dining rooms. The device of the period room to display a collection of furniture in a usable way always remained an unusual choice for collectors. Nonetheless, two canonical collectors' houses grew in the United States in the interwar period, hugely influential in establishing the field of American decorative arts, first among cognoscenti and then as public museums. Another two, similar-but-different adorned houses, deserve reference because their inhabitants wrought what could well be called artwork houses with collections of largely nonelite material.

The first was Henry Mercer's house, Fonthill, in Doyleston, Pennsylvania; it was the product of a systematic approach to collecting, from the 1890s to the 1920s, everyday relics of the preindustrial age. Privately wealthy, Mercer worked at the University of Pennsylvania Museum as curator of prehistoric archaeology. Leaving the museum in middle age, he began to apply archaeological perspectives to collect and study the handmade tools and mundane products of old America, which he valued with an Arts and Crafts ethic. He also took up the almost defunct tradition of Pennsylvania German redware pottery, focusing on decorative glazed terracotta tiles. He opened the Moravian Pottery and Tile Works in 1899, hand press-molding lines of figurative and patterned tiles, "cheap enough to sell and artistic enough to rival the old ones" (Leach 2008). They were widely used in public and private settings, including adorning his own remarkable reinforced concrete castle, Fonthill, completed in 1912. To house his expanding collection, he had a second concrete castle built nearby, seven stories tall, with a multistory atrium surrounded by built-in niches to contain, and fixtures to hang, the collection; it was finished in 1916, though the collection continued to grow. On his death in 1930, Mercer bequeathed this building and its contents to the Bucks County Historical Society, which continues to maintain and open it as the Mercer Museum. He gave a life interest in Fonthill to his housekeeper, who had married the manager of the Tile Works. The house finally came fully into the public domain in 1976, and is managed by the Bucks County Historical Society as a house museum, together with the Mercer Museum.

A more fanciful counterpart was shaped by Charles Paget Wade at Snowshill Manor in the English Cotswolds. He purchased it semiderelict after World War I, funded by family-owned sugar plantations in the Caribbean. The house became the setting for his lifelong collecting of "vanished artefacts," continuously rearranged according to his own principles of "design, colour and workmanship" (Wade 2002, 159). This is essentially an Arts and Crafts agenda but dedicated less to moral living than to profoundly aesthetic play. Wade lived in a cottage in the courtyard, similarly densely decorated and without electricity (though with a large boiler system for heating). He gave his life to adorning the manor house with thematic tableaux and atmospheric fantasy; here he entertained the arty and the literati, often with dress-up charades. Wade transferred the house to the National Trust in 1951, where it continues to captivate visitors.

A similar finely tuned spatial intelligence induced Henry Sleeper—a Boston bohemian affluent enough to build a house and collection, even though he died deep in its debt—to find his metier building and decorating his picturesque summer house, Beauport, in Gloucester, Massachusetts. Here, from 1907, he merged architectural salvage and an interest in American antiques to cast his new house as charmingly old, and themed rooms in period styles in a romantic variation on the Colonial Revival aesthetic (Curtis & Nylander 1990; NPS 2003). Beauport's fame grew first among Sleeper's artistic friends, who included Isabella Stewart Gardner, and then among their friends, creating a fashionable demand for his services as a designer and decorator. The house was profiled in popular magazines such as *House Beautiful*, often presented inaccurately as a restoration and acclaimed for its Americanist character (Riegler 2009). Yet the editor of (US edition) *Country Life* wrote more truly in 1929, "This house is paramount perhaps as a composition. Its creator is more than a mere collector. He is more than an antiquarian. He is at heart an artist" (Townsend 1929, 42). The assertion points to Sleeper's eye for the vernacular and popular interspersed with high style, and artful collections grouped by color, which are still beloved today, that keeps his house among the most popular in the portfolio of Historic New England. That this specimen of an adorned house survived its creator's death in 1934 is due to profound appreciation then and since. It was purchased in toto by Woolworth heiress Helena McCann, who made minimal changes; her heirs donated the house just eight years later to the then–Society for the Preservation of New England Antiquities. Reappearing on the cover of ultrachic *World of Interiors* in 2006, Sleeper's taste continues to address the rhetorical question put by *Country Life* seventy-five years before: "Who can estimate the far-reaching influence that such a house will have upon the taste of a nation?" A primary answer is the democratization of the collector aesthetic in the United States, employing relatively humble antiques and articles of folk culture (Stillinger 2011, 34–35).

Henry Francis du Pont—super-rich fifth generation of the DuPont chemicals fortune—lighted upon his life's work in 1923, having visited Sleeper at Beauport, and pioneer collector of American folk arts, Electra Havemeyer Webb, in Shelburne, Vermont. He engaged Sleeper to help him furnish a new house on Long Island with American antiques, envisaging it as a future museum, and transferred the vision to a new scale when he inherited the family mansion, Winterthur, Delaware, in 1927. Here du Pont added his own Metropolitan Museum–style American wing to the old house, specifically designed for 175 period rooms presenting largely southern regional variations on elite styles (with the exception of a Sleeperesque pine kitchen and an unequalled collection of Pennsylvania Dutch vernacular material). Rooms were shaped by the availability of salvaged paneling and other architectural elements. Du Pont prided himself on archaeologically precise detailing, though he managed to find historic sources to justify changes, exemplified by extending the Montmorenci staircase from a circular, one-story flight to an elliptical, two-story form that met modern building safety regulations (Cantor 1997, 161). Du Pont was not only extremely rich but also lucky to remain rich through the Depression, when many significant pieces came onto a shallow market. Yet he also bid many a record price for items of outstanding quality and provenance, competing with the handful of other major collectors of American furniture.

The combination of conviction and money generated a new canon of American-made decorative arts as masterpieces of a characteristically American aesthetic. Unchallenged as "the greatest collector of his generation," du Pont was acclaimed for his connoisseurship and his flair in arranging each room vignette (Stillinger 1980, 222–27). He and his family lived among the collection (though summering in Long Island and wintering in Florida) until 1951, when they moved into a smaller house on the estate and Winterthur officially opened as a museum. Du Pont continued collecting to add furnished rooms but also developed the infrastructure of a modern museum: air conditioning, authoritative staff and catalogs, a reference library, a conservation studio, a graduate program in decorative arts, a materials conservation program. Today Winterthur stands monumentally at the museum end of the

The Pennsylvania German Room, Winterthur, 1938. H. F. du Pont brought Pennsylvania German vernacular culture to the attention of (largely New England–focused) folk art collectors in the early twentieth century.
Stereo-photo courtesy of the Winterthur Library, Winterthur Archives

spectrum of collectors' house museums, an encyclopedia of the difference of colonial and republican style from European norms.

At another point on the spectrum of adorned houses stands La Cuesta Encantada (the Enchanted Hilltop), now usually known as Hearst Castle, in San Simeon, California. Its patron, William Randolph Hearst, was derided as "the Great Accumulator" by dealer Joseph Duveen, but an era more tolerant of creative pastiche has begun to rehabilitate him as a collector, "extravagant, amusing, intuitive and voracious" (Levkoff 2008, 24). Already a wealthy man, he came into a large inheritance in 1919 and, in the same year, engaged the brilliant, eclectic architect, Julia Morgan, to build a flamboyant country house on a family property. Hearst was already a collector of European architectural salvage, furniture, sculpture, and tapestries, which he envisaged incorporated into a castle and several guesthouses. Morgan proposed Spanish sixteenth-century style, blocky but draped with intricate decoration, enclosing rooms that would incorporate European paneled walls, coffered ceilings, banks of choir stalls, and elaborate chimneypieces. Hearst kept a network of specialist agents who acquired immense quantities of antiques on his behalf; much remained in warehouse storage for years, but all was photographed and cataloged, by which means Morgan selected pieces for use. She described the avalanche of materials arriving continuously at the site; miraculously, she unified them on a luxurious scale into a fantasy suitable for Hearst's Hollywood clique (Kastner 2000). Hearst Castle was a life-long project, but it was only the biggest of five houses the magnate built, and one Welsh castle he purchased in the roaring 1920s—all of them insatiably furnished with the collections.

The expense was colossal, and when the Depression crippled the Hearst Corporation's mining, publishing, and movie empires, Hearst faced financial disaster. Building stopped, and throughout the 1930s the Corporation was restructured, much of it liquidated. Hearst kept his houses and never ceased collecting, but in 1938–1942 his five-story New York warehouse of art, antiques, and antiquities was put to auction and then to sale via the department store Gimbels. Europeans couldn't buy in the war years, and the works realized nothing like their cost, even though the sale made $11,000,000 toward the corporation's debts (Kastner 2000, 186–87). Hearst himself claimed that about half his collections had been sold up. By the end of World War II, his finances had recovered and Hearst made a few further developments to the Castle, where he lived until 1948. His collecting now turned to donations of objects and money to the nascent LA County Museum of Art. After he died in 1951, the Hearst Corporation presented Hearst Castle and practically all its contents to the state of California in 1958; it is now managed by the Department of Parks and Recreation. Hearst's reputation for manipulative media ownership, reactionary politics, outrageous debts, sybaritic luxury, and undisciplined collecting tainted Hearst Castle among commentators for many years, though it never discouraged the visiting public (Harris 2007, 219; Levkoff 2008, 212–21; see also TripAdvisor reviews). Its aura of Hollywood glamour and excess propels Hearst Castle toward the further divide between house museum and theme park: on the other side stands Disneyland's first Sleeping Beauty Castle, opened in 1955. Both constitute peaks of American enchantment.

The Modern Art Collector's House

Jim Ede's house and collection, Kettle's Yard in Cambridge, survives as house museum due to a vision of connecting young people to modern art in homely surrounds. Ede was an arty young man in London in the 1920s, who found junior jobs at the National Gallery and then the Tate Gallery to support his young family, and made a career as "a friend of artists." It enabled him to collect contemporary art on a shoestring by chance, gift, exchange, soft talking, and living very frugally. Thus he gathered small works and drawings by his English modernist friends and their European friends. He took on a role as unofficial curator of contemporary art at the Tate, which he eventually gave up in 1936. The Edes departed for Morocco, later France, and lived by writing and lecturing in the United States. In their early sixties, they returned to England, with a dream of establishing something like Dumbarton Oaks, Washington, DC, an art research library and collection presented to Harvard University in 1947. They came serendipitously to Kettle's Yard in Cambridge, and transformed four derelict cottages into a modest modern home, moving in in 1957. Here Jim held open house from 2 to 4 p.m., inviting students and local artists to drop in to talk art in an informal setting (Ede 1984).

The interior brought a bohemian Mediterranean touch to Osbert Lancaster's bracket of "Cultured Cottage" modernism, the walls hung with small paintings, framed drawings, and domestic-scale sculpture (Lancaster 1939, 62–63). Jim Ede found his element, curating the house with austere sensitivity to light, balance, and stillness. Homely furniture, bookcases of paperbacks, potted plants, and exquisitely placed shells and pebbles—all still in place—add a gently humane resonance to the collection. The Edes presented the whole to Cambridge University in 1966, staying on until retirement in 1973. In that time, Kettle's Yard grew into a beloved local place. It has been carefully enlarged several times, adding galleries for a vigorous program of contemporary exhibitions, as well as education, theater, storage, and administrative spaces. A recent essay concludes with a warm assessment of the place of Kettle's Yard: "Ede was a curator whose judicious sensitivity allowed an understated but exquisite collection to take on a pivotal position in the history of British modernism" (Slingsby 2012).

Jim Ede's story constitutes an idiosyncratic take on the post–World War II trajectory of art collecting. A number of important changes to old patterns emerged in this period (Stourton 2007, 9–11). With Ede a notable exception, thanks to increasing wealth, art collecting has become available to a far wider segment of Western populations, including the cultivated bourgeoisie as well as the super rich. In light of the finite quantum of Old Master paintings, collecting has shifted decisively to contemporary art. And for reasons much less clear, collecting and collections have moved out of the private household into the public domain. Collecting art remains a prestigious activity, sustained by the aura of discerning taste and fortified by the prices of artworks. Most collectors still enjoy their acquisitions at home, but the projection of self that underwrites most collecting is boosted by new public presences, from loans to published catalogs to privately owned public galleries—the so-called ego-seums (Alberge 2010). A handful occupy houses designed as museums, with an eye for conversion to public use at some point in the future. The following example presents a further variation, via a characteristically postmodern conceit.

The Lyon Housemuseum in suburban Melbourne is introduced online as "a combination of museum scaled spaces and residential settings, juxtaposing paintings and installations with the house's living spaces and domestic furniture" (Lyon Housemuseum 2014). Melbourne architect Corbett Lyon began collecting in 1990, guided by an influential dealer to invest in young Australian artists. Ten years later he designed a family house composed around opposite white and black cubes, following the conventions of large, neutral spaces in which to display, respectively, paintings and installation artworks and video art. Conventional domestic spaces wrap around and between the display galleries. Since 2009 the Lyon family has developed a museum-style suite of opening days, currently twice a month; school programs as booked; occasional concerts and lectures; access to a library nook; publications; and biennial turnaround of works. The gesture of regular public access to a private home (paid ticket) is presented as a benevolent act of sharing the pleasures of art; the concept of living in a museum is described as an act of "delineating meaning in art as an integral part of framing and living a life" (van Schaik 2011, 1).

In the larger context of the history of collectors' house museums, it is hard not to see the self-conscious appropriation of the museum as a domestic space fully meriting the label *ego-seum*.

CHAPTER SIX

⌒

Social History House Museums

The tide of social history that began to rise in British and American academe in the 1960s took some twenty years to reach institutional museums, including house museums. But just as conventional, politically framed historiography was already fed by certain streams of economic history and the history of the common people, a few house museums already existed, focusing on the living conditions of the nonelite, the unfamous, the poor, the humble, the insignificant. The wellsprings of this trend were folklife, local history, and postmedieval and colonial archaeology, which rapidly morphed into historical and industrial archaeology. In the second half of the twentieth century, the small world of museums was reshaped, socially, culturally, environmentally, and intellectually. Among the universe of changes, representation of "the common man" took new prominence. Then, in the 1960s–1970s, the historiography of the humble took a startling turn, illuminated by the "new social history." The difference and energy of the new perspective can be characterized, first, by its politically oppositional character, bringing to the fore the historic significance of ordinary people and everyday life, and second, by a social justice agenda aiming to give voice to the historically excluded. Studying the history of the oppressed and suppressed opened up new themes—the poor, the working class, slaves, women, immigrants—to be analyzed with new tools, particularly quantification derived from large bodies of data and the emotional clout of oral history. The findings slowly opened up new kinds of houses for museumization.

Histories are constructed in line with the dominant values of their times. Thus the contexts of historical interest in the common people shifted in the light of twentieth-century social change. The interpretive character of the history of house museums can be observed in the following account, for museums in general react to intellectual shifts rather than initiate them. Museums of all types may be effective in transmitting new ideas to the public and reinforcing their lessons, but they do it more in sync with ideology than at the cutting edge of social change. Hence historic houses found themselves out of step with contemporary directions in historiography, while on the verge of an especially resonant shift in museology. The old genre had been established to focus on histories shaped by elite political interests. They were framed by government, war, and ruling-class culture, perceived in material terms as relics of the great, the expensive apparatus of military technology, and the luxury goods that embellished elite life. In Britain, the chronology of centuries was conceptualized in royal reigns, weighted toward ancient glories, and expressed in the house format of stately homes, described in chapter 8. In the New World, colonials began to reshape the histories that informed museums in the late nineteenth century, having already consigned Indigenous people to the nonhistory of ethnographic museums. Relics of early politics and trophies of European claims to colonized land entered nascent public collections, along with colonial imagery of settlement. House museums developed in the twin perspectives of patriotism associated with national heroes—described in chapters 2 and 3—and white settlement marked by a spreading frontier—described in the vocabularies of vernacular design and grand family houses in chapters 4 and 8. This chapter addresses the impact of the new social history and its predecessor modes of folklore/folklife and industrial/historical archaeology by tracing their interpretive focuses.

Folklife and Archaeology as Frames of History in House Museums
House museums before World War II addressed history almost entirely in the Carlylean mode of honoring heroes for their exceptional qualities in shaping or saving the nation. In Britain, common people played a minimal role in this narrative, beyond gratitude and admiration for the norms established by heroic individuals. In the United States, however, the sense of a national history achieved by the agency of the common man had been a fulcrum of ideological positions since the Revolution. Hence a culture of valorizing the founding fathers and other pioneers as Everyman (and occasionally Everywoman) motivated a collecting and exhibiting genre from the mid-nineteenth century onward of personal and domestic goods that represented humble folk in the public sphere. The egalitarian potential of this history

made by the common man had significant consequences for American interest in the history of unaristocratic houses and furnishings. It enabled the relics and dwellings of practically anonymous people to be honored in civic view, in ways that preceded the invention of national history museums in the British world. Indeed, the history of exhibiting domestic assemblages of unassuming old furniture, often under the title "New England kitchen" to represent the values of the good old days, can be traced as a proto-museum display of common people's lives (see, for example, the 1907 period rooms in the Essex Institute, Salem). These modest spectacles began as fund-raising events organized by women's committees to make money for Union veteran relief during and after the Civil War. The patriotic capacity of the "kitchen" trope ignited adoption by subsequent generations of women's associations, a story picked up later in this chapter.

Interior of the New England Kitchen at the Centennial International Exposition, Philadelphia, 1876. The (spacious) one-room log cabin built for the purpose at the Exposition was well endowed with windows for good viewing of the American Everywoman's domestic history.
Steel engraving in *Frank Leslie's Illustrated Historical Register of the United States Centennial Exposition, 1876* (New York, 1877), 90.

At the same time around the turn of the twentieth century, new social science disciplines were taking specialist shape to articulate the study of society—among them, anthropology, archaeology, and folklore, all with some degree of historical perspective. As modes of knowledge production, they overlapped in concepts and techniques that enabled systematic study of unremarkable people and mundane lives, and were particularly applicable to the central museum business of material culture. In practice, the embryonic disciplines that contained possibilities for understanding history as the product of the common man were variously taken up, based on exposure and opportunity as much as intellectual or political conviction. To write now about folklore, anthropology, and archaeology in this formative era constructs an apparently inevitable rationale, which cannot be sustained much beyond the purpose to illustrate how modern ideas about history became relevant in the modest sphere of house museums. But with this aim and its limits in mind, the following discussion traces the similar yet different circumstances in which the exhibition of houses as museums of history took shape.

Folklore-folklife manifested out of older fields of popular antiquarianism in the early to mid-nineteenth-century period, and gradually professionalized in the early twentieth century. On respective sides of the Atlantic, practitioners investigated ancient Celts and Romans, and ancient Indians and Puritans, simultaneously contributing to the emergent distinctions between archaeology and anthropology as well as folklore. In its modern substance, folklore studies traced the histories of "surviving" cultural identities, largely in the expressive media of mythic, oral literatures, and to a lesser degree in practices of belief that often generated material production. The first generations of theoretically informed research have since been dissected for glosses of exoticism, nostalgia, nationalism, and racism, and the same values also imbued the popular sphere of interest in folklore-folklife. This was the register in which items of housing and daily life came to be collected by amateurs and exhibited in context, in room and house museum re-creations. Some of these gradually took on modern professional museum standing.

The typological lens of British folklife study at this time was "bygones," which decisively cast folklife in the past as preindustrial and rural. Bygones came into focus in contrast with the urbanizing, industrializing developments of the late eighteenth- and early nineteenth-century period, culminating in the popular taste for Olde England at the turn of the twentieth century. Collecting bygones occupied a spectrum of activity from hobby to obsession. Its most prolific practitioner, Dr. John Kirk of Pickerings, Yorkshire, made commercial and domestic bygones the core of what is now the York Castle Museum. He gave his collection to the City of York on the promise of display space in the old Female Prison and installed it there in period room settings and novel streetscapes where masses of objects can be viewed, set in late Victorian shop windows. The exhibitionary device of "Kirkgate" has been much copied, and the original revised several times since it opened in 1938, most recently in 2012. By today's standards, Kirk was a collector of the vacuum-cleaner school; he kept few notes on sources, locations, or provenance. The enduring value of his collection and its display owes much to the retro-application of social history perspectives on material culture—a revisionist process that was widely applied to old house museums and their collections in the last decades of the twentieth century.

Models of collecting practice began to shift from the antiquarian to the systematic at the National Museum of Wales, where from 1927 Iorwerth Peate began to catalog what were known as "the folk collections." Initially a subset of archaeology, folklife material became a museum department in 1936, and expanded into the St. Fagan's Folk Museum in 1948 (having been interrupted by World War II). Peate had already published *The Welsh House: A Study in Folk Culture* (1940), and he began to develop a museum of traditional housing forms and other structures, including late medieval rural houses and a row of iron-workers' houses of about 1800. The St. Fagan's program generally followed Scandinavian open-air museum mode, presenting discourses of "craft" and "folk" to define the folklife approach to history. These tended to constrain folklore studies to regions with particularly distinctive folk cultures, especially indicated by language, such as the first folklife museum in Britain, Henry Kelley's cottage in Creagneash on the Isle of Man, opened in 1938 (Kavanagh 1990, 24–27).

Concepts of folk culture collecting and museumization took a different trajectory in the United States. Here, the prehistoric diversity of Indigenous peoples, and the multiculture of immigrants, prompted investigations by amateurs and proto-professionals that fed the disciplined advent of folklore, archaeology, and anthropology, with characteristic collecting outcomes. The interpretation of American Indian cultures located them as ethnographic others in prehistory, suitable for anthropology or natural history museums. By contrast, those European settlers arriving in America in the preindustrial era, who reestablished traditional cultures in cohesive, rural communities, could be understood as premodern within the United States and hence fodder for folklore. As such communities declined under the pressures of modernization, the more attractive of their material productions underwent an aestheticization in certain arty circles, becoming recognized and collected as folk art in the mid- to late nineteenth century (Stillinger 2011). At the same time, the cultures of enslaved Africans, having been construed as primitive to begin with and crudely hybrid to follow, occupied a blind spot in the national consciousness, even to ethnographers. Having been ruthlessly suppressed and held in bondage without possessions for two centuries, black American slave life remained outside the idea of collectable culture until folklorists of the post-Emancipation era began to recognize the immense black oral culture of story and music. But no museum systematically collected vernacular black material culture until the 1970s (Vlach 1991, xiii–xvii).

Hence the homely bygones that represented folk culture in the United Kingdom were less collected as "folk" products than as historic relics in the United States, except within the mindset of folk art. Meanwhile, the diffuse relationship between folklore and archaeology enabled museum-based investigators to consider material culture found in historic, aboveground contexts as knowledge equivalents to that from prehistoric or anthropological excavations. While never a large branch of research in the turn of the twentieth-century period in the United Kingdom or the United States, its practitioners generated some notable intellectual achievements that informed the concept of home-based history exhibited in houses.

Henry Chapman Mercer, a wealthy scion of old Philadelphia, constitutes an exceptional specimen of this proto-disciplinary connection. He made an intellectual switch from the archaeology of prehistoric tools with the University of Pennsylvania Museum to privately collecting the preindustrial tools of Bucks County, Pennsylvania (Reed 2000). In the 1890s–1900s Mercer resuscitated the nearly extinct tradition of Pennsylvania German redware pottery by opening the Moravian Pottery and Tile Works in Doylestown to produce press-molded tiles, with historic, patriotic, and naturalistic motifs, happily appealing to the Arts and Crafts aesthetic of the time. These he used to decorate a new house, Fonthill Castle (1908–1912), and a museum, the Mercer Museum (1913–1916), both constructed of exposed, reinforced concrete in an idiosyncratic style. Mercer described his work as archaeology and never used the term *folk*; he regarded his collections as objective evidence of the history of eastern Pennsylvania, recovered through techniques of typological analysis. Its significance for museum historiography was a vision of history made by the common man, cataloged and presented under the title "Tools of the Nation-Maker." Mercer died in 1930. He left his museum and his house (they are about a mile apart) in trust to the Bucks County Historical Society, with a life interest in the house to his works manager and his housekeeper. The latter died in 1975, when Fonthill Castle also came into the public domain as a house museum under the mantle of the historical society. Considered as a whole, the museum and the castle could be analyzed as a collector's house and as an artwork, an adorned house. It is presented in this chapter as a house museum that presents a thread of historical understanding of the common people because Mercer himself so envisaged it. In this light it demonstrates a discourse that was to become influential in the house museumscape, even though Fonthill itself came relatively late to public awareness.

More influential in constructing a practice of everyman history buttressed by archaeology and folklore studies were the great historical villages that opened in the 1930s: Colonial Williamsburg, Greenfield Village, Old Sturbridge Village, Historic Deerfield. The concept of the village format focused primarily on buildings, and houses in particular, as media for the interpretation of American history via the experience of everyday people. Colonial Williamsburg has been extensively documented as a history museum authenticated by its original location and fabric, and even though its intellectual history is less well known, it constitutes the exemplary interwar case of the meeting of the new disciplines to construct historical knowledge via houses and other built structures. Writing about the early deployment of archaeology on the site, one expert prefers to describe it as "unstructured excavation" in support of architectural research (Poole 2001). This may have been rudimentary archaeology, but the Williamsburg project began literally to construct a history authorized by old walls in situ, genuine antique furniture, and portraits of the forefathers. These items of material reality presented visitors with evident guarantees of the Revolutionary foundation myth. Folklore, or rather folk art, was also present in the first period of Williamsburg reconstruction, though more thanks to Rockefeller patronage than curatorial intent. Abby Aldrich Rockefeller, wife of the project's benefactor, had taken up the folk art taste in the early 1930s, and she installed some of her collection—mainly portraits—in the Ludwell-Paradise house from 1935. When she died in 1948, having gifted the collection formally, her husband recognized that it represented the early nineteenth century rather than the 1770s of the Restoration (as the site was known to its staff) and established a new museum outside the historic area as the Abby Aldrich Rockefeller Folk Art Collection, later Museum. The place of the "folk" in the Williamsburg vision remained artisanal for another thirty years.

The historical values presented there deftly appropriated the Revolutionary past to reinforce contemporary conservative narratives. At the same time, thanks to their scale and relatively liberal funding, the historic villages became the breeding and proving grounds of professional practice in managing historic houses as a form of museum. The villages and their counterpart solo house museums took shape as responses to American circumstances and values, and these can be tracked in the history of house museums established by women's lineage societies.

Patriotic Visions of American Identity

The concept that the ancestors of America were fundamentally Everyman, and that his efforts were central to every beginning from the Pilgrim Fathers to the Patriots of the Revolution to both sides of the Civil War, mobilized a very different cast of characters than was possible in the Old World. Everyman became available as the exemplary hero of the nation. This resource was seized by the host of women's lineage associations—northern, southern, and black—that adopted the cause of promoting American nationalism (as each group understood it) in the post–Civil War period, and for the next fifty years. The moral and cultural authority allowed to middle-class women promoted activism, whose nationalist element soon came to focus on patriotic monuments and practices. Prominent among them was the establishment of historic house museums (West 1999; Morgan 2005). Seizing on the elision

The Oliver Ellsworth Homestead, Windsor, Connecticut, c. 1910s. The "spinning room" exhibits the arch-emblem of colonial female virtue, the spinning wheel, displayed with further rural and domestic equipment to emphasize the impression of proper industry. This postcard was published by the Daughters of the American Revolution, Connecticut chapter, which still operates the house museum.
Postcard, private collection.

of "house" and "home" and the double application of "home" to family and nation, houses were museumized from the 1880s to the 1930s at a tremen-dous rate. The Mount Vernon Ladies Association had modeled the peak of success. It was copied by proponents who deployed the universalist aura of Everyman, filtered by native-born ancestry claims, to establish the ideal of representative patriotism. Two in particular developed large portfolios of house museums managed by local chapters, as well as supporting other groups to open historic houses: the Daughters of the American Revolution (DAR), established in 1890, and the more exclusive National Society of the Colonial Dames of America (NSCDA), founded a year later.

A fiftieth anniversary survey of the DAR's historic houses in 1941 re-corded more than two hundred houses of historic significance owned by local chapters, plus a further fifty managed on behalf of city and state agencies (Barrington 1941). Some had belonged to gentlemen—for example, Grouse-land, Vincennes, Indiana, built in 1804 as the home of William Henry Har-rison, governor of Indiana Territory (and later, short-lived ninth president of the United States). A local DAR chapter acquired the house in 1911 and furnished it; in 1999 it was leased to a new foundation to maintain viability in a broader community (Sarell 2010). Others belonged to plain Ameri-cans—for example, the log cabin in Owosso, Michigan, built for lawyer Elias Comstock in 1836, purchased by a DAR group in 1920 to exhibit domestic relics of early settlers. Some houses achieved complete scenarios of period rooms; others contained random antiquarian collections. The majority of such houses (including the Comstock cabin, which still stands) disappeared as museums, but in the first half of the twentieth century they amounted to a visible and influential body of house museums. By museumizing dwell-ings generally more distinguished for their antiquity than their inhabitants, the DAR transferred the ethos of the hero's house to the simpler mode of demotic ancestor veneration. Ancestors define smaller communities than heroes, but their less exceptional public stature brings them very close to the imagination of the common man in the present. Celebrated in domestic settings, the other constituents of family—female, young, and old—were also enabled to occupy legitimate places in national history.

Meanwhile, the National Park Service had been established in 1916 with a focus on wilderness preservation and "scenic nationalism" (Bodnar 1992, 170). It was early responsible for a small number of historic sites (such as Winsor Castle, Pipe Spring National Monument, a ranch house in north-west Arizona fortified against Indians in the 1860s). Not until 1933 did the organization focus seriously on history when it acquired responsibility for all federal historic sites. The NPS maintained a strong patriotic agenda constituted by a portfolio of battlefields, cemeteries, and monuments. An increasingly professional staff approached the growing historic holdings with the embryonic apparatus of cultural resource management: thematic criteria for selecting sites; a commitment to public education; deliberate interpretive goals; research-led reconstructions; historic structure reports; and museum technology for powerful communication. The need to coordinate operations across a far-spread estate demanded systematizing concepts. The organization's perspective on its continent-wide suite of historic sites framed a strongly nationalist interpretive vision, populated by the foot soldiers, as well as the heroes, of American history. Themes to address the educational role of historic places had to be big enough to be flexible as well as specific: exploration and settlement; development of the early colonies; westward expansion, as well as wars and government. In these lights, the apparatus of NPS knowledge production in the 1930s took shape in the *Field Manual for Museums*. A chapter dedicated to historic house museums articulated the requirement that house histories should be interpreted to connect to the large themes of American history, either as an exemplar of lifestyle—by association with a great American—or as the scene of "epochal or dramatic" events. If furnished, they should be in styles consistent with the period of historic significance; the furniture was to be placed as if for use rather than display; and the whole was to be interpreted by guides or guidebooks rather than labels (Burns 1941, 255–59). Such prescriptions required the engagement of academically trained historians with a vision of the interpretive potential of material culture.

Tensions between the DAR and the NPS approaches to house museums illustrate the emerging split between antiquarian sensibility and professional mentality, exemplified in the case of Moore House, Yorktown, Virginia. In 1781, in the drawing room of this modest plantation house, the terms were negotiated for the British surrender to the colonial patriots, and hence the end of fighting the American Revolution. With this association, the house became a key site of Colonial National Park, a triangle between Yorktown, Jamestown, and Williamsburg. The house was restored in 1931–1934, and a careful furnishing plan was researched to interpret it. When the DAR offered to furnish the Surrender Room, the NPS anticipated cash donations to buy the appropriate antiques. The women of the DAR, however, envisaged a more personal selection by individuals who would give fine pieces of furniture. Despite a curator's inventory of the right kind of material, the room was ceremoniously opened in 1938 with more, and more elaborate, items than historical research showed would have been likely. NPS staff gave in gracefully to the ladies (Lewis 1993, 223–26).

The visual language of a house furnished in such heady old style fed the consumer appetite to join in by adopting its forms. The more obsessive end of the spectrum of patriotic taste sought American antiques to furnish their lives in the national values. Those who appreciated modern comforts as well as a nationalist aura could buy the Colonial Revival in both house design and furnishings. Stylish goods being at the dearer end of the price spectrum, living a colonial-style life was a choice for those with discretionary income. It was also the prerequisite for a car in which to tour the colonial landscape and inspect house museums. This market responded eagerly to Colonial Williamsburg's offerings of licensed reproduction pieces, launched in 1936. (Now more concerned with items inspired by eighteenth-century taste, it continues to bring in a helpful stream of profit, as well as satisfying visitor desires to connect themselves with Williamsburg values.)

Impact of Archaeology after World War II

The traumas of the world wars precipitated two critical outcomes in the history of house museum representation of the nonelite in the United Kingdom. The first was the peri-nationalization of the stately homes of the aristocracy (presented more fully in chapter 8); counterintuitively, this eventually opened an interpretive route to "downstairs" life, discussed further on. The second was the new directions forged by postwar archaeology, which in the course of reconstruction revealed individual specimens of vernacular antiquity and large landscapes of industrial working-class experience, including housing.

"Postmedieval" (assertively nonclassical) archaeology played a new role in the reconstruction of bombed cities and the provision of new housing estates in postwar Britain. Reconstruction exposed, frequently destroyed, sometimes rescued, and in the long run permanently altered popular attitudes toward nonelite heritage. Archaeological techniques began to be applied in some rescue and development situations, such that in the 1960s, industrial archaeology and building archaeology were claimed as new disciplinary specializations. They constituted and were constituted by the rising idea of "heritage" as a category of incorporating and managing the past in the present. Their products were expressed in individually museumized buildings, in museums of relocated buildings, and in entire museumized sites. As had occurred in the United States, the large sites assembled the critical mass of opportunity and expertise, and thus became seedbeds of practice and theory and later of formal training and education. Museumized houses in these environments were inexplicitly understood as the history of people's lives, for the major interpretive direction in this time of technological upheaval was toward industrial and manufacturing themes, as illustrated by the following cases.

The Weald and Downland Open Air Museum in West Sussex began in the mid-1960s as a rescue operation conducted by a group of enthusiasts of local vernacular timber structures. Its founding genius, Roy Armstrong, ascribed his motivation to observing the loss of a fourteenth-century hall house enclosed in an anonymous farmhouse in the course of postwar Crawley New Town development (Leslie 1990). The group obtained a site on the West Dean estate in 1966 and began to acquire the dismantled timbers of various medieval structures; it opened formally in 1969 with seven buildings, mainly houses. The museum's success is outstanding, set in a contextualizing vision of the South Downs landscape, rural life and industry, and research and training programs in the conservation of historic timber structures. A costumed interpreter ethic, partly inspired by experimental archaeology and partly by the Scandinavian tradition of open-air museums, has now informed visitors for many years, and merges seamlessly with modern social history display modes. The museum has motivated and informed the conservation and museumization of many further ancient vernacular houses.

Dismantling Bayleaf Farm in situ, Chiddington, Kent, 1968. Built in the early 1400s for tenant farmers, Bayleaf Farm was reconstructed in 1972 at the Weald and Downland Open Air Museum. Now furnished with reproductions, it is activated by costumed interpreters undertaking ordinary domestic business.
Photo courtesy of the Weald and Downland Open Air Museum, near Chichester.

On the industrial heritage front, thanks to systematic regional planning, the historic significance of the Ironbridge area in Shropshire was recognized and preserved as a cradle of key elements of the Industrial Revolution. It was acknowledged as a cultural resource via the development of Telford New Town, leading to the creation in 1968 of the Ironbridge Gorge Museum Trust. When the site opened to visitors in 1973, it centered on the iron-smelting and iron-casting village of Coalbrookdale, and its most famous product, the 1781 Iron Bridge. By 1986, when Ironbridge was inscribed on the World Heritage List, the Trust managed 375 listed buildings, seven Scheduled Ancient Monuments, and two Sites of Special Scientific Interest. The largest were furnaces, factories, and warehouses, now transformed into museums. Over the years, terraced housing for industrial workers was also introduced to display, as was a grander house of the ironmaster Darby family. In the framework of presenting a "landscape of industry," workers and their families constituted one of a package of fundamental interpretive themes. Others include the geology that provided raw materials, the river that formed communication and transport links as well as a power source, and the "industrial vernacular" buildings housing industrial activity and its human workers (Alfrey & Clark 1993). Archaeologically meticulous standards of investigation and documentation fed a range of management and interpretive strategies, including stabilization, conservation, restoration, and adaptive reuse. This suite of treatments came to define the developing field of cultural heritage management, with repercussions for historic house museums in the following decades.

The rising profile of the industrial past had also stimulated local historical groups throughout Britain to take action to preserve sites endangered by the pace of postwar reconstruction. Several small-scale industries, in which machines occupied the upper floor of tenement houses, were museumized by volunteers in the 1960s and early 1970s in Newtown, Powys; Golcar, West Yorkshire; Ruddington, Nottinghamshire; and Kilbarchan, Scotland. Larger industrial sites such as Quarry Bank Mill near Manchester, and New Lanark near Glasgow, were museumized at the same time, though their large scale required long periods of gradual restoration. Quarry Bank, a water-powered cotton spinning mill established in 1784, early drew on "apprentice" labor— in reality, abandoned children, rehoused in a dedicated residence beside the mill. The mill and much of the estate closed in 1959, having been given to the National Trust. The stark Apprentice House was opened in the 1980s to depict the children's lives. In the 2010s the Trust moved to display one of the units of worker housing constructed in the 1820s and 1830s in the village of Styal, and to open the mill owner Greg family house.

In all these sites, housing was prominent—indeed, integral—in the meaning of the conserved structures. The relationship of loom chamber to spartan living quarters, and of factory to company housing, made the connection between family or child labor and industrial production in unadorned terms. It both presaged and informed the social history turn on the museum horizon. As specimens of the realities of economic history, these worker cottages, tenements, and boardinghouses demonstrated historical contexts more pointed than most house museums of the time. It might be said they showed that economic history was practically indistinguishable from social history.

The case of Lowell, Massachusetts, demonstrates the history of the museumization of redundant, historic industrial infrastructure in the United States. In particular for the purpose of this chapter, sites at Lowell display the role of archaeology in legitimizing the site through scholarship. The city's vast textile industries, founded in the 1820s and surging throughout the nineteenth century, had slumped from the 1920s. Post–World War II urban renewal focused at first on "slum" clearance and the demolition of abandoned factories, but in the 1970s it was redirected to the possibility of preservation as the vehicle of city revitalization. A vision of Lowell's ethnic working-class heritage, and the mobilization of federal government funds by an influential senator, paved the way for the National Park Service to develop its first urban park in 1978 (Weible 2011). Archaeological works undertaken in the 1980s and 1990s were specifically framed to investigate class differences between skilled and unskilled mill workers, and the supervisory and managerial segment of overseers and company agents (Mrosowski, Ziesing, & Beaudry 1996). In practice, the findings took a low profile. The canal system that powered machinery and transported goods had been identified as significant technological heritage, and preserving it became the focus of the site's operations. Remaining factory buildings were gradually rehabilitated, and infill for modern-standard living and services was constructed, funded by private capital. New industries were attracted to the city and thrived in the 1980s, drawing in new and newer generations of immigrant workers. The surviving Boott Cotton Mill was equipped with 1920s looms and a museum of Lowell's industrial history, and a boarding house with re-creations of mill girl housing in the 1840s period opened in 1989. In the economic field of urban development, Lowell emerged as a notable demonstration of the compatibility of development with preservation. On a micro scale, historians have criticized the NPS emphasis on technology at the expense of human histories that carry the confronting politics of labor, gender, and ethnicity (Blewett 1989, 281; Weible 2011, 91–92). Nonetheless, Lowell National Historical Park was profoundly influential in applying social history perspectives to museumizing the span of industrial buildings, including housing.

The New Social History Reaches House Museums

In the long run, it has not been found easy to deploy the fundamental museum practice of making material histories into the field of social history (Fleming, Paine, & Rhodes 1993, 6, 9, 28). In the United Kingdom, the shift was marked by the emergence of the Social History Curators Group in 1982. Looking back on thirty-five years of activity, SHCG members claimed that social historians led the way in the democratization of museums, with a focus on working-class history that gradually broadened into comprehensive local history (Broadbent 2012; Fleming 2012). In the United States, the social history perspective was strongly promoted by the American Association for State and Local History (AASLH). Its monthly magazine *History News* began to carry articles, usually by academics, advocating women's and black people's history in museums (e.g., Pleck 1982; Buchanan 1984). Fewer, but enthusiastic, were case studies of house museums de-romanticizing their history and planning more inclusive interpretation (e.g., Floyd 1981).

By the early 1980s, social history had begun to percolate from universities into historic sites and museums, largely carried by graduates moving into the growing professional domains of heritage and museums. The focus on ordinary people's lives and its viewpoint of "history from the bottom up" resonated intellectually and politically, launching new themes for exhibition and interpretation—if relevant objects could be located. Collections in the tradition of "bygones" constituted a reservoir of the more nostalgic types of the material culture of everyday life. At the same time, the absence of the material culture of the marginal and the powerless launched proactive and contemporary collecting. Sound specimens often proved challenging to locate, since goods were contingently scarce among people with few or no resources. Whatever they owned tended to be used up, worn out, or passed on, lacking the quality or prestige to warrant the long-term keeping that eventually fills museums. Curators developed new analytical techniques, such as reading objects "against the grain" to expose traces of the excluded in existing collections (e.g., a linen tablecloth could be one woman's dowry and another woman's daily work) and "reading in" the maker or user of a surviving item (e.g., a hand-sewn shirt could represent a wretched seamstress's life as well as an immigrant's wardrobe for a new world). Historic photographs and oral histories proved especially eloquent in presenting social history in museums but, in doing so, made the point that social history works more effectively in museums as an interpretive stance than as a field of collecting.

On the house museum front, the fundamental shortage of the dwellings of the marginal challenged the mobilization of social history. While collections of the material culture of labor, gender, and race have grown, much of their evidentiary power depends on context and provenance—in other words, on the personal stories they illuminate. Much the same pots and pans communicate different histories in the contexts of the kitchen of a great house or of a log cabin, as the property of a widowed laundress or of an aspirationally genteel woman, or located in late eighteenth-century Scotland or mid-nineteenth-century California. A growing focus on interpretive "stories" aimed simultaneously to introduce the agency of ordinary individuals and to contextualize them via the new historiography. Usually generated in universities, social history drew especially on statistical techniques powered by computerized analysis of the records of social control (censuses, court documents, institutional reports), employment (factory wage books, business accounts, military rolls), and property (rate and rent books, inventories). Such records made both typical and exceptional individual cases visible, and statistics showed trends that reshaped understandings of common people's lives. The Marxist perspective on labor as the source of the wealth that supports material existence and shapes consciousness was especially apt in uncovering the history of working people. Further, its political dimension of restorative justice for the fundamental creators of wealth resonated with the rise of social justice and identity politics. Throughout the 1980s, though none too fast, the social history paradigm and its findings infused new themes into historic house interpretation. In the frame of house and home, the theme of labor inevitably focused on women's work, as determined by class distinctions within the domestic environment. In the United States, domestic labor encompassed the further suppressed history of enslaved people. Now the demand for the museum history of both women and the enslaved was invigorated by new research and strengthened by the contemporary politics of civil rights.

As to be expected, social history on the theme of the everyday life and work of women took root early on in house museums. The domestic sphere was always a female domain, but female historic invisibility was (and is still) projected in the very title of many a house museum by presenting the house as a man's property rather than a gendered workplace—for example, Blundell's Cottage (in Canberra, Australia, to take an example close to my heart) could be (but isn't) presented restoratively as "Flora and George Blundell's Cottage," the site of an immigrant tenant farmer-couple's married life. Within house museums, representations of women's real span of work were (and often continue to be) frozen in the conventions of kitchen and nursery. The social history difference is less in the furnishing of these spaces than in the interpretation of the work that took place in them and the social relations between workers and other inhabitants. Explicitly feminist insights into women's labor are still scarce, though not as challenging to the popular imagination as they might have been in the 1980s. Also still rarely presented are the physical labor of reproduction; the social labor of child socialization; the emotional labor of palliating the stresses of male work outside the home (sometimes extending to violent victimization); the economic labor of making cash out of small businesses like poultry and boarders; and the symbolic labor of representing family honor through religious observance, cleanliness, and manners. Such histories—truly, herstories—cannot speak through furnishings alone.

One aspect is taking a higher profile, slowly. In a 1970 brochure, *Tips on Living History Demonstrations*, a NPS writer doubted that visitors to a Virginia mansion "would accept interpretation from a domestic." He used the feminine pronoun and entirely suppressed the possibility of a woman or man of color in the role (Kay 1970, 22). Yet the presence of employed women workers in domestic settings soon furnished a vigorous new trope in house museums: the history of servants became visible. Visitors were perhaps primed by the success of the television series *Upstairs, Downstairs*, shown around the world from 1971 to 1975. In the United Kingdom, two National Trust country house properties opened service rooms to the public in the early 1970s, though more as documents in themselves than with social history–informed interpretation to hand. "Probably the first kitchen to be shown by the National Trust" emerged at Cotehele in Cornwall in the 1970s, reconstructed according to an engraving of the 1840s, and an unusual collection of servant portraits and biographical records kept by the Yorke family inspired the interpretive direction of Erddig, Wales, established in 1973 and carried through to this day, where visits commence in the service outbuildings and move on through the servants' work rooms toward the stately apartments of the owners (Waterson 2011, 79, 195–96). The social history difference between these examples and one of the few published accounts of the process is demonstrated by house curator Patricia West's efforts in 1984 to show how integral was the labor of a laundress and a ruffle iron to the political reputation of President Martin Van Buren. The program at Van Buren's house, Lindenwald, near Albany, New York, was resisted by house trustees as a secondary and trivial story (West 1986, 91; West 2014).

The kitchen at Cotehele, Cornwall, 1997. The kitchen was re-created with reproduction items in the 1990s. It is based on a drawing by Cornish artist Nicholas Condy, one of sixteen lithographic plates in a guidebook to Cotehele, undated but published in the 1840s. Photo by Andreas von Einsiedel, 1997, courtesy of National Trust Images.

More than twenty years later, another house curator began to survey the interpretation of domestic service at post–Civil War house museums (Pustz 2010). She traced a rising practice of interpreting servants in the 1990s but found that even in the mid-2000s, the theme of domestic service lacked critical approaches. Exhibits and stories still privileged house-owner families, and kitchens (the most frequently presented servants' room) were displayed in static, period room mode. Many guides resisted the starker realities of social history stories, just as they hesitated over the blunt term *servant*, often preferring the euphemisms *help* or *hired girl*. Individual site histories contained plenty of evidence of immigration and ethnicity, but the stories of servants told on tours were composed more around quaint domestic technology than around servants' living conditions, and least around working conditions. Jennifer Pustz's informants noted that visitors reacted positively to interpreta-

tion of the servant dimension in house museums, perhaps because they iden‐
tified more with servants than with rich house owners (2010, 39–67). Her
findings underline the necessity of presenting a deliberate and well-informed
story line to carry counternarratives to the mythic "warm parlour of the past"
(Bickford 1985). But, as people familiar with house museum interpretation
will acknowledge, the thirty to sixty minutes of a guided tour, and the word
limits of brochure text for self-guiding, constrain the depth and complexity
of information that can be provided to visitors. Hence the popularity and
utility of audio-visual orientation before the site visit begins.

Pustz proposes a handful of techniques to remedy slight or uncritical
presentations of domestic service, illustrated by case studies. An important
preliminary is to reclaim servants' spaces for public access. The lesser rooms
of museumized houses only too easily become offices and storage, thus per‐
petuating the invisibility of the service side of a historic household. She
demonstrates how tours presented from servants' perspectives can dispute the
master narrative of households wealthy enough to buy in service. Restorative
interpretation strategies include personalizing the role of the house guide as
a servant, who can cast information about "upstairs" and "downstairs" condi‐
tions as a different discourse to that of the master or mistress of the house.
Offering specifically themed "behind the scenes" or "nooks and crannies"
tours can also be a convenient mode of presenting rooms and contents at the
margins of the big histories of many houses; they may be less frequent than
regular tours, adding to the attractive sense of broaching what is generally
hidden. Yet another strategy flows from a museum management commitment
to represent equally the lives of all house inhabitants, as illustrated by a long
program of research and grant funding to implement changes at Maymont in
Richmond, Virginia. Reviewers on travel websites describe appreciation of
this kind of detail; their oft-noted familiarity with another British TV series,
Downton Abbey (shown globally between 2010 and 2015), might explain
why they don't realize how unusual it is in house museum practice.

In the United States, the goal of equal representation contains the bitter
struggle of race in every aspect of life and history. In the 1970s, social his‐
tory methods applied to the records of slavery via quantification based on
sales, legal and tax documents, and identifying personal details in plantation
diaries and slave narratives, and they began to produce radical new histo‐
ries of American slavery. They contested racist dogma, wishful myth, and
euphemism, but like other aspects of the black struggle for civil rights, the
evidence of revisionism was and is acknowledged selectively by individuals
and institutions. The reality is painful: that the white institution of slavery
denied black humanity and degraded people to chattels; that free Americans

of North and South owned slaves; that even a few free black people owned slaves; and that the plantation economy of the South depended on enslaved labor. It is unsurprising that to address the history of slavery in house museums was resisted and suppressed; the shame is that it largely continues to be so (Grim 2015, 47–63).

Many houses of the arch-heroes of the United States, the presidents, exemplify the dilemma. At its crux is the contradiction that patriots in the cause of the freedom of all men could be slaveholders. The Mount Vernon Ladies Association avoided the inconsistency by focusing on the republican virtues of George Washington rather than his ownership of enslaved people. Not until 1949, when archaeologists were called on to identify the location of Washington's greenhouse for reconstruction, did the question arise of the structure's two wings, which were shown to be barracks-style slave quarters. Other quarters composed of cottages had stood nearby and out on the plantation lands. These could be held to have been the cozy cabins of popular myth, but four large dormitories, apparently lined with built-in bunk beds, cast such an unsympathetic light on the president that the MVLA preferred to use the space for the shop, archaeological finds, offices, and storage space. Even one room sparsely furnished in 1951 remained undisplayed until 1962, ten years after the reconstruction of the building. Not until 2010 were the other uses of the greenhouse wings displaced and the dwelling barracks reinstated (Pogue 2004, 2010). Meanwhile, a single representative log cabin for a slave family was constructed on the farm site in 2007. The tide of popular demand for the acknowledgment of George Washington (and Martha Washington, in her own right) as owners of enslaved people had also been addressed, in 1983, with a memorial on the site of the slave cemetery; an archaeological survey of the cemetery began in 2014. The topic of slavery is now treated via dedicated tours of the site and substantial online coverage.

Archaeology had also been the vehicle of making public the presence of enslaved workers at Monticello, where a slave quarter named Mulberry Row was excavated in 1957 and 1979, and again in the 1990s–2000s. The excruciating case of Thomas Jefferson as the author of the Declaration of Independence, with its invocation of men's freedom, equality, and right to life and liberty, had long been disturbed by claims that the widowed Jefferson fathered the children of a young enslaved woman, Sally Hemings. Exemplifying the jarring stages of how a presidential house museum adapted to shifting politics buttressed by social history is the story of how the Thomas Jefferson Foundation ignored the charge for many years but eventually embraced it. A genetic investigation undertaken in 1998, and a subsequent historical research review, convinced the foundation to acknowledge the profound ramifications of African American presence at Monticello with incorporation in site interpretation, specialist tours, and continuing archaeology of the slave quarter, as well as homecoming visits by Jefferson's formal and informal descendants. Historian of the presentation of slavery, Lois Horton, suggests that the frank recognition of interracial relations actively enhanced public regard for the site (L. Horton 2006).

Mount Vernon and Monticello, focusing on houses, outhouses, and their landscapes, demonstrate the effects of late twentieth-century shifts in presenting social history at significant houses. The barometer of the winds of social history can also be tracked usefully in two great institutions, Colonial Williamsburg and the National Park Service, which deal with grand as well as humble houses. As large, old organizations, they contain notable evidence of eras of thinking about historical presentation in the light of experience.

Colonial Williamsburg's first in-house interpretation document, "Teaching History at Colonial Williamsburg: A Plan of Education," was introduced by research head Cary Carson in 1982, under the theme "Becoming Americans," explained as a process of the cultural transformation of the colony of Virginia (Carson 1998). He records that its developers felt the tropes of room settings seemed unable to carry the large themes of history, especially the labor of ordinary, indeed enslaved, folk. Thus the marks of social history began to emerge in a program of personal stories and interpreter action throughout the historic center of the town. The new approach was heralded by the appointment of four African American interpreters in 1979; their role was literally to add color to the re-creation of a period when half the population of Williamsburg was black. Today there are some eighty African American role players, and they are critical to Colonial Williamsburg's historical credibility. Subsequent editions of "Becoming Americans" expanded to include "more African-Americans, more Native Americans, more women, more of the common sort, more of the dailyness of life" (Tyler-McGraw 1998, 54). The third iteration in 1998 acquired a subtitle, "Our Struggle to Be Both Free and Equal," embracing topics that span historical and modern values that continue to engender controversy. At this time, the mode of interpretation at Colonial Williamsburg moved decisively to theater, effectively situating houses and furnishings as sets and props (a theme taken up in chapter 7 on the infinite project of authenticity in historic house museums).

The National Park Service is older, bigger, and more bound by procedure than the private foundation that is Colonial Williamsburg. The motors of policy drove the national historic site portfolio since the 1930s, informed by internal and external expertise and much practice on the ground. The history of the NPS shows it as a model agent of the business of historic site and museum management. Among procedures and policies, the NPS grappled early with the need for interpretation to optimize public understanding of its historical parks. In 1982 the breezes of the social history movement fanned the first new thematic framework for decades, ambitiously titled *History and Prehistory in the National Park System and the National Historic Landmarks Program* (revised in 1987) (NPS 1987). It was followed by *History in the National Park Service: Themes and Concepts* (1994, revised 2000). (The decentralization of National Park management in the early 2000s means there is no longer a master policy.) Analyzing changes in these documents reveals shifts mobilized by new directions in the discipline. Attempts to list Everything in History tend to prove more wishful than workable, but they do serve as a gauge of park or landmark representation of historical topics. The 1980s documents listed thirty-four themes. In response to social history perspectives, theme XXX, "American Ways of Life," addressed the daily life perspectives typical in house museums. Theme XXXI, "Social and Humanitarian Movements," approached surging interest in identity politics such as women's rights, abolitionism, civil rights, and reform, among others, which bring conceptual critique to daily life. Colored by history's cultural turn, the 1994/2000 themes were constructed to rise above the taxonomy of the earlier frameworks by exchanging them for a Venn diagram of eight linked spheres, though they still contained taxa of historic subjects. All four systems described the reinvention of old, and the foundation of new, parks and landmarks that fulfilled a restitutional agenda of house museums representing women's and African American history. Among them were the Women's Rights National Historic Park (WRNHP) in Seneca Falls, New York—consisting largely of three heroines' houses—and the Martin Luther King Jr. Historic Site, in Atlanta, Georgia—including the great man's birthplace home—both in 1980. These sites have grown since their foundation, with the full apparatus of visitor centers, interpretive programs, and associated monuments.

Social history perspectives inform the presentation of these houses to a large degree. The three houses preserved in the WRNHP were inhabited in the 1840s by Elizabeth Cady Stanton (with husband and seven children), Mary Ann M'Clintock (with husband and five children), and Jane Hunt (with husband and six children). These three and two other women were the instigators of the Declaration of Sentiments drafted in the M'Clintock parlor (on a mahogany tea table, now in the collection of the National Museum of American History) and ratified by one hundred women at the Convention on Women's Rights held in the Wesleyan Chapel in July 1848. The Chapel and Visitor Center now introduce the major themes of the women's rights movement, while ranger-led interpretation introduces the perennial challenge of women managing family and domestic lives at the same time as political organizing. It was likewise in the house where Martin Luther King was born and grew up in Atlanta, Georgia, and the nearby Ebenezer Baptist Church, where Dr. King was copastor with his father until his death. What emerges from current interpretation in both parks is the vision of the protagonists, which feeds the next development in museums' aims to present ever more real histories: a more explicit and political register of civil rights and social justice.

Beyond Social History to Social Justice

Social history research into the categories of working class, black, and women's lives enlarged the scope of the domestic world that constitutes the central theme of house museums. The act of extending representation of the oppressed for the sake of larger, more inclusive interpretation coincided with the rise of the discourse of human rights; it projected socially aware museums into the politics of social justice. The contention that museums of all kinds can and should mobilize to combat social inequality is now documented in several anthologies of the early twenty-first century (e.g., Sandell 2012; Janes & Conaty 2005; Marstine, Bauer & Haines 2013). The politico-ethical idea flowered in the wake of the previous decade of professional assertions that museums should function less as introverted collection repositories and more as sites in the public domain, where ideas are aired and contested in history, science, and art (e.g., Weil 1999). The shift was borne along by the concurrent managerial reorientation to visitors as consumers of cultural goods that address their own lives, to local community as the sphere of museum programming, and to curatorial authority as a power to be shared among stakeholders in the interest of democratizing museum resources (e.g., Weil 2002). As the civil rights of inclusion shifted from radical politics toward policy and law, some museums and house museums chose to develop purposeful social justice agendas.

The Lower East Side Tenement Museum (LESTM) in New York City stands as the epitome of this trend. Key to its strength was the foresight of activist founders in starting from scratch, working strategically, and steadily building resources. The idea to develop a museum of the history of immigrants who settled on the Lower East Side took shape in 1988 with the identification of a time-capsule tenement building at 97 Orchard Street. It is estimated to have housed some seven thousand souls between 1863 and 1935, when the owner locked the front door rather than pay for improvements. Since all it contained was the abandoned detritus of sixteen empty apartments, the interpretation plan proposed re-creating apartments in the names of individuals representing periods of immigration. The first opened in 1992, representing a German-Jewish family who lived there in the 1870s; five more have followed, all based on real inhabitants, informed by scrupulous social history research. The LESTM building has been stabilized for public access safety, and it is visited in groups conducted by guides who mediate discussions on immigrant experience then *and now*. The museum's campaigning objectives manifest here; founder Ruth Abram writes, "We were activists who had come to believe that our best contribution to the ideas we hold dear could be made through history, and specifically, through historic sites. We accepted our roles as formers of public conscience" (Abram 2005, 38).

Similar complexes of working-class housing were museumized in the same 1990s period in Australia and the United Kingdom, employing the same modes of tightly focused social history to re-create typical dwellings, while applying archaeological standards in maintaining part of each complex in as-found condition. Susannah Place in Sydney and the Inge Street back-to-backs in Birmingham interpret the living conditions of their cities' poorest from the 1840s to the 1970s. Both mobilize the evidence of fine-grained urban social history, and the spirit of social justice infuses their interpretive media; yet they seem tame by comparison with the bold aura of the LESTM. The difference is personal interpretation, presented as only a skilled guide can, by conjuring the experience and emotion of visitors to connect past with present. It comes as no surprise that LESTM mastermind Abram also conceived and launched the International Coalition of Sites of Conscience, a network of more than two hundred institutions, whose mission is "to activate the power of places of memory to engage the public in connecting past and present in order to envision and shape a more just and humane future" (http://www.sitesofconscience.org/about-us/). A surprising proportion of the network's member sites are inhabited places: workhouse, gulag camp, slave barracks, the Anne Frank house, the houses that constitute the US Women's Rights National Park. They underline the deep resonance of the dwelling as a locus of living, and therefore of meaningful evidence of situations of injustice. Bringing them to public attention via museum exhibition opens new sites in the public sphere for information, conversation, and debate.

The motivational politics of promoting social justice is buttressed on the spectrum of museum activism by the practical, therapeutic interventions that Lois Silverman names "the social work of museums" (2010). She offers a myriad of examples, such as museum-based programs to introduce and unite Catholic and Protestant children in Ulster and Palestinian and Jewish children in Jerusalem; family encounters with disaster preparedness in Taipei and child abduction risk in Washington, DC; fostering green design in family homes via exhibitions in Norfolk and Sydney; diverting young vandals in Wolverhampton and spray-can graffitists in Newcastle-upon-Tyne. Such programs are driven by institutional awareness of the realities of lives in which museums would seem to have little relevance. To explain the potential, Silverman cites John Cotton Dana's Newark Museum as the fount of service-oriented museums, where he prescribed in 1917, "Learn what aid the community needs; fit the museum to those needs" (Silverman 2010, 139). Among historical cases, she includes the Hull House Museum of Labor, a unit of the Hull House Settlement founded in Chicago's Near West Side by social activist Jane Addams in 1889. The Museum of Labor was a museum of the traditional crafts of immigrant women, deskilled and demoralized by industrial work. The museum's claim to the value and virtue of traditional skills expressed Addams's assertion of the truly radical position that cultural rights were as important as economic and political rights in the Americanization of immigrant labor in the decades around the turn of the twentieth century.

Today, only two structures of the Settlement remain. One is the Residents' Dining Hall; the other is the Hull Home, in which Jane Addams's bedroom is re-created. Over the mantelpiece, in its historic location, hangs a portrait of a young woman, whose identification offers an exemplary study of restorative justice in a house museum (Lee & Lopez 2014). The portrait had been in storage when Hull House was museumized; it depicted Mary Rozet Smith, and the challenge emerged: How to describe her significance in the Hull House Settlement? She had been a prominent financial patron of the Settlement, and she often stayed there for periods of weeks but lived with her parents for many years. But Smith was also the lifelong companion of Jane Addams, who considered the two of them married; their coupledom was acknowledged throughout their circle. In 2006 it was not clear whether labeling Smith's portrait with her relationship to Addams would undermine Addams's public reputation. Her historic achievements lay in social activism and public policy, for which she was both watched by the FBI and awarded the Nobel Peace Prize. Staff at Hull House Museum therefore set up an alternative labeling experiment, offering three texts to identify Smith's portrait and requesting public feedback. The *Chicago Tribune* described the project as "Outing Jane Addams" (Schoenberg 2007). Some responders argued that the private life of Smith and Addams was irrelevant to the Settlement story, but the majority favored the franker approach. The latter now contextualizes the presentation of Addams in tours of the house and identifies the intimate significance of Smith's portrait.

Jane Addams's bedroom at Hull House, Near West Side, Chicago, 2010. The re-creation of Jane Addams's private space now illustrates her private life and love for Mary Rozet Smith, who was painted by Alice Tyler Kellogg in 1897.
Photo by Charles Rex Arbogast, courtesy of AP via AAP.

Acknowledging the political ramifications of private life in the public world points up the social justice of acknowledging gender politics, in house museums as much as any cultural institution. Having browsed the websites and guidebooks of hundreds of house museums, I concur with Josh Adair's analysis of "the (non-)representation of gay men in the museums they called home"—that gay men's lives and creativity as collectors and preservers have been silenced by boards, curators, docents, and, indeed, themselves (Adair 2010, 265). Coy references to unmarried uncles, lifelong bachelors, and eccentric solitaries perpetuate a prurient stereotype of sexual activity as the defining element of living gay, in response to the conventional prejudice against atypical gender behavior. Adair argues that the evidence of subjects' lives should be sufficient to identify unacknowledged gay men's museumized houses. To do so would, he advocates, confront the distortions, untruths, and abuses of homophobia, which deformed many lives. That this can be asserted at all is a function of changing human rights consciousness, via the slow decriminalization of male homosexuality (England in 1967, Australia in 1994, the United States in 2003). Its closeted history had distinctive impacts on several species of house museum. More than a few country houses in the

United Kingdom were significantly enhanced by an occasional generation of ownership by men who would today be described as gay, though many were also married and fathers. In the baddest of old days, some were driven into exile by capital charges of sexual transgression, as was William Bankes of Kingston Lacy, Dorset, in 1841. Bankes's scandalous escapades are noted in his house's interpretation today, perhaps the fruit of earlier law reform in the United Kingdom than elsewhere. He was but one of nine generations of wealthy aristocratic owners, and the larger context of his interpretation on site focuses on his important contributions to the house's redesign, luxurious decoration, and exotic collections. This is fair and true, but it is noteworthy that British interpretation of country houses consistently foregrounds their architectural, collection, and garden design significance ahead of the private life even of notable gender-atypical inhabitants. Referring to Vita Sackville-West of Sissinghurst and the Ladies of Llangollen at Plas Newydd, Alison Oram explores the convolutions of time and ideas that can be uncovered in historic house museums. Interestingly, she comes to the conclusion that the heritage industry in Britain does not promote a unified and conservative approach to sexuality; rather, she argues that gay visitors who care to look may find themselves constituted there as a counterpublic among dominant others (Oram 2011).

By contrast, most museums tend to maintain the aura of heteronormativity, even in houses that were specifically conserved by gay people. In the relative absence of multigenerational houses, this is the case at more than a few houses preserved for the sake of their design and/or furnishings. In fact, neutered accounts of unmarried aesthetes who collected art or bequeathed their houses as museums (represented in this book by Philip Johnson of the Glass House and Patrick Gwynne of the Homewood) can be called a typical trope of displacement that accompanies homophobic prejudice. A case study can be made of Charles Gibson Jr. as a man whose gender atypicality bore conspicuously on the maintenance and eventual museumization of his family's 1860 house in Boston. He left the house, furnishings, equipment, services, and collections, as well as an endowment, to the Gibson Society Inc., which he founded in 1936 when the Society for the Preservation of New England Antiquities declined his offer of the house. The Gibson House opened as a museum in 1957, having been inhabited by three generations. It has been assessed within the formal heritage system as a rare specimen of a largely intact, furnished row house of the mid- to late nineteenth century, significant for architecture, design, and historic lifestyle (Hessney 2000, 17). The man who ensured its transition is described by a recent magazine writer as "a patrician bon vivant" and by the curator as "a very eccentric lifelong bachelor" (Brown

2015). Adair might respond that the lifestyle so described, and the house he bequeathed, constitute sufficient evidence to justify identifying Gibson as a gay man. Meanwhile, euphemisms enable the journalist cited above to sidestep sexuality issues by quoting the curator about the managerial decision to avoid acknowledging Charles Gibson's private life: it is a well-honed conceptual and linguistic mechanism that effectively suppresses the possibility of non-normative sexuality. But even if interpretation that denies his sexuality is an act of abuse, should justice be thrust by others upon the man, his house, and its management? This clash of perspectives illustrates Richard Sandell's careful view that human rights themes in museums comprise a dynamic field in which particular, local agendas will frequently clash with universalist ideals, and that it may require long periods of negotiation to adopt a convincing commitment to social justice (Sandell 2012, 195–97).

A long time coming is certainly the case in house museums with a history of enslaved residents. Despite a spate of new interpretations of the slave presence in many American house museums, surveys in the 1990s documented what its authors called a "shocking degree of social forgetting" at the majority of museumized great estates and grand houses built on the slave economy. Jennifer Eichstedt and Stephen Small visited 122 former plantations now presented as house museums, mainly in Virginia, Georgia, and Louisiana (Eichstedt & Small 2002). Crediting museums with the discursive power to construct identities, they note that practically all plantation sites use white-centric rhetoric to valorize a southern culture of civility, honor, grandeur, and tragedy, concomitantly suppressing black presence and history. By contrast, they analyze a handful of black-centric museums (unsurprisingly, *not* plantation mansions) presenting the counternarrative of resistance against brutality, resilience encountering injustice, and dignity in the face of inhumanity (Eichstedt & Small 2002, 7, 233). The researchers produced a forthright typology of interpretive strategies at plantation mansion sites. Most extreme is perfunctory reference to slavery or even total silence on the topic, which they name "symbolic annihilation and erasure." They further distinguish between "trivialization and deflection" via distorting frames of reference and language (e.g., "faithful slave") and "segregation and marginalization of knowledge," referring to acknowledgment of the presence of enslaved people but hived off on a separate tour. They name the least racialized interpretive tours "relative incorporation"; this category refers to interpretive frameworks with explicit presentation of white inhabitants as slaveholders. Its characteristics include frank acknowledgment that white comfort and profit came at the cost of the enslaved, the impression that the theme of slavery permeates both site and tour, and the admission that information about individual slaves is presented to personalize their experience (Eichstedt & Small 2002, 10–11, 205–13). This is a devastating review of a period in which authoritative knowledge of the historical scale of slavery had become available but continued to be ignored. It manifests the deep persistence of real and symbolic racist violence in house museums in the United States, despite legal redress in the civil rights era.

In fact, more than a decade later, reviewing the websites of house museums that Eichstedt and Small visited shows that nowhere does the theme of slavery frame the presentation of an entire site, despite the causal agency of the enslaved and their presence as 50–90 percent of plantation residents. Little context of the historical statistics of owners and estates informs the genre of plantation museums, such as that ownership of more than fifty slaves defined a planter aristocracy of some ten thousand families in the South, and that the wealth created by an enslaved workforce of more than a hundred people made some three thousand families super rich. Given that Eichstedt and Small assessed a tiny number of sites as practicing the justice of "relative incorporation" of the presence of the enslaved within sites' mainstream interpretation, it is an unavoidable conclusion that in plantation museums, the impact of social history, let alone the trend toward an explicit social justice agenda, has been minimal. A rare estate they noted as effective is Montpelier in Orange, Virginia, family home of James Madison, fourth president and "Father of the Constitution." A key element of Montpelier efforts to present this history even-handedly comes by explicitly referring to *white* as well as black people, pointedly applying a linguistic marker of race to all inhabitants. Eichstedt and Small further recorded that the audio-guided tour addresses the contradiction of a slaveholding proponent of "freedom," considerably complicating the persona of national hero James Madison (2002, 214–18). These are marks of moving beyond the historic site function of giving evidence of the past to the critical museum agenda of changing understanding in the present.

Meanwhile, in Britain, the social justice stream that emerges from social history in museums discovered the presence of the profits of slavery in the United Kingdom, first in maritime museums in the 1990s and soon after in many country houses that had been funded and sustained by the profits of Caribbean plantations (Smith, Cubitt, & Fouseki 2011). Stimulated by the 2007 bicentenary of the abolition of the slave trade in the British Empire, a number of country houses revisited their interpretations to explore previously unspoken connections. The Lascelles family of Harewood House in West Yorkshire had recently discovered and transferred to public archives a remarkable cache of documents concerning the family's eighteenth-century businesses in shipping, imports and exports, and Caribbean sugar, underwritten by the slave trade. They took a proactive stance in the 2007 commemorations by introducing small displays of slavery-related items throughout the house, and holding a Caribbean festival in the grounds. Responding to the same impetus, English Heritage amended the listings of twelve buildings to show how England's involvement in the slave trade is reflected in the historic built environment. The agency also published a volume of conference papers exploring the links between slavery-based wealth and the English country house, and ways such history could be presented to the public today. Among the contributors, Caroline Bressey reframes the social history agenda of uncovering the presence of the excluded as a struggle against racism, provoking the need to challenge the whiteness of British country houses. It remains to be added that Bressey notes the absence of continuing interpretation of slave-based fortunes after 2007 (Bressey 2013, 116, 121).

As a postscript, a plantation house museum claiming to be the first interpreted primarily from the enslaved point of view opened in late 2014: Whitney Plantation, in Wallace, Louisiana. The site is the private project of an individual, John Cumming, motivated, according to the historian with whom he has worked since 2000, by a sense of personal obligation to make reparation to black history (Amsden 2015). Whitney Plantation addresses the common absences of evidence with relocated slave cabins and interpretive sculpture.

The adoption of social history in house museums accentuated awareness of the degree to which interpretation molds presentation, stressed by claims to new levels of authenticity. Passive consumption of museum authority and its apparently "natural" rhetoric frequently blinds both staff and visitors to the ideological implications of the presentation of great persons and their domestic circumstances, or the cultural meanings of domestic design, or the importance of elite collections shown *in situ domesticu*, or the history of personal and social circumstances of individuals in their home environments. But as house museum management and/or curators embarked on ever more purposeful agendas such as inclusive histories and social justice, the charged content of new interpretive perspectives provoked debates on the ethics of interpretation. That is the nub of problematized histories in house museums, though it has long been articulated under the aegis of the idea of authenticity. But authenticity is an inescapably artful topic, addressed via a multitude of applications; the next chapter takes a stand and documents the techniques that social history museum curators have marshaled to make their point.

~

CHAPTER SEVEN

Authenticity

Material Reality, Negotiated Understanding

For a concept that seems so self-evident, the hazards of authenticity are many. Dictionaries explain authenticity as the characteristics of genuineness, implying that authenticity in objects and places means they are original and credible, and that the people or agencies that authenticate objects and places are trustworthy and reliable. The topic is especially important in the field of museums, which stand as public filters and guarantors of authenticity in art and history. Museums therefore have a responsibility to understand, assess, and interpret authenticity to their publics, both visitors and the broader communal sphere of culture. The history of museums' relationship with authenticity shows it is overwhelmingly shaped by a modernist perspective on the materiality of collections. By contrast, the critique of postmodernism proposes a view of culturally constructed collections whose authenticity emerges as forms of knowledge. The tension between the two concepts generates a more complex view of how museums authorize material authenticity and authorize the public to believe it. The following history presents a summary; more comprehensive investigations can be found in Phillips (1997), Starn (2002), Lindholm (2008), and Jones (2010).

The need for judgments of authenticity in the premodern world was met by faith, and the agencies that determined it were the church and the market. The church authorized faith in forgiveness, resurrection, and other miracles, addressing the fears and hopes of humanity. The market, essentially the market for luxuries, established the parameters of value by rarity and beauty, addressing the desires of those who could afford to buy. Church and market have never been equivalent in power or reach, but as the standard-setters for values requiring authenticity, they engaged in similar practices. Both were impacted by the rise of scientific modernism, a bundle of ideas that generated new structures for judging authenticity, including the museum. Both church and market (or economy) accommodated modernist approaches with modifications in old beliefs and practices. Museums invented new processes to demonstrate authenticity, starting with comparative taxonomy and the expertise of connoisseurship, and engaging scientific procedures of physical investigation on an ever more detailed scale. These techniques produced standards that were sometimes mistaken but, as scientific (or pseudo-scientific) knowledge, stood to be corrected. Museum standards were useful in the market as an external validation of commercial claims, but less usable by the church, where they appeared to undermine the claims of faith—though faith persists, and can still outweigh science in some circumstances. The intellectual challenge of postmodernism emerged in the light of anthropological awareness of other cultures' knowledges. By asserting that dominant modernist forms of knowledge are absolutist and exclusive, it demonstrates the political agendas of communications between contesting interests. The perspective that knowledge is a cultural construct brought into focus the relativity of multiple knowledges, and recognition that individuals, societies, and their institutions create and alter understandings of the world in political contexts. On one hand, this approach undermined the old certainty of authenticity, but, on the other, it opened up ways of negotiating genuineness between parties according to circumstance—thus explaining how faith is still a meaningful element in many a judgment of authenticity.

Everyday museum practice regarding authenticity is dualistic, employing both materialist and constructivist approaches, according to need. Scientific knowledge of the physical composition of an object might be required to discover or verify information about it, or to plan conservation treatment or exhibition exposure. But thinking about the constructivist possibilities in the minds of visitors might suggest interactive exhibition techniques or programs for particular visitor segments. The late twentieth-century shift in museum priorities from collections to audiences lifted the latter to unprecedented prominence in planning and management. The visitor focus inaugurated a strategic role for postmodern perspectives on the agency of visitors in creating their own satisfying knowledge and experience/visit, while meeting the organization's intellectual and financial goals. This truth applies to house museums, too.

The methodology of this book, splitting the category into subclasses on the basis of the founding motivation, identifies a range of applications of authenticity, which led me to this chapter. What follows is a survey of ideas about authenticity in the different types of house museum, and of the technical quest for authenticity in social history houses. Hence I present my own understanding of the nature of authenticity in house museums: authenticity can be understood as a bargain about the genuineness of material objects and intangible knowledge, co-constituted by museum staff and visitors in the form of knowledge and experience. The motive of this bargain is to establish a yardstick by which to gauge whether the products of the museum are credible. It matters because the museum is more than a cluster of objects and buildings; it is an experience-forming, knowledge-making apparatus whose product must be consumed in order to realize its purpose—that is why the visitor's judgment of credibility is so important. Different house museum types illustrate a spectrum of transactional environments in which authenticity is acknowledged and appreciated (or not).

On a scale from less to more interactive negotiations about authenticity, they are:

1. the hero's house, where both material authenticity and intangible experience are guaranteed by faith
2. the artwork house, whose authenticity is defined by aesthetics suspended between faith in the authority of taste and conviction of the visitor's own taste
3. the collector's house, where the market authorizes authenticity of objects, the museum authorizes the authenticity of the presentation, and the visitor mobilizes her or his own taste
4. the social history house, in which material authenticity is often scarce or nonexistent, opening the way for a repertoire of interpretive techniques to construct knowledge whose credibility depends very much on the visitor's own values
5. the country house, whose material authenticity is sustained by its connection to ancient power structures mediated by more or less professional authority, the credibility of which is open to visitor evaluation

Authenticity in Heroes' Houses

As argued in chapter 2, the bedrock of the museumization of the houses of culture heroes is shared faith in the genuine nature of material evidence exhibited to honor the subject, and in this respect, parallel to the presentation of sacred objects and stories in churches. The long history and vast apparatus of religious faith supports the confidence of believers and clergy (notwithstanding the fact that there is a long history of challenge by members of both

Sir Walter Scott's desk and chair, Abbotsford, watercolor by William Smith, 1904.
Plate in *Beautiful Britain Abbotsford* (London, 1912).

parties). The transfer of faith to the civil religion of nationalism constitutes an easy vehicle to attach similar credibility to other ideals of the kind. In this process, the museum and its regime of rational knowledge support faith in secular relics via a circuit of self-fulfilling claims: if it's the real evidence, its place is in the museum, and if it's in a museum, it must be real. At the same time, a number of wry commentators have confessed that the absurdities that a critically inclined visitor identifies in a hero's house don't necessarily undermine the satisfactions of visiting (Goldhill 2011, 122; Trubek 2011, 147). What is faith, and what is wishfulness?

In fact, museum practice shows that curators and visitors can both engage fruitfully with inauthentic presentation in certain circumstances. In the case of heroes with humble dwellings, structures may survive but with no contemporary furnishings, so the interiors are often retro-furnished with similar or reproduction items. It's significant that visitor reviews rarely note or question authenticity in these cases. This suggests that public desire for material authenticity can be satisfied either by the museum aura of credibility or by the four solid walls of a house, or perhaps that it is much less important than the visitor's own interest in, or sense of the aura of, the inhabitant. This very issue was tested by specialist marketers on the childhood home of New Zealand writer Janet Frame, investigating consumer responses to a re-creation installed in the (genuine) house. They drew conclusions about the signals and qualities that make frank inauthenticity palatable, indeed pleasurable, to some visitors (Hede & Thyne, 2010). Frame lived with her family in the modest brick cottage in Oamaru from 1931 to 1943, when she left for college; family life here was often the subject of her writing. The house was purchased by well wishers and transferred to a trust in 2005. In the absence of any Frame-associated furnishings other than a later-period desk, the decision was taken to interpret the house by "reframing" the interior spaces with pieces acquired to match records and memories, including the author's, shortly before she died. Hede and Thyne found that careful explanation of the philosophy of reframing at the start of the tour encourages visitors to negotiate the re-created rooms, enhanced by the freedom to wander and touch. The introduction at the door urges them to project their own readings of the books, and personal nostalgia for modest homes, onto the room settings. Hede and Thyne concluded that these cues help many visitors to an imaginative connection with Frame and a heightened awareness of New Zealand literature, rising above any discomfort about the authenticity of the place (2010, 700–701). Nonetheless, web-based visitor reviews include some who are not convinced: "Not worth it, stories made up to make it seem interesting, but are completely unfactual and false" (JacquiFodie 2014). The frank approach and the disbelieving response equally demonstrate the practical flexibility of negotiating authenticity in heroes' houses.

Authenticity in Artwork Houses

The bargain of the authenticity of artwork houses is similar to the case of heroes' houses in being steeped in faith, but it is a calibrated faith, subject to two powerful ideas about the nature of art. One line of thought stresses the value of the designer's personal mark on the house and perhaps the signs of antiquity, both demonstrated by the presence of original fabric. This view contains a strand of romanticism that values the artwork house for essentialist qualities, even if compromised by destructive history. It therefore tends to the antirestoration or leave-as-is standard of care. The other perspective values the intellectual program of the house design in its purest form. It is more cerebral than emotional and seeks to understand the full scope of house style and decoration, and hence regards the marks of time as impediments to be corrected. Restoration is its strategy, ranging from well informed to conjectural. The two value systems diverge over the professional decisions of material preservation of the museumized house: whether or how much to restore or reconstruct it. (The same tensions apply in the conservation of fine and decorative artworks.) Houses are big and complex by comparison with paintings and sculpture, though they may be similarly fragile. Hence it is common to subdivide the house conceptually by considering conservation treatments in relation to components rather than the total house—for example, exterior/interior, structure/furnishings, house/setting. Visitors apply their own predilection for conservation or restoration as the frame of their individual conviction about the house's authenticity. But in the modernist practice of museumizing houses for their aesthetic quality, the predominant approach has been restoration, tending toward the extreme of total re-creation.

This taste has its own history. Until the later nineteenth century, architects were not shy about revising the work of their predecessors, whether for convenience or fashion. But the Gothic Revival movement endowed medieval buildings with the essence of beauty, virtue, and national character and set the scene for the struggle between the elimination of accretions via restoration and maintenance of the ancient fabric via stabilization. Restoration guided by expert knowledge (contingent as it is) has always predominated in practice, though the romance of valuing original materials and workmanship captured the high ground of architectural conservation theory, from Ruskin to the Venice Charter of the International Council on Monuments and Sites (ICOMOS). The allure persists of ever-growing historical and scientific knowledge of the details and finishes that enhance the kind of houses considered worth museumizing as artworks: more restoration than conservation is still common (Jokilehto 1999, 303–5). An important example is the rise in the 1980s of historical studies of domestic interiors, which opened curatorial eyes to contemporary views of decor and furnishing (Thornton 1984; Seale 1979). At the same time, a further outcome of archaeological attention to historic buildings sparked new understanding of the materials and forms of historic finishes and colors. Specialist heritage architects were quick to recover the techniques. Scraping for sequences of interior and exterior paint colors and searches for wallpaper fragments hidden behind fittings revealed evidence of historic decorative schemes that had been suppressed by eighty years of the anti-Victorian taste for white modernism. A new awareness arose of interiors as originally experienced by the inhabitants of historic buildings, especially as perceived by fire, candle, and gaslight. The reproduction of wallpapers and carpets based on "archaeological" evidence (i.e., surviving specimens) became a mark of scrupulous standards in the conservation of the authentic—and its reproduction. The insight precipitated a new visual language for house museums and other restored buildings, and generated a new professional specialism in historic interiors (Ponsonby 2007, 168–70). Authenticity demonstrated by immaculate simulation became a measure of high-quality restoration and reproduction in house museums, popularly acclaimed as "return to former glory."

A current example is the Martin house in Buffalo, New York, designed by Frank Lloyd Wright in 1903–1905 and under restoration from 1996 to 2017. The site was originally composed of six linked buildings: the main house; a smaller house; a conservatory linked to the main house via a glasshouse-style "pergola" walkway; a carriage house/garage with chauffeur's quarters; and a gardener's cottage. The owner was ruined in the 1929 stock market crash; after he died in 1935, his family could not afford local taxes and they abandoned the property, which reverted to the City of Buffalo. The buildings succumbed to ruin and all but the two houses were demolished in 1962; however, interest in the significance of the site began to revive. The Martin House Restoration Corporation, formed in 1992, acquired the smaller house and developed a staged conservation plan, beginning work in 1997; the main house joined the Corporation in 2002. There followed years of repairs and restoration: roof and gutter work; drainage work; rebuilding the pergola, conservatory, and carriage house; acquiring the gardener's cottage; and masonry work on the main house. A Miesian visitor center opened in 2009, and the final stage of interior fittings reconstruction began in 2010. The Corporation also acquired many of the fifty-five pieces of furniture designed by Wright for the house, as well as other furnishings he approved, a large suite of *ukiyo-e* woodblock prints he selected, and some of the 394 panels of "art glass" (windows, doors, sidelights, skylights, etc.) in sixteen groups of patterns. Some missing pieces of furniture were reproduced from Wright's drawings, and the fragile *ukiyo-e* prints were painstakingly replicated via digital printing on Japanese paper (Bayne et al. 2012). The overwhelming tenor of public reviews of the Darwin Martin house restoration is enthusiastically positive (see the TripAdvisor website). Professional comments are also affirmative, though occasional pieces raise the existential question that underlies the continuing argument between restoration and conservation: "Once a landmark piece of architecture is gone, is it better to re-create it or let its absence tell the story? Does re-created experience trump the value of authenticity? Does the presence of facsimile buildings undermine the integrity of original ones?" (Jacobs 2009). This author can't bring herself to condemn the beautiful labor of re-creating the Martin house, despite her consciousness of the dark edge of reproduction. It is a telling specimen of the anxieties of a negotiated assessment of authenticity.

Darwin D. Martin House Complex, Buffalo, New York, 2005. Frank Lloyd Wright certainly intended his houses as *Gesamtkunstwerk*. The capacity to view the entire Martin House site restored, rather than merely the parts remaining in 1992, would probably have pleased his sense of appropriate public admiration.
Photo courtesy of the Martin House Restoration Corporation.

Authenticity in Collectors' Houses

It was noted in chapter 5 that there are two styles of collections museumized within the houses where they were formed and displayed: those comprising the most valuable and prestigious artifacts in Western culture—namely, fine arts—and those gathered to adorn a house, most frequently though not exclusively antique furniture. Even though the former are not for sale, they are guaranteed authentic by their market value. The latter may also be expensive but are intended to be meaningful in their collective character, as established by the collector. Two more conditions can be considered as standards of authenticity in collectors' houses: the integrity of the house and of the creative unity of the collection as presented to the public. A peak manifestation of wealth that fine art house museum collections seem to acknowledge, but not feel constrained by, is the logic of the historic authenticity of setting. The Wallace Collection, for instance, has been rearranged twice since installation in 1900, evidencing a tacit bargain between visitors and institution based on the primacy of the artworks. The fact is, relatively few house museum buildings and collections came to museum status exactly as they were at the time of donation; many were considerably altered during the transition to public status, as was the Wallace. The Frick Museum is unusual in having been endowed to continue collecting, and the collection has nearly doubled in size since Frick's death. His own vision for the museum included enlargement as soon as the house shifted from a home to a museum in 1935, and there have been several extensions since then. Yet change at the Wallace and the Frick appears not to contest any of the concepts of authenticity mentioned above, a perspective that points to public satisfaction with predominantly aesthetic rather than historic value in the collections.

Sir John Soane's Museum and the Isabella Stewart Gardner Museum are more typical of collectors' houses, being conserved today in much the same condition as their benefactors left them, both having been bequeathed with that condition. No. 13 Lincoln's Inn Fields and Fenway Court are by far the most idiosyncratic and romantic collector's house museums, where rooms were designed around certain works, and their placement has become as memorable to visitors as the works themselves. This point is marked in Gardner's museum, where empty frames are still in place on the walls to indicate the absence of thirteen works stolen in 1990. Yet both organizations have recently expanded their buildings, with strategic references to their founders' intentions. Soane had intended No. 13 to be the public museum, with the two flanking houses used respectively for library and staff accommodation and income-producing rent. In his time, Soane used parts of all three houses, including a multihouse back office for his architectural practice. In the period 2011–2016, the museum carried out a plan far beyond Soane's vision, remaking No. 12 to provide new visitor, collection, and exhibition services and a lift to make the whole complex accessible for the first time. In No. 13, Soane's own apartments, including his architectural model room, have been restored, and No. 14 now houses education and seminar rooms, the research library, and other access to Soane's collection of drawings. The collector could hardly have imagined today's interest, though there's no doubt he would relish it. So would Gardner, whose museum was enlarged by a politely stylish, separate building constructed in the back garden in 2009–2014 to provide expanded services for visitor reception and programs. Activities fostered by Gardner herself, such as recitals and drawing, had become risky in the original house spaces due to vastly increased visitation. The case was doubtless made to trustees that these very considerable developments would be in line with the intentions of the original collectors (the Gardner extension required judicial approval), but apparently not invoking any aspect of authenticity: that aspect of the museum houses appears to be a given in the evidence of visitor reviews of both house museums.

By contrast, the authenticity of the display and its house container is extremely important among the subclass of collection-adorned houses. A key difference is in the market value of the goods comprising the collection. Old Master fine art is such a separate category from the relatively unsophisticated tastes of science and the exotic to be seen in Rosalie Chichester's Arlington Court and the Harper-Crewes's Calke Abbey, or the Arts and Crafts taste that shapes the collections in Charles Paget Wade's Snowshill or Henry Mercer's Fonthill, or even the expensive antiquarian tastes of Frank Green's Treasurer's House and Henry Francis du Pont's Winterthur (see chapter 5). In these cases, the mind of the collector (demonstrated by the exact placement of the display) is so evidently primary in appreciating the purpose of these house collections that maintaining or reinstating an original layout is a significant responsibility of those who manage them in trust for the public. Thus visitors sense the idiosyncrasy of the collector and, with their own opinions, reap the product of the museum bargain of authenticity.

Authenticity in Social History Houses

Social history house museums are fundamentally different from other forms of house museum identified by this book's typology. The types discussed above and below were museumized in the materialist understanding that the structure and/or its contents themselves constitute the significant meaning that justifies preservation: the house/furnishings as its/their own evidence. This conviction guided most house museumizations. But it was difficult to find the dwellings of socially marginal people, the subjects of the social history focus, for museumization, because such people hardly ever owned property, and the cheap houses they inhabited rarely survive undisturbed through time. Since the necessary material scarcely existed, the project to present social history houses to the public engineered standards and compromises that would seem to infringe even the variables of authenticity discussed above. It pushed expectations about authenticity into a different dimension, where *interpretation* constitutes the effective social history house museum. Thus its products unexpectedly collided with postmodernist analyses of heritage culture to illuminate the furthest reaches of house museum agency today. The techniques of social history house museums are recounted in the next part of this chapter, beginning with the quest for indigenously furnished, intact houses, the challenges of retro-creating houses, and the span of interpretive modes applied to house museums: archaeological, experimental, living history, and theatrical vehicles to construct understandings of social history. All of them conceive the eye and other senses of the visitor as crucial components in the credibility of the story presented, aiming to shock, astonish, captivate, charm, and move the spectator in order to engage and convince.

The risks to the museum's reputation for authenticity, and to visitors' capacity to make judgments about history, were probed by Edward Bruner's ethnographic study of Lincoln's New Salem, a town established and abandoned in prairie Illinois in the 1830s and reproduced a hundred years later as a project of the Civilian Conservation Corps. It was for years self-styled (though no longer) as an "authentic reproduction." This conundrum set Bruner to describe modulations of "authenticity" in the site and elsewhere, arriving at the spectrum of verisimilitude, genuineness, originality, and authority (Bruner 1994, 399–401). The historical rationale for reviving New Salem was the six years Abraham Lincoln spent in the town in his twenties, developing his credentials as American Everyman on the way from log cabin to White House. Bruner concluded from his observations of visitors and their interactions with costumed interpreters, in the reproduced streets and dwellings of New Salem, that they engaged in semiformal dialogues, enabling visitors to experiment playfully with alternatives to the (generally minimal) history they knew. He identified three themes: nostalgia for the prairie town origin myth; confirmation of the American vision of progress; and celebration of the spirit of community—all of it, "the raw material (experiences) to construct a sense of identity, meaning, attachment, and stability" (Bruner 1994, 410–11). New Salem's visitors were shown to be unfazed and untroubled by reproductions and capable of interacting with them for substantial hedonic satisfactions.

Authenticity in Country Houses

Country houses in the British meaning refer to the great houses of the nobility, located on inherited estates, discussed in chapter 8. Due to social and economic changes, many became impossible to maintain around the turn of the twentieth century and thereafter, and some turned to tourism by opening the grander parts of the house for public visiting. In their traditional role as symbols of wealth and power, many country houses are monuments of architectural high style, set in beautiful gardens, splendidly furnished, and decorated with multigenerational collections of artworks, some as rich as the best museums. These singular houses further offer visitors the fantasy charms of access into the once exclusive world of aristocratic privilege, with associated history, myth, and a deep nationalist essence of Old England. Country houses now open to the public, whether by a family of hereditary owners or a professional organization working in trust, raise few questions on the grounds of authenticity in material presentation. Some people are disturbed by the absence of a resident aristocratic family, feeling that the loss of traditional use makes the house less meaningful: this variant on the theme of authenticity is not shared by any other type of house museum. Not all country houses are open to the public, and not all can or want to be called museums, but enough fit my definition of a house museum to warrant considering the ramifications of ideas about authenticity in their public manifestations. These are generally credible in both material and constructivist aspects of authenticity as perceived by managers and visitors.

British country houses have been so successful as museums that in the wider British world, where no hereditary aristocracy ever existed, many a grand historic house on a landed estate (or once in that situation) has been museumized with the country house model in mind. Such formerly colonial houses are often richly designed and furnished and occasionally sustain multigenerational contents, but in sociological comparison should be thought of as gentlemen's houses. The slippage in meaning allowed by the term *country house* when used outside the United Kingdom is the least of the challenges to their ontological authenticity. Not only is the practice of male primogeniture irrelevant, but so is the taxation regime that recognizes the cultural significance of keeping country houses and their contents together and makes it viable.

The foregoing survey of aspects of authenticity commonly applied to house museums shows how polymorphous the idea is in practice. By presenting it as a standard that is not only produced and consumed materially but also co-constituted by museum and visitor creativity, it is possible to challenge its apparently categorical quality. Nonetheless, the modernist habit of seeking an absolute authenticity draws both museums and visitors into an endless quest for total and perfect interpretation of the past. Here it is timely to recall the assessment of David Lowenthal, who has thought more about the problem of heritage and authenticity than most people. He presents three principles: that the past is gone and irretrievable; that it nonetheless remains vital and relevant to the present; and that it is impossible to avoid changing its remnants. His advice to make these truths usable in museum and heritage management is to acknowledge our human fallibility, but also our capacity to learn by trying (Lowenthal 2008, 4–6).

Authenticity in Social History: A Record of Heroic Techniques

House museums are not alone in what Raphael Samuel called "resurrectionism," meaning the quest to revive the authentic past via heritage. His play on the article of Christian faith and the practice of body snatching for dissection suggests he had no sympathy with museum techniques to present history in ever more realistic ways. In fact, Samuel was both a progenitor of social history and a student of the means to present and affirm the lives of the historically oppressed and excluded (Samuel 1994). His joke thus introduces an ironic edge to the desire to bring the past into the present. The second part of this chapter traces the history of the sincere and inventive, if ultimately impossible, quest for authenticity in social history house museum practice. It begins with a group of material realities, and moves on to show how further techniques are in fact interpretive devices that invoke a connection with authentic material.

Preserving Houses with Indigenous Furnishings

An important museumizing response to the conventional standards of authenticity in house museums emerged in the 1980s–1990s via the preservation of a handful of nonelite houses complete with "indigenous" or "intact" furnishings—that is, as installed by the inhabitants. One of the first cases to become well known was the 1892 Glasgow apartment occupied by Miss Agnes Toward from 1911 to 1965, shared for twenty-eight of those fifty-four years with her mother. The dwelling was owned by the Towards and furnished with genteel comfort. Uninhabited for the last ten years of Miss Toward's life, it was purchased in 1975 complete with furnishings, by a sensitive spirit who recognized its integrity and maintained it until selling to the National Trust for Scotland in 1982 (Hepburn 1999). Another specimen was preserved in Canberra, Australia, where the middling bourgeois significance of the Calthorpes' house was recognized by a granddaughter, who pushed for it to be preserved for the sake of its remarkably intact furnishings and equipment. The house was built and furnished in 1927, the life's product of Mrs. Della Calthorpe, a long-lived, meticulous housekeeper who kept not only the receipts from her initial house-furnishing spree but also the generations of technology in the kitchen: a wood stove, a gas stove, and an electric stove. (Such behavior might verge on the obsessive, but social history curators cherish it.) Mrs. Calthorpe lived in the house for fifty-two years; she died in 1979. It was then acquired by local government in 1984 (Bickford 1987). A third example is Mr. Straw's House in Worksop, Nottinghamshire: the duplex house (half inhabited by the Straws, half by tenants) of a successful grocer's family since 1923. Two unmarried sons lived there for a total of sixty-seven years, changing nothing after their parents' deaths in the 1930s. Occupied until 1985, it was opened to the public by the National Trust five years later (Anon. 1993). The survival of another, very humble, furnished house is due to community action in the village of Navenby, Lincolnshire, which rallied to preserve Mrs. Hilda Smith's cottage, her home for seventy-three years

Mrs. Hilda Smith's Cottage, Navenby, Lincolnshire, 2012. A long-time single woman of the lower middle class could rarely expect to purchase her own house in the early twentieth century. This modest dwelling meant the security of property ownership for Mrs. Smith (née Craven).
Photo courtesy of the Friends of Mrs. Smith's Cottage.

(Anon. 2008). The mid-nineteenth-century brick cottage is thought to have been built as accommodation for seasonal rural labor: only a single skin of bricks thick, it was without stairs. Mrs. Smith used a kind of ship's ladder to ascend to the bedroom until her nineties. An electric light was installed in the 1930s; a single cold water tap (no sink) and a toilet inside were added in the 1960s. She died in 1995, and the house was acquired by a trust (Mrs. Smith's Cottage Museum), though the parlous quality of construction and cost of conservation has closed it to visitors.

These examples can astonish modern spectators, and their authenticity, understood as unmediated evidence of the occupant's lifestyle, is a major reason. Accustomed to the standard of living of their youth, Mr. Straw and Mrs. Smith declined most modern services out of satisfaction with the old ways, and Miss Toward and Mrs. Calthorpe found little need to update or dispose of what worked perfectly well for their whole lives. When such dwellings move into the museum sphere, visitors' faith in the integrity of museum practice is usually sufficient to satisfy them of its authenticity. But practitioners are aware that with the best will in the world to maintain as-is, the museumization of each site alters the assemblage from that known by the inhabitant: preliminary interventions such as cleaning, tidying, and stabilizing may have minimal impact, but repairs for the sake of collection or visitor security can be invasive, however well disguised. Whether, or to what degree, these intrusions compromise authenticity is a question that degenerates into Zeno's paradox of infinitely miniscule changes that seem to make finite reality impossible. Hence it is a standard of ethical management to acknowledge the inevitability of change and avoid the term *authentic*, even with qualification.

Though Mrs. Smith's cottage, in particular, was designed to house working-class labor, the fact that she owned it in her own right locates her among the others, as lower-middle to middle-class property holders. Even so, their modest tastes in consumption stand as witnesses to the material expressions of homely thrift and its impact on lived lives. On a public scale, the identification and museumization of houses with indigenous collections of furnishings has intensified a more totalizing awareness of the domestic world by social history curators. Post–World War II specimens have already begun to emerge for museumization, such as the Hardmans' House in Liverpool: the studio, workshops, office, and home of a pair of professional photographers from 1948, museumized in 2004. Survivor houses such as this will continue to be revealed thanks to private ownership, long widowhood, and a lack of heirs. As such, they cannot be expected to encompass the living conditions of the poor and poorest, as the social history paradigm seeks.

A second group of significantly intact houses belonging to less-than-elite inhabitants evolves via the veneration of heroes. The lifetime or mature-age house of a culture hero may be translated into a museum at death, or death of an heir—a juncture where fame justifies preserving the dwelling and furnishings, or a good proportion of them, untouched. Thus the everyday material culture, which is usually culled out of an estate, sometimes survives, intended as relics, but also constitutes further slices of authentic material history. At the upper middle end of the scale in this scenario is Sarah Orne Jewett's family house in South Berwick, Maine, inhabited by the author for sixty years, preserved by her sisters, and transferred by their heir to the Society for the Preservation of New England Antiquities in 1931. Rudyard Kipling's house, Bateman's, in East Sussex, is of similar class, though monogenerational; it was bequeathed to the National Trust in 1939. Maggie L. Walker (1867–1934), daughter of an ex-slave mother and a Northern abolitionist father, and the first female president of a bank in the United States (Saint

Luke Penny Savings Bank, established in 1903 and surviving in merged form until 2009), purchased an appropriately grand house in the early twentieth-century black center of Richmond, Virginia, where she lived with her children and their families (Ruffins 2003, 76–79). The Walker family preserved it until sold, complete with furnishings, to the National Park Service in 1979. I introduce these three houses as "less-than-elite" to acknowledge a spectrum of subelite domestic culture, for they are certainly not "nonelite." However, the fact that there is meaning in contrasting the Jewett, Kipling, and Walker houses with the very opulent houses that constitute a majority of house museums with significant indigenous-authentic furnishings contains its own truth: that the poor and their houses do not survive through time.

Retro-Furnishing Houses

The Jewett, Kipling, and Walker houses were museumized in the spirit of hero commemoration, but they fulfill a parallel agenda in the perspective of social history, demonstrating the agency of individuals to construct homes with the expressive capacity of presenting the owners' dreams of the good life. The ecology of furnishings that accumulate in a life (especially a life comfortably above subsistence level) has logic relative to the individuals who assembled it, which can be called authenticity. It is sometimes possible to reproduce authentic furnishing schemes thanks to graphic evidence, but it often falls to little more than stereotype. The reliable provenance created by heroic association thus contributes important evidence of the diversity of taste and means through time. The density and idiosyncrasy of these collections are as precious as the archaeological domestic assemblages of Pompeii, and like the example of Pompeii, they amount to time capsules of homely minutiae.

But houses with large proportions of in situ furnishings are very scarce, unavoidably introducing the specter of compromise with originality. Such pragmatic dimensions of presenting "authentic" domestic history have been discussed throughout the literature of house museum practice (e.g., Coleman 1939, 72–75; Burns 1941, 255–69; Lewis 1976, 191–99; Shafernich 1993; Carruthers 2003, 90–95; Ponsonby 2007, 157–90). Curatorial compromises emerged on the grounds of common sense and drifted into common use with little analytical attention. Ralph Lewis, whose curatorial career with the National Park Service spanned thirty-six years, recounts telling examples (1993, 223–27). The path was well trodden when the agenda of social history asserted the need for houses representing historically excluded social groups: the practical alternative was compromise via restoration and reproduction. The difference is their relativity on a spectrum from "original" (indigenous or provenanced) to "restored" (similar) to "reproduced" (replica) material, judged according to the professional principles and techniques of historic preservation (see, for example, the US Secretary of the Interior's *Standards for Preservation, Rehabilitation, Restoration, Reconstruction*, National Park Service 2001). Restoration may repair damage, reinstate absent parts, and address modern concerns with safety and convenience; reproduction replaces known originals, with a greater or lesser degree of compromise. In general, restoration is a common mode with furnishings, equipment, and decoration due to their relative transience. Nonetheless, philosophical, aesthetic, historical, and political perspectives often haunt the compromise with the authenticity of original material.

The National Park Service approached the issue via an increasingly formal process, which effectively masked the degree of compromise. The 1941 *Field Manual for Museums* dedicated a chapter to historic house museums, of which it then managed thirty-five. Ned J. Burns, chief of the Museum Branch, recommended that a house should be furnished as it was in its heyday or its significant era; that original furnishings were preferred, but that period pieces or reproductions could satisfy in some circumstances; and that furnishing should follow a researched plan and expert advice. "Far too often a hasty selection of furnishings is made and as a result, a heterogeneous accumulation takes the place of an orderly and pleasing atmosphere," he wrote in the voice of experience, which echoes to this day. And with the Yorktown, Virginia, Moore House doubtless in mind, he added that if an individual or society offers to help, there should be controls and agreements (Burns 1941, 257). The Moore House was the site of the effective end of the Revolutionary War, where the Articles of Capitulation were negotiated in 1781. It suffered badly in the Civil War, was repaired for the centenary of the battle of Yorktown in 1881, and became the first major restoration project of the National Park Service in the early 1930s. The intensive historical, physical, and comparative study undertaken became the prototype of the NPS's modern historic structure report, and a similarly careful furnishing plan was prepared. Patriotic societies were keen to assist, and though theoretically under NPS curatorial control, the rooms rapidly became finer than envisaged, and the labels more filled with the details of donors (as described in chapter 6).

The NPS turned its attention to systematic furnishing plans in 1958 with an order that plans should contain six basic elements: an interpretive purpose; a narrative of the historic occupants; an account of contemporary furnishings for the nominated period; a specification of furnishings for the house; floor plans and elevations marked with the location of each piece; and notes on sources and costs (Lewis 1993, 238). In 1976, Lewis elaborated on the process with a series of pointed questions about the benefit of furnishing a historic house—whether furnishing is the optimal way of interpreting it, whether it can be furnished accurately, and whether maintaining or reintroducing furnishings will facilitate access by visitors (Lewis 1976, 184). Proving the mighty bureaucracy of the NPS, he followed up with a new checklist of ten stages, of which he acknowledged only the last three were under the control of the individual site curator embarking on furnishing. They turned on the Historic Furnishing Plan, requiring thorough research, "enlightened understanding" of life in the period, and "considerable interpretive insight" (Lewis 1976, 189). The NPS stress on the interpretive purpose of furnishing a house museum placed the subject as a responsibility of the Interpretation and Visitor Services Division, established in 1964. The expertise that subsequently grew in this environment was fed by experienced curators drawn in from Park practice, and came to host an extensive materials conservation section. The National Park Service decentralized in the 1990s–2000s, and this specialist expertise was distributed to regional centers.

Updating the corporate body of professional expertise, a new edition of the National Park Service *Museum Handbook* was published in 1998, with additional chapters in 2007, specifically addressing the use of collections in historic furnished structures (including but not limited to houses). They confirmed the primary interpretive purpose of historic furnishings on the ground that objects not only frame evidence of historic people, events, and processes but also set "a tone of authenticity" that, it is hoped, will enable visitors to feel "the presence of history" (NPS 1998, 8.32). The pursuit of historic authenticity continues, though its limits are recognized by frequent admonitions that re-creations should be clearly presented as such. Evidence of professional and public satisfaction with its standards, NPS methods, especially Historic Furnishing Reports and Plans, have spread into wide use throughout the house museum field (Brooks 2002, 129–30). A consortium of federal and state agencies plus individual museums developed standards and guidelines for historic furnished interiors in 2006 to define and share knowledge, evidence of the professionalization of house museum development (NPS NER 2006, 22–114). Still, the craft of the historic furnishings curator in the United States is little analyzed; a rare commentary comes from Carol Petravage, pointing out the temptations of connoisseurship that can obscure interpretive purpose (1998, 151–58). Underlining the rise of philosophical and practical standards is the growth of specialist libraries such as the pioneering Winterthur Library, where collections of trade catalogs, advisory and prescriptive literature, and ephemera concerned with household goods and their use are mined for reliable detail in house museum settings. The impact of such libraries cannot be underestimated.

The modern craft of managing furnishings in historic house environ- ments in the United Kingdom springs from the mid-twentieth-century work of the National Trust and the Country Houses Scheme, pollinated by the Department of Furniture and Woodwork at the Victoria & Albert Museum. Both were informed by British traditions of fine furniture manufacture and restoration, conditioned by the growth, since the mid-nineteenth century, of appreciation for the history and style of antique furniture. These factors, touched on in previous chapters and manifesting again in chapter 8, located British house curatorship practice primarily in elite houses, and responded to standards of presentation prescribed by the disciplines of art history and art conservation. In times when these fields were led by the conviction that the most important aspect of their work was the artist's and/or patron's original vision for the piece or the ensemble, there was a clear rationale to represent furnishing schemes at the moment of initial installation or peak completeness. The concept of a spectrum of stages in the life of a domestic interior opens up the possibility of plausible variants of authenticity. Hence the goal emerged to reassemble dispersed suites of furniture, artworks, and ornaments (a continuing task) and to restore their appearance to the se- lected date.

High-quality restoration of interiors became a marker of National Trust professionalism, its polished perfection contributing perversely to criticism of restored environments as beautiful corpses. Perfection also provoked an antiaesthetic: a taste for ruins, for the patina of use, and for quirky irregu- larities of manufacture, which connects to the historic antirestorationism of John Ruskin and William Morris, and to the modern concept of "the social life of things" (Appadurai 1986). The archival and archaeological principle that meaning can be found in the relationships of objects in assemblages joined this vortex of ideas about the significance of the imperfect or irregu- lar to justify an alternative mode of conservation: the leave-as-is approach to presenting historic interiors (Ponsonby 2015, 44–46). The conservation of Calke Abbey in 1985–1989 and Brodsworth Hall in 1988–1990 by the National Trust and English Heritage, respectively, pioneered the concept of stabilization as viable management for complex furnishing assemblages (Allfrey 1999). The Calke-Brodsworth style of purism has applications only in very particular circumstances, so it will never be a common mode of house presentation. It does, however, represent the logical endpoint of the gamut of modes to conserve authentic historic furnishing schemes.

Interpretation and Reconstruction

Preserving, restoring, retro-furnishing, and stabilizing original historic houses are techniques with materialist dimensions that anchor them to the physically authentic existence of house museums. At the same time, the motive of individuals and groups who museumize houses is to mark aspects of history they believe to be significant enough to merit attention in the public sphere. Their goal is to mobilize authentic material as evidence of their truth-claim, trusting that the reality of bricks and mortar (or wattle and daub) can convince visitors to see and agree with the larger ideas they commend. This is a typical manifestation of the social process of the construction of heritage, articulating the value of the past in the present via structures with the capacity to persist through time. It rests solidly on the idea of authenticity as original material, but what carries it across the gap between walls and floors to the objective of acknowledged values is the process of heritage interpretation.

A famous definition of heritage interpretation was devised by Freeman Tilden, a writer and editor for the National Park Service in the 1950s: "An educational activity which aims to reveal meanings through the use of original objects, by firsthand experience, and by illustrative media, rather than simply to communicate factual information" (Tilden 1957, 8). This definition is still very useful, as long as it's understood that the meanings proffered in each interpretive act are created socially and contextually, and are not singular truths. The delivery model that Tilden had in mind was the Park Ranger explaining large ideas about ecology and environment, illustrated by the stones, leaves, and feathers that can be picked up in the course of a walk. These real objects appear to prove the main message, or at least to demonstrate it convincingly. By linking their authentic nature to the science (or faith or politics) of the interpreter's words, visitors with a basically positive attitude toward the topic can feel they achieve insight and new knowledge about the topic. In this way, heritage interpretation is key in fulfilling the Park Service mission: "To preserve unimpaired the natural and cultural resources and values of the National Park System for the enjoyment, education, and inspiration of this and future generations."

The ranger-guided walk is just the beginning of interpretive techniques that invoke the palpable presence of the subject, be it environment, art, science, or history. Insofar as the furnishing modes discussed above convey meanings by their presence in a house museum, they too constitute interpretive techniques. For the bulk of house museums without much or any original furnishing, a range of further heritage management processes should be considered more as interpretation than as curatorial expertise. This is because a furnished interior is intended to rise above mere spectacle, to communicate the significance that the house is asserted to embody or represent. Thus we come to reconstruction, experimental archaeology, living history, and museum theater. Each mode contains real discipline and expertise, but the aim of critically reviewing the idea of authenticity in house museums demands that they be considered here as methods of communication rather than as fields of practice in themselves.

Thus, although apparently a contradiction in terms, a primary technique to achieve authenticity in house museums is the interpretive reconstruction (Ponsonby 2015, 46–47). The desire to enable experience of the past in spatial forms that are unavailable other than via archives or archaeology has inspired generations of romantics, pedagogues, and museum makers. The apotheosis of all three is Colonial Williamsburg, where, in the 1920s, the Rev. W. A. R. Goodwin observed that the town's historic center contained numerous authentic buildings dating to the eighteenth century, which with some judicious demolition, restoration, and reconstruction could represent the germinal environment of American patriotism as a site for the improvement of modern citizens. With the resources of J. D. Rockefeller Jr. behind the project, it launched as Williamsburg Restoration Inc. in 1929, with a plan to create a museum precinct within the town to the period of the 1770s. The 731 buildings were removed, 81 were reconstructed, and 413 were restored on their original sites (Whiffen 1958, v). Among those judged to contain sufficient historic fabric to be called original, and to be restored, were Bruton Parish Church (Goodwin's pastoral base), the Court House, and the College of William and Mary. The reconstructions, based on historical, archaeological, and comparative architectural research, began with the Raleigh Tavern in 1931, the Virginia Capitol in 1934, and the Governor's Palace in 1935: they are key to the institutional claim to authenticity. In these six public sites the colonial experience of religion, law, education, free society, government, and despotism was represented as a crucible of freedom-loving American republicanism. Embedding the big themes in the carefully pruned, restored, and reconstructed town fabric physically connected eighteenth-century Virginia style to the twentieth-century patriotic agenda.

The 1930s years of building cast the Williamsburg project as essentially architectural, orienting staff and contractor knowledge toward a new domain of applied architectural history for the purposes of historic preservation. The need for historical and archaeological expertise was admitted slowly. But from inexperience in applying technical findings to the goal of large-scale restoration and reconstruction, the professional staff of the Williamsburg

Restoration developed the first historic preservation studio in the United States, and the organization's reputation rose by sharing knowledge and exporting specialists to develop restoration sites elsewhere. Implicit in the project was the conviction that the artifice of the entire reconstruction would be guaranteed by expertise; its credibility would be guarded by a number of advisory boards; and the whole operation would be underwritten by the authentic presence of original fabric. Managerial excellence and proven resource would guarantee the integrity of the message of inspirational Americanism (Hosmer 1981; Yetter 1988; Greenspan 2002). The elasticity of the notion of authenticity stretched wide, rather than deep, at Williamsburg, and it has proved a very palatable conception in American restoration practice.

Colonial Williamsburg is now approaching its centenary, and its record as a manager of the past has influenced generations of visitors and of international heritage management practice. Not without criticism: the rising heritage movement castigated Williamsburg's reputation as the archetype of American historical representation. Ada Louise Huxtable began a long critical relationship in 1963, with a *New York Times* piece that condemned the organization for demolishing the unwanted past in favor of restoring and reconstructing a desired past, arguing that the product was a selective fantasy (Huxtable 1963). Other critics began to note analogies with Disneyland and contrasts with competitor historical villages. By the bicentennial year, 1976, the tasteful charm and pristine cleanliness of Williamsburg seemed shallow to many visitors; they also observed the absence of slavery in its history and of African Americans in its presentation (Greenspan 2002, 142–47). In the long run, the shift to the paradigm of social history and associated new focus on history education addressed these challenges (as discussed in chapter 6). Meanwhile, the heritage movement nurtured new philosophical and technical standards in historic preservation procedures, and Williamsburg-style wholesale restoration and reconstruction declined in professional standing. At the same time, a new generation of converts to the heritage critique were already on the job, galvanized by Ivor Noel Hume's professionalization of historical archaeology. Their influence on the development of the 1980s phase of reconstructions was grounded in purposeful adherence to educational objectives in planning, and informed by historically revisionist approaches to design, but still dedicated to excavating something materially authentic.

Such voices draw on experience to contribute to the reflexive analysis of evolving heritage practice. The critiques of fantasy, on the one hand, and obsession with authenticity, on the other, are acknowledged and defended, respectively, on the basis of historical relativism and the social history-led commitment to inclusive education. Reevaluation of the Colonial Revival

Governor's Palace garden, Colonial Williamsburg, 1934. The uncritical production of Colonial Revival charm has been somewhat tamed by social history research since the 1990s.
Postcard, private collection.

aesthetic infusing the 1930s restoration era points out that it was of its time, expressing contemporary knowledge and values, and argues that, eighty years later, it is unjust and unhelpful merely to dismiss it (e.g., Lounsbury 2011; Chappell 2002). At the same time, revisions emerged, beginning with a controversial, plainer refurnishing of the Governor's Palace in 1981 and continuing today, for example, with a program of repainting in mineral colors the exteriors of many formerly white buildings (Hood 2000; Chase 2014). Tackling the ethics of reconstruction, a review of Williamsburg's record grapples with the negotiation between reconstruction as a powerful mode of interpretation and its high potential to mislead visitors by "sliding down the slippery path of speculation towards the netherworld of fantasy" (Noel Hume, quoted by Brown & Chappell 2004, 47). Inconveniently, local historical fantasies such as geometric box hedge gardens tend to be identified in retrospect, when rationales made at the time are long forgotten. It's part and parcel of intergenerational revisionism, enmeshed in the conviction that new readings of old records and reexamination of archaeological findings can bring reconstruction ever closer to the perfection of authentic historical reality. In practice, with some humility, Williamsburg revisionists acknowledge today that they tread where others have trod before, and that in improving the presentation of the past, they again introduce present values. Thus Williamsburg architectural historian Carl Lounsbury riffs on the risks of an institution founded on other generations' visions of history, with an apocryphal scheme for warning signs about authenticity around the site: "Now entering the Colonial Revival Area: this is how people in the 1930s imagined the eighteenth century. Do not mistake it for a past that cannot be recaptured" (Lounsbury 2011, 251).

Experimental Archaeology, Living History, and Museum Theater

Colonial Williamsburg currently calls itself the world's largest living history museum. In claiming the mantle, it asserts directions that its archaeological research division helped to invent: the project popularly known as experimental archaeology. Emerging in the mid-twentieth century, often with an academic agenda, the methodology of experimental archaeology merged easily into the frame of living history, such that any distinction between the two is in the minds of practitioners more than apparent to visitors. The common objective of practical authenticity stimulated and justified the surge of reconstructed or re-created dwellings presented in open-air museums (Anderson 1991, 87–99). Prehistoric archaeology in the United Kingdom and the United States had long studied from the Bronze Age to the Pilgrim Fathers. Out of the remains, experimental archaeologists generated reconstructions, which picked up the living history idea: it came to inform many conventional house museums.

A primal source of the trend is Butser Ancient Farm in Hampshire, established in 1972 and operating until 1989 as an experimental research program into Iron Age agriculture and domestic life. An adjacent site was developed in 1976 for public access as an open-air museum, and a third site followed in 1991, with Iron Age roundhouses and early Romano-British structures for trialing and interpretive purposes (Reynolds 1979, 1999). Butser inspired a number of further ancient British houses and farms, not usually identifying as house museums but satisfying my definition sufficiently to include them as expressions of the mode as well as to acknowledge the impact of archaeological experiments on articulating the likely realities of ancient life. The lure of reconstruction animated by reenactment sparked popular interest, and it was fed by British television reality documentaries showing modern people volunteering to live the life of the Iron Age, as in *Living in the Past* (1978) and *Surviving the Iron Age* (2001). Their success bred a genre of fly-on-the-wall television series in the archaeologically correct living history mode, set in various historic times and circumstances, beginning with *The 1900 House* in 1999 (McCrum & Sturgis 1999). Spin-offs followed around the English-speaking world and in Europe. Academic historians have since analyzed the conviction that participating in, or simply watching, embodied experience of the past provides deeper understanding of living in the past than archive sources can; they conclude that it makes a different rather than "truer" understanding (McCalman & Pickering 2010). However understood, it is clear that the ethic of the real-time experience of living history excites the imagination of viewers, and reorients their expectations of personal experience in conventional, static house museums.

Archaeologically informed living history also emerged in the United States, where the initial experimental subjects were the Indigenous people of the land. The history of an early example, Chucalissa Indian Village near Memphis, Tennessee, demonstrated the rising issue of the civil and cultural rights of Indigenous people. The excavated site of Chucalissa opened to the public in 1956, complete with reconstructed houses representing a Mississippian settlement of the fifteenth century; displays were amplified by dioramas of shamanic rituals and excavated burials. (Chucalissa was the biggest tourism attraction in Memphis before the death of Elvis Presley.) But the standards of professional archaeology began to fall in line with the temper of the indigenous cultural rights movement, subsequently mandated by the 1990 Native American Graves Protection and Repatriation Act (NAGPRA). Chucalissa management had covered the graves in 1985, and the reconstructed village, increasingly regarded as inauthentic and old-fashioned, was closed in the early 2000s in favor of a museum with a hands-on archaeology lab (Gorman 2013). Nonetheless, other archaeologically inspired sites continue to thrive under the banner of the open-air museum.

The most self-consciously archaeological case transposed the experimental focus into historic time: Plimoth Plantation near Boston aims to reproduce life in 1627, seven years after the arrival of the Pilgrim Fathers in America (Anderson 1991, 45–52). Plimoth became enormously influential in the museum world thanks to the shift piloted by Assistant Director James Deetz. From 1967, an existing open-air village was rebuilt, relandscaped, and refurnished on the basis of historical and archaeological research, bolstered by the lessons of experimental practice. The interpretive perspective was initially in the conventional third-person mode of explaining historic ways of life to visitors, but as staff took on historical characters, they came via role play to first-person interpretation. It suited the institutional commitment to authenticity and was popular with visitors, who proved very willing to participate in "the sense of a different reality—the reality of another time" (Deetz 1991, 15). Paradoxes emerged, potentially subverting the ideal of the authentic seventeenth century, such as the weathering of the

A Pilgrim lad pushes a barrow at Plimoth Plantation, 1975. Work that takes characters out into the woods or fields is today more often accompanied by a musket than a sword. It's not known whether this is the fruit of further research or inconvenient experience.
Photo by, and courtesy of, Charles G. Kellogg.

village buildings, making them seem quaintly old instead of raw and new. Another distortion of modernity follows the turnover of interpretive staff, who tend to be young and casual, with the consequence that there are few middle-aged people or children evident as inhabitants of Plimoth. The site's communicative transformation from costumed, third-person interpretation to profoundly embodied, first-person performance was analyzed by a two-season participant, Stephen Snow, as an organic development in the quest for authenticity (1993, 21–48). He concludes that the Plimoth experiment constitutes a new genre of cultural performance with special application for those who sense the personal motivation of pilgrimage in their visit, while also providing a satisfying recreational attraction in the rituals of postmodern tourism (Snow 1993, 206–12).

Living history without recourse to archaeological reference points shares the goal of "making history come alive" (Anderson 1991, 3–12). The developers of living history almost everywhere looked first to the Nordic folk museums, and then to the great US historical villages of the interwar period (Rentzhog 2007, 236–87). A distinction lies between the Skansen concept of specimen houses interpreted within an open-air museum and those village re-creations aiming to present total environments. The village idea, profoundly informed by the 1930s re-creations, exerted an almost irresistible logic in the development of living history sites and historical villages at the cost of an unhistorical predominance of trade workshops, retail shops, and civic structures over dwellings (Young 2006). It is a characteristic inconsistency of art(ifice) imitating life in the setting of heritage, and it is not the only one.

As an interpretive mode, the totalizing world of impeccably re-created life risks the trap of perfectionism as an end in itself. It poses the paradoxical question: Is it possible to have enough, or even too much, authenticity? The fallacy of the ultrarealist approach is often recognized by visitors, well informed by the reality techniques of filmmaking and the hyper-reality of computer games; yet it seems not to disturb either understanding or pleasure. In fact, visitors to living history sites have been documented by many observers as deliberately engaging playfully with the dual time of then and now (Snow 1993, 180–82; Bruner 1994, 411; Rutherford-Morrison 2015). This highlights two important insights about "visiting the past." First, visitors willingly suspend disbelief for the sake of an engaging experience; second, though they participate in activities and demonstrations, visitors do not actually step into anachronistic character (with the exception of school groups, clothed or at least hatted both for personal connection and for ready identification around the site). In a living history environment, visitors remain in the present as entangled observers of the past. That this voluntary dualism doesn't undermine the quality of their experience suggests that "enough" authenticity may not need to be "total" authenticity.

In the United States, much living history is enacted in rural settings, and adds an important population segment to the modern inclusive social history agenda. Agricultural life is a source of national myths everywhere and justifies many a museum, thanks to the conviction that the countryside nurtures native spirit uncorrupted by the sins of modernity. The ideological push to demonstrate the purity of rural life coincides neatly with the microscale of living history in rural settings; hence stereotypes haunt the presentation of daily life (see the illustrations in Anderson 1991). Conventional limits and their inherent values have been criticized practically since the emergence of the living history genre, at least in part provoked by its claim of authenticity (e.g., Leone 2009; West 1986). While gendered and racialized lives constituted historical reality, the uses of museums today require challenging the power of now-unacceptable social relations via interpretation that goes beyond authentic microenvironments. Examples are the Old World Wisconsin collection of ten historic farms of various immigrant nationalities, and the long-running "Follow the North Star" runaway slave drama at Connor Prairie, near Indianapolis, Indiana, in which visitors flee from slave hunters through houses and outbuildings. There was a time when living history museums subtitled themselves "authentic reproductions" (as at Lincoln's New Salem, previously mentioned). In 2016, this claim has disappeared, and whether for accuracy, fashion, or rebranding, terms such as *interactive history* are rising in the subtitles of American living history sites. It's a good phrase, addressing the capacity of visitors and downplaying the need for authenticity.

The practice of site-based living history is not the same in the United Kingdom as in the United States. Rural culture epitomized by farm sites dominates the type in America. By contrast, the numerous historic farms in the United Kingdom offer living history embodied in historic, now-rare, breeds of animals rather than human reenactors. Focusing on humans, industrial history is a much bigger "living" theme in the United Kingdom, and meticulously costumed interpreters thrive in a number of large site museums of in situ, relocated and replica buildings. Foremost is the complex of Beamish, the North of England Open Air Museum, in County Durham, which has grown and diversified since opening in 1972 (Rentzhog 2007, 225–35). It now presents a "1900s Town" composed of relocated and replica buildings, mainly shops and workshops, plus a terrace row housing domestic businesses: a dentist's front-room surgery and a music teacher's genteel parlor. In another corner of the Beamish site is a coal mine and associated "1900s Pit Village"; here another terrace houses a Methodist family, an immigrant Irish Catholic family, and a woman widowed by a mine fatality. In yet another quarter of the site, the World War II home front is presented in a farmhouse living on wartime rations, with cottages inhabited by Land Girls of the Women's Land Army and a family of city wartime evacuees. In these settings, well-defined characters interpret stories whose specificity can carry challenging historical themes of labor, religion, and politics as well as demonstrating the historic material culture of ordinary life.

The spectrum of costumed interpretation in museum settings, and its furthest expression as living history, translates into another sphere through the lens of performance studies. This shift in perspective introduces an important outcome for the idea of authenticity: that visitors can apprehend another kind of understanding via the aesthetics of theater (Kirschenblatt-Gimblett 1998, 248). In this view, art authorizes emotion as a channel of perception, whereas other interpretive techniques operate in the domain of cognition. Restoration, reconstruction, experimental archaeology, and living history can incite the mindfulness of wonder, shock, and empathy, but the impact created by theatrical performance is licensed by imaginative sensation. The very term *theatrical* contains a dangerous whiff of fantasy that could seem in opposition to the rationality of other modes of heritage interpretation (Snow 1993, 132–48; Magelssen 2007, 116–19). That fear is hard to reconcile with Tilden's principles of interpretation, the third of which positions interpretation as "an art which combines many arts," while the fourth famously asserts, "The chief aim of interpretation is not instruction but provocation" (Tilden 1957, 9). Fortunately, suspicion is countered by a bundle of research demonstrating that museum theater engages emotion and intellect, with measurable increases in recall and empathy (Jackson & Rees Leahy 2005; Kidd 2011).

In practice, theatrical performance had already moved into the interpretation of social history via individuals (such as Dot McCree, progenitor of the Young National Trust Theater in 1978) and the broader Theatre in Education movement, beginning in the 1960s; its momentum coalesced into the International Museum Theater Alliance in 1990 (Jackson 2013). In Britain, the Historic Royal Palaces has employed a company of actors, Past Pleasures, since 1987, at the Tower of London and Hampton Court Palace; other companies also develop and perform interpretive theater. Dramatic vignettes of a day in history happen around the site throughout each day, for visitors to follow or chance upon. They are introduced by a master of ceremonies, who sketches the context and instructs visitors when to take off their hats, bow, and shout "God save the King!" Dressed in high-quality costumes, the actors may follow a script as well as extemporize. Their performances are hugely appreciated, according to Internet reviews.

Dramatic (performance) and postdramatic (participatory) presentations are equally popular within museum and site organizations for their capacity to introduce complex historical contexts, present contestant positions of dilemma, and evoke affective responses that heighten awareness (Jackson & Vine 2013, 4–12). The maximum demonstration of this claim was so devastatingly effective that it has never been repeated: the 1994 presentation of a slave auction at Colonial Williamsburg. Cary Carson, longtime head of interpretation, recounts the event as a counterpoint case study throughout a long article tracing the site's approaches to interpretation (Carson 1998, 19–20, 43–45, 51). The decision to enact a slave auction was made by members of the African American interpretation department, and they prepared the script; Christy Matthews Coleman, who managed it, later described the group's motivation to push boundaries, to engage with contention (Carson 1998, 20). In the event, black and white activists, communities, and visitors were horrified by the apparent condoning of racist history by the museum, and there were pleas and threats to stop it. Nonetheless, the actor-interpreters were determined. The event commenced with the banality of auction regulations; then a woman was sold to her free black husband; a man was sold high, for his carpenter skill; and a pregnant couple was sold, separately. There were silence and tears in the audience. Afterward, a black objector told a television interviewer, "Pain had a face, indignity had a body, suffering had tears. We saw all of that" (Carson 1998, 51). Evidently the episode had been traumatic for all involved; afterward, the actor-interpreters concluded it was too draining to offer again. Later, the event was criticized for failing to engage the "emotionally engaged but passive" audience in further discussion, and for sanitizing the presentation by not including beating, stripping, and other horrors (Stupp 2011, 81). Yet if shocking observation is not enough to press an audience into contemplating the historical conditions of evil and its continuing ramifications, it's hard to imagine what could be effective. If this critique can be sustained, museum and site interpretation is a hopeless project, contrary to many accounts.

To my mind, a more than adequate sufficiency of popular and scholarly evidence exists that the spectrum of (hi)story-telling media deployed in house and site museums has an objective effect on visitors that enlarges experience, stimulates imagination, and challenges understanding. The agenda may be clothed in an educational mission, but that phrase hides the ways in which visitors make use of heritage resources to activate pleasurable encounters for leisure. It also masks the satisfactions of informal learning as the motivation for visiting museums and sites. The consumers of this kind of cultural product show signs of being less in need of assertions of authenticity than its producers. This is due not least to the high degree of trust that the (American and Australian) public assigns to museums, little knowing how much energy and ingenuity goes into ensuring, or hoping to ensure, authenticity (Rosenzweig & Thelen 1998, 91; Ashton & Hamilton 2007, 78). The lesson of the odyssey of authenticity in museums lies in its constant reprocessing by the organs of heritage.

CHAPTER EIGHT

⁓

The English Country House

The English country house is a species of house museum unique to the United Kingdom. While the phrase *country house* can mean "a house in the country," in practice it refers to the great houses of the aristocracy and wealthier gentry, defined in distinction to a "town house" in London. The vision it evokes today is a site of ancestral grandeur, open for the public to see magnificent art, architecture, and gardens.[1] This kind of country house is the inspiration of numerous grand house museums in the New World: there may well be as many "English country house–style" house museums in the rest of the British world as in England itself. The global influence of the original model is a further reason to consider local and global derivative English country houses as a taxonomic category in this study.

There is a long habit of resistance in the United Kingdom to naming country houses that are open to the public for fee-paying visitation as "museums." The thought was abhorred when a country house rescue scheme was first proposed at the annual general meeting of the National Trust in 1934: "Nothing is more melancholy than to visit these ancient houses after they have been turned into public museums. . . . If they are to be preserved, they must be maintained, save perhaps for a few great palaces, for the uses for which they were designed," said the eleventh Marquess of Lothian, who subsequently left Blickling, one of several ancestral houses he inherited, to the Trust (Gaze 1988, 121). As the Country House Scheme took shape during and after the years of World War II, it became an article of faith in the National Trust that houses become "inert when deserted by the ancient families;

at best half-alive when lived in by usurping parvenus; and wholly dead when inhabited by no one but a custodian" (Lees-Milne 1992, 16). The conviction that museumization means death is old and persistent. It has been shown to be most strongly held among people who don't actually visit museums (Merriman 1991, 62), though it is doubtless also colored by the anguish of owners who could not afford the upkeep of their houses and had to part with them. But a generational and professional shift in National Trust management at the turn of the twenty-first century decisively refocused country houses as historical documents of social life, design, and landscape rather than as relics of the aristocracy. Today the aura of family occupation is emphasized mainly in the privately owned houses, whose websites frequently include images of the current family in residence. This device presents a gesture of the traditional owners offering to share with the (admission-paying) public sites that are popularly regarded as quintessential English national heritage. The welcome fails to mention that, in exchange for certain minimums of public access, the owners can access government grants to help with expensive heritage conservation, and can avoid or ameliorate succession taxes.

Some seven hundred privately owned country house estates band together for lobbying and marketing purposes in the Historic Houses Association (it also represents smaller houses and many gardens, in Scotland and Ireland as well as England, currently totaling about 1,600 sites); most of this group is open for a limited summer season of public visiting. Some, such as Chatsworth, Castle Howard, and Harewood House, where ownership has shifted to a nonprofit trust, have adopted the full professional apparatus of museology and heritage management. A smaller but higher-profile fraction of great country houses is owned by government and charitable nonprofit agencies. Their epitome is the statutorily established National Trust, with about 150 great country houses. The other major ownership agencies are local authorities, with about a hundred, and English Heritage, with some twenty (Musson 2012, 74). Some 30 percent of the National Trust's houses are still inhabited by families who once owned them, a circumstance explored further in this chapter. None of the local government or English Heritage houses are occupied other than in the service quarters or outbuildings.

A family in residence is the basis of the distinction that such houses are "living": "I feel passionately that great houses die when there is no one to live in them," writes Lady Emma Barnard, who lives in an apartment of Parham Park, Sussex, acquired by her great-grandparents in 1922 (Kirk 2009, 180). The special magic of occupation by traditional owners is adduced by the Historic Houses Association, exemplified in the report *The Disintegration of a Heritage: Country Houses and Their Collections, 1979–1992*: "It is the lived-in quality of the country house that contributes so much to the refreshment of visitors and the *genius loci*" (Sayer 1993, 20). If the spirit of family occupation of a house enabled all families to apply for conservation assistance from government, the difference might be sustainable. But in practice, the "life-giving" continuity of people whose family once owned the place smacks of the mystification of ancestry and wealth. That said, it is undeniable that the idea of resident aristocrats is popular with many visitors. Still, inhabited or not, if the house satisfies the conventional standards of a museum by maintaining a cultural resource, open to the public and not for profit, then it is meaningless to maintain that it is not a museum.

This chapter acknowledges that not all country houses are museums, and generally concerns itself with the country houses that have adopted the standards and practices of professional museology, usually as a means of survival, but with real commitment to the satisfactions of presenting and interpreting a remarkable cultural heritage to the public. As Barnard also writes, "To live here is a very great privilege and a great responsibility. . . . It is such a joy that so many others can come here, so that Parham can make a place in their hearts as well" (Kirk 2009, 180–81).

Visiting the Country House

There is a long tradition of outsiders visiting aristocratic country houses to admire their architecture and collections (Tinniswood 1989). It thrived as a genteel phenomenon of the later eighteenth century, as a new fraction of the population acquired the discretionary income to support the leisure of touring. Respectable folk arriving in carriages could apply to the housekeeper to be shown around the great rooms, for a small consideration. At first, these visitors were accommodated with a sense of noblesse oblige deriving from the tradition of hospitality to strangers. But as numbers rose, owners and housekeepers of the most popular country houses introduced the elements of modern tourism management, such as opening hours and booked tickets, to cope with the number of enthusiastic visitors. The spread of railways and public holidays in the Victorian period expanded the market. Adrian Tinniswood cites the opening of a new railway in 1849, delivering five hundred "respectable, orderly and well-dressed individuals" to Rowsley Station, three miles from Chatsworth, where they were taken by omnibus and admitted in groups of twenty for free. Some visitors saw the duke in the house and in his carriage and were thrilled, indicating the more deferential relationship of the working class to His Grace than the civility of equal culture expressed by the genteel middle-class visitors (Tinniswood 1989, 144–45).

Chatsworth House, 1913. Chatsworth presents an archetype of the English stately home, seat of the noble Cavendish family since the 1540s. Nearly abandoned in the mid-twentieth century, Chatsworth was revived as a tourist destination under curatorial management, with a highly effective marketing base.
Postcard, Wikimedia Commons.

A step above and ahead of such aristocratic openness was the model of royalty. Queen Victoria announced the year after her coronation that the State Apartments of Hampton Court Palace should be open to the public for free, after a century of genteel admission paid to the housekeeper: a visit cost one shilling in 1737. Having excluded the proletariat for so long, opinions disagreed on the wisdom of permitting them free access, but the right was keenly taken up. While an 1841 Select Committee on National Monuments noted that visitors were numerous and "the propriety of their demeanour has fully warranted this accommodation," metal barriers around furniture and grilles over pictures were introduced by 1857. Hampton Court was less than an hour from London on the Southwest Railway and attracted around two hundred thousand visitors every year between 1850 and 1870 (Thurley 2003, 317–20; Tinniswood 1989, 131–32).

Tourism as the main mode of country house visiting soared from 1949, when the Marquess of Bath opened Longleat, enlarged with a suite of attractions including (leased) lions; it expanded in 1966 into a full-scale safari park (Littlejohn 1997, 80–83). The demand to visit country houses developed in line with modern tourism after World War II. The product was reshaped at the same time, due to the owners' need to make their expensive-to-maintain assets profitable. The Duke of Bedford wrote an amusing but hard-nosed account in 1971: *How to Run a Stately Home*. Here he claimed to be mystified by visitors' expectation of special magic in a present, visible duke, but added that since he was not a charity, he was very grateful that sales increased 50 percent when he was at work behind the souvenir counter (Bedford 1971, 32). He added a safari park to Woburn Abbey some years after opening, and soon acknowledged that three-quarters of his visitors came to the park rather than the house, noting that the game park solved all his financial problems. The duke wrote light-heartedly, but his experience of tourism operations was well founded. His analysis of visitor motivation, "Why do they come?" (he suggests a romantic fantasy to identify with the owner), aptly precedes modern theoretical models of identity formation via tourism, and his focus on "good loos, and plenty of them" is really pragmatic (Bedford 1971, 103, 114).

The country house visit can be defined bluntly as public access to the house—as a family, a peer group, or sometimes a packaged experience. The rationale is well explained as commodified hedonistic fantasy. A tour to a country house is the entrée to spacious privilege and tasteful riches, where visitors can imaginatively cast themselves as players, sharing or deploring ("I love/hate the yellow sofa") and costing and evaluating ("I would/wouldn't give ten pounds for that") the material trappings of aristocratic culture. Increasingly, country houses have opened the "below stairs" world of servant life in response to the popular interest in the social history of life in the country house, and it is clear that visitors equally enjoy the exposure of the workings of the grand life. However, it must be said that contemplating the world of chamber pot emptying and hearth blackening is hedonistic more in the sense of exercising the imagination than in fantasizing about possession. Laurajane Smith found that some modern English visitors clothe their visits to country houses in their own family histories of service, with unsurprisingly critical views on the old order of domestic social relations (Smith 2006, 155–58). Similarly, the TV reality history show of 2002, *The Edwardian Country House*, demonstrated that the modern volunteer subjects who were assigned to live and work as servants found social relations in the great house a sour experience (Gardiner 2002, 266–68). Modern visitors seem capable of trying on the multiple personae of the country house, imagining themselves in different roles and drawing confident conclusions about the experience.

The difference in responses between historic and modern country house visitors points to the crux of the presentation of country houses as museums: the opening up of private privilege to public consumption via tourism. It is a particularly complex site of cultural production because, though country houses were always intended for display as well as for dwelling, the original intent was display to a select audience of social equals and local inferiors—an assertion of status directed toward both audiences. Modern tourism, drawing on the concept of country houses as national heritage, now situates the country house museum as a place for all to know as democratic equals. The objective of display intended to validate aristocratic inclusion or assert servile exclusion via a culture of deference has been displaced to the cultural domains of aesthetics and social history. That is to say, what is admired today is the magnificence of architecture, furnishings, and gardens, and the intricacies of life—high and low—in the house, rather than the lords who owned and practiced it. Observing and imaginatively appropriating such varieties of cultural practice separates modern country house tourists from visitors in the era of the feudal politics that inspired their construction and decoration.

The shift in country house visiting from a ritual of rank and deference to a commodified experience of fantasy projection, art appreciation, and historical exhibition coincides with the technologies of mass tourism. Leisure was a key environment of country house visiting in its heyday, and while the sociology of tourism proposes that the social aspects of leisure are generally more important than the substance, the object of the visit frames the experience. The visit of duke to duke, or rising political man to duke, or genteel Victorian family to ducal country house, were different in terms of invited and uninvited motivation, but they enacted particular social relationships between the aristocrat and his or her visitors, within the environment of the country house. Since leisure and culture have ceased to be elite preserves, the major personal and social interactions that occur in modern country house visiting today are those within the visiting group, and with the house's attendant staff.

Dean MacCannell's perspective that tourism is a search for authentic experience suggests how the country house visit works in our times (MacCannell 1999). Whether driven by fantasy or cultural experience, visitors to country houses today focus on the representation of history, style, and/or life in the house and grounds, generating new or intensified knowledge or feelings about the self. In this way the visit is an act of cultural production, in a particular setting that is also a special (even sanctified) object—the house. Visitors construct an experience shaped by interpreting what they see as aesthetically or imaginatively different from the everyday, which can propel them into new intellectual or sensory directions. The authenticity of the experience can never really be so, because under the conditions of tourism it is inevitably staged to a greater or lesser degree. Furnishing layout, the picture hang, ornaments, and carpets are arranged to facilitate conservation and security along with access, as well as to produce frozen moments of "authentic" historicity. Similarly, "below stairs" presentations are contingently and obviously anachronistic in an era of few, if any, household servants. Family or caretaker quarters, not to mention administration offices, remain discreetly off stage, separate from the public.

Luckily, a body of research now indicates that what MacCannell named "staged authenticity" does not undermine the effectiveness of country house visiting. Even if tourists continue to seek authenticity, postmodern awareness informs them that what they find is a construct. Tourists of the twenty-first century can acknowledge that events are "staged but not necessarily inauthentic"—staged, but still meaningful, enjoyable, and worthwhile (Chhabra, Healy & Sills 2003, 715–16). The dining table set with porcelain, silver, and flowers, the butler's pantry equipped with decanters of whiskey-colored liquid, the opulently re-created swagged damask curtains, are techniques of scenography, demarcated by a velvet rope or carpet track. And as with the experience of attending a play, country house visitors suspend disbelief to engage to a greater or lesser degree with the story of the place, making idiosyncratic and shared connections with all the staged dimensions of the house: front region, back region, and crossovers of behind the scenes (MacCannell 1999, 94–104).

Perhaps the foregoing should be rewritten, qualifying the experience to *willing* country house visitors, those who *want* to create a hedonistic imaginative experience for themselves. This doesn't necessarily mean imagining the self as duchess or gardener, but implies an affective interaction with characters and/or their material culture. It is the zone in which the visitor can be said to engage in identity construction, extending and exploring the mental web within which humans exercise their perception of the world. One might incorporate a painting that appeals, another might fantasize about the great bed or imagine the labor of cleaning the room. Guided tours, brochures, and guidebooks may be part of the engagement, but structured information is far from the limits of how visitors apprehend the house space. The resistant visitor will never be engaged in this way, though he or she may find satisfaction in cynicism. The virtue of heritage visiting is that it is generally voluntary, with the exceptions of adolescent school groups and reluctant partners. Even they can be drawn in by gifted interpreters.

The Aristocratic Context of the Country House

To open up the portmanteau phrase *English country house* reveals a spill of riches within a modest linguistic container. It is an understatement to call the palaces of the English nobility on their ancestral lands "houses in the country"; the context needs to be expanded. It has a five-hundred-year history, effectively the modern history of England and its ruling class, filled with revolutions and evolutions in politics, economy, technology, and society. The key factors of the country house as a microcosm of English power began with possession of estates large enough to make rents that kept the owner rich (the *Returns of Owners of Land,* also known as the "New Domesday Book," reporting to Parliament in 1873–1876, specified more than ten thousand acres as the measure of a great estate). The estate needed to be populous enough to vote for him or a family member to represent them in Parliament, and intricate enough for a range of social relationships focusing on the great house and its lord. The owner of these conditions was not always a titled peer of the realm (Beckett 1986). In fact, the greater gentry, the rank that could be acknowledged into aristocratic social (if not power) relations (people whom the "New Domesday" defined as owning three thousand to ten thousand acres), constituted a large part of the demographic that owned country houses (Wilson & Mackley 2000, 7–9). This upper gentry lived by the code of deference to hereditary authority and in as noble a manner as possible: the aristocracy was the zenith of desirable lifestyle.

There was no reliable way to enter the aristocracy other than the king's or queen's favor. Upward mobility into the sphere where caste became hereditary was less common than myth suggests (Stone & Stone 1984, 20). Where it happened, elevation to the nobility was draped in wealth and nurtured by personal service (often of a financial kind) to the monarch. It often occurred so late in a career that the second generation enjoyed the fruits of prestige more than the founder. An invariable step in the course of constructing a new aristocratic lineage was to acquire large-scale property and a country house (Beckett 1986, 66–70). It could be a brand new house; the makeover of an old place, newly acquired; or a smaller house that had been in the family when it was more gentry than nobility, as long as it was surrounded by ample acres.

Estates and their country houses were (somewhat) protected through time by the English practice of primogeniture and sometimes by the law of entail to a specific line. Thus the eldest son inherited the entire estate, to the exclusion of younger siblings, who dwindled to gentry status (Thompson 1963, 64–71). The duty of preserving and improving the estate constituted the central and sacred value of aristocratic esprit. Today, the power and influence of the peerage has definitively passed. By the end of the twentieth century, British nobles no longer owned the majority of land, possessed the wealth of the nation, or controlled the government, which could still have been said at the end of the nineteenth century (Cannadine 1990, 692).

Country houses expressed an important index of aristocratic power, and their fate in the past five centuries carries the story of people as well as land and buildings.

In medieval England, a fortified castle protected a feudal lord's landholding, which issued from the monarch, to reward and pacify the nobility who were his counselors and warriors. In the long century of Tudor and Elizabethan rule, fortifications became less necessary than grandeur, and the country house as now known took shape. Successful or effective aristocrats enlarged, remodeled, and built more grand residences on their property, and they invested in fine furnishings and decor as symbols of their wealth and taste; equally, incapable generations could waste it. New or would-be aristocrats asserted their privilege with land acquisition and house building, first stimulated by the dissolution of the monasteries in the 1530s and consequent land redistribution by sale and royal favor. The peaks and troughs of the king's or queen's fortune were thereafter refracted throughout the land in the splendor of aristocratic architecture.

The progress of the smart, lucky, and ambitious could be remarkable. In the Tudor-Elizabethan era, they built the first English houses to be influenced by European Renaissance ideas, some so splendid they came to called "prodigy houses" for their spectacular size, glittering glass windows, and classical motifs (Summerson 1993, 61–95). Take, for instance, Sir Francis Willoughby, who became the unexpected heir of two manors, extensive lands, and coal mines in several counties, all of which made him a wealthy country gentleman. He commissioned a sumptuous modern house, Wollaton Hall, the most ornate of the English prodigy houses, with Italian, French, and Dutch influences enclosing a fantasy Gothic heart. The cost nearly ruined him and his estate, but his heirs occupied the house until the late nineteenth century, when the industrial presence of nearby Nottingham drove them to prefer more salubrious houses.

In a later period, Robert Walpole created himself from a mister and MP of the Norfolk gentry to first minister to George I and George II, and was eventually created an earl. In a long career of political survival, he invested hugely in Houghton Hall, to the point that the cost of its fittings nearly ruined his estate. Such was the quality of his possessions that his art collection was sold after his death to Catherine the Great and still hangs in the Hermitage in St. Petersburg. Houghton was designed and decorated by masters. Spaces such as the stucco-decorated Stone Hall and the Carrara-paneled Marble Parlour exemplify the grandeur that was the purpose of the status-asserting country house. Walpole invited government ministers to "congresses" of hunting, dining, and politicking at Houghton—the ancestor

Wollaton Hall, Nottingham, drawing by Thomas Allom. Wollaton was constructed in the 1580s. The stately symmetry, large windows, and outward-looking focus characterize it as an English Renaissance style, interpreted at the periphery of the classical world.
Lithotint in S. C. Hall, *The Baronial Halls and Ancient Picturesque Edifices of England,* vol. 1 (London, 1858).

of the country house party, where the atmosphere of prestige massaged ambition and manipulated political strategy.

And the practice continued. By the nineteenth century, the upwardly mobile encompassed entrepreneurs and financiers as well as statesmen from the gentry, and their wealth drew them inevitably toward country house construction as markers of their power. One whose new country house made him fit to be visited by royalty was William Armstrong, a Newcastle engineer, inventor, and industrialist whose armaments companies supplied international wars of the later nineteenth century. In 1869 he had Cragside built, a massive modern-Tudor pile in a picturesque rocky valley, powered by hydroenergy for electricity. It was furnished opulently and received business visitors such as the shah of Persia, the king of Siam, and the prince and princess of Wales. Armstrong was raised to the peerage as Baron Armstrong of Cragside in 1887 (Thompson 1963, 293, 297).

This is the sense in which Mark Girouard aptly called English country houses "power houses" (Girouard 1978, 2–12). Country houses existed in tandem with town houses, the London palaces of the aristocracy. In the early seventeenth century, the Stuart kings abandoned the medieval tradition of nomadic progress around the country to call on nobles to reassert fealty, and the court became regularly established in London and surrounds. As the power of Parliament grew under the Georges, the nobility found a further need to be in London, where their heirs commonly represented the family seat in the House of Commons, until they succeeded to titles and seats in the House of Lords. The Palace of St. James, commissioned by Henry VIII, was the principal residence of the monarch from 1698, though George III bought Buckingham House in 1761 as a more private home, and upon accession in 1837, Queen Victoria made it her official residence. The house was enlarged and remodeled into the palace of today in many stages, mainly of the late nineteenth and early twentieth centuries.

From the turn of the eighteenth century, a secure royal dynasty, long periods of peace, and growing economic productivity encouraged the lords of the land to match their country houses with appropriately grand London town houses (Sykes 1985; Port 1998). But as many country houses slid into the category of liabilities rather than assets around the time of World War I, town house owners succumbed to the lure of land value as their properties were sought as development sites in modern London. Though widely lamented for the loss of fine buildings, the need for residential magnificence had diminished. In the twenty-first century, some ten aristocratic London houses remain standing. Apart from those owned by the royal family, just one still houses an aristocrat, though it is largely a public museum in the care of English Heritage: Apsley House, the home of the first Duke of Wellington; the family of the eighth duke maintains an apartment in a wing.

But the country house was always the home base of aristocratic power, the symbol of the fundamental currency, land. Land brought in rents from tenant farmers, profits from the landowner's own estate production, and sometimes from forestry and mineral resources. But it required vast extra income to build or improve great houses. In the early modern period, that money came from perquisites in royal office and spoils of war, the traditional service of the nobility to the Crown. By the eighteenth century, aristocratic land ownership extended to colonial properties producing new kinds of wealth; the profits of many Caribbean plantations funded waves of country house rebuilding in the United Kingdom (Dresser & Hann 2013). Yet another source of income for some arrived in the nineteenth century, when property that had been on the fringes of London and other swelling cities was developed for housing, bringing in high-density rents. New industries, communications, and businesses needed capital that the more adventurous aristocratic capitalists could provide, and on which they sometimes made triumphant returns. And throughout history, the aristocracy enriched or rescued its fortunes by marrying heiresses. Whether noble or not, a fortune cast a highly acceptable aura around a rich woman, for her money was not tied up in land, and upon marriage, it came under the control of her husband.

However, economics and democracy slowly displaced aristocratic power in Britain, starting in the late nineteenth century. The "New Domesday" was the first national survey of large land-holdings since William the Conqueror's time; it showed publicly—and embarrassingly—how concentrated were aristocratic landholdings, and how huge their unearned rentier incomes. At the same time, agricultural production from the colonies was undermining domestic production, reducing the value of farmed land. Meanwhile, the Third Reform Act of 1884–1885 doubled the electorate (though still excluding all women and about 40 percent of men). Reform of the House of Lords in 1911 abolished the Lords' power to veto money bills and reduced their power to block other bills. Both Labour and Conservative governments increased wealth taxes. The carnage of World War I wiped out a generation of heirs and sent the aristocracy into mourning. Prices, rentals, values, and confidence slipped in a rural depression that persisted until World War II.

It is difficult today to understand how land could lose its economic value, political weight, and social prestige, but less difficult to recognize how country houses could become unviable assets (Waterson 1985, 13–22; Beckett 1986, 474–81). The maintenance of large houses and grounds required the constant attention of an army of skilled workers; their operation as family homes was based on a hierarchy of domestic servants whose labor constituted the power plant of the house. New standards of comfort such as good lighting, hot water, and central heating needed electricity and plumbing that were expensive to retrofit. Expressive as they were of status, country houses and works of art did not generate wealth; they tied up capital that could only be realized by sale. For many, the country house became a burden. From the 1880s to the 1920s, houses were sold to new generations of self-made plutocrats, English and American, and for uses such as schools and hotels. If no one wanted to buy, houses were sold for scrap value; the photographic record of houses in stages of abandonment and demolition is truly grim (Strong et al., 1974).

Some houses were ruined; some were reborn. In 1920 Sutton Scarsdale Hall was sold for salvage, from the paneled staterooms to the roof lead; it was eventually consolidated as a ruin in 1942. The fate of its paneling tells a subplot in the history of country house decay: the dispersal of architectural elements. Acquired by a London dealer, three rooms were sold on to the

Sutton Scarsdale period room at the Philadelphia Museum of Art. Director Fiske Kimball acquired this paneled interior in 1928 as the setting for a collection of English paintings and decorative arts. Research into its provenance at PMA indicates that additional paneling was inserted and the giant order lifted on high pedestals to make the ensemble fit the gallery space. The carving on the overmantel was added by the salvage dealer, Roberson. Museum-specification doors further interrupt the original configuration (Harris 2007, 298).
Photo courtesy of the Philadelphia Museum of Art.

Philadelphia Museum of Art. Another came into the possession of William Randolph Hearst, was mutilated as a stage set, and later given to the Huntingdon Library (Harris 2007, 112, 236).

A happier story is that of Parham Park, an Elizabethan house, somewhat altered by its late Victorian heirs. It was sold in 1922 to the younger son of an immensely rich industrialist who had been created a baronet. Over forty years, his architect undertook such meticulous restoration that only his records of all stages of work prove what is old and what is new (Kirk 2009, 145). Parham was refurnished with salvaged paneling, appropriate furniture, and a large collection of artworks, specially focusing on then-unfashionable Tudor and Stuart portraits (Hearn et al., 1998, 8).

World War II has been said to be what finally destroyed the stately homes of England (Littlejohn 1997, 49). A few houses sustained bomb damage. The major agent of destruction was wartime requisition as homes for children, schools, and government departments evacuated from the cities, as well as bases for military agencies, hospitals, and, worst of all, barracks for troops. Even though artworks were removed to storage and paneling boarded up, houses where troops were billeted suffered from fires accidental and intentional, destructive highjinks, and lack of maintenance. Returned to their owners in poor condition, recompensed by the government but unable to spend it due to national austerity and the shortage of building materials, over a thousand country houses were demolished after the war (Robinson 1989, 249–53).

The Country House in the Post–World War II Public Domain

The transformative episode in the museum career of the country house in English history is the shift from private residence and symbol of landed power to icon of national heritage and popular tourism. In a period of fifty years—the 1930s–1980s—shaped by two world wars and their aftermaths, a consensus emerged that the cultural significance of country houses merited some degree of state support. As a political decision it was fraught, for both Labour and Conservative governments, with the risk of seeming to support ancestral privilege.

The parameters of state funding for country houses developed slowly, shaped by post–World War II policies in urban and country planning, buttressed by tax reforms, and urged on by a coalition of aesthetes and historians. The "Report of the Committee on Houses of National Importance" (known as the Gowers Report), issued in 1950 by a Labour government, was implemented in reduced form in 1953 by a Conservative government. It introduced the Historic Buildings Council to administer grants for maintenance and repairs to private owners and to the National Trust, in exchange for a specified number of days open to the public—the basis of the system that obtains today. Thus, on the whole, government avoided property ownership but took control of development. Meanwhile, the British economy gradually recovered from the war, and by the later 1950s a growing affluence spread through much of society, enabling a new public leisure market, in which country houses, both privately and National Trust–owned, participated with vigor.

The prehistory of this transition lies not only in the roots of the country house malaise of the late nineteenth-/early twentieth-century period. Peter Mandler makes the argument that it relates also to the development of a concept of *English* heritage (Mandler 1997, 7–17). The losses of country houses in the 1890s–1910s were largely ignored at the time: he ascribes this absence to a sense of national identity that, in the last glory days of empire, had no need of history and preferred a nostalgic taste for "Tudorbethan"

Olden Times. The ideal quivered to a bucolic national imaginary focused on a countryside of green fields, villages, castles, and ancient houses; it was at odds with, and efficiently suppressed, the dark realities of a century of industrialization, and it framed a vision of what the troops would be fighting for in World War I. This was the taste regime in which the National Trust was established in 1895 for the preservation of the countryside and vernacular buildings. Precisely in this perspective, the Trust's first large house, Barrington Court, had more romance than historic or aesthetic significance: a Tudor structure that had sunk in fortune to a farm shed, it was acquired in 1907 despite prescient misgivings about expensive maintenance (Waterson 1994, 51). Informed interest in the secular buildings of the late medieval period was nurtured by *Country Life* magazine, starting up in 1897. Amid coverage of racing, property, and "girls in pearls," the magazine carried a regular piece on old English country houses, which shifted within a few years from sentimental to serious architectural history (Watkin 1980, 104). *Country Life*'s authoritative writing was accompanied by professional architectural photography, making visible the significance of historic houses in a newly respectful way. By this means, country houses began to be perceived as central to the "rural-historic" essence of England, infusing the national discourse that is now thoroughly incorporated into heritage (Watson 2013).

The sense of a national past represented by Tudor and Jacobean country houses expanded after World War I to incorporate the neoclassical Georgian mansions also disappearing from London and the countryside. Victorian specimens were even later to be adopted into the country house pantheon. But to find ways to respond to their abandonment required a novel articulation of country houses as a national public good along the lines of the royal palaces—Hampton Court, Holyrood House, and the Tower of London—which had been open to the public since the mid-nineteenth century. The justification for state support was invoked via the rhetoric of art and architectural history, embellished with a low-key patriotic claim to essential Englishness. The project was undergirded by the logic of the modern museum, holding that public exposure to both topics was a worthy endeavor, even though the word *museum* was despised and denied in relation to country houses.

The mobilization of the National Trust as the agent for government to forego inheritance taxes in exchange for public access to approved country houses was a deft, though not simple, mechanism of establishment politics. A reluctant Treasury aimed to quantify the potential tax loss by requiring from the Trust's Country Houses Committee a list of houses "of undoubted merit." James Lees-Milne was the young secretary of the Committee; more than fifty years later he described how this defining list, numbering 230, came together hastily in 1936. He reflected that though it was the product of the best-informed minds at the time, many more important buildings were then simply unknown (Lees-Milne 1992, 7). Country house owners were not eager to transfer ownership of their stately homes, plus estate or cash endowment, to the National Trust in exchange for an apartment in the house and no more maintenance and repair bills—until after World War II. Lees-Milne later wrote portraits of fourteen houses and their owners, whom he visited in the 1940s and 1950s to introduce the possibility of participating in the Country Houses Scheme. He found some pathetic, others heroic, practically all facing impossible costs for maintenance, let alone repairs, to their ancestral mansions. Owners who signed on to the Scheme were simultaneously despairing and relieved to take advantage of the National Trust policy that encouraged families to continue to live in their houses for the sake of the "ineffable spirit essential to the legendary purpose of country houses" (Lees-Milne 1992, 16). While the advocates of the Scheme argued in favor of public access to national art to justify its mission, the Trust's sympathies lay profoundly with the donors; both sides shared the subtle relationships of the well-connected elite. In the context of the Trust becoming landlord not only to aristocrats but also to estate tenants, the absence of the latter in the contemporary and historic commentary on the transition is conspicuous.

As the postwar recovery strengthened, the National Trust demonstrated there was an eager demand for what the British Tourism Authority soon presented as "the treasure houses of Britain." Some of the first generation of private country house entrepreneurs realized the potential of treating country house visiting as a leisure choice, glossed with historical grandeur, tasteful appreciation of art, and aristocratic glamour. They also discovered a demand for comforts and entertainments, leading to the introduction of zoos, butterfly houses, museums of historic vehicles, playgrounds, and cafés and restaurants, all of which offered more profits than did tickets to see a historic house. Additional attractions were adopted to various degrees, and some houses converted entirely to amusements, which became a very lucrative business in the late twentieth century. Warwick Castle introduced popular medieval-themed events and activities in the 1970s so successfully that the Greville family happily sold out to an entertainment company in 1978. Alton Towers had opened its gardens for many years before the Talbot family sold it in 1918; purchased by a business consortium as a garden venue, the buildings were stripped and sold for scrap. After World War II, the leisure function was enlarged with a huge model railway, and in the 1970s it was totally redeveloped as a theme park of spectacular rides, bought and sold several times by big investment companies. The semiruined house still looms at the edge of the site, half picturesque, half spectral.

There was no more doubt that tourism could pay, and public familiarity with the emerging narrative of "heritage" enfolded country houses into popular culture. Nonetheless, more country houses were demolished in the 1950s than ever before, and half as many again in the 1960s–1970s: mainly the battered residue of wartime abuse, foregone maintenance, and inheritance taxes. In 1974, the scale of the loss was presented in a paradigm-shifting exhibition at the Victoria & Albert Museum, *The Destruction of the Country House, 1875–1975*. The tragedy of noble ruins depicted in stark, black-and-white photographs and the implicit destruction of aristocratic culture in Britain attracted middlebrow attention; importantly, the show's catalog documented the continuing demolition of country houses in the language of national heritage (Adams 2013). The show tapped into the growing movement in support of urban conservation, which gave a less exclusive context to the residences of the English elite. At the same time, it pitched country houses as supreme collective artworks of Englishness, unmatched in the world for variety and richness (Harris 1974, 15). This line, first launched in modest form by the Gowers Report, has proved enduringly potent.

The theme of heritage in danger was in its first popular flush in the 1970s, and it was harnessed by the newly formed Historic Houses Association of private owners of country houses to point up the inadequacies of government funding for houses not invited into, or resisting, National Trust protection. Its vehicle was a study by *Country Life* architectural writer John Cornforth, titled "Country Houses in Britain: Can They Survive?" His analysis of visitation showed that the biggest, most businesslike country houses attracted the largest numbers of visitors, and that the extensive rump of less spectacular and less organized houses had no hope of covering the costs of maintaining a historic estate complex (Cornforth 1988). The Historic Houses Association campaigned then, and still, for implementation of further recommendations of the Gowers Report, especially tax relief for expenditure on repairs and maintenance. It funded another project in 1990–1993, surveying the extent of country house alienation from family ownership, as well as associated sales of estate land and house collections (Sayer 1993). The 1990s figures show the limits of making a profit from country house tourism and event hosting sufficient to keep up both house and family, other than by becoming a big, diversified operation located conveniently to a major city. About ten privately owned sites fulfill these conditions today. It seems that just one country house of the first rank, Badminton House, is not open to the tourist public at all. That said, several of Britain's richest individuals and families accept the grants that have been called "outdoor relief for the rich" and open their country houses the minimum number of days required per year (Thompson 1963, 18–20).

Sayer's findings included the chagrined reflection that "a number of private owners now feel that the success of the National Trust makes it harder for them to compete for visitors" (Sayer 1993, 45). This belies the transformation among both visitors and house museums that developed with the rise of heritage as a domain of public culture from the 1970s. Maintaining connections with the past by preserving personal objects, public buildings, whole environments, and the traditions that accompanied them turned out to be much more broadly meaningful than anyone involved had anticipated (Lowenthal 1985). The popular demand for action to save and access heritage brought voluntary associations such as the National Trust, and more radical campaigners, to new prominence. Membership of the Trust swarmed, reaching a million in 1981 and two million in 1990. National Trust management had to change, not only to adapt to new influence and income but also to satisfy its supporters. Harold Nicolson cosily deprecated the National Trust in 1949 as "a group of amiable, aristocratic amateurs" (overlooking their access to the levers of establishment power), and staff salaries were so low that new employees were asked frankly about their genteel private resources into the 1960s: "Can you afford to work for us?" (Gaze 1988, 150, 240). The first art advisor (curator), conservator-housekeeper, public relations officer, and educator were appointed just before and throughout the 1970s. Site services to visitors rose in organizational priority, ensuring decent toilets, tearooms with locally made edibles, and shops with country-themed products, now making a considerable profit. Members facilitated it all with volunteer labor. The Trust's reputation as an agent of heritage conservation was high, and strongly identified with saving country houses for public access. By the 1980s, the National Trust and country houses had come to seem a natural connection. Market research in 1992 showed a third of the adult population of the United Kingdom had visited a country house that year, more than any other kind of heritage site (Mandler 1997, 411).

The National Trust entered the era of managerialism toward the end of the 1980s, represented by the 1986 appointment as director-general of Jennifer Jenkins, the first woman and the first nonlandowner in the position. Gingered by member-activists, she led a reorientation toward the countryside rather than country houses, attempting to shift the Trust's public image from elite culture to the rural-historic landscape. It included a new approach to country house estate and farm buildings, bringing attention to thousands of vernacular structures within house ensembles and landscapes. An example is

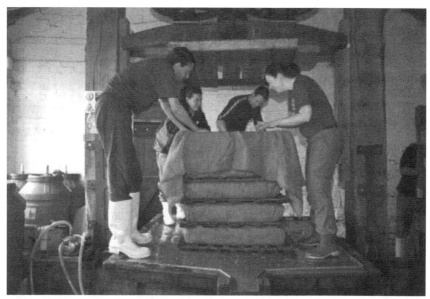

Volunteers make apple cider at Killerton Estate, 2009. The very large Killerton Estate in Devon offers many opportunities for volunteers to join the gardening and countryside care teams. Such activities satisfy multiple contemporary aims of the National Trust: local and visitor engagement, continuing traditional use of the site, conservation of its vernacular and industrial aspects, and being outdoors in the countryside.
Photo by Ross Hoddinott, courtesy of National Trust Images.

the 1990s discovery of a circa 1450 cottage enclosed in Marker's Cottage in the village of Broadclyst, part of the estate of Killerton House, Devon, which had come to the Trust in 1944.

In 2001 the National Trust became the largest nongovernment land-holder in Britain, thanks to its early, continuous commitment to landscapes of environmental as well as aesthetic and historic significance. Gardens and estate parks have always been hugely popular with visitors, even more than houses, and especially since parks tend to be admission-free and child friendly. In this, they satisfy a large proportion of members and visitors, and usefully divert and spread the load of visitor impact on historic fabric. The countryside vision was confirmed during the directorship of Fiona Reynolds, 2001–2012, with focuses on environmental sustainability, family outdoor health and leisure, and community engagement, matched by a return to devolved management. A paradigm shift toward museum professionalism in house presentation and public programs took hold, somewhat more slowly than in the wider UK museum world, but marking a profound break with previous Trust convictions. It was regretted by old hands, even as they admired the new scholarship and conservation standards, and diehards remain today to write letters to newspaper editors about "dumbing down" (Cornforth 1998, 12–13, 146). By the turn of the millennium, the National Trust had become a savior of last resort for country houses; since 2000, just three have entered the fold: Tyntesfield, near Bristol (2002); Godolphin House in Cornwall (2007); and Seaton Delaval, near Newcastle upon Tyne (2009), the first and last assisted by massive public fund-raising campaigns. Current programs focus on the "spirit of place" to be found in great houses, estate farms, and natural environments that comprise the cultural landscapes of the British countryside.

Presenting the Country House as a Museum

No house translates directly from everyday inhabitation to museumhood; the process is a drastic alteration. The house transforms from a home for residents, via the intervention of specialists, to a spectacle for visitors. Its new purpose is sustained by the material fabric of the building, furnishing, and collections, which come to stand for absent humans. The functions of most of the apparatus are evident to visitors, but they usually require rearrangement, or sometimes replacement or removal, in order for visitors to observe them clearly, and for secure, convenient access. This is the business of house presentation: making it visible, accessible, public. The further stage of communicating the distinction and significance of the house and its elements is carried by interpretation that offers a framing discourse to the whole site.

The practice of presenting country houses (and most other types of house museum) is shaped by the circumstances under which they came into institutional ownership. The majority of houses that move into museumhood do so following the death of the owner and/or last inhabitant; they tend to be run down and in need of major curatorial attention before they can be exhibited to the public. There is likely to be internal and external deterioration; damage due to lack of maintenance; abandonment of main rooms following the inhabitant's retreat into one or two smaller rooms; few or no modern services because the old ways were regarded as good enough; and buildup of normally ephemeral stuff where the inhabitant lost the will or capacity to dispose of it. Some houses are tidied up, cherry-picked, or totally cleared by heirs who cooperate, or don't, with the agency that inherits management of the house. Thus the museumization of houses can be said to begin with a kind of editorial process, undertaken by architects and curators; Paul Eggert, book historian and editorial theorist, compares it directly to the work of historical and literary editing (Eggert 2009, 15–16). It is understood more by convention and experience than by rules, though some agencies have policies to guide conservation interventions. The following surveys a gamut of presentational issues and techniques (excluding the history of architectural conservation) to show their power as mediators of the knowledge constructed by house museums. Older practices can be traced, but, for my purposes, the presentation of country houses essentially evolved after World War II.

The primary presentational perspective has been always aesthetic. All the initial 230 National Trust Country Houses Scheme houses were identified for their merit in architectural history and/or exterior and interior design. Since the currency of post-Tudor country house prestige was style, this shorthand for wealth and taste depended on expensive labor and materials, set in the conspicuous extravagance of parklands dedicated to leisure. Interior decor designed for display focused on the most public rooms. The adornments and fittings of the English country house existed to be seen. Even in an age when aristocratic privilege commands less sway than it did in the past, the cultural capital of magnificent design and collections demonstrates the traditions of English power. With this purpose in mind, it doesn't matter whether beholders understand the history and aesthetics of the decor as long as they appreciate that it represented plenty of money.

The second frame of country house presentation displays a hint of domesticity amid the grand environment. It used to be suggested in privately owned houses by the presence of the BBC *Radio Times* and ashtrays on side tables, or in more recent years by a television in a family drawing room otherwise furnished with Old Master paintings. The dissonance of the articles of common life suggests that the users of the room are ordinary people, yet somehow different because they live with high art. The Historic Houses Association often asserts in its annual reports that stately homes presented as inhabited by people with ancestral connections to the site are more popular than apparently uninhabited houses. By contrast, in National Trust houses where a traditionally associated family still lives on site, there is a preference for privacy; the cozy devices that hint at daily use make no show. There are advocates of the old school who maintain that the character of inherited property is diminished without the occupation by a traditional owner. Simon Jenkins, chairman of the Trust in 2008–2014, is noted for recommending a compulsory pram and labrador in the front hall of every Trust property (Knox & Harris 2012, 15). Ironically, the person with the longest living connection to a country house today may well be a pre–World War II kitchen or laundry maid, a generation nearly extinct. Still, the common touch evidenced by *Radio Times*, putative labrador, or oral history in the presentation of a country house is embodied humanity, real people with whom visitors may compare and contrast their own life experience. This idea certainly informs the current interpretive appetite for personal narratives.

The third presentation frame is the social history of working and private life in the country house. History as the lens for presenting country houses once meant genealogy and its intersections with national greatness. The popularity of social history transformed not only the subject matter of country house history but also the mode of conveying it via interpretation. The interpretive mode is the major knowledge mechanism of contemporary country house presentation, via a raft of media. It developed in contrast to the guidebook, produced since the late eighteenth century for the segment of visitors seeking improvement as well as sensation. Under the influence of museum catalogs of the later nineteenth century, house guidebooks evolved a style of exhaustive listing that implied the importance of everything on display and the expectation that visitors would look at and appreciate it all. Some people did, and do (readers of this book are likely to be in this category). A new generation of National Trust house guidebooks challenged the power of such expectations from the 1990s by addressing the demand for cheaper, smaller, illustrated narrative guides. Curmudgeons still occasionally rail after the loss. Yet the common critique that interpretation is selective and trivial neglects to note that history may be accused of the same failings: selectivity is a human way to think, though it doesn't discourage people from trusting that their facts are holistic and meaningful.

Some houses come to the threshold of museumization well clothed with furniture, collections, outbuildings, gardens, and parks. They might also be charged with quantities of conventional history, most commonly national, biographical, and architectural history. Others arrive with less material content or context, or even none beyond the house itself. But there is always contextual history in and around a house, even if it's partial or opaque. Understanding the physical and historical dimensions of museumization is critical for developing its presentation, even more for interpretation. The following examples expand some historical processes of country house presentation and interpretation.

Blickling Hall came to the National Trust in 1940 as a notable Jacobean house, with extravagant modeled plaster ceilings and a major eighteenth-century library. It had been used for the previous ten years by Lord Lothian, its last owner, as a country house of retreat from political life in London, so it had an apartment furnished in 1930s comfort, with the tapestry-hung state rooms and a long gallery above. James Lees-Milne described preparations to open the latter part in 1947, assisted by the late donor's private secretary and a London decorating firm. He describes how rotting silk hangings were replaced with the only available cheap stuff for several years, and how he was tempted to remove "lumpish" Victorian bookcases in the long hall. Others defended their presence as evidence of the growth and use of the house through time, and the advice, he later decided, was "eminently right, I now see, though I still find them ugly and inappropriate to their setting" (Lees-Milne 1992, 33–41). This recognition is a moment of truth for the curators of historic houses. It defines the spectrum of "leave as is" and the "rule of taste" mode of connoisseurship in arranging historic house furnishings; in practice they are employed in tandem. Lees-Milne was involved with opening further rooms in 1957 and 1962. Throughout, he followed the then-conventional National Trust focus on the historical aesthetics of the house and its furnishings. By assuming common knowledge and making little effort to explain the elite culture of tapestries and other costly decorations, the connoisseur's presentation of Blickling confirmed the values of hierarchy and social order that undergirded the English country house. Presentation styles can change, but sometimes values don't. The latest 2015 interpretation applied to re-creating Lothian's private rooms, bringing theatrical media to an installation suggesting preparations for a house party dinner, with casually arranged whiskey glasses and ashtrays; the sounds of gramophone music and servant gossip; the smells of cigar smoke, cooking, and Lord Lothian's Christian Science preference—orange juice. Volunteers in costume encouraged visitors to make themselves at home with 1930s newspapers. These were more loaded props than it might seem, for Lothian was part of the aristocratic "Cliveden Set," who hoped that Hitler could be appeased, right up to the declaration of war in 1939. Though he instantly abandoned this idea, and died on duty as British ambassador to the United States, Lothian's story is still awkward to tell, and appears undermined by the house-party atmosphere.

The presentation of country houses that arrive at museumhood naked and unfurnished opens different directions in presentation and interpretation. The case of Clandon Park in Surrey evidences the high era of National Trust practice in redecorating and refurnishing a largely empty house (Ponsonby 2015, 34–36). It was described as splendid, cold, and bare when presented to the Trust in 1956 (Cornforth 1988, 64–65), and thus it came to the hand of John Fowler, decorator to high society since the 1930s. Fowler grew famous between the wars for "de-granding" formal interiors with color, warm textiles, and comfortable sofas amid the antiques (since known as "country style"). After World War II, he revived many country houses for private owners, and in his later years often worked for the Trust at token cost. At Clandon and several other largely empty houses, Fowler's technique was to accentuate architectural forms and details, especially the plasterwork, with shades of color and marbling, informed by historical practice and a creative eye. Clandon was furnished with a few Onslow family pieces and portraits, augmented by a bequest from a collector of high-quality but smallish-scale furniture and Chinese porcelain and carpets, arranged by Fowler. It is useful to read the evaluation, fifteen years later, by his friend, *Country Life* editor and National Trust Committee member John Cornforth, that "his solution is not a historical one, but it makes visitors look at what matters" (Cornforth 1988, 217). With this comment, Cornforth also acknowledges the scholarly work on historic house decor developing at the Victoria & Albert Museum's Department of Woodwork at the same time as Fowler's influence. In the long run, archaeological standards of physical investigation and the analysis of country house archives transformed the presentation of country (and other) houses in England and the world (see chapter 4). (Tragically, Clandon was reduced to a shell by a fire in 2015.)

A multitude of contradictory elements intervenes between the historic and current visit to the country house, reshaping the experience. Today, tourism allows uninvited guests to pore through the house and garden, admiring, criticizing, and gossiping, followed by tea in the stables and a little souvenir shopping on the way out: a thoroughly postmodern experience. That this could be a viable and satisfying mode of visiting country houses would have been unimaginable by the pre– and post–World War II advocates of saving country houses. The era has passed when country houses fulfilled the roles for which they were built, and their pleasures, luxuries, intricacies, and mysteries have joined the public imaginary of heritage knowledge and fantasy. On the consumption side of this exchange, demand for experiencing historic sites and their settings (such as country houses) is shaped by changes in time use and discretionary funds for leisure, the availability of personal transport, the spread of middle-class values, and public interest in popular history and culture, largely informed by TV and films. On the production side, country house managers now construct experiences for visitors using developments in conservation expertise, interpretive techniques that engage different audience segments, perspectives informed by social history, and customer services that add comfort to the visit.

What I describe above is pure museumization. In these terms, conventional museums themselves have made or are making the transition from cultural authority to cultural commodity, in response to societies that no longer want or need authoritative expertise other than to create hedonic experiences. This does not remove historic sites and other forms of museums from the nets of ideology, but it points out that they convey different forms of essentially nationalist conviction communicated in the subtler forms of discourse. "Heritage," viewed as a national resource shared, if not owned, by all, appears to blend high serious purpose with appropriate democracy. It did not take long for critics to dissect the contexts of heritage to demonstrate how its manifestations reinforce conventional relations of power and influence in national, racial, and economic frames. Some despaired and mocked its roots in a future-denying taste for nostalgia (Wright 1985; Hewison 1987). The more nuanced analysts examined the application of "heritage" and the historical disciplines it nourishes to validate present values and practices by reference to the past. And the most humane showed how "heritage" is inevitably subverted by personal associations and meanings and used as much for performances of memory and attachment as for rituals of citizenship (Samuel 1994; Smith 2006). The country houses of England that made the transition to house museumhood under the aegis of heritage created a contemporary genre of remarkable museum effect.

The Country House in the New World

The political purpose of the English country house to signify power, display wealth, and model cultural authority had global application to members of the ruling elite of the Empire's one-time dominions. The major British difference was the long persistence of hereditary power and dynastic solidarity embodied in the country house, which never achieved currency elsewhere. But large, lavish houses constructed for the elite of the New World learned from the country house archetype, and its elements can be tracked in the houses of the rich and powerful of the colonies and former colonies, with some curious and baleful consequences when such houses were museumized.

The most direct likeness manifested in the Old South, the southern five of the original thirteen American colonies. A few dynastic estates survived until the Civil War (very occasionally longer) since settlement in the seventeenth century, though the golden age of house building occurred in the middle decades of the eighteenth century. The profits that funded plantation estate and house development at this time were derived from enslaved labor (as was true for some British country houses). All of the eighteenth-century plantation houses can be classified in the category of "gentlemen's houses," so named by Steven Hague in an original study of small Georgian classical houses in Britain and its Atlantic colonies (Hague 2015). The character of gentleman was the estate of honor that could be claimed by colonials, justified by the polite culture of gentility, where gentility was a function of self-made financial and cultural capital more than inheritance. Hague's parameters of the gentleman's house category are Georgian style, two-and-a-half to three stories tall, with five to seven bays of windows, of double pile plan, and

Westover Plantation, Charles City County, Virginia, 1939. William Byrd II (colonial politician, planter, diarist, and founder of Richmond) had Westover built in the 1750s. This gentleman's house is the quintessential James River plantation dwelling: a plain Georgian block, flanked by dependencies, decorated with a broken ogee pediment doorway taken almost directly from the pattern book, *Palladio Londinensis*, of 1738.
Photo courtesy of the Library of Congress, Prints & Photographs Division, HABS VA, 19-WEST, 1–1.

opening into a hall with a handsome staircase: a house that enabled living like a gentleman (Hague 2015, 4). This house was a visible statement of the assets and authority underwritten by land ownership, and as in England, resources were consolidated by strategic alliances within a de facto aristocracy of less than a hundred families (Moss 1990, 11–17). A very few families managed to maintain occupation by lineal descent; Shirley Plantation, on the James River, Virginia, claims to be the longest family-owned business in the United States, having housed eleven generations of the Hill-Carter family.

The string of plantation houses along the north side of the James River in Charles City County, Virginia, illustrates the history of Old Southern landed culture from its earliest years, and its peri-museumized existence today. Belle Air, Shirley, Berkeley, and Westover are all located on land settled in the seventeenth century, though it took another two or more generations to suppress Powhatan Indian presence, establish the slave economy, and dedicate the profits of tobacco planting to life in gentlemanly houses. All the houses were damaged in the Civil War, and all but Shirley were rehabilitated in subsequent decades by new owners. They began opening their gardens to the public in 1929. All now rely to some degree on tourism, as well as estate farming, rents and businesses, and external earnings (Hermanson 2014). As in the United Kingdom, a historic house can be a rich asset but an uncertain income.

An important difference bearing on the kind of history represented to visitors is evident between privately owned plantation houses and those in public ownership. As depicted by Hermanson, the narrative of family antiquity and happy childhood experience permeates the James River cases, whereas the contrast of a slavery-acknowledging history in plantation houses in the public sphere is striking. Colonial antiquity, family history, and architectural significance are prominent in the presentations of Drayton Hall, near Charleston, South Carolina (National Trust, since 1974, and Drayton Hall Preservation Trust, 2015); Hampton Plantation, McClellanville, South Carolina (South Carolina State Park Service since 1971); and Snee Farm, Mount Pleasant, South Carolina (National Park Service, since 1990). (These examples are selected for their public ownership, location in the Old South, and pre–Civil War establishment.) The three are associated with nationally and locally famous families, and all have architectural significance as gentlemen's houses. At all three sites the findings of archaeology present the fragile material evidence of the enslaved experience that made the plantations viable for white owners. The slave presence is also highlighted by the banal evil of chattel lists of humans, presented in signs and brochures. Two sites offer programs celebrating Gullah culture, the intangible heritage of Africans in Low Country Carolina; such evidence is very discrepant with the houses full of fine antiques.

Meanwhile, in the imperial Anglosphere, the continuity of governing power was controlled by statute from the foundation of the Empire's colonies, where government operated in the British monarch's name, represented by a regular turnover of incumbent governors. When colonial governments became democratic and even independent, the leader's term remained finite, so there was no need for individuals to keep up a great house in the colonial or national capital because the state provided an appropriate dwelling to house the regular turnover of power. The Governor's Palace in Williamsburg (reconstructed for museum purposes in 1933–1935) was a very early specimen; the rest of the former British Empire likewise features Government Houses, some still inhabited by the head of state and some museumized. As the domestic seats of state authority, they were centers and symbols of political power in a way functionally similar to the country houses of the

British aristocracy. But an important difference between the British and the former colonial "power houses" emerged with the concept of heritage and museumization. Transformation in terms of heritage presented Government Houses as key in the growth of postcolonial identity, but it is a historic rather than a cultural identity. Such houses in the New World sometimes become museumized; by contrast, English country houses had museumization thrust upon them.

Government Houses were grand in relation to other colonial houses, and grander ones were sometimes built as colonial importance grew. But even the biggest and best colonial houses never matched the scale, opulence, and lordly image of English town or country houses. It is therefore ironic and misleading that the aura of the aristocratic country house touches a multitude of house museums in the New World via the dynamic of museumization. I call this delusion "the revenge of the country house." There has been a dismaying tendency to exaggerate the grandeur of almost any big, old house that is proposed for museumization, unless it has a clearly specified mission as a house museum. It happens too often that historic houses are saved from destruction because they are big and old, without much understanding whether they are important. Houses that survive in this way tend to be at the grander, more formal end of the architectural spectrum of their times. When it comes to rationalizing them as museums, they are often found to have been the residences of wealthy citizens, a couple of generations distant from the first settlers in the area, where a family managed to hold onto, or buy into, land that eventually enabled descendants to build a fine house. These residents can then be formulated as an "old family" of the district, notable for houses such as belonged to the daughter of the first judge in the town, or to the settler whose house became an inn that later spawned a brewery fortune, or to a landowner (whether or not connected to earlier owners) whose comfortable homestead has now been encircled by town or suburban development. There are endless variations on these retro-rationalizations (and not-infrequent exceptions) among house museums, which ascribe a kind of historic genealogy to a house deemed suitable for museumization. Associated furnishings rarely remain in situ, so the house tends to be dressed with finer antique furniture than it probably ever contained. The primal chronology, colored by multigenerational inhabitation, blurs into a myth that this was an influential household in the district, and is therefore museum worthy today. The magic of a hundred years of age, or depending on local history, two hundred or three hundred years, casts the whole place into the imaginary of ancestral grandeur—*almost* an English stately home. Many such houses began their museum careers under amateur management, where the theme of gracious and pedigreed antiquity can satisfy local myth making. If the house survives into professional management, its rationale is likely to be revised in line with social history approaches to presenting local memory.

A third aspect of the image of the English country house comes into play to confuse the museumization of great houses of the rich and powerful in the New World. Riches never hurt aspirants to gentlemanly status, and making money via professional skill, canny trading, or successful manufacturing was a far more viable trajectory in the colonies than in old England. Immigrants to the New World, aside from those coerced as slaves or convicts, expected to better their lot: no one immigrates who is content at home. The kind of house chosen by would-be genteel rising Americans, Anglo-Indians, and Australians was deliberately not in a vernacular tradition but followed polite English taste, as described by Hague. Thus, while the seekers of religious freedom in America initially had in mind the eternal rewards of practicing their faith correctly, earthly rewards in the form of gentlemen's houses soon became available to the energetic and their heirs. These cases expose the process of "re-Anglicization," the generational slippage among New Englanders toward a more accommodating religion, eased by affluence toward the English model and epitomized by building and furnishing fine houses (Deetz 1991; Conforti 2006, 163–99). Likewise the Quakers of Pennsylvania managed to include advanced elegance into the precept of consuming "the best sort but plain" (Tolles 1959).

The gentleman's house type can be found throughout the British world in the eighteenth and nineteenth centuries, augmented by neo-medieval styles after the 1840s. Many Government Houses are gentlemen's houses. In the United Kingdom, this kind of small, classical house occasionally becomes a museum to commemorate a hero (e.g., Wordsworth's birthplace in Cockermouth, Cumbria), but the form is too small for the level of style, collection, or ancestral grandeur that otherwise justifies museumization in the British context. It has a different significance in formerly colonial worlds. In places where survival mandated basic, even primitive, housing for most people, importing stylish hardware and furniture to fit out a house built of stone (a material almost always available locally) and fronted with a classical order helped to place the man who could afford it at the top of the social scale. Discrepancies in personal gentility and the scale of built style could become grist for mockery by some, but big fish could easily dominate small colonial ponds. The Williamsburg Governor's Palace exemplifies the important place of the small classical house in the colony of Virginia, and the subsequent museumizing tendency to dress it up when it was reconstructed in the 1930s. Graham Hood, chief curator of Colonial Williamsburg, gave a revealing account of the shock and resistance by management and the public when the palace was refurnished much more simply in 1981, based on rereading the inventories on which the initial scheme had been developed (Hood 2000). It was among the first revisionist exercises in house museum presentation in the United States, followed by the rest of the world.

Along with the gentlemen planters' houses of the Old South, there is another sense in which English and colonial "power houses" coincide, though for different reasons and with different historical outcomes. The rich and powerful in the colonies frequently maintained a house in the country as well as a house in the city, as did the English aristocracy. In the American case, it is generally more apt to call it a summer house. (The London town house was especially the base for parliamentary sittings and the social season in the winter, and in that sense a seasonal house, too.) In the northern United States, summer houses were predominantly of the small classical house type, known from the mid-eighteenth century as a villa. The forthright designer A. J. Downing wrote in his pattern book *The Architecture of Country Houses*, "What we mean by a villa, in the United States, is the country house of a person of competence or wealth sufficient to build and maintain it with some taste and elegance" (1850, 257). Within a day's journey from the big cities, a country house such as Stenton, in Germantown near Philadelphia, is a characteristic eighteenth-century modest Georgian specimen, and Lyndhurst, up the Hudson River from New York City, is characteristic of the nineteenth— not least in its romantic Gothicism and its doubled enlargement after only twenty years. Summer villas survive in the United States much better than town houses, for the same reason as English country houses: the value of city real estate trumps the comfort and sentiment of even the most lavish urban mansions. Hence a disproportionate segment of grand American house museums were summer houses of the rich.

Yet even beyond the temptations of clearance for land value, each generation of American moguls generally sought to build its own palaces. The arch example is the Vanderbilt dynasty of New York, which had twenty-five town and country houses built between the 1870s and 1920s; they were not unique. The last of their eight mansions raised on "Millionaire's Row," Fifth Avenue, was demolished in the 1950s, but six of the third generation's country houses are house museums today. Marble House and The Breakers in Newport, Rhode Island, summer resort of the Gilded Age, are the most spectacular among the spectacles now managed by the Preservation Society of Newport County (since 1963 and 1971), and another, Rough Point, was subsequently owned by the Duke family and occupied seasonally until 1993 (opening publicly in 2000). Further Vanderbilt country houses are the well-furnished Vanderbilt Mansion in Hyde Park near Poughkeepsie,

New York (managed by the National Park Service since 1940); the Spanish Colonial Revival Eagle's Nest in Long Island, New York (open since 1950, with notable marine scientific collections); and Biltmore Estate, Asheville, North Carolina, still owned by a Vanderbilt descendent and open as a tourism attraction since 1930. Biltmore House, completed in 1895, remains at the top of Wikipedia's list of the largest houses in the United States; the list's statistics bear exploring. More than half of the list is in the Northeast and Mid-Atlantic states; twelve houses have been demolished; fifteen have moved into educational use; and twenty-one are museumized. This leaves about half inhabited by very rich moderns, who continue to build "power houses." Bluntly, the maintenance, let alone conservation, of enormous, grandiloquent houses costs more than public and charitable agencies can invest; they need the sensational money of the mega-rich to conserve and endow them for use as public resources.

It is hard not to be in love with country houses, English or anywhere else. There is a plethora of books on magnificent architecture and captivating gardens, with more glorious color images than the most pitiless researcher can resist. Visits to country houses enchant the eye and tickle the imagination. History, character, and high style are expressed in palaces, follies, and gardens, wonderfully equipped with gilt furniture, tapestries, and luscious paintings, proffering a seductive sense of private privilege to the reader or visitor. The great houses of the New World can be similarly entrancing. While it is possible to contextualize them in the blunt light of history, their place in the schematic range of house museums is, for many visitors, probably more sensuous. Others might continue to share the fantasy of American Arts and Crafts aesthete and Harvard professor Charles Eliot Norton, who, in an 1889 magazine article, regretted the absence of "hereditary homes" in the United States. He cited the spirit of equality and distribution of property, the change in standards of living, the diffusion of wealth and material comfort, the rapid settlement of America's vast territory, and the growth of old and new cities as undermining "a high type of civilization" represented by the lack of old homes (Norton 1889, 636–38). The temptation and the fallacy of this position is to pretend that British culture was much different. In admiring hereditary houses, Norton conceived himself as sharing in that higher civilization, whereas the rest of us know that when we visit country houses, we are playing at it.

Note

1. I regret to acknowledge that this chapter woefully ignores the importance of gardens and park estates in the economy and ecology of country houses.

~

CHAPTER NINE

The Significance, Insignificance, and Future of House Museums

Having laid out a typology of house museums and narrated origins, distinctions, and challenges in practice shaped by history and ideology, I come to a last, ignominious, category: insignificant house museums. Sometimes I lack the fortitude to mention this large rump. But its real presence and ramifications within the dispersed totality of house museums amounts to another way to present a theme that has haunted the industry for twenty years, and especially in the aftermath of the Great Recession: "Are there too many house museums?" I will return to this question, but begin with "insignificance" as a means of presenting the problem in terms of heritage value or significance. This constructs the problem as a standard of professional practice, which some might argue diminishes the place of community stakeholders. The limits will become evident, but the perspective clarifies directions for house museums in the broad sphere of cultural heritage management.

It is helpful to understand the modern history of managing the movable and immovable remains of the past in the Western tradition, which began with a focus on portable objects attributed with value for one reason or another. They were removed from their sources and presented to the public as exemplary evidence, aggregated in museums—a new kind of institution in which new disciplines of knowledge were cultivated, beginning with the natural sciences, joined by art, ethnography, and archaeology. Museums observed the Western bifurcation of knowledge in nature and culture, and in the field of culture they grew characteristically informed by new, nineteenth-century approaches to the past, molded by archaeology (Diaz-Andreu 2007).

The critical point to observe here is that selected objects became perceived as capable of representing the entirety of characteristics of the past. This elision meant that there was less need to preserve places of the past because they could be recalled via objects, carefully arranged in special institutions— that is, museums. Places are more finite resources than objects and often required for continuing purposes such as the growth of cities or the development of industries, at the expense of preexisting uses or of native landscapes. The common taste for preserving historic and natural environment places in the Anglophone world is a mid- to late twentieth-century development (*pace* many old roots), which have coalesced under the name *heritage*. Heritage preservation is one of the remarkable phenomena of recent history, unpredicted, seemingly radical even in the 1970s, and explained by a profusion of theories (Lowenthal 1985; Fairclough et al. 2008). Its impact has been huge.

The title *heritage* is (in English) less associated with objects than with places. Today the word is generally understood as referring to sites and the structures built on them, identified for conservation by regulatory processes mainly in the field of land-use planning in order to represent the past in the present. A whole apparatus has evolved, organizing regulation, management, standards, publicity, and public support, and its evolution has paid little attention to the extant and continuing apparatus of managing historic objects via collection into museums. In fact, the bifurcation of both the concept and the management of historic places and objects is marked and perpetuated in separate professional bodies, exemplified by ICOM, the International Council on Museums, and ICOMOS, the International Council on Monuments and Sites. Yet the philosophy of preserving objects and places to represent the past is derived from much the same intellectual sources and operates with much the same objectives. At a crossover of the two modes, house museums have existed for a hundred-and-fifty-plus years, demonstrating the commonality of historic objects and places in the practice of heritage management.

Using the word *heritage* to describe objects *and* places is highly evident in the emergence of the phrase *movable cultural heritage* to refer to objects (though this awkward term has failed to gain much popularity). The utility of enlarging the subjects referred to as heritage to incorporate a third field of the-past-in-the-present—traditional knowledge and practice—has established use of the term *intangible heritage* (a risingly popular phrase). Much of the content of this domain is still called folklore, but it is clear that the older discipline is following the route into heritage. The picture of heritage as a body of theory, practice, and discourse that applies to objects, places, *and* traditions is not yet widely adopted, though it is contained or inferred in the field of critical heritage studies. The subjects of heritage management and studies will continue to be informed by history, archaeology, art history, architecture, anthropology, sociology, and materials science but will achieve greater public awareness as a unified front than by remaining in the separate tracks established by the historical development of museums, heritage, and folklore. The Skansen concept of houses and furnishings (movables) museumized together with sounds, tastes, and other sensory experiences demonstrates the power and energy of the convergence model of heritage.

Returning to the notion of "insignificant house museums," the following analysis shows how management practice in place heritage can be deployed to identify existing and new house museums as worth the time, energy, and money required to sustain a viable monument of the past in the present, or not. Values-based heritage management takes a holistic view of a site in order to establish the values ascribed by stakeholders to make the place significant; the aim of protecting, conserving, and interpreting those values drives the policy and interventions laid out in the consequent conservation management plan (Avrami, Mason, & de la Torre 2000). The useful concept of the technique is its embrace of intangible value, in all its subjectivity and contestability, as the rationale of heritage preservation, thus acknowledging that heritage is less a perfectly restored structure than a medium of embracing meaningful aspects of the past. The principle can also apply to museumized collections, as presented in the Australian manual *Significance* (Russell & Winkworth 2001). The process of cultural significance assessment is a tool for prioritizing recognition and hence resources. But while the concept of evaluating significance in relation to thematic and comparative fields is relatively straightforward, the problem of the threshold of significance is less clear. The simplest filter is geographic: local, national, international, all the way up to world standard, characterized by "outstanding universal value," the criterion for inscription on the World Heritage List (Jokilehto 2008, 7–15). Other filters could relate to relevance to a community and institutional capacity. Making such judgments requires practical wisdom, acquired through experience and collegial reflection (and open to interpretation). This is the basis on which I recognize a set of insignificant house museums. If I don't investigate it very closely, it's because my methods are large scale, remote, and inevitably subject to errors—and because the conditions that reduce many a house museum's significance have been explored in the professional literature discussed below, explaining how optimistic plans can degenerate. It is true that responding to the analysis of insignificant house museums can be painful to individual and communal interests.

Are There Too Many House Museums?

The need for house museum euthanasia has been a wry lament among professionals around the world for a long time, which is to say that house museum people have long been aware of an excess of sites, or to be precise, an excess of ineffective sites. The issue appears to have been first put publicly in an article in the US National Trust's *Forum Journal*, titled "Historic House Museums: Struggling for Survival" (Elsler 1996). The seriousness of the issue resonated through a string of well-informed conferences between 1998 and 2007. They expressed a crisis in professional confidence in house museums, and the spectrum of views put forward still frames the problem. The issues raised were not new, but in articulating them publicly and attempting to address them head on, the American house museum scene took stock of itself in an unprecedented way. The themes generated are broadly relevant to house museums throughout the English-speaking world.

"American House Museums" was the title of a symposium held in Philadelphia in 1998. Speakers represented the nonprofit sector (the cradle of American house museums), one of a nest of suburban mansions, a state agency, and a for-profit house museum business. All contributors agreed that historic house museums were facing a bleak future, identifying a public perception of house museums as exclusive and backward looking; a focus on collection and preservation management at the expense of engagement with visitors; and an economic environment of sparse resources getting thinner. Experienced voices agreed that most house museums can barely fund their operational costs. At the same time, the speakers asserted a suite of benefits flowing from house museums, vivid to themselves, their staff, and volunteers, if not to visitors: house museums as valuable community resources and local amenities, as affirmative visitor experiences via immersive exposure to history, and as important educational resources. These expressions of faith did not blind the speakers to the urgency of change. The future was projected to include strategic planning for creative, entrepreneurial, and cost-effective business; partnerships with community organizations to spread the load; more diverse representations and interactive programming, especially to explore difficult histories; and a shift to a marketing orientation based on customer needs and wants. The Philadelphia symposium laid out experiences and ideas representing the modern boom in historic houses, and exposed a disturbingly hollow core, held together by optimistic conviction.

Many of the same issues were also being raised in the larger sphere of museums. Conventionally oriented toward aspects of elite, white culture, and focused on the increasingly professionalized processes of collections management, conservation treatment, and exhibition design, orthodox museum practice was a major object of the critique of the new museology that arose in the late 1980s (Hudson 1998; Weil 1999). At the same time, both government and not-for-profit public policy shifted toward contemporary currents of managerialism in a neoliberal economic climate (in the United Kingdom, Thatcherism; in Australia, economic rationalism). In the capitalist United States, the ruthless agenda of the market grated on the tradition of philanthropy that formed the financial backbone of many museums. For museums in the British sphere, the Thatcherist/rationalist logic demanded new approaches to museums as businesses, with products and markets to be managed in an entrepreneurial style that mandated more attention to offering museum experiences for which customers would be prepared to pay enough to support operational costs. These trends coincided to promote new attention to visitors and their desires, expressed in a priority shift among museum managers from collections toward visitor services such as interpretation and education programs, and a serious move to develop new visitor markets (Alexander 1999). The language to articulate these aims could be put, usually separately, in terms of social justice *and* financial viability, and it conveys these directions today.

Meanwhile, in 2002, the American Association for State and Local History (AASLH) and the National Trust organized a summit on "the house museum malaise" at Kykuit, the Rockefeller mansion in Hudson Valley, New York. It was introduced with a bald statement: "Many, if not most, historic sites are struggling for survival, and the quality of preservation and maintenance of many such sites has declined precipitously" (George 2002). Referring to an old study, blunt facts were reiterated: 54 percent of house museums surveyed attracted less than five thousand visitors per annum; 65 percent had no full-time staff; and 80 percent operated on budgets of less than $50,000. Also looming was a storm of deferred maintenance, threatening the stewardship of historic properties, pointed out as the central purpose of historic preservation. Some unflattering truths were acknowledged: the sameness of house museums; dubious period room re-creations; endless guided tours; the "don't touch" mentality; and the lack of connection between houses and their local communities. Some were ascribed to problems that emerged out of the very structures established to support house museums, especially the pressure to implement professional standards with far-from-professional resources. And yet conviction maintained that house museums are worthy objects, with the emotional capacity to move, inspire, connect, and engender pride, empathy, and identity. The lessons of the Kykuit conference shifted the conception of house museums as resources not only for communicating civic values but also for enriching imaginative fantasy, thus adding creative and recreational aspects to visiting. It also made the special characteristics of the house museum doldrums explicit and public.

A second summit was held at Kykuit in 2007, reviewing the failures and successes of historic house museums in ever more detail. Kykuit II issued findings and recommendations (Vogt 2007, 20–21). Many were expressed in the rising terminology of sustainability and laid out clear directions. Effective stewardship requires financial sustainability, and sustainability begins with community support as well as a willingness to change in order to address supporters' needs. It was forcefully asserted that "the long-accepted tourism business model is not a sustainable business model for most historic sites," and that "serving the needs of the local community (not the tourist audience) is the most valuable and most sustainable goal for most historic sites." This was an incisive finding because it rejected the received wisdom that cultural tourism is the route to viable incomes for house museums other than the most important "destination houses" such as Mount Vernon. The Kykuit II recommendations projected that meeting local demands for cultural and educational services is the most sustainable way to preserve a historic house, even at the expense of the museum function, and that in some cases the most effective stewardship is to return a house to private ownership.

These and further options were examined in an important study, *New Solutions for House Museums* (Harris 2007). Donna Harris identified a variety of crucial scenarios in house museum decline: aging boards; lack of endowment or financial reserves; dwindling attendance; increased competition; and questionable relevance to local communities. Using eight case studies of vulnerable house museums, she surveyed a range of alternative directions, including sharing the load via co-stewardship agreements or mergers, ownership transfers, short- and long-term leases, and sale to a private owner, under covenant. Meanwhile, recognizing the validity of such issues, the AASLH had obtained federal funding to develop the Standards and Excellence Program for History Organizations (StEPS), a self-assessment schedule launched in 2009. The program aimed to guide boards or management committees to make improvements in governance, audience awareness, interpretation quality, and long-range planning; in 2012 it became an entry pathway into the demanding Museums Accreditation Program of the American Alliance of Museums (AAM). No one foresaw the global recession that erupted in 2008, with its devastating impact on local government and charitable funds for museums and house museums. Cuts in state and local government services, and shattered investment incomes, meant that many house museums (in fact, all types of museums) suffered paralyzing, amputating, and even terminal experiences.

And yet in 2012, retired National Trust president Richard Moe wrote an iteration of an article he had published ten years before, under the same title, "Are There Too Many House Museums?" The earlier article presented a blunt survey of house museum problems: there are *so many* of them, so much the same, so largely representing dead, rich, white men, and costing so much to operate and maintain (Moe 2012, 56–60). The 2012 article observed with frustration that little had changed: "There are still thousands of historic house museums in the United States, mostly run entirely by dedicated volunteers, which are financially strapped, struggling for visitors, and badly in need of repair" (Moe 2012, 55). Moe's assessment can be demonstrated by inquiry on discussion lists. An exemplary finding is the case of the Hezekiah Alexander House in Charlotte, North Carolina, a plain stone house of 1774, the oldest surviving house in Mecklenburg County. The Daughters of the American Revolution leased it for museumization in 1949; the Daughters established a foundation in 1969 and raised a heroic $200,000 to restore the

Hezekiah Alexander House, Charlotte, North Carolina, 1936. Old, vernacular houses are always at risk of destruction by time or design. This one was recorded by professional photographer Johnston's decade-long Carnegie Survey of the Architecture of the South. Its reputation as the oldest in the district makes it typical museumization material.
Photo by Frances Johnston, courtesy of the Library of Congress, www.loc.gov/pictures/resource/csas.02856/.

house, but they ran into financial difficulties building a new visitor center. In the next thirty years, management cycled between local government and the foundation, which had succeeded in raising an endowment of $3 million. A $7 million new museum building was constructed in 1999 and the site was renamed the Charlotte Museum of History. But visitation declined, and the director's position turned over five times in twelve years. The city closed the museum and house in 2012, retrenched staff, and distributed the collections to other institutions. In 2016 "an exciting new preservation project" for the house was promised. While tracing a museum's history can help to understand its course in time, and while to understand is to forgive, there comes a time when "museum" is not the right solution for a historic house.

No one can say how often this scenario has occurred since 2008, though when the American Alliance of Museums (AAM) surveyed museums in 2010, two-thirds reported moderate to severe financial stress; in 2012, just over half were still in the same difficulties (Bell 2012). And for every house museum closed, it is certain that hundreds cut back opening hours, programs, and staff. Global financial crisis is an extreme way to cull the evident excess of house museums in the United States, but in the long run, the invisible hand of the market may prove to have shaped the future.

Meanwhile, in the United Kingdom . . .
Some of the same sustainability issues existed in the United Kingdom, but since there are relatively fewer house museums, the jeremiad of too many has only ever been applied to country houses; the foibles of their viability were addressed in chapter 8. However, the 2008 financial crisis launched brutal attrition on all museums in the United Kingdom, darkly suspected by some to be prolonged by the hand of government in the interests of reducing cultural expenditure in the long term. Recovery has now been further undermined by the likely economic impact of the British exit from the European Union. Since salaries constitute the largest expenditure of most cultural agencies, when costs must be cut, staff constitutes the bottom line for making significant savings. In the United Kingdom, years of successive budget cuts have been so severe that they will play out for many years to come in national and local government houses and museums. In this environment, the dire impact on museums follows from two characteristic factors. First is the degree of instrumentalist cultural policy adopted by the national government after World War II, and especially in the 1980s–2000s. The second condition affecting the recent history of UK house museums is the highly networked management of many public heritage and museum agencies.

The postwar ethic of the welfare state to provide for the economic, social, and cultural well-being of its citizens was unpicked by Conservative governments in the 1980s. In response, cultural sector public management recast the arts (including heritage) as a job- and wealth-producing industry with outputs in urban regeneration, tourism, and community development (Alexander 1999). This construction changed the face and place of UK museums as elements of state apparatus, with economic as well as cultural responsibilities. When Labour took government in 1997, museums, including house museums, were accustomed to policy-promoting functions, and many found the new commitment to multiculturalism and social cohesion fit the disciplinary directions of social history quite naturally, as well as the ever-present imperative for audience development (Sandell 2003). The long-range effectiveness of the inclusiveness policy in museums is doubtful, but it forced many to analyze their product and its markets, with a salutary shake-up in attention to local communities. The example of Kedleston Hall in Derbyshire demonstrates the mechanism and its outcomes. Lord Curzon, viceroy of India from 1899 to 1905, installed his Eastern Museum on the ground floor when he inherited the house; a project in 2004 allowed Indian women's groups and college students from Derby to get to know the collection and produce interpretive writing, a textile artwork, and a dance performance, all exhibited in 2005–2006 (Prudames 2004). The outcomes of such means of serving society by catering to culturally diverse and socially marginal visitors are difficult to evaluate, but they offer an alternative to the strategy of restitutional representation adopted in the United States (surveyed in chapter 6).

The second factor affecting the recent history of UK house museums is the intricacy of networked public and private heritage and museum agencies. The National Trust is not the proprietor of all British house museums, as often popularly perceived. But given the peculiarities of its nature as a membership association, a huge charity, and the largest private landowner in England, it is efficiently managed, thanks to economies of scale and strategic planning informed by ambitious goals. As an example, the Trust grasped the nettle of site sustainability early, with focuses on family activities, local produce in its cafés and stores, and green power generated on site via biomass and hydroelectricity. With a fair exposure to investment returns, the Trust has slowed since the recession. Happily, sources such as the Heritage Lottery Fund enable new major works, epitomized by the grant of £7.75 million for a huge project that started at Knole in west Kent in 2013: building repairs; improved environmental controls; opening abandoned rooms and attics; urgent conservation work on paintings, textiles, and furniture; establishing a conservation studio in a fifteenth-century barn previously used for parking and storage, and a learning center in seventeenth-century haylofts; plus new visitor comforts. Winning big funding today involves demonstrating social and economic benefits to the region, such as sensitive involvement of local people, opportunities for jobs and training, and new services or perspectives that extend the impact of the site. The scale of the grant and the works indicates the complexity of managing not only a peak of English country house culture but also its social context.

At the national level of cultural funding, governments since the Thatcher decade in the 1980s–1990s aimed to lighten the load of annual grants-in-aid to museum and heritage organizations by increasingly requiring them to become self-supporting. Since then, British museums have increased their proportion of earned income via special exhibition admission charges, venue rentals, and cafés and shops, proving ever more vital since the recession. The same agenda of self-sufficiency informed the government decision in 2015 to split off the larger, property-managing part of English Heritage as a self-

Bolsover Castle, Derbyshire, 2008. Bolsover scarp has been defended by a castle since the twelfth century, though ruined and rebuilt several times. Industrial pollution degraded it badly in the nineteenth and twentieth centuries, and it was presented to the Ministry of Works (ancestor of English Heritage) in 1943. Parts have been stabilized and repaired, but the seventeenth-century country house, pictured, remains roofless.
Photo by Andrew Knowles, UK: DSC02629, CC BY 2.0, https://commons.wikimedia.org/w/index.php?curid=15565830.

sufficient trust while maintaining a small government organization under the name Historic England to fulfill statutory requirements. English Heritage's existing membership scheme demonstrated viable popular support for its four-hundred-plus sites, which are popularly distinguished from National Trust properties as the nation's ruins. This is not entirely the case: (roofed) houses such as Audley End in Essex, the Little Castle at Bolsover Castle in Derbyshire, and Charles Darwin's Down House in Kent are managed by English Heritage along with its portfolio of ruins.

A further quantum of historic houses and sites was, until the recession, concentrated in the portfolio of local government and largely managed by city and county museums services with relative efficiency and flexibility. However, as just one segment of the multitude of services provided by local authorities, house and other museums rate fairly low in the pecking order of funding priorities (Lawley 2003). Here at the bottom of the government funding system, the attrition of cultural services has been most severe, simultaneously affecting galleries, libraries, archives, and the arts. The Museums Association has documented the impact of budget cuts on museums since 2010. It reported that 51 percent of museums had reduced staff numbers in 2011; 42 percent in 2012; 37 percent in 2013. Over the same years, income was down at 58 percent, 51 percent, and 49 percent of museums (Museums Association 2013). In 2015 the Cuts Survey noted the cumulative impact on local authority budgets was starting to threaten museum buildings and collections, with industrial sites the most vulnerable, and more in the north than the south (Museums Association 2015). Today, many city and county museums services include house museums at risk of closure. For instance, five museums closed in Lancashire in 2016, and another six are on notice in 2017; among them are the oldest surviving town house in Lancaster, the Judges' Lodgings, and the Lancaster Cottage Museum. Groups defending the museums predict that once closed, they are unlikely to open again.

In a second strategy of retrenchment, following the national example of transforming heritage management into a charity, local governments have sought interest groups to take over houses and museums as independent trusts. On a small scale, Ford Green Hall in Stoke-on-Trent, an important sixteenth- and eighteenth-century farmhouse that faced closure by the City Council in 2011, was reconstituted under the management of a charitable trust in 2014. In the same region, Staffordshire County Council had leased Shugborough Hall from the National Trust since 1966; in 2016 the Council calculated that it was more worthwhile to surrender the lease than to keep it up for another forty-nine years. On a larger scale, nine museums formerly managed by Birmingham City Council merged in 2012 as the Birmingham

Museums Trust, though ownership remains with the Council; sites include Aston Hall, Blakesley Hall, and Soho House. This large movement from government to private management, relying significantly on volunteer labor, constitutes a paradigm shift in British heritage conservation, and a tipping point in the administration of public cultural resources (Babbidge 2015). The new model may sustain house museums for another epoch—or the current American phenomenon of too many unsustainable house museums may emerge over time in England.

Meanwhile, ironically, some house (and other) museums have never looked better, and new sites have opened in the midst of the bleakness, thanks to the tightly focused munificence of the Heritage Lottery Fund (HLF), established in 1994. It directs 20 percent of a proportion of all National Lottery ticket purchases to heritage projects (the remainder to the arts, sports, charities, and environmental causes); by 2014 the HLF had distributed more than £6 billion to museums and heritage organizations. Multimillion-pound grants have enabled large-scale conservation works at houses such as Abbotsford and Tyntesfield, as well as much smaller projects that have revived houses with new programs oriented to the now deeply embedded social goals of multiculturalism and social inclusion. The HLF (like many big funders and philanthropists) gives essentially for projects and capital works, in the expectation that improved structures will equip the organization to meet recurrent operational costs. (The idea seems like common sense, but experience shows that it encourages expansion without the funds to develop and keep up staff services.) The HLF also offers matching grants to develop endowment funds, designed to bring further private money into the heritage sector. Such strategies are the instruments of modernizing policy to develop the resilience that is projected to take cultural heritage off the books of government. It's not a bad idea in itself, but it's evidence of the profound switch in public management approaches to culture as a niche market rather than a public good.

Who and What Are House Museums for Today?

The purposes and desirability of house museums appear to be deeply embedded in the popular mind throughout the English-speaking world. As proof, consider the clockwork response to announcements of the sale or demolition of the birthplace of hero X, or the best built house of style Y, or the mansion-and-collection of millionaire Z: make it a house museum! Professionals in the field wince, knowing the costs and risks all too well. It would seem to be a significant expression of public support. Or is it a virtuous but meaningless habit? Who wants house museums, and what for? Ways of addressing these questions are numerous, but not conclusive. They begin with the resource of new knowledge derived from visitor studies.

There is little evidence specifically about house museum visiting or visitors. Visitor trends observed in the generic family of museums must serve, with caveats that a distinctive profile of house museums is not well defined in the public mind and that house museums generally share the disadvantages of being smaller and less visible among the totality of museums. The recent state of museum visitation as measured by official statistics shows very small declines in the United States, and small rises in both museum and heritage visiting in the United Kingdom (Department for Culture, Media & Sport 2013, 20; National Endowment for the Arts 2013, 20). The US figures trend gradually down (since 1992) and the UK trend goes gently up (since 2008); both document the continuing predominance of white, highly educated attendance at museums. There is some evidence that efforts to make museums attractive to nonwhite or non-Anglo audiences are having a small positive impact, but the slightness of change is disappointing.

Finer detail about museum visitors began to emerge in the 1990s, when many museums invested in programs of visitor research and exhibition evaluation (Hooper-Greenhill 2006). As market intelligence, visitor research contained data so specific that it could be considered commercial-in-confidence; at the same time, the findings constituted important evidence in the realm of public culture, and some was shared in professional and scholarly formats (e.g., Doering 1999). Thus knowledge about museum visitors and visiting circulated, such that the museum world is today incomparably better informed about its visitors: not only concerning demographic characteristics and socioeconomic status but also concerning the psychographics of lifestyles and motivations in visiting. There is some knowledge, too, of museum nonvisitors. As a consequence, it is no longer adequate to refer to "the general visitor," who evaporated under analysis via the marketing technique of segmenting visitors according to their tastes and values. Despite suspicion of stereotyping, the intuitive aptness of findings seems disarmingly tenable. Hence categories such as "cultural connoisseurs," "learning families," and "self-developers" inform the development of services, activities, and comforts that will help different visitors appreciate the experiential product of the house museum.

The findings of visitor research have reshaped understanding of visitors' agendas for, and behavior in, their museum excursions. The insight that most visitors seek recreation and a sociable outing more than "education" as such was particularly important and influential (Hood 1983; Falk & Dierking 1992, 11–20). It shows that a social experience of informal, free-choice learning in the museum, comfortably located on the same arc as cultural tourism and "edutainment," is a desirable form of leisure to many visitors and potential visitors, with inflections according to family life cycle. Shifting from the historical idea of the improvingly educational museum to a new frame as the learning-for-leisure museum is a conceptual (and not universal) reorientation. It is acute at the museum end of the relationship, where staff plans experiences for visitors to have in mind the maximization of visitor satisfaction. To test the outcome, larger organizations conduct market evaluations of visitors' experience to measure the organization's effectiveness as a host. The National Trust in England, for instance, measures the proportion of visitors who rate their experience "very enjoyable"; the 2014–2015 *Annual Report* recorded it at 60 percent, rising to 96 percent for the rating "enjoyable/very enjoyable" (National Trust 2015, 9). The figures testify to the capacity of a historic house or garden visit to give pleasure to visitors. (They also prove the concept of a visit as more than inspecting a historic interior or landscape: it must address the tourism essentials of satisfactory car parking, wayfinding, ticketing, information, cafés, and shops.)

At the consumer end, the profile of museum visitors remains persistent. Time and time again, higher education and middle age have been found the most reliable predictors of museum visiting. But in contrast to the stalwarts, Hood (1983), Merriman (1991), and Bennett (1994) identified a substantial residuum of museum nonvisitors, between 40 and 60 percent of the population studied. Merriman noted that within this group there is no specific antagonism toward museums, just different preferences. Bennett goes further and points to indifference, with the unusually explicit observation that there is a substantial fraction of the population "beyond the reach of any kind of policy initiative or marketing strategy, and this needs to be recognized" (Bennett 1994, 55).

The most useful explanation of these two ends of the visitor spectrum is the sociological perspective that describes museum visiting as an index of cultivation, a flexing of personal cultural capital as a resource in the field of social mobility (Bourdieu, Darbel, & Schnapper 1997). Merriman and Bennett interpret the scale of interest in museum visiting as a function of the possession of cultural capital, a position with which I concur. Cultural capital functions as an asset of social power, but not necessarily in tandem with matching levels of economic capital. In the middling zones of wealth, cultural capital constitutes a resource of legitimacy and aspiration, soaking down to the upper zone of the working class. Today, the varieties of knowledge that undergird competence and confidence for social mobility can be metaphorically summarized in the taste for museums, which implies easy familiarity with a range of cultural experiences.

This view of museum visiting demonstrates remarkable continuity with the history of the civic museums of the nineteenth century. Various species of museum, including house museums, were pitched by dominant factions of the rising middle class to improve not-unwilling workers in the middle-class image. Museum visiting never offered instant social transformation, serving more as a ritual affirming cultural competence. But this show of and desire for cultural capital still constitutes an important flow in the stream of ideas that inform contemporary museums. As Simon Knell observes, the commitment to education, cultivation, and civilization itself is the source of museums' moral authority (Knell et al. 2011, 5).[1] It is not by chance that it is the very stuff of the cultural capital that defines middle-class-ness. In fact, the "improvements" of cultural capital can apply to the resource itself as much as to the visitors who take it in: new and different knowledge can be legitimized by putting it on display in a museum. Museum visiting is—still—a taste of the middle class, but as a means of self-improvement it can now be taken as leisure, making it that much more palatable. Simultaneously, the range of cultural content exhibited in museums has enlarged to include popular fields such as films and fashion. Film and television costumes make very congenial displays in house museums: far more sturdy than historic clothing, offering impeccably perfect reproduction styles, and deliciously familiar to visitors. For example, Jane Austen's House Museum in Chawton, Hampshire, is often inhabited by one or two items of film costume. On a much bigger scale, costumes from the TV series *Downton Abbey* circulate the globe to show in museums and house museums, such as at Biltmore, Winterthur, and the Driehaus Museum, a collector's house in Chicago, in 2014–2016, and in Melbourne, Rippon Lea, a National Trust mansion, has cultivated an exhibition specialty in local film and TV series costume (including *Downton Abbey* in 2017). Visitors simply love costumes.

History indicates that the reformist mission of civic museums in the nineteenth century transmuted, subtly and not totally, via the discourse of education toward a new ideal of socially equitable museums in the late twentieth century. Hence, while the analysis of museum visiting as a classed and classing practice is convincing to sociologists, it is politically unacceptable in the cultural apparatus of liberal democracies, especially in the era of multiculturalism and social inclusiveness. This view acknowledges that museums were and still are constructs of the middle-class taste for learning and cultivation, with the effect that museums still require advanced cultural capital in

Rippon Lea, Melbourne, 2015. Visitors relished costumes from the Australian TV series *Miss Fisher's Murder Mysteries*. This mansion was a regular site in the series. The exhibition included specimen fabrics for handling, replicas for dressing up, and a "sewing room" where visitors could sketch new designs for Miss Fisher.
Photo by Jessica Hood, 2015.

order to consume and enjoy them. Cultural participation statistics continue to demonstrate this truth. That is to say, not even museums that adopt the view of visiting as a leisure choice, and plan exhibitions and programs that will be appreciated by different segments of their visitor bases, can expect to attract 100 percent of civil society. Put this way, the notion that a cultural institution could or should be universally attractive is implausible. Yet museum discourse contains a formidable ethic to this effect, underlain today by sensitivity to the charge of exclusivism: museums must be for everyone. The sheer impossibility of this logic facilitated the recasting of the instrumentalist British social inclusion goals of the 1990s. In the 2010s the quest emerges for a narrative to demonstrate that museums create value that makes a difference in the public domain, via the intrinsic value of the museum experience (Scott, Dodd, & Sandell 2014, 16–27). In other words, the challenge to articulate the benefits to individuals and society of spending money on preserving and operating house museums continues to require new rationales. Those who love museums need no persuading, but there are plenty more who are less convinced; for them, the problem is a subset of justifying public expenditure on culture, the arts, and heritage.

Museum advocates currently address the challenge in two major directions: culture as an economically productive field (e.g., Arts Council England 2014), and culture as a form of public value, or "planned outcomes which add benefit to the public sphere" (Scott 2013, 2). The former seeks museum potential to participate in the creative industries, or cultural economy. Though the potential seems intuitively correct, the house museum product of a visitor experience is difficult to monetize beyond an admission fee, books, and souvenirs because there is no means of reproducing the experience in ways that can be sold other than as a tour in person (Hesmondhalgh 2013, 16–18). And so, apart from mobilizing the real estate potential of the house as a venue for events and film shoots, most house museums find themselves outside the powerhouses of the creative economy. Hence the second direction for vindicating museums is called to demonstrate that the public sphere of civil society benefits by the activities of museums. The evidence of investigations into visitors' own perceptions points toward the satisfactions of belonging to or integrating with communities by sharing experiences facilitated by the museum. This might include sensitive and difficult issues, and different attitudes to the viewer's own, as well as highly pleasurable or wondrous perspectives, all of which may inform or shift the individual's perception (Selwood 2010, 35–50). While some house museums certainly mobilize such valuable experiences in visitors' hearts and minds, the intention to do so is not yet a standard goal; it ought to be.

The Future of House Museums

This chapter has so far suggested a grim outlook for house museums—or rather, for museums in general. Among all the woeful conditions impacting museums in recent years, none is exclusive to house museums. The entire family of museums is destabilized and threatened by the financial challenges of adequate, sustainable income. Certain museums are doing (relatively) well, generally because they have found ways to fit within the economy of leisure and tourism and to invest in further infrastructure to enlarge the experience of the place/site itself, and so it is with house museums too.

Some house museums cross the threshold of fame to become "destination sites," capable of attracting visitors by their very fame: they might be called the celebrities of house museums, famous for being famous. It's not a predictable transition. The conditions of fame are infamously fickle: a profoundly important national symbol that guarantees an enduring stream of pilgrims; a national anniversary that attracts government and philanthropic funding; a starring role in a television drama or film that stimulates public enthusiasm; a crystallization in the zeitgeist of fashion that captures tastemaker and popular attention; a very gifted and lucky director—such lucky chances can reinforce the historic value of a house museum with the aura of fame that attracts visitors, philanthropy and grants, services, and more visitors. It usually helps to be big in order to get bigger, and it also helps to be located in a tourism center or on a popular tourist route.

Shakespeare's birthplace and Washington's Mount Vernon exemplify the hero category of this happy class. It is only too tempting for admirers of further heroes to imagine that their man or woman exerts the same magnetism. Few do, alas, except to the cognoscenti and true believers. But the relative success of thematic tours such as literary England and the National Historic Trails system in the United States demonstrate that the right note is there for house museum marketers to make resonant. That said, there is a distinct trend in heroic house museumizations toward celebrating artists' lives in their houses and studios. Most recently opened in the United States are Chaim Gross's apartment and studio in Greenwich Village, New York City (2009); Winslow Homer's house and studio in Scarborough, Maine (opened 2012); and Donald Judd's Soho, New York, and Marfa, Texas, properties (2013). In the United Kingdom, J. M. W. Turner's villa, Sandycombe, in then-rural Twickenham, was acquired by a trust in 2014, some two hundred years after the artist designed it for himself and his father. It is in need of substantial conservation before it can open as a museum, but it will do so with a collection of Turneriana gathered and donated by the last owner of the house.

The artwork and collector genres of house museums contain many specimens of recent ascendancy into house museum stardom, exemplified by the renaissance of Sir John Soane's Museum and several houses designed by Frank Lloyd Wright. The enlargement and development of new services at the Frick Collection and the Wallace Collection demonstrate the capacity of old institutions to expand to meet new tides in public interest. The species of modernist houses now moving into museumhood as artworks in themselves taps into current trends of advanced interest and may soon prove their attraction with investment in interpretive and service facilities. Social history houses might be said to have pioneered the virtues of growing big, impelled by necessity: they tend to be small houses to begin with and simply unable to absorb the level of visitation necessary to become viable attractions. Thus a new or additional building on or near the house site is a necessity for many house museums to grow as institutions, as at Robert Burns's Birthplace Museum and Wright's Martin House. Even palaces rarely have spare space suitable for the modern apparatus of visitor reception, education and meeting rooms, halls for concerts and talks, interpretive exhibitions, cafés, shops, and user-friendly toilets.

Collectors' house museums show every chance of strengthening their positions, thanks to the popular prestige of capital-A Art collections. An example is the John and Mable Ringling Museum of Art in Sarasota, Florida; bequeathed to the state in 1927, and enduring legal turmoil until 1946 to become public property, it has achieved the stability to develop since reorganization in 2000. The complex is based on John Ringling's Venetian-inspired mansion, Ca' d'Zan, together with his own art museum; the site also now includes a circus museum, an eighteenth-century Italian theater from Asolo, and contemporary art galleries. Effectively, a cultural complex of wider interest overtook the house museum; it was recently rebranded as "The Ringling," a fashionable conceit of nomenclature that may be viable locally but is mystifying in the larger world. Its growth represents the history of museums that morph from private collections, initially envisaged as the individual's legacy to the state but increasingly presented as celebrating the donor in situ at home.

Unexpectedly, the extreme vanity project of collectors' live-in house museums of contemporary art or antique decorative arts is surging in Australia—and probably the rest of the world. Since writing about the Lyon Housemuseum in chapter 5, a second has opened in Melbourne: the Justin Art House Museum. Melbourne is also the location of a town house bequeathed to the state by William Johnston, an antiques dealer, in 1986, and something similar opened in Adelaide in 2016, under the name the David Roche Foundation. Beleura, a mid-Victorian summer house on the seaside edge of Melbourne, was left to a foundation in 1996; its last owner was a musician and composer without any art-collecting interest, an absence that has been rectified by its current museum managers in the form of a growing collection of modernist ceramics now placed around the house. Assets such as these sites possess might once have been offered to public museums, but they have become more selective in their collecting and more crowded with donors' names. The capacity of the modern wealthy to share their private collections in situ, or pre- or postmortem, and the growing sense that collections justify house museums appear to be feeding a new age of house museums in Australia.[2]

But such directions are unlikely for most house museums. Among the older types of hero shrines and vernacular characterizations of national identity, the typical advocacy of small interest groups organized as trusts or foundations has not often managed to create wider popular support for their causes. Those that have been absorbed into networked organizations such as the National Trust or the National Park Service have (until recently) demonstrated stronger chances of survival. At the same time, historic house networks have become reluctant to acquire further properties. Like art museums, house museum networks now collect to strategic agendas. They operate enough houses of the traditionally valued and usually available types, and of course the networks are not the only agencies in the field, boosted by the multitude of individually constituted house museums. What counts as a surfeit of house museums is a function of national conditions. In the United Kingdom, stately homes seem innumerable in the visitor destination mix. In the United States, colonial houses and neostately homes appear to be sated categories; for example, Harris counted 275 house museums in and around Philadelphia, of which more than a hundred are eighteenth-century gentlemen's houses (Harris 2007, 9).

The turn toward local "relevance" recommended by museum professional and service organizations is not an easy fix, and may well be a chimera. A central problem is, as Nina Simon points out, that for relevance to be a museum-attractive characteristic, it needs to be identified by the visitor, not the museum (Simon 2016). Among recent tactics to claim relevance has been the introduction of vegetable gardens into the grounds of former country houses that today find themselves ringed by inner-urban density, as at Wyck in Philadelphia and Woodlawn Plantation near Washington, DC. It is an attractive idea with fine interactive potential; yet, in the only-too-modern environment of urban social blight, its message that fresh veggies are good for you sits discomfortingly in the reformist tradition of nineteenth-century museums. This is the relevance of do-goodism, not relevance defined by locals.

Does an exhibition theme of personal identity with the visitor make a house relevant? There is evidence for and against this question. The potential attraction of identity-likeness possesses the logic of connection on a personal scale. Where the oppressed are featured as key players in a house's stories, some sites have certainly risen in esteem for the representational achievement of public statements of "other" characters in history. They actively draw special interest visitation, such as lesbians to Plas Newydd (not the National Trust house of the same name), Wales, for the sake of the Ladies of Llangollen (however little the present house resembles theirs). On a larger scale, it can be argued that themes in national and global histories, especially emigration and war, contain epic potential for large-scale relevance to individuals, families, and nations. Stories of labor immigration from country to city, south to north, and poor Europe to thriving United States or lucky Australia frame the experience of practically everyone in the New World, and wherever industrial modernity took root. The consequences for individuals and societies of fighting or enduring wars, dying or surviving, and reestablishing families afterward touch the lives of everyone in the modern world. The impact of war was vividly demonstrated in some house museum short-term installations marking the centenary of World War I. For instance, in 2014–2016, the National Trust house Dunham Massey Hall, near Manchester, transformed its saloon into the fifteen-bed hospital it housed in the later war years, complete with a makeshift operating theater beside the great stairs, where there had been a bathroom with running water. Yet few house museums employ the history of big events to contextualize individuals or generations of inhabitants, perpetuating the vision of the family home as the locus of private life. Thus they flout the microeconomic principle of the household as the basic unit of social construct and the feminist lesson that the personal is political. Much more should be considered and implemented on these fronts.

Other models of community relevance generate uses for historic houses that are so distantly connected to the museum tradition that they might be called generic community centers rather than museums. One such is the National Trust property Sutton House in Hackney, London. Beside interpreting the five-hundred-year-old Tudor building with activities for school students, Sutton House partners with specialists to offer programs ranging from family learning oriented to children's skills in literacy to alternative culture pop-up cinema events, such as Amy Grimehouse club nights. The House operates a café and caters for forty weddings a year. These kinds of mixed educational, social, and commercial functions bring welcome income to many a house, though most conveniently to houses without historic furnishings. But it raises the question: How flexible can a house museum get? A variation on the theme of wider social uses developed (slowly) to preserve four mid-nineteenth-century and later houses in Weeksville, Brooklyn, New York. It was a village built and inhabited by free black people since the 1830s, "rediscovered" in 1968, when the site became known as the Hunterfly Road Houses. In 2005 the houses were incorporated as museum pieces in the Weeksville Heritage Center, now Brooklyn's largest African American cultural institution. The Heritage Center surrounds the houses with community infrastructure dedicated to arts, literacy, local history, and a preservation program with the aim of strengthening cultural identity. Both Sutton House and the Hunterfly Road Houses present their sites as the heritage of the people who live nearby, though their business is much more than heritage preservation. They stretch the concept of a house museum, reducing the degree to which "museum" can be said to be their core business. Yet it may be the realistic way to preserve historic houses.

In this context it is appropriate to refocus on the nature of museums in general. Older professional definitions focused on the centrality of collecting and collections; newer definitions stress the social environment they aim to serve by collecting. I proposed at the beginning of this book that a house museum is "a dwelling, museumized and largely presented in its domestic function," subsuming the collecting aim by referring to a house museum's implicit museum character. My line contains the implication that the house itself is the primary object of the museum's collecting practice. I do not mean to exclude or diminish the significance of its contents, which are critically important if they are indigenous to the house—less so if they are not. But I do intend to assert that a fundamental purpose of a house museum is the preservation and interpretation of the house itself. If a museumized house is inadequately protected by its management as a museum, the ethical priority is to preserve the house by some other means. Hence I rejoice in the extended services that Sutton House and the Hunterfly Road houses can offer to their communities. I praise the successes of the house museums whose celebrity earns them visitors and funding to keep up their good work. I honor the determination of smaller organizations that manage to sustain their special sites. And I mourn the conditions described at the beginning of this chapter that lead to the decline of care by staff and budget cuts. These sad and dangerous conditions make me turn to Harris's *New Solutions for House Museums* (2007) with hope. But though the book earned a second print run, its eminent good sense does not seem to have propelled much movement for change. Failing house museums have proved reluctant to bite the bullet of adapting to another function, even in very straightened times. So it seems that insignificant house museums will persist because there is neither a will for change nor a commitment to rational programs of preservation. By comparison with the demolition of historic houses for redevelopment, the decline of some house museums is more an embarrassment than a disaster, but it is sad and unnecessary.

To my own surprise, I observe that the improving national mission of nineteenth-century house museums persists to this day. Even the trials of the past twenty years have had little effect in altering the nature of house museums. This is heroic persistence, as exemplified by insignificant houses. Nonetheless, changes have emerged, crucially via the shift to locate and represent domestic social histories, which may have been the saving grace of the species of house museums. By unpacking and historicizing the total phenomenon, I have come to see that the existential specificity of the structures in which humans dwell mandates a role that could have strangled the museological management of historic houses, but doesn't, necessarily. The original genre of house museum, the hero's house, possesses ritual significance that remains meaningful. The concept of the artwork house has acquired renewed presence as the archetype of designs that define, identify, and matter in the world today. The unlikely domestication of museum-framed collecting and exhibiting is now turbo-charged by the wealth to indulge egos as big as any of the great house collectors, and it thrills spectators. The country houses of England ride again as the peak of national artistic achievement, still imitated in concept, style, and scale around the world. The sustainability of any and all will never be easy, but house museums are worth it.

Notes

1. *Middle class* has always been contentious to define, and the concept of "class" has very different connotations in the United Kingdom and the United States. I hope readers will permit me to skate by in this context, with an impressionistic meaning of *middle class* today as middling, neither very rich nor very poor, but with a positive degree of cultural capital. See Anat Shenker-Osorio, "Why Americans All Believe They Are 'Middle Class': A Taxonomy of How We Talk about Class and Wealth in the United States Today," *Atlantic*, August 1, 2013, http://www.theatlantic.com/politics/archive/2013/08/why-americans-all-believe-they-are-middle-class/278240/; "Huge Survey Reveals Seven Social Classes in UK," *BBC News*, April 3, 2013, http://www.bbc.com/news/uk-22007058.

2. I intend to follow up this phenomenon!

Bibliography

Abram, Ruth J. 2005. "History Is as History Does: The Evolution of a Mission-Driven Museum." In *Looking Reality in the Eye: Museums and Social Responsibility*, edited by Robert R. Janes and Gerald T. Conaty, 19–42. Calgary: University of Calgary Press.

Ackroyd, Peter. 2002. "Introduction." In *18 Folgate Street: The Tale of a House in Spitalfields*, edited by Dennis Severs, vii–xi. London: Vintage/Chatto & Windus.

Adair, Joshua. 2010. "House Museums or Walk-In Closets? The (Non)Representation of Gay Men in the Museums They Called Home." In *Gender, Sexuality and Museums*, edited by Amy K. Levin, 264–78. Abingdon: Routledge.

Adams, Ruth. 2013. "The V&A, the Destruction of the Country House and the Creation of 'English Heritage.'" *Museum and Society* 11, no. 1: 1–18.

Alberge, Dalya. 2010, July 10. "Art Collectors Build Museums to Let Public See Private Hoards." *Guardian*. http://www.theguardian.com/artanddesign/2010/jul/11/modern-art-collectors-private-museum.

Alexander, Victoria. 1999. "A Delicate Balance: Museums and the Market-Place." *Museum International* 51, no. 2: 29–34.

Alfrey, Judith, and Catherine Clark, eds. 1993. *The Landscape of Industry: Patterns of Change in Ironbridge Gorge*. London: Routledge.

Allfrey, Martin. 1999. "Brodsworth Hall: The Preservation of a Country House." In *Managing Historic Sites and Buildings: Reconciling Presentation and Preservation*, edited by Gill Chitty and David Baker, 115–25. New York: Routledge.

Allfrey, Martin, and Amber Xavier-Rowe. 2012. "Conserving and Presenting Brodsworth Hall: New Approaches for a Sustainable Future." In *Proceedings of "The Artifact, Its Context and Their Narrative," Joint Conference of ICOM-DEMHIST and Three ICOM-CC Working Groups*, edited by Kate Seymour and Malgorzata

Sawicki. Los Angeles, Getty Research Institute. http://www.icom-cc.org/ul/cms/fck-uploaded/documents/DEMHIST%20_%20ICOM-CC%20Joint%20Interim%20Meeting%202012/06-Allfrey-DEMHIST_ICOMCC-LA_2012.pdf.

Alpers, Svetlana. 1991. "The Museum as a Way of Seeing." In *Exhibiting Cultures: The Poetics and Politics of Museum Display*, edited by Ivan Karp and Steve Lavine, 25–32. Washington: Smithsonian Institution Press.

Altick, Richard D. 1978. *The Shows of London*. Cambridge, MA: Harvard University Press.

American Classical Homes Preservation Trust. Accessed December 3, 2015, http://www.classicalamerican.org/html/history.html.

Amsden, David. 2015, February 26. "Building the First Slavery Museum in America." *New York Times Magazine*. http://nyti.ms/1zK43Qg.

Anderson, Jay. 1991. *A Living History Reader, Vol. 1: Museums*. Nashville: American Association for State and Local History.

Andrews, Corey. 2004. *Literary Nationalism in Eighteenth-Century Scottish Club Poetry*. Lewiston: Edwin Mellen Press.

Anon. 1928. "Cedar Grove." *Bulletin of the Pennsylvania Museum* 23, no. 118: 4–14.

Anon. 1984. *From Threshold to Rooftree: The Haddington Home of Jane Welsh Carlyle*. Edinburgh: Pentland Press.

Anon. 1993. *Mr. Straw's House, Nottinghamshire*. London: National Trust.

Anon. 1995 [facsimile 1896]. *Illustrated Memorial Volume of the Carlyle's House Purchase Fund Committee*. London.

Anon. 1996. *Arlington Court, Devon*. Swindon: National Trust.

Anon. 2008. *Mrs. Smith's Cottage: A Souvenir Book*. Navenby: Friends of Mrs. Smith's Cottage.

Appadurai, Arjun, ed. 1986. *The Social Life of Things: Commodities in Cultural Perspective*. Cambridge: Cambridge University Press.

Arts Council England. 2014. *The Value of Arts and Culture to People and Society: An Evidence Review*. http://www.artscouncil.org.uk/sites/default/files/download-file/Value_arts_culture_evidence_review.pdf.

Ashton, Paul, and Paula Hamilton. 2007. *History at the Crossroads: Australians and the Past*. Sydney: Halstead Press.

Avrami, Erica C., Randall Mason, and Marta de la Torre. 2000. *Values and Heritage Conservation: Research Report*. Los Angeles, CA: Getty Conservation Institute. http://hdl.handle.net/10020/gci_pubs/values_heritage_research_report.

Babbidge, Adrian. 2015. "Museums and Heritage." *Cultural Trends* 24, no. 1: 21–27. doi: 10.1080.09548963.2014.1000602.

Bachelard, Gaston. 1994 [1958]. *The Poetics of Space*. Boston: Beacon Press.

Baldry, A. L. 1904. *The Wallace Collection at Hertford House*. London: Goupil & Co.

Barnes Foundation, Philadelphia, 2016. http://www.barnesfoundation.org/about/history/albert.

Barrington, Lewis. 1941. *Historic Restorations of the Daughters of the American Revolution*. New York: Richard Smith.

Bates, Charlotte Fiske, ed. 1882. *The Cambridge Book of Poetry and Song.* New York: Thomas Y. Crowell.

Bayne, David, Michele Phillips, Deborah Lee Trupin, and Eric Jackson-Forsberg. 2012. "Keeping It Real: The Relationship between Curator and Conservator in Furnishing a Historic Interior." In *Proceedings of "The Artifact, Its Context and Their Narrative," Joint Conference of ICOM-DEMHIST and Three ICOM-CC Working Groups,* edited by Kate Seymour and Malgorzata Sawicki. Los Angeles, Getty Research Institute. http://www.icom-cc.org/ul/cms/fck-uploaded/documents/DEM-HIST%20_%20ICOM-CC%20Joint%20Interim%20Meeting%202012/04-Trupin_Phillips-DEMHIST_ICOMCC-LA_2012.pdf.

Bearss, Edwin C. 1971. *The Hoover Houses and Community Structures: Historic Structures Report, Herbert Hoover National Historic Site, West Branch, Iowa.* http://www.nps.gov/history/history/online_books/heho/hsr/index.htm.

Beckett, J. V. 1986. *The Aristocracy in England 1600–1914.* Oxford: Basil Blackwell.

Beckett, John. 2002. *Byron and Newstead: The Aristocrat and the Abbey.* Newark: University of Delaware Press.

Bedford, John. 1971. *How to Run a Stately Home.* London: Andre Deutsch.

Bell, Ford W. 2012. "How Are Museums Supported Financially in the U.S.?" http://photos.state.gov/libraries/amgov/133183/english/P_You_Asked_How_Are_Museums_Supported_Financially.pdf.

Bellah, Robert N. 1967. "Civil Religion in America." *Daedalus* 96, no. 1: 1–21.

Bennett, Mary. 1964. *Sudley: The Emma Holt Bequest.* Liverpool: City Council.

Bennett, Tony. 1994. *The Reluctant Museum Visitor: A Study of Non-Goers to History Museums and Art Galleries.* Redfern, NSW: Australia Council.

Bennett, Tony. 1995. *The Birth of the Museum: History, Theory, Politics.* London: Routledge.

Bennett, Tony. 2004. *Pasts Beyond Memory: Evolution, Museums, Colonialism.* London: Routledge.

Bickford, Anne. 1985. "Disquiet in the Warm Parlour of the Past: Calthorpes House Museum, Canberra." In *History and Cultural Resources Project: Part 2: Seminar Papers.* Canberra: Committee to Review Australian Studies in Tertiary Education.

Bickford, Anne. 1987. *Calthorpes' House Museum Guide.* Canberra: Australian Government Publishing Service.

Bills, Mark. 2001. "Display and Exhibition in the Victorian Era." In *Art in the Age of Queen Victoria,* edited by Mark Bills, 42–52. Bournemouth: Russell-Cotes Art Gallery and Museum.

Black, Barbara. 2000. *On Exhibit: Victorians and Their Museums.* Charlottesville: University Press of Virginia.

Black, Graham. 2005. *The Engaging Museum: Developing Museums for Visitor Involvement.* Abingdon: Routledge.

Blewett, Mary H. 1989. "Machines, Workers and Capitalists." In *History Museums in the United States: A Critical Assessment,* edited by Warren Leon and Roy Rosenzweig, 262–93. Urbana: University of Illinois Press.

Blunt, Alison, and Robyn Dowling. 2006. *Home*. London: Routledge.

Blunt, Anthony. 1979. "The History of the House and Collections." In *Treasures from Chatsworth: The Devonshire Inheritance*, 17–21. Washington: International Exhibition Foundation.

Bodnar, John. 1992. *Remaking America: Public Memory, Commemoration, and Patriotism in the Twentieth Century*. Princeton, NJ: Princeton University Press.

Bosley, Edward. 2002. *Gamble House: Greene and Greene*. 2nd ed. New York: Phaidon Press.

Boswell, David, and Jessica Evans, eds. 1999. *Representing the Nation: Histories, Heritage and Museums*. London: Routledge/Open University.

Bourdieu, Pierre. 1977. *Outline of a Theory of Practice*. Cambridge: Cambridge University Press.

Bourdieu, Pierre. 1986. *Distinction: A Social Critique of the Judgment of Taste*, translated by Richard Nice. London: Routledge & Kegan Paul.

Bourdieu, Pierre, Alain Darbel, and Dominique Schnapper. 1997 [1966]. *The Love of Art: European Art Museums and Their Public*. Cambridge: Polity Press.

Bowe, Nicola Gordon, ed. 1993. *Art and the National Dream: The Search for Vernacular Expression in Turn-of-the-Century Design*. Dublin: Irish Academic Press.

Bressey, Caroline. 2013. "Contesting the Political Legacy of Slavery in England's Country Houses." In *Slavery and the British Country House*, edited by Madge Dresser and Andrew Hann, 114–22. Swindon: English Heritage.

Bridal, Tessa. 2004. *Exploring Museum Theatre*. Walnut Creek, CA: AltaMira Press.

Broadbent, Jennifer. 2012. "People and Places: Developments in Social History 1989–2011." *Social History in Museums* (Social History Curators Group) 36: 26–31.

Brooks, Bradley C. 2002. "The Historic House and Furnishings Plan: Process and Product." In *Interpreting Historic House Museums*, edited by Jessica Foy Donnelly, 128–43. Walnut Creek, CA: AltaMira Press.

Brown, Iain Gordon. 2003. "Scott, Literature and Abbotsford." In *Abbotsford and Sir Walter Scott: The Image and the Influence*, edited by Iain G. Brown, 1–28. Edinburgh: Society of Antiquaries of Scotland.

Brown, Marley, and Edward Chappell. 2004. "Archaeological Authenticity and Reconstruction at Colonial Williamsburg." In *The Reconstructed Past: Reconstructions in the Public Interpretation of Archaeology and History*, edited by John H. Jameson, 47–63. Walnut Creek, CA: AltaMira Press.

Brown, Nell Porter. 2015, January. "Preserving Heirs and Graces." *Harvard Magazine*. http://harvardmagazine.com/2015/01/preserving-heirs-and-airs.

Bruggeman, Seth C. 2009. *Here, George Washington Was Born: Memory, Material Culture and the Public History of a National Monument*. Athens: University of Georgia Press.

Bruner, Edward M. 1994. "Abraham Lincoln as Authentic Reproduction: A Critique of Postmodernism." *American Anthropologist*, New Series 96, no. 2: 397–415.

Bryant, Julius. 2003. *Kenwood: Paintings in the Iveagh Bequest*. New Haven, CT: Yale University Press.

Bryant, Julius. 2004. "Kenwood's Lost Chapter." *Apollo* 159, no. 505: 40–44.

Buchanan, Sandra. 1984, February. "The Mitchell House: A Maryland Museum Combines History and Architecture to Tell the Story of a 19th-Century Black Family." *History News* 39, no. 2: 12–15.

Burns, Eric. 2007. *Virtue, Valor and Vanity: The Founding Fathers and the Pursuit of Fame*. New York: Arcade.

Burns, Ned J. 1941. *National Park Service Field Manual for Museums*. Washington, DC: US Government Printing Office.

Campbell, Colin. 1987. *The Romantic Ethic and the Spirit of Modern Consumerism*. Oxford: Basil Blackwell.

Campbell, Joseph. 1949. *The Hero with a Thousand Faces*. New York: Pantheon.

Cannadine, David. 1990. *The Decline and Fall of the British Aristocracy*. New Haven, CT: Yale University Press.

Cannadine, David. 2014. "Pictures Across the Pond: Perspectives and Retrospectives." In *British Models of Art Collecting and the American Response*, edited by Inge Reist, 9–25. Farnham: Ashgate.

Cantor, Jay. 1997. *Winterthur*. Expanded edition. New York: Harry N. Abrams.

Cantwell, A. W., Nan Rothschild, and James B. Griffen, eds. 2009. *The Research Potential of Anthropological Museum Collections*. New York: New York Academy of Sciences.

Carlyle, Thomas. 1841. *On Heroes, Hero-Worship and the Heroic in History*. ElecBooks Classics. http://www.elecbook.com.

Carruthers, Annette. 2003. "House Museums and Domestic Life Displays in Scotland." *Scottish Economic and Social History* 23, no. 2: 85–98.

Carson, Cary. 1991. "Living Museums of Everyman's History." In *A Living History Reader, Vol. 1: Museums*. Edited by Jay Anderson, 25–31. Nashville: American Association for State and Local History.

Carson, Cary. 1998. "Colonial Williamsburg and the Practice of Interpretive Planning in American History Museums." *Public Historian* 20, no. 3: 11–51. doi: 10.2307/3379773.

Casa del Herrero, Santa Barbara, CA. http://www.casadelherrero.com.

Casper, Scott E. 2008. *Sarah Johnson's Mount Vernon: The Forgotten History of an American Shrine*. New York: Hill and Wang.

Chappell, Edward. 2002. "The Museum and the Joy Ride: Williamsburg Landscapes and the Specter of Theme Parks." In *Theme Park Landscapes: Antecedents and Variations*, edited by Terence Young and Robert Riley, 119–56, Dumbarton Oaks Colloquium on the History of Landscape Architecture 20. Washington, DC: Dumbarton Oaks.

Chase, Dawn. 2014. "A House of a Different Color." http://whatsnew.history.org/2014/08/a-house-of-a-different-color/.

Chhabra, Deepak, Robert Healy, and Erin Sills. 2003. "Staged Authenticity and Heritage Tourism." *Annals of Tourism Research* 30, no. 3: 702–19. doi: 10.1016/S0160-7383(03)00044-6.

Chitty, Gill, and David Baker, eds. 1999. *Managing Historic Sites and Buildings: Reconciling Presentation and Preservation*. London: Routledge.

Coleman, Laurence Vail. 1939. *The Museum in America: A Critical Study*. Washington, DC: American Association of Museums.

Conforti, Joseph A. 2006. *Saints and Strangers: New England in British North America*. Baltimore: Johns Hopkins University Press.

Coote, Jeremy, and Anthony Shelton, eds. 1992. *Anthropology and Aesthetics*. Oxford: Clarendon Press.

Cornforth, John. 1988. *The Search for a Style: "Country Life" and Architecture, 1897–1935*. London: Andre Deutsch.

Cosgrove, James, ed. 2004. *House for an Art Lover*, 2nd ed. Glasgow: House for an Art Lover.

Court, Franklin E. 1992. *Institutionalizing English Literature: The Culture and Politics of Literary Study, 1750–1900*. Stanford, CA: Stanford University Press.

Coward, Noel. 1938. "The Stately Homes of England." *Operette*. Wikipedia.

Crawford, Robert. 1998. *The Scottish Invention of English Literature*. Cambridge: Cambridge University Press.

Crawford, Robert. 2000. *Devolving English Literature*, 2nd ed. Edinburgh: Edinburgh University Press.

Crook, John Mordaunt. 1999. *The Rise of the Nouveaux Riches: Styles and Status in Victorian and Edwardian Architecture*. London: John Murray.

Crowley, David. 2001. "Finding Poland in the Margins: The Case of Zakopane Style." *Journal of Design History* 14, no. 2: 105–16. doi: 10.1093/jdh/14.2.91.

Curtis, Nancy, and Richard Nylander. 1990. *Beauport: The Sleeper-McCann House*. Boston: Society for the Protection of New England Antiquities.

Davidoff, Leonore. 1973. *The Best Circles: Society, Etiquette and the Season*. London: Croom Helm.

Deetz, James. 1991. "The Changing Historical House Museum: Can It Live?" In *A Living History Reader, vol. 1: Museums*, edited by Jay Anderson, 15–17. Nashville: American Association for State and Local History.

Department for Culture, Media & Sport. 2013. "Ch. 3: Museums and Galleries." *Taking Part 2012–13, Quarter 4*. https://www.gov.uk/government/statistics/taking-part-201213-quarter-4-statistical-release--2.

Diaz-Andreu, Margarita. 2007. *A World History of Nineteenth-Century Archaeology: Nationalism, Colonialism, and the Past*. Oxford: Oxford University Press.

Doering, Zahava D. 1999. "Strangers, Guests or Clients? Visitor Experiences in Museums." Conference paper delivered at *Managing the Arts*, Weimar. https://www.si.edu/content/opanda/docs/Rpts1999/99.03.Strangers.Final.pdf.

Doss, Erika. 1999. *Elvis Culture: Fans, Faith, and Image*. Lawrence: University Press of Kansas.

Dowey, Bill. 1995. *A Brief History of Malibu and the Adamson House*. Malibu: Malibu Lagoon Museum.

Downing, A. J. 1969 [1850]. *The Architecture of Country Houses*. New York: Dover.

Doyle, Brian. 1989. *English and Englishness*. London: Routledge.

Dresser, Madge, and Andrew Hann, eds. 2013. *Slavery and the British Country House*. Swindon: English Heritage.

Dubrow, Gail Lee, and Jennifer B. Goodman, eds. 2003. *Restoring Women's History through Historic Preservation*. Baltimore: Johns Hopkins University Press.

Duncan, Carol. 1995. *Civilizing Rituals: Inside Public Art Museums*. London: Routledge.

Duncan, Carol, and Alan Wallach. 1980. "The Universal Survey Museum." *Art History* 3, no. 4: 448–69.

Ede, Jim. 1984. *A Way of Life: Kettle's Yard*. Cambridge: Cambridge University Press.

Eggert, Paul. 2009. *Securing the Past: Conservation in Art, Architecture and Literature*. Cambridge: Cambridge University Press.

Eichstedt, Jennifer L., and Stephen Small. 2002. *Representations of Slavery: Race and Ideology in Southern Plantation Museums*. Washington, DC: Smithsonian Institution Press.

Elsler, Jennifer. 1996. "Historic House Museums: Struggling for Survival." *Forum Journal* 10, no. 4: 42–50.

Emerson, Ralph Waldo. 1907 [1856]. "Heroism." In *Essays*, 136–55. New York: Charles Merrill Co. http://www.gutenberg.org/files/16643/16643-h/16643-h.htm#Page_139.

English, Shirley. 2005, May 19. "After 200 Years Scott House Leaves Family." *The Times*.

Fairclough, Graham, Rodney Harrison, John H. Jameson, and John Schofield, eds. 2008. *The Heritage Reader*. London: Routledge.

Falk, John, and Lynne Dierking. 1992. *The Museum Experience*. Washington, DC: Whalesback Books.

Fedden, Robin, and Rosemary Joekes, eds. 1984. *The National Trust Guide*, 3rd ed. London: Jonathan Cape.

Filmer-Sankey, William. 1998. "History of the Victorian Society." *Victorian*, no. 1.

Fitch, James Marston. 1982. *Historic Preservation: Curatorial Management of the Built World*. Charlottesville: University Press of Virginia.

Fleming, David. 2012. "Social History in Museums: 35 Years of Progress?" *Social History in Museums* (Social History Curators Group) 34: 39–40.

Fleming, David, Crispin Paine, and John G. Rhodes, eds. 1993. *Social History in Museums: A Handbook for Professionals*. London: HMSO.

Floyd, Candace. 1981. "Legend versus History: Raynham Hall Redirects Interpretation from Romance to Documentary." *History News* 36, no. 6: 14–15.

Fox, Levi. 1997. *The Shakespeare Birthplace Trust: A Personal Memoir*. Norwich: Shakespeare Birthplace Trust.

Frazer, James. 1890. *The Golden Bough: A Study of Magic and Religion*. http://www.gutenberg.org/etext/3623.

Frye, Northrop. 1957. *Anatomy of Criticism*. Princeton, NJ: Princeton University Press.

Gable, Eric, and Richard Handler. 1996. "After Authenticity at an American Heritage Site." *American Anthropologist*, New Series 98, no. 3: 568–78. http://www.jstor.org/stable/682724.

Gallas, Kristin L., and James DeWolf Perry. 2015. *Interpreting Slavery at Museums and Historic Sites*. Lanham, MD: Rowman & Littlefield.

Gardiner, Juliet. 2002. *The Edwardian Country House*. London: Channel 4.

Garnett, Oliver. 1998. *20 Forthlin Road*. London: National Trust.

Garnett, Oliver. 2000. *Calke Abbey*. Swindon: National Trust.

Garnett, Oliver. 2003. *Mendips*. London: National Trust.

Gaynor, Suzanne. 1984. "Changing Interiors at Hertford House." *Antiques Collector* 11, no. 84: 74–79.

Gaze, John. 1988. *Figures in a Landscape: A History of the National Trust*. London: Barrie & Jenkins, in association with the National Trust.

Gefen, Gérard. 1998. *Composers' Houses*. New York: Vendome Press.

Geisler, Michael E., ed. 2005. *National Symbols, Fractured Identities: Contesting the National Narrative*. Middlebury, VT: Middlebury College Press.

Gell, Alfred. 1992. "The Technology of Enchantment and the Enchantment of Technology." In *Anthropology and Aesthetics*, edited by Jeremy Coote and Anthony Shelton, 40–63. Oxford: Clarendon Press.

George, Gerald. 2002. "Historic House Museum Malaise: A Conference Considers What's Wrong." *History News* 57, no. 4: 21–25.

George Washington Birthplace National Monument: Long Range Interpretive Plan. 1999. National Park Service.

Gerle, Janos. 1993. "What Is Vernacular? Or, the Search for the 'Mother-Tongue of Forms.'" In *Art and the National Dream: The Search for Vernacular Expression in Turn-of-the-Century Design*, edited by Nicola Gordon Bowe, 143–54. Dublin: Irish Academic Press.

Gill, Hermon. 1957. *Cook's Cottage: The History of Cook's Cottage and Voyages of Captain James Cook*. Melbourne: Melbourne City Council.

Girouard, Mark. 1978. *Life in the English Country House: A Social and Architectural History*. New Haven, CT: Yale University Press.

Goldfarb, Hilliard T. 1995. *The Isabella Stewart Gardner Museum: A Companion-Guide and History*. Boston: Isabella Stewart Gardner Museum.

Goldhill, Simon. 2011. *Freud's Couch, Scott's Buttocks, Bronte's Grave*. Chicago: University of Chicago Press.

Gorman, Joshua. 2013. "Universalism and the New Museology." In *New Directions in Museum Ethics*, edited by Janet Marstine, Alexander A. Bauer, and Chelsea Haines, 76–89. Abingdon: Routledge.

Graham, Brian. 2002. "Heritage as Knowledge: Capital or Culture?" *Urban Studies* 39, nos. 5–6: 1003–17. doi: 10.1080/00420980220128426.

Greenspan, Anders. 2002. *Creating Colonial Williamsburg*. Washington, DC: Smithsonian Institution Press.

Grim, Linnea. 2015. "'So Deeply Dyed in Our Fabric That It Cannot Be Washed Out': Developing Institutional Support for the Interpretation of Slavery." In *Interpreting Slavery at Museums and Historic Sites*, edited by Kristin L. Gallas and James DeWolf Perry, 47–63. Lanham, MD: Rowman & Littlefield.

Hague, Stephen. 2015. *The Gentleman's House in the British Atlantic World, 1680–1780*. Basingstoke: Palgrave Macmillan.

Hall, Melanie, ed. 2011. *Towards World Heritage: International Origins of the Preservation Movement, 1870–1930*. Farnham: Ashgate.

Hall, Michael. 2002. *Waddesdon Manor: The Heritage of a Rothschild House*. New York: Harry N. Abrams.

Hall, Michael. 2014. "'Le Goût Rothschild': The Origins and Influences of a Collecting Style." In *British Models of Art Collecting and the American Response*, edited by Inge Reist, 101–15. Farnham: Ashgate.

Halleck, Fitz-Greene. 1882. "Burns: To a Rose Brought from Near Alloway Kirk, in Ayrshire, in the Autumn of 1822." In *The Cambridge Book of Poetry and Song*, edited by Charlotte Fiske Bates, 249–51. New York: Thomas Y. Crowell.

Harris, Donna. 2007. *New Solutions for House Museums: Ensuring the Long-Term Preservation of America's Historic Houses*. Lanham, MD: AltaMira Press.

Harris, John. 1974. "Gone to Ground." In *The Destruction of the Country House, 1875–1975*, edited by Roy Strong, Marcus Binney, and John Harris, 15–100. London: Thames & Hudson.

Harris, John. 2007. *Moving Rooms: The Trade in Architectural Salvages*. New Haven, CT: Yale University Press.

Hearn, Karen, Robert Upstone, Giles Waterfield, Tate Gallery and Historic Houses Association. 1998. *In Celebration: The Art of the Country House*. London: Tate Gallery.

Hede, Anne-Marie, and Maree Thyne. 2010. "A Journey to the Authentic: Museum Visitors and Their Negotiation of the Inauthentic." *Journal of Marketing Management* 26, no. 7–8: 686–705. doi: 10.1080/02672571003780106.

Heidegger, Martin. 1993. "Building Dwelling Thinking." In *Basic Writings from Being and Time (1927) to The Task of Thinking (1964)*, edited by D. F. Krell, 343–63. London: Routledge.

Hemans, Felicia. 1827, April. "The Homes of England." *Blackwood's Edinburgh Magazine*.

Hepburn, Lorna. 1999. *The Tenement House*. Edinburgh: National Trust for Scotland.

Herbert Hoover National Historic Site: General Management Plan and Environmental Assessment. 2004. National Park Service.

Hermanson, Marisa. 2014. "The Ties That Bind." *Virginia Living*. http://www.virginialiving.com/home-garden/the-tie-that-binds/.

Hesmondhalgh, David. 2013. *The Cultural Industries*, 3rd ed. London: Sage.

Hessney, David. 2000. "Gibson House." *NPS: National Historic Places Nomination*. http://www.nps.gov/nhl/find/statelists/ma/Gibson.pdf.

Hewison, Robert. 1987. *The Heritage Industry: Britain in a Climate of Decline*. London: Methuen.

Higonnet, Anne. 2009. *A Museum of One's Own: Private Collecting, Public Gift*. Pittsburgh: Periscope.

Hildebrand, Grant. 1991. *The Wright Space: Pattern and Meaning in Frank Lloyd Wright's Houses*. Seattle: University of Washington Press.

Hill, Kate. 2005. *Culture and Class in English Public Museums, 1850–1914*. Burlington, VT: Ashgate.

Hilyard, Rupert. 2000. *Treasurer's House*. Swindon: National Trust.

Hinds, James R. 1968. *Frederick Douglass Home: Cedar Hill: Historic Structures Report, Part II (Historical Data)*. Washington, DC: National Park Service.

Hoare, Quintin, and Geoffrey Nowell Smith, eds. 1971. *Antonio Gramsci: Selections from the Prison Notebooks*. London: Lawrence & Wishart.

Hobsbawm, Eric. 1983. "Introduction: Inventing Traditions." In *The Invention of Tradition*, edited by Eric Hobsbawm and Terence Ranger, 1–14. Cambridge: Cambridge University Press.

Hobsbawm, Eric, and Terence Ranger, eds. 1983. *The Invention of Tradition*. Cambridge: Cambridge University Press.

Hodgdon, Barbara. 1998. *The Shakespeare Trade*. Philadelphia: University of Pennsylvania Press.

Hofland, Mrs. Barbara. 1919. *Popular Description of Sir John Soane's House, Museum and Library*, edited by Arthur T. Bolton. Oxford: Arthur Hall.

Holler, Manfred J., and Barbara Klose-Ullmann. 2010. "Art Goes to America." *Journal of Economic Issues* 44, no. 1: 89–112. doi: 10.2753/JEI0021-3624440105.

Holleran, Michael. 2001. *Boston's "Changeful Times": Origins of Preservation and Planning in America*. Baltimore: Johns Hopkins University Press.

Holmes, Charles. 1928. *Pictures from the Iveagh Bequest and Collections*. London: Iveagh Bequest.

Hood, Graham. 2000. "Palace Days: Recollections of Dismantling the Most Beautiful Rooms in America." *Colonial Williamsburg Journal* (Winter). https://www.history.org/foundation/journal/Winter00_01/palace.cfm.

Hood, Marilyn. 1983, April. "Staying Away: Why People Choose Not to Visit Museums." *Museum News*, 50–57.

Hooper-Greenhill, Eilean. 2006. "Studying Visitors." In *A Companion to Museum Studies*, edited by Sharon Macdonald, 362–76. Oxford: Basil Blackwell.

Horne, Donald. 1984. *The Great Museum: The Re-Presentation of History*. Sydney: Pluto Press.

Horton, Lois E. 2006. "Avoiding History: Thomas Jefferson, Sally Hemings and the Uncomfortable Public Conversation on Slavery." In *Slavery and Public History*, edited by James Oliver Horton and Lois E. Horton, 135–49. New York: New Press.

Hosmer, Charles B., Jr. 1965. *The Presence of the Past: A History of the Preservation Movement in the United States before Williamsburg*. New York: G. P. Putnam's Sons.

Hosmer, Charles B., Jr. 1981. *Preservation Comes of Age: From Williamsburg to the National Trust, 1926–1949*. Charlottesville: University Press of Virginia.

Howard, Peter. 2003. *Heritage: Management, Interpretation, Identity*. London: Continuum.

Howarth, Thomas. 1952. *Charles Rennie Mackintosh and the Modern Movement*. London: Routledge and Kegan Paul.

Hudson, Kenneth. 1998. "The Museum Refuses to Stand Still." *Museum International* 51, no. 1: 43–50.

Hughes, Peter. 1981. *The Founders of the Wallace Collection*. London: Wallace Collection.

Hull, Howard. 2010, July. Director of Brantwood. Personal communication.

Hutner, Gordon. 1999. *American Literature, American Culture*. New York: Oxford University Press.

Huxtable, Ada Louise. 1963, September 22. "Dissent at Colonial Williamsburg." *New York Times*.

Ingamells, John. 2004. "Wallace, Sir Richard, Baronet (1818–1890)." In *Oxford Dictionary of National Biography (Online)*. Oxford: Oxford University Press. http://www.oxforddnb.com/view/article/28538.

International Coalition of Sites of Conscience. "About Us." http://www.sitesofconscience.org/about-us/.

International Museum Theatre Alliance. http://www.imtal-us.org/FAQ-about-museum-theatre.

Jackson, Anthony. 2013. "Education or Theatre." In *Learning through Theatre: The Changing Face of Theatre in Education*, 3rd. ed., edited by Anthony Jackson and Chris Vine, 21–40. London: Routledge.

Jackson, Anthony, and Helen Rees Leahy. 2005. "'Seeing It for Real . . . ?' Authenticity, Theatre and Learning in Museums." *Research in Drama Education* 10, no. 3: 303–25. doi: 10.1080/13569780500275956.

Jackson, Anthony, and Chris Vine, eds. 2013. *Learning through Theatre: The Changing Face of Theatre in Education*, 3rd ed. London: Routledge.

Jacobs, Karrie. 2009. "Wright-ish." *Metropolis* 29, no. 3: 44–47. http://www.metropolismag.com/October-2009/Wright-ish/.

JacquiFodie. 2014. *TripAdvisor*. http://www.tripadvisor.com.au/ShowUserReviews-g255677-d4154952-r293137706-56_Eden_Street_The_Childhood_Home_of_Janet_Frame-Oamaru_Otago_Region_South_Islan.html#.

James, William. 1917 [1880]. "Great Men and Their Environment." In *Selected Papers on Philosophy*, 165–97. London: J. M. Dent & Sons.

Jameson, John H., ed. 2004. *The Reconstructed Past: Reconstructions in the Public Presentation of Archaeology and History*. Walnut Creek, CA: AltaMira Press.

Jameson, Mrs. 1844. *Companion to the Most Celebrated Private Galleries of Art in London*. London: Saunders and Otley.

Janes, Robert R., and Gerald T. Conaty, eds. 2005. *Looking Reality in the Eye: Museums and Social Responsibility*. Calgary: University of Calgary Press.

Jenkins, Simon. 2003. *England's Thousand Best Houses*. London: Penguin.

Jenrette, Richard Hampton. 2005. *Adventures with Old Houses*. Charleston: Wyrick & Co.

Jenrette, Richard Hampton. 2013. "About Us." American Classical Homes Preservation Trust. http://www.classicalamerican.org/html/history.html.

Jervis, Simon Swynfen. 2013. "In Institutional Hands: Ham House, the Victoria & Albert Museum and the National Trust." In *Ham House: 400 Years of Collecting and Patronage*, edited by Christopher Rowell, 383–96. New Haven, CT: Yale University Press.

Jokilehto, Jukka. 1999. *A History of Architectural Conservation*. Oxford: Butterworth Heinemann.

Jokilehto, Jukka. 2008. "What Is OUV?" *Monuments and Sites* XVI: 7–99.

Jones, Sian. 2010. "Negotiating Authentic Objects and Authentic Selves: Beyond the Deconstruction of Authenticity." *Journal of Material Culture* 15, no. 2: 181–203. doi: 10.1177/1359183510364074.

Kaplan, Wendy. 1993. "The Vernacular in America, 1890–1920: Ideology and Design." In *Art and the National Dream: The Search for Vernacular Expression in Turn-of-the-Century Design*, edited by Nicola Gordon Bowe, 53–68. Dublin: Irish Academic Press.

Kastner, Victoria. 2000. *Hearst Castle: The Biography of a Country House*. New York: Abrams.

Kavanagh, Gaynor. 1990. *History Curatorship*. Leicester: Leicester University Press.

Kay, William Kennon. 1970. *Keep It Alive! Tips on Living History Demonstrations*. National Park Service, Visitor Services Training. https://archive.org/details/keepitalivetipso00kayw.

Keeble, Trevor. 2006. "Introduction." In *The Modern Period Room: The Construction of the Exhibited Interior*, edited by Penny Sparke, Brenda Martin, and Trevor Keeble, 1–7. London: Routledge.

Kidd, Jenny. 2011. "Performing the Knowing Archive: Heritage Performance and Authenticity." *International Journal of Heritage Studies* 17, no. 1: 22–35. doi: 10.1080/13527258.2011.524003.

Kimball, Sidney Fiske. 1922. *Domestic Architecture of the American Colonies and of the Early Republic*. New York: Charles Scribner's Sons.

Kimball, Sidney Fiske. 1926a. "Philadelphia's 'Colonial Chain.'" *Art and Archaeology* 21, no. 4: 150–55.

Kimball, Sidney Fiske. 1926b. "Mount Pleasant: A Branch Museum of American Art on the Eve of the Revolution." *Bulletin of the Pennsylvania Museum* 22, no. 105: 197–215.

Kindred, Bob. 2007. "Introduction." In *Conservation of Modern Architecture*, edited by Susan Macdonald, Kyle Normandin, and Bob Kindred, 1–8. Shaftesbury: Donhead.

Kirk, Jayne. 2009. *Parham: An Elizabethan House and Its Restoration*. Chichester: Phillimore.

Kirschenblatt-Gimblett, Barbara. 1998. *Destination Culture: Tourism, Museums and Heritage*. Berkeley: University of California Press.

Knapp, Mary. 2016. *Miracle on Fourth Street: Saving an Old Merchant's House*. New York: Girandole Books.

Knell, Simon, ed. 1999. *Museums and the Future of Collecting*. Aldershot: Ashgate.

Knell, Simon. 2000. *The Culture of English Geology: A Science Revealed through Its Collecting*. Aldershot: Ashgate.

Knell, Simon, Peter Aronsson, Arne Bugge Amundsen, Amy Jane Barnes, Stuart Burch, Jennifer Carter, Viviane Gosselin, Sarah A. Highes, and Alan Kirwan, eds. 2011. *National Museums: New Studies from Around the World*. London: Routledge.

Knox, Tim, and John Harris. 2012. "Confessions of a Country House Snooper: Tim Knox Interviews John Harris." In *Looking Ahead: The Future of the Country House*, edited by Giles Waterfield and Rebecca Parker, 8–17. London: Attingham Trust (60th Anniversary Conference). http://www.attinghamtrust.org/wp-content/uploads/2012/08/Conference-Papers1.pdf.

Kramnick, Jonathan Brody. 1998. *Making the English Canon: Print-Capitalism and the Cultural Past, 1700–1770*. Cambridge: Cambridge University Press.

Lancaster, Osbert. 1939. *Homes, Sweet Homes*. London: John Murray.

Laniel, Mariel. 2008. "Revisiting a Great Man's House: Virginia Woolf's Carlylean Pilgrimages." *Carlyle Studies Annual* 24: 117–28.

Lasic, Barbara. 2009. "'Splendid Patriotism': Richard Wallace and the Construction of the Wallace Collection." *Journal of the History of Collections* 21, no. 2: 173–82. doi: 10.1093/jhc/fhp009.

Lawley, Ian. 2003. "Local Authority Museums and the Modernizing Government Agenda in England." *Museum and Society* 1, no. 2: 75–86.

Le Corbusier. 2007 [1923]. *Toward an Architecture*, translated by John Goodman. Los Angeles: Getty Research Institute.

Leach, Mallory. 2008. "Henry Chapman Mercer." Biographies in *Literary and Cultural Heritage Map of Pennsylvania*. Penn State University Libraries. http://pabook.libraries.psu.edu/palitmap/bios/Mercer__Henry_Chapman.html.

Lee, Lisa, and Lisa Junkin Lopez. 2014. "Participating in History: The Museum as a Site for Radical Empathy, Hull-House." In *Jane Addams in the Classroom*, edited by David Schaafsma, 162–78. Urbana: University of Illinois Press.

Lees-Milne, James. 1945. "The Country House." In *The National Trust: A Record of Fifty Years Achievement*, edited by James Lees-Milne, 61–77. London: Batsford.

Lees-Milne, James, ed. 1945. *The National Trust: A Record of Fifty Years Achievement*. London: Batsford.

Lees-Milne, James. 1992. *People and Places: Country House Donors and the National Trust*. London: John Murray.

Leon, Warren, and Roy Rosenzweig, eds. 1989. *History Museums in the United States: A Critical Assessment*. Urbana: University of Illinois Press.

Leone, Mark. 2009. "The Relationship between Artifacts and the Public in Outdoor History Museums." In *The Research Potential of Anthropological Museum Collections*, edited by A. W. Cantwell, Nan Rothschild, and James B. Griffen, 301–13. New York: New York Academy of Sciences.

Leslie, Kim. 1990. *Weald and Downland Open Air Museum: The Founding Years, 1965–70*. Singleton, Sussex: Weald and Downland Open Air Museum.

Leuchtenburg, William F. 2009. *Herbert Hoover*. New York: Henry Holt.

Levin, Amy K., ed. 2010. *Gender, Sexuality and Museums*. Abingdon: Routledge.

Levkoff, Mary. 2008. *Hearst the Collector*. New York: Harry N. Abrams.

Lewis, Ralph H. 1976. *Manual for Museums*. Washington, DC: National Park Service.

Lewis, Ralph H. 1993. *Museum Curatorship in the National Park Service, 1904–1982.* Washington, DC, Department of the Interior: National Park Service. http://www. nps.gov/history/history/online_books/curatorship/toc.htm.

Lindgren, James. 1995. *Preserving Historic New England: Preservation, Progressivism and the Remaking of Memory.* New York: Oxford University Press.

Lindholm, Charles. 2008. *Culture and Authenticity.* Oxford: Wiley-Blackwell.

Littlejohn, David. 1997. *The Fate of the English Country House.* New York: Oxford University Press.

Loewen, James W. 1999. *Lies Across America: What Our Historic Sites get Wrong.* New York: Touchstone.

Lossing, Benjamin John. 1870. *The Home of Washington, or, Mount Vernon and Its Associations, Historical, Biographical and Pictorial.* Hartford, CT: A. S. Hale.

Lounsbury, Carl R. 2011. *Essays in Early American Architectural History: A View from the Chesapeake.* Charlottesville: University Press of Virginia.

Lowenthal, David. 1985. *The Past Is a Foreign Country.* Cambridge: Cambridge University Press.

Lowenthal, David. 2008. "Authenticities Past and Present." *CRM: The Journal of Heritage Stewardship* 5, no. 1: 6–17. https://www.nps.gov/CRMJournal/Winter2008/view.html.

Lyon Housemuseum. 2014. http://lyonhousemuseum.com.au/concept/.

MacCannell, Dean. 1999. *The Tourist: A New Theory of the Leisure Class,* 3rd ed. London: Macmillan.

Macdonald, Sharon. 2005. "Enchantment and Its Dilemmas: The Museum as a Ritual Site." In *Science, Magic and Religion: The Ritual Processes of Museum Magic,* edited by Mary Bouquet and Nuno Porto, 209–27. New York: Berghan Books.

Macdonald, Susan, Kyle Normandin, and Bob Kindred, eds. 2007. *Conservation of Modern Architecture.* Shaftesbury: Donhead.

Mackintosh, Barry. 1969. *Booker T. Washington National Monument: An Administrative History.* National Park Service.

Macleod, Dianne Sachko. 1996. *Art and the Victorian Middle Class: Money and the Making of Cultural Identity.* New York: Cambridge University Press.

Magelssen, Scott. 2007. *Living History Museums: Undoing History through Performance.* Lanham, MD: Scarecrow Press.

Mallett, Shelley. 2004. "Understanding Home: A Critical Review of the Literature." *Sociological Review* 52, no. 1: 62–89.

Mandler, Peter. 1997. *The Fall and Rise of the Stately Home.* New Haven, CT: Yale University Press.

Marling, Karal Ann. 1987. *George Washington Slept Here: Colonial Revivals and American Culture, 1876–1986.* Cambridge, MA: Harvard University Press.

Marling, Karal Ann. 1993. "Elvis Presley's Graceland, or the Aesthetic of Rock'n'Roll Heaven." *American Art* 7, no. 4.

Marling, Karal Ann. 1996. *Graceland: Going Home with Elvis.* Cambridge, MA: Harvard University Press.

Marsh, Jan. 2004. "Chichester, Rosalie Caroline (1865–1949)." *Oxford Dictionary of National Biography (Online)*. Oxford: Oxford University Press. http://www.oxforddnb.com/view/article/45578.

Marstine, Janet, Alexander A. Bauer, and Chelsea Haines, eds. 2013. *New Directions in Museum Ethics*. Abingdon: Routledge.

Marston Fitch, James. 1982. *Historic Preservation: Curatorial Management of the Built World*. New York: McGraw-Hill.

Matthews, Rosemary. 2009. "Collectors and Why They Collect: Isabella Stewart Gardner and Her Museum of Art." *Journal of the History of Collections* 21, no. 2: 183–89. doi: 10.1093/jhc/fhp019.

Mauss, Marcel. 1990. *The Gift*, translated by W. D. Halls. London: Routledge.

Maynard, W. Barksdale. 2000. "'Best, Lowliest Style!' The Early-Nineteenth-Century Rediscovery of American Colonial Architecture." *Journal of the Society of Architectural Historians* 59, no. 3: 338–57.

McCalman, Iain, and Paul Pickering, eds. 2010. *Historical Re-Enactment: From Realism to the Affective Turn*. Basingstoke: Palgrave Macmillan.

McCarter, Robert. 2006. *Frank Lloyd Wright*. London: Reaktion Books.

McCrum, Mark, and Matthew Sturgis. 1999. *The 1900 House*. London: Channel 4 Books.

McKay, Harriet. 2004. "Patrick Gwynne's The Homewood." http://www.c20society.org.uk/botm/the-homewood/.

McKay, Harriet. 2006. "The Preservation and Presentation of 2 Willow Road for the National Trust." In *The Modern Period Room: The Construction of the Exhibited Interior*, edited by Penny Sparke, Brenda Martin, and Trevor Keeble, 154–64. London: Routledge.

McLeod, Stephen A., ed. 2010. *The Mount Vernon Ladies' Association: 150 Years of Restoring George Washington's Home*. Mount Vernon, VA: Mount Vernon Ladies' Association.

Meem, Deborah T. 2000. "The Ladies of Llangollen." In *Readers' Guide to Lesbian and Gay Studies*, edited by Timothy Murphy, 334–36. Chicago: Fitzroy Dearborn.

Merriman, Nick. 1991. *Beyond the Glass Case: The Past, the Heritage and the Public in Britain*. Leicester: Leicester University Press.

Meyer, Bruce. 2007. *Heroes: The Champions of Our Literary Imagination*. Toronto: HarperCollins.

Moe, Richard. 2012. "Are There Too Many House Museums?" *Forum Journal* 27, no. 1: 55–61.

Morgan, Francesca. 2005. *Women and Patriotism in Jim Crow America*. Chapel Hill: University of North Carolina Press.

Morristown National Historical Park: Long Range Interpretive Plan. 2007. National Park Service. http://www.nps.gov/morr/parkmgmt/upload/morr-lrip-2007.pdf.

Moss, Roger W. 1990. *The American Country House*. New York: Henry Holt.

Mrozowski, Stephen, Grace Ziesing, and Mary Beaudry. 1996. *Living on the Boott: Historical Archaeology at the Boott Mills Boardinghouses, Lowell, Massachusetts*. Amherst: University of Massachusetts Press.

Mrs. Smith's Cottage Museum, Navenby. http://www.mrssmithscottage.co.uk.

Muensterberger, Werner. 1994. *Collecting: An Unruly Passion: Psychological Perspectives*. Princeton, NJ: Princeton University Press.

Murphy, Kevin D. 2002. "The Villa Savoye and the Modernist Historic Monument." *Journal of the Society of Architectural Historians* 61, no. 1: 68–89. http://www.jstor.org/stable/991812. doi:10.2307/991812.

Murphy, Timothy, ed. 2000. *Readers' Guide to Lesbian and Gay Studies*. Chicago: Fitzroy Dearborn.

Museums Association. 2013. "Cuts Survey." http://www.museumsassociation.org/download?id=1019920.

Museums Association. 2015. "Cuts Survey." http://www.museumsassociation.org/campaigns/funding-cuts/cuts-survey.

Musson, Jeremy. 2012. "The Crisis in Country Houses in Local Government Care." In *Looking Ahead: The Future of the Country House*, edited by Giles Waterfield and Rebecca Parker, 72–83. Attingham Trust 60th Anniversary Conference. http://www.attinghamtrust.org/wp-content/uploads/2012/08/Conference-Papers1.pdf.

National Endowment for the Arts. 2013. *How a Nation Engages with Art: NEA Research Report #57*. Washington, DC: National Endowment for the Arts. https://www.arts.gov/sites/default/files/highlights-from-2012-sppa-revised-oct-2015.pdf.

National Park Service. 1982, rev. 1987. *History and Prehistory in the National Park System and the National Historic Landmarks Program*. Washington, DC: National Park Service. https://www.nps.gov/parkhistory/online_books/thematic87/index.htm.

National Park Service. 1994, rev. 2000. *History in the National Park Service: Themes and Concepts*. Washington, DC: National Park Service. http://www.nps.gov/nhl/learn/themes/ThematicFramework.pdf.

National Park Service. 1998. *Museum Handbook, Part III, Museum Collections Use*. https://www.nps.gov/museum/publications/handbook.html.

National Park Service. 2001. *The Secretary of the Interior's Standards for the Treatment of Historic Properties: Guidelines for Preserving, Rehabilitating, Restoring and Reconstructing Historic Buildings*. http://www.nps.gov/tps/standards/four-treatments/standguide/index.htm.

National Park Service. 2003. *National Historic Landmark Nomination: Beauport*. pdfhost.focus.nps.gov/docs/NHLS/Text/03000641.pdf.

National Park Service Northeast Region. 2006. *Northeast Region's Guidelines for the Treatment of Historic Furnished Interiors*. Charlestown, MA: Northeast Museum Services Center, National Park Service.

National Trust. 2015. *Annual Report 2014–15*. http://www.nationaltrust.org.uk/documents/annual-report-2014-15.pdf.

Norman, A. V. B. 1962. "Arms and Armour at Abbotsford." *Apollo* LXXVII, no. 7: 525.

Norton, Charles Eliot. 1889, May. "The Lack of Old Homes in America." *Scribner's Magazine*, 636–41.

Obee, Hannah. 2008, June. "The Golden Age Returns." *Apollo* 167, no. 555: 60–66.

Oliver, Basil. 1945. "Country Buildings." In *The National Trust: A Record of Fifty Years Achievement*, edited by James Lees-Milne, 78–96. London: Batsford.

Oram, Alison. 2011. "Going on an Outing: The Historic House and Queer Public History." *Rethinking History* 15, no. 2 : 189–207. doi: 10.1080/13642529.2011.564816.

Otte, T. G. 2011. "The Shrine at Sulgrave: The Preservation of the Washington Ancestral Home as an 'English Mount Vernon' and Transatlantic Relations." In *Towards World Heritage: International Origins of the Preservation Movement, 1870–1930*, edited by Melanie Hall, 109–37. Farnham: Ashgate.

Ousby, Ian. 1985. *Literary Britain and Ireland: Blue Guide*. London: A&C Black.

Page, Thomas Nelson. 1910. *Mount Vernon and Its Preservation, 1858–1910*. New York: Knickerbocker Press for Mount Vernon Ladies' Association.

Palmer, Susan. 2002. *The Soanes at Home: Domestic Life at Lincoln's Inn Fields*. London: Sir John Soane's Museum.

Pearce, Susan M. 1992. *Museums, Objects and Collections: A Cultural Study*. Leicester: Leicester University Press.

Pearce, Susan. 1995. *On Collecting: An Investigation into Collecting in the European Tradition*. London: Routledge.

Pearce, Susan, Rosemary Flanders, Mark Hall, and Fiona Morton, eds. 2002. *The Collector's Voice, vol. 3: Imperial Voices*. Aldershot: Ashgate.

Peate, Iorwerth. 2011 [1940]. *The Welsh House: A Study in Folk Culture*. Burnham-on-Sea: Llanerch Press.

Pessen, Edward. 1984. *The Log Cabin Myth: The Social Background of the Presidents*. New Haven, CT: Yale University Press.

Peterson, Gloria. 1968. *An Administrative History of Abraham Lincoln Birthplace National Historic Site Hodgenville, Kentucky*. National Park Service. http://www.nps.gov/history/history/online_books/abli/adhi/adhi.htm.

Petravage, Carol A. 1998. "When Values Collide: Furnishing Historic Interiors." In *Preservation of What, for Whom? A Critical Look at Historical Significance*, edited by Michael A. Tomlan, 51–58. Ithaca, NY: National Council for Preservation Education.

Pevsner, Nikolaus. 1968. *Charles R. Mackintosh, Studies in Art, Architecture and Design*. London: Thames and Hudson.

Pfeiffer, Brian. 2012, January. "A Return to Splendour." *Apollo* 175, no. 594: 50–56.

Phillips, David. 1997. *Exhibiting Authenticity*. Manchester: Manchester University Press.

Pitcaithley, Dwight T. 2001. "Lincoln's Birthplace Cabin: The Making of an American Icon." In *Myth, Memory and the Making of the American Landscape*, edited by Paul Shackel, 240–54. Gainsville: University Press of Florida.

Pleck, Elizabeth. 1982. "More Than Pots and Pans: The New Women's History Re-Examines Daily Life." *History News* 37, no. 4: 38–39.

Pogue, Dennis J. 2004. "Interpreting Slavery at Mount Vernon." *American History* 38, no. 6: 58–59.

Pogue, Dennis J. 2010, September 1. Personal communication.

Ponsonby, Margaret. 2007. *Stories from Home 1750–1850*. London: Ashgate.

Ponsonby, Margaret. 2015. *Faded and Threadbare: Historic Textiles and Their Role in Houses Open to the Public*. Farnham: Ashgate.

Poole, Andrea Geddes. 2010. *Stewards of the Nation's Art: Contested Cultural Authority 1890–1939*. Toronto: University of Toronto Press.

Poole, Meredith M. 2001. "A Short History of Archaeology at Colonial Williamsburg." http://research.history.org/research/archaeology/history.

Port, M. H. 1998. "Town House and Country House: Their Interaction." In *The Georgian Country House: Architecture, Landscape and Society*, edited by Dana Arnold, 117–38. Stroud: Sutton.

Praz, Mario. 1964. *An Illustrated History of Furnishing from the Renaissance to the Twentieth Century*. New York: George Braziller.

Preziosi, Donald. 2006. "Art History and Museology: Rendering the Visible Legible." In *A Companion to Museum Studies*, edited by Sharon Macdonald, 50–63. Oxford: Basil Blackwell.

Proshansky, Harold, William Ittelson, and Leanne Rivlin, eds. 1976. *Environmental Psychology: People and Their Physical Settings*, 2nd ed. New York: Holt, Rinehart & Winston.

Prudames, David. 2004. "Untold Story Project Brings Kedleston Hall's Indian Past to Life." http://www.culture24.org.uk/history-and-heritage/art24349.

Pucci, Suzanne Rodin, and James Thompson, eds. 2003. *Jane Austen and Co: Remaking the Past in Contemporary Culture*. Albany: SUNY Press.

Pustz, Jennifer. 2010. *Voices from the Back Stairs: Interpreting Servants' Lives at Historic House Museums*. De Kalb: Northern Illinois University Press.

Quodbach, Esmée. 2009. "'I Want This Collection to Be My Monument': Henry Clay Frick and the Formation of the Frick Collection." *Journal of the History of Collections* 22, no. 2: 229–40. doi: 10.1093/jhc/fhp008.

Raleigh, John Henry. 1963. "What Scott Meant to the Victorians." *Victorian Studies* 7, no. 1: 7–34.

Reed, Cleota. 2000. "Mercer, Henry Chapman." *American National Biography Online*. http://www.anb.org/articles/14/14-00407.html.

Reist, Inge, ed. 2014. *British Models of Art Collecting and the American Response*. Farnham: Ashgate.

Rentzhog, Sten. 2007. *Open Air Museums: The History and Future of a Visionary Idea*. Östersund, Carlssons/Jamtli.

Reynolds, Peter J. 1979. *Iron Age Farm: The Butser Experiment*. London: British Museum Publications.

Reynolds, Peter J. 1999. "Butser Ancient Farm." In *The Constructed Past: Experimental Archaeology, Education and the Public*, edited by Peter Stone and Philippe Planel, 124–35. London: Routledge.

Rice, Charles. 2007. *The Emergence of the Interior: Architecture, Modernity, Domesticity*. Abingdon: Routledge.

Riegler, Shax. 2009. "The Legacy of Henry Davis Sleeper." *The Magazine Antiques* 176, no. 6: 46–48.

Robbins, Daniel, Reena Suleman, and Pamela Hunter. 2003. *Linley Sambourne House*. London: Royal Borough of Kensington and Chelsea.

Roberts, George, and Mary Roberts. 1959. *Triumph on Fairmount: Fiske Kimball and the Philadelphia Museum of Art*. Philadelphia: J. B. Lippincott.

Robinson, John Martin. 1989. *The Country House at War*. London: Bodley Head.

Rogers, Alla Harman. 1928. *The History of Mount Vernon: America's Patriotic Shrine*. Washington, DC: National Art Service.

Rosenzweig, Roy, and David Thelen. 1998. *The Presence of the Past: Popular Uses of History in American Life*. New York: Columbia University Press.

Rothschild, Ferdinand. 2007 [1897]. "Bric-a-Brac." *Apollo* 165, no. 545: 54–77.

Rothschild, Mrs. James de. 1979. *The Rothschilds at Waddesdon Manor*. London: Collins.

Rousseau, Jean Jacques. 1762. "Civil Religion." *The Social Contract, or Principle of Political Right*, Book IV, part 8.

Rowell, Christopher, ed. 2013. *Ham House: 400 Years of Collecting and Patronage*. New Haven, CT: Yale University Press.

Ruffins, Fath Davis. 2003. "Four African-American Women on the National Landscape." In *Restoring Women's History through Historic Preservation*, edited by Gail Lee Dubrow and Jennifer B. Goodman, 58–80. Baltimore: Johns Hopkins University Press.

Russell, Roslyn, and Kylie Winkworth. 2001. *Significance: A Guide to Assessing the Significance of Cultural Heritage Objects and Collections*. Canberra: Heritage Collections Council.

Rutberg, Carl. 2010. "A 'Boston Marriage' on Staten Island." *Historic Houses Trust-New York City* (Fall).

Rutherford-Morrison, Lara. 2015. "Playing Victorian: Heritage, Authenticity, and Make-Believe in Blists Hill Victorian Town." *Public Historian* 37, no. 3: 76–101.

Rutter, Frank. 1913. *The Wallace Collection*. Boston: Small, Maynard and Co.

Ryskamp, Charles, Bernice Davidson, Susan Galassi, and Edgar Munhall. 1996. *Art in the Frick Collection*. New York: Harry N. Abrams.

Samuel, Raphael. 1994. *Theatres of Memory, vol. 1: Past and Present in Contemporary Culture*. London: Verso.

Sandell, Richard, ed. 2002. *Museums, Society, Inequality*. London: Routledge.

Sandell, Richard. 2003. "Social Inclusion, the Museum and the Dynamics of Sectoral Change." *Museum and Society* 1, no. 1: 45–62.

Sandell, Richard. 2012. "Museums and the Human Rights Frame." In *Museums, Equality and Social Justice*, edited by Richard Sandell and Eithne Nightingale, 195–215. Abingdon: Routledge.

Sandell, Richard, and Eithne Nightingale, eds. 2012. *Museums, Equality and Social Justice*. Abingdon: Routledge.

Sarell, Daniel. 2010, August 1. Grouseland Foundation. Personal communication.

Sayer, Michael. 1993. *The Disintegration of a Heritage: Country Houses and Their Collections, 1979–1992.* Norwich: Michael Russell.

Schoenberg, Nara. 2007, February 6. "Outing Jane Addams." *Chicago Tribune.* http://articles.chicagotribune.com/2007-02-06/features/0702060273_1_hull-house-mary-rozet-smith-lesbian.

Schwartz, Barry. 1987. *George Washington: The Making of an American Symbol.* New York: Free Press.

Scott, Carol A. 2013. *Museums and Public Value: Creating Sustainable Futures.* Farnham: Ashgate.

Scott, Carol, Jocelyn Dodd, and Richard Sandell. 2014. "User Value of Museums and Galleries: A Critical View of the Literature." Leicester: Arts and Humanities Research Council.

Seale, William. 1979. *Recreating the Historic House Interior.* Nashville: American Association for State and Local History.

Sears, John F. 1989. *Sacred Places: American Tourist Attractions in the Nineteenth Century.* Amherst: University of Massachusetts Press.

Selwood, Sara. 2010, July. "Making a Difference: The Cultural Impact of Museums: An Essay for the National Museum Directors' Council." London: Sara Selwood Associates. http://www.nationalmuseums.org.uk/media/documents/publications/cultural_impact_final.pdf.

Severs, Dennis, ed. 2002. *18 Folgate Street: The Tale of a House in Spitalfields.* London: Vintage/Chatto & Windus.

Seymour, Kate, and Malgorzata Sawicki, eds. 2012. *Proceedings of "The Artifact, Its Context and Their Narrative," Joint Conference of ICOM-DEMHIST and Three ICOM-CC Working Groups.* Los Angeles, Getty Research Institute. http://www.icom-cc.org/269/#.V0OVZZN97vH.

Shafernich, Sandra. 1993. "On-Site Museums, Open-Air Museums, Museum Villages and Living History Museums: Reconstructions and Period Rooms in the United States and the United Kingdom." *Museum Management and Curatorship* 12: 43–61.

Shumway, David R. 1994. *Creating American Civilization: A Genealogy of American Literature as an Academic Discipline.* Minneapolis: University of Minnesota Press.

Silverman, Lois. 2010. *The Social Work of Museums.* New York: Routledge.

Simon, Nina. 2016. *The Art of Relevance.* Santa Cruz, CA: Museum 2.0.

Slingsby, Thomas. "Collector in Focus: Harold Stanley Ede." Aiden Meller Galleries. http://www.mellermerceux.com/collector-in-focus-harold-stanley-ede/4695/ (accessed 25 April 2012—now disappeared).

Smith, Anthony. 1996. "History and Modernity: Reflections on the Theory of Nationalism." In *Representing the Nation: Histories, Heritage and Museums,* edited by David Boswell and Jessica Evans, 45–60. London: Routledge/Open University.

Smith, Charlotte. 2002. "The House Enshrined: Great Man and Social History House Museums in the United States and Australia." PhD thesis, University of Canberra.

Smith, H. Clifford. 1933. *Sulgrave Manor and the Washingtons.* New York: Macmillan.

Smith, Laurajane. 2006. *Uses of Heritage*. London: Routledge.

Smith, Laurajane. 2009. "Deference and Humility: The Social Values of the Country House." In *Valuing Historic Environments*, edited by Lisanne Gibson and John Pendlebury, 33–50. Farnham: Ashgate.

Smith, Laurajane, Geoff Cubitt, and Kalliopi Fouseki, eds. 2011. *Representing Enslavement and Abolition in Museums: Ambiguous Engagements*. New York: Routledge.

Snow, Stephen. 1993. *Performing the Pilgrims: A Study of Ethno-Historical Role-Playing at Plimoth Plantation*. Jackson: University Press of Mississippi.

Society for the Protection of Ancient Buildings. 1877. "Manifesto." http://www.spab.org.uk/what-is-spab-/the-manifesto/.

Staiff, Russell, Robyn Bushell, and Steve Watson, eds. 2013. *Heritage and Tourism: Place, Encounter and Engagement*. London: Routledge.

Starn, Randolph. 2002. "Authenticity and Historic Preservation: Towards an Authentic History." *History of the Human Sciences* 15, no. 1: 1–16. doi: 10.1177/0952695102015001070.

Stephen, Leslie. 1892. *Hours in a Library*, 2nd ed. London: Smith, Elder and Co.

Stillinger, Elizabeth. 1980. *The Antiquers*. New York: Alfred A. Knopf.

Stillinger, Elizabeth. 2011. *A Kind of Archaeology: Collecting American Folk Arts, 1876–1976*. Amherst: University of Massachusetts Press.

Stone, Lawrence, and Jeanne C. Fawtier Stone. 1984. *An Open Elite? England 1540–1880*. Oxford: Clarendon Press.

Stone, Peter, and Philippe Planel, eds. 1999. *The Constructed Past: Experimental Archaeology, Education and the Public*. London: Routledge.

Stourton, James. 2007. *Great Collectors of our Time: Art Collecting since 1945*. London: Scala.

Strong, Roy. 1997. *The Roy Strong Diaries 1967–1987*. London: Weidenfeld and Nicolson.

Strong, Roy, Marcus Binney, and John Harris. 1974. *The Destruction of the Country House, 1875–1975*. London: Thames & Hudson.

Stroud, Dorothy. 1984. *Sir John Soane, Architect*. London: Faber and Faber.

Stupp, Jason. 2011. "Slavery and the Theatre of History: Ritual Performance on the Auction Block." *Theater Journal* 63, no. 1: 61–88. doi: 10.1353/tj2011.0009.

Summerson, John. 1978. *Georgian London*. London: Barrie & Jenkins.

Summerson, John. 1981. *A New Description of Sir John Soane's Museum*. 5th rev. ed. London: The Trustees.

Summerson, John. 1993. *Architecture in Britain, 1530 to 1830*, 8th ed. New Haven, CT: Yale University Press.

Sykes, Christopher Simon. 1985. *Private Palaces: Life in the Great London Houses*. London: Chatto & Windus.

Taylor, Lou. 2004. *Establishing Dress History*. Manchester: Manchester University Press.

Thane, Elswyth. 1967. *Mount Vernon: The Legacy: The Story of Its Preservation and Care since 1885*. Philadelphia: J. B. Lippincott.

Thomas, Julia. 2012. *Shakespeare's Shrine: The Bard's Birthplace and the Invention of Stratford-upon-Avon*. Philadelphia: University of Pennsylvania Press.

Thompson, F. M. L. 1963. *English Landed Society in the Nineteenth Century*. London: Routledge & Kegan Paul.

Thornton, Peter. 1984. *Authentic Décor: The Domestic Interior 1620–1920*. London: Viking.

Thornton, Peter. Obituaries. *Daily Telegraph*, February 24, 2007; *Independent*, March 12, 2007.

Thurley, Simon. 2003. *Hampton Court: A Social and Architectural History*. New Haven, CT: Yale University Press.

Tilden, Freeman. 1957. *Interpreting Our Heritage*. Chapel Hill: University of North Carolina Press.

Tinniswood, Adrian. 1989. *A History of Country House Visiting*. Oxford: Basil Blackwell.

Tolles, Frederick B. 1959. "'Of the Best Sort but Plain': The Quaker Esthetic." *American Quarterly* 11, no. 4: 484–502.

Tomlan, Michael A., ed. 1998. *Preservation of What, for Whom? A Critical Look at Historical Significance*. Ithaca, NY: National Council for Preservation Education.

Townsend, Reginald. 1929, February. "An Adventure in Americana: Beauport: the Residence of Henry D. Sleeper, Esq." *Country Life*: 34–42.

Trevor-Roper, Hugh. 1983. "The Invention of Tradition: The Highland Tradition of Scotland." In *The Invention of Tradition*, edited by Eric Hobsbawm and Terence Ranger, 15–42. Cambridge: Cambridge University Press.

Trubek, Anne. 2011. *A Skeptic's Guide to Writers' Houses*. Philadelphia: University of Pennsylvania Press.

Turner, Graeme. 2006. *Understanding Celebrity*. London: Sage.

Tyler-McGraw, Marie. 1998. "Becoming Americans Again: Re-envisioning and Revising Thematic Interpretation at Colonial Williamsburg." *Public Historian* 20, no. 3 (Summer): 53–76.

Tylor, Edward B. 1958 [1873]. *The Origins of Culture* and *Religion in Primitive Culture*. New York: Harper and Brothers.

Vale, Lawrence J. 2008. *Architecture, Power and National Identity*, 2nd ed. London: Routledge.

van Schaik, Leon. 2011. *Meaning in Space: Housing the Visual Arts, or, Architecture for Private Collections*. Melbourne: Lyon Housemuseum.

Vanderbilt, Kermit. 1986. *American Literature and the Academy*. Philadelphia: University of Pennsylvania Press.

Vergo, Peter, ed. 1989. *The New Museology*. London: Reaktion Books.

Victor, Adam. 2008. *The Elvis Encyclopedia*. New York: Overlook Press.

Vlach, John Michael. 1991. *By the Work of Their Hands: Studies in Afro-American Folklife*. Charlottesville: University Press of Virginia.

Vogt, Jay. 2007. "The Kykuit II Summit: The Sustainability of Historic Sites." *History News* 62, no. 4: 17–21.

Wade, Charles Paget. 2002. "Haphazard Notes, 1945." In *The Collector's Voice, vol. 3: Imperial Voices*, edited by Susan Pearce, Rosemary Flanders, Mark Hall, and Fiona Morton, 157–60. Aldershot: Ashgate.

Wainwright, Clive. 1989. *The Romantic Interior: The British Collector at Home, 1750–1850*. New Haven, CT: Yale University Press.

Wallace, Michael. 1986. "Visiting the Past: History Museums in the United States." In *Presenting the Past: Essays on History and the Public*, edited by Susan Porter Benson, Stephen Brier, and Roy Rosenzweig, 137–61. Philadelphia: Temple University Press.

Wallach, Allan, and Carol Duncan. 1980. "The Universal Survey Museum." *Art History* 3: 447–69.

Waterfield, Giles. 1999. "Paintings from the Russell-Cotes Art Gallery and Museum, Bournemouth." *The Magazine Antiques* 155, no. 6: 858–65.

Waterson, Merlin, ed. 1985. *The Country House Remembered: Recollections of Life between the Wars*. London: Routledge & Kegan Paul.

Waterson, Merlin. 1994. *The National Trust: The First Hundred Years*. London: National Trust & BBC Books.

Waterson, Merlin. 2011. *A Noble Thing: The National Trust and Its Benefactors*. London: Scala.

Watkin, David. 1980. *The Rise of Architectural History*. London: Architectural Press.

Watson, Nicola. 2006. *The Literary Tourist: Readers and Places in Romantic and Victorian Britain*. Basingstoke: Palgrave Macmillan.

Watson, Nicola, ed. 2009. *Literary Tourism and Nineteenth-Century Culture*. Basingstoke: Palgrave Macmillan.

Watson, Steve. 2013. "Country Matters: The Rural-Historic as an Authorised Heritage Discourse in England." In *Heritage and Tourism: Place, Encounter and Engagement*, edited by Russell Staiff, Robyn Bushell, and Steve Watson, 103–26. London: Routledge.

Weible, Robert. 2011. "Visions and Reality: Reconsidering the Creation and Development of Lowell's National Park, 1966–1992." *Public Historian* 33, no. 2: 67–93. doi: 10.1525/tph.2011.33.2.67.

Weil, Stephen E. 1999. "From Being *about* Something to Being *for* Somebody: The Ongoing Transformation of the American Museum." *Daedalus* 128, no. 3: 229–58.

Weil, Stephen E. 2002. *Making Museums Matter*. Washington, DC: Smithsonian Institution Press.

Weintraub, Alan, and Alan Hess. 2005. *Frank Lloyd Wright: The Houses*. New York: Rizzoli.

Wellman, Judith. 2003. "'It's a Wide Community Indeed': Alliances and Issues in Creating Women's Rights National Historical Park, Seneca Falls, NY." In *Restoring Women's History through Historic Preservation*, edited by Gail Lee Dubrow and Jennifer B. Goodman, 230–47. Baltimore: Johns Hopkins University Press.

West, Patricia. 1986. "The New Social History in Historic House Museums: The Lindenwald Example." *Museum Studies Journal* 2: 22–26.

West, Patricia. 1999. *Domesticating History: The Political Origins of America's House Museums.* Washington, DC: Smithsonian Institution Press.

West, Patricia. 2014, June 3. Personal communication.

Wharton, Edith, and Ogden Codman Jr. 1898. *The Decoration of Houses.* London: Batsford.

Whiffen, Marcus. 1958. *Public Buildings of Colonial Williamsburg.* Williamsburg: Colonial Williamsburg.

Wildman, Thomas. 1857. *Newstead Abbey: Its Present Owner, with Reminiscences of Lord Byron.* London: Longman.

Wilson, Richard, and Alan Mackley. 2000. *Creating Paradise: The Building of the English Country House, 1660–1880.* London: Hambledon.

Wilson-Costa, Karyn. 2009. "The Land of Burns: Between Myth and Heritage." In *Literary Tourism and Nineteenth-Century Culture,* edited by Nicola Watson, 37–48. Basingstoke: Palgrave Macmillan.

Wood, Mary I. 1912. *The History of the General Federation of Women's Clubs.* New York: Northwood Press.

Woolf, Leonard, ed. 1966. *Collected Essays.* London: Chatto and Windus.

Woolf, Virginia. 1966. "Mr. Bennet and Mrs. Brown." In *Collected Essays,* edited by Leonard Woolf, 319–27. London: Chatto and Windus.

Woolf, Virginia. 1975. "Great Men's Houses." In *The London Scene: Five Essays,* 23–29. New York: Random House.

Wright, Patrick. 1985. *On Living in an Old Country.* London: Verso.

Yetter, George. 1988. *Williamsburg Before and After: The Rebirth of Virginia's Colonial Capital.* Williamsburg: Colonial Williamsburg Foundation.

Young, Iris Marion. 1997. *Intersecting Voices: Dilemmas of Gender, Political Philosophy and Policy.* Princeton, NJ: Princeton University Press.

Young, Linda. 2003. *Middle Class Culture in the Nineteenth Century.* Basingstoke: Palgrave Macmillan.

Young, Linda. 2006, July. "Villages That Never Were: The Museum Village as a Heritage Genre." *International Journal of Heritage Studies* 12, no. 4: 321–38.

Young, Linda. 2007. "Is There a Museum in the House? Historic Houses as a Species of Museum." *Museum Management and Curatorship* 22, no. 1: 59–77. doi: 10.1080/09647770701264952.

Young, Linda. 2008. "The Contagious Magic of James Cook in Captain Cook's Cottage." *ReCollections* 3, no. 2: 123–42.

Young, Linda. 2012. "House Museums Are Not All the Same." In *Proceedings of "The Artifact, Its Context and Their Narrative," Joint Conference of ICOM-DEMHIST and Three ICOM-CC Working Groups,* edited by Kate Seymour and Malgorzata Sawicki. Los Angeles, Getty Research Institute. http://www.icom-cc.org/269/#. V63akZMrKjg.

Young, Linda. 2012. "Magic Objects/Modern Objects: Heroes' House Museums." In *The Thing about Museums: Objects and Experience, Representation and Contesta-*

tion, edited by Sandra Dudley, Amy Jane Barnes, Jennifer Binnie, and Jennifer Walklate, 143–58. London: Routledge.

Young, Linda. 2015. "Literature, Museums and National Identity; or, Why Are There So Many Writers' House Museums in Britain?" *Museum History Journal* 8, no. 2: 229–46. doi: 10.1179/1936981615Z.00000000052.

Young, Terence, and Robert Riley, eds. 2002. *Dumbarton Oaks Colloquium on the History of Landscape Architecture*. Washington, DC: Dumbarton Oaks.

Index

Sleeper, Henry, 139, 140
Smith, Laurajane, 24, 209
Snee Farm (Mount Pleasant, SC), 231
Snowshill Manor (Gloucestershire), 117, 139, 184
Soane, John: museum, 120–21, 138, 183, 254
social history house museums, 145–74; authenticity of, 184–85
social inclusion, 23–24, 159, 167, 248, 253
social justice, 9–10, 27, 145, 167–74, 241; restorative justice, 56, 160, 169; restitutional justice, 245
"social life of things," 90, 159, 193
Society for the Preservation of New England Antiquities, 49, 94–95, 97, 100, 106, 139, 171, 189. See also Historic New England
Society for the Protection of Ancient Buildings, 94, 95, 111
Soho House (Manchester), 248
sources of house museums, 99, 116, 119, 131, 187
Spanish Colonial Revival, 107–8, 235
St. Fagan's Folk Museum (Cardiff, Wales), 92, 149
Standen, East Grinstead, 88, 111
Stanton, Elizabeth Cady, house (Seneca Falls, NY), 81, 166
Stenton (Germantown, PA), 234
Stickley, Gustav, 108
Strong, Roy, 106
style: high, elite, or academic, 88, 89, 96–113, 126, 225; middle class, 127, 136; in national identity, 87–89; popular culture, 89, 108, 112; vernacular, 88, 90–96
Sudley House (Liverpool), 128
Sulgrave Manor (Northampton), 47
Sullivan, Louis, 101
Surviving the Iron Age, 198
Susannah Place (Sydney), 168

sustainability: environmental, 223, 245; socioeconomic, 28–29, 242, 244, 259
Sutton House (Hackney, London), 257
Sutton Scarsdale Hall (Derbyshire), 216–17, *217*

Taliesin (Wisconsin and Arizona), 102
taste, professional, 132, 227
Theatre in Education, 203
Thornton, Peter, 104–6
tourism to house museums: critique of, 242; history of, 37–57, 122, 207; modern, 103, 113, 122, 126, 185–86, 208–10, 220–21, 228, 231, 235, 245, 254; postmodern, 200, 210–11, 250
Treasurer's House (York), 137–38, 184
Tubman, Harriet: Brick House (Auburn, NY), 80
Turner's Villa (Twickenham), 254
Tylor, Edward B., 34
Tyntesfield (Bristol), 224, 248

Upstairs, Downstairs, 161
US presidents' houses, *13*, 43–52, *44*, 49, 82, 153, 161, 164, 173

value of house museums: and community engagement, 14, 76, 81, 167, 169, 257–58; conventional, 185, 223, 240, 248–49; critiques of, 241–42, 253; and economic development, 245; and social justice, 9–10, 27, 145, 160, 167–74
Vanderbilt houses, 234–35
Van der Rohe, Mies, 107
vernacular culture and style, 88, 90–96
Victoria & Albert Museum: historic houses, 104–6, 193
Victoria Mansion (Portland, ME), 88, 110–11
Victorian Society, 99–100
Victorian style, 98–100
Villa Savoye (Poissy, Paris), 101

~

About the Author

Linda Young is a historian by discipline and a curator by trade; she has taught aspects of heritage and museum studies for more than twenty years at the University of Canberra and Deakin University in Melbourne. Her research revolves around domestic and personal goods in the nineteenth-century British world. Her PhD began as an analysis of several house museum collections and was revised as *Middle Class Culture in the Nineteenth Century: America, Australia and Britain* (2003). On the principle that historians have responsibilities to the local past, she wrote *Lost Houses of the Molonglo Valley* (2007) about the pre–federal capital region's domestic history. The current book explores the history of a museum form that connects with the subjects of both of the other books.